THE RISE OF METHODISM:
A SOURCE BOOK

THE RISE OF METHODISM:
A SOURCE BOOK

by

Richard M. Cameron, Ph.D.
Professor of Church History
in
Boston University School of Theology

PHILOSOPHICAL LIBRARY
New York

EVELYNAE GRAY CAMERON
CONIVGI DILECTISSIMAE
HVNC LIBRVM
QVI PRAESERTIM NON SVVS SED EORVM EST
DEDICAT AVCTOR

TABLE OF CONTENTS

TABLES

TABLES

ACKNOWLEDGMENTS

A book — any book, but especially such an one as this — is like a meal which, as we are often told, is made possible only by the combined labor of many persons, most of whom never cross the ken of him who enjoys it. But that should not excuse him from the happy duty of expressing his appreciation to those near at hand, without whose cheerful help the "symposium" could have assumed neither form nor substance.

I owe and hereby render hearty thanks to Bishop Lewis O. Hartman, who not only made the resources of the Library of the New England Methodist Historical Association available to me, but read this book in manuscript and gave valuable aid in discussion and suggestion. Dr. James R. Joy, Librarian of the New York Methodist Historical Society gave generously of his time in helping me to its treasures. My debt to Dr. Janette E. Newhall and the staff of the Boston University School of Theology Library has been especially heavy since I began this work, but indeed it has been accumulating through many earlier years. The same should be said also of the staffs of three Harvard University Libraries: the Widener Memorial, Houghton and the Andover-Harvard Theological Library. I am grateful to the staff of the Library of Wesleyan University at Middletown, Conn., for permission to use their copy of Woodward's pamphlet on the Religious Societies, unique, I believe, in this country.

The painstaking transcription and typing was done by Mrs. Ruthe Leigh and Mr. Edward V. Sherwin. The very dull but very necessary work of verifying texts and references was shared by Robert Hibbard, John Neff, Richard Chartier, B. J. Coates (students at Boston University) and Evelyn Cameron. To all of them I am deeply indebted, as also to E. K. Brown and to Evelyn Gray Cameron, most patient and co-operative of wives, for reading proof, and to Dr. Lindsey Pherigo of Scaritt College for making the index.

The compiler of a source book especially is indebted to many publishers for permission to reproduce material from their publications, and this one is no exception. Acknowledgment of such indebtedness is made at the proper places in the footnotes. But I am glad here to add my name to the long list of students of Methodism whose debt to the Epworth Press in London is inexpressible. I am especially grateful for their permission to reproduce the many passages herein from their monumental standard editions of the Journal and Letters of John Wesley, as well as shorter quotations from several other works published by them.

PREFACE

The story of the early years of Methodism is one of the most stirring epics of Christianity since the Reformation. It is fitting that it should often have been retold by masters not only in the fields of history and religion, but of literature as well. Never, however, has it been better told than by the men who were themselves making the story as they wrote. The first Methodist leaders—the Wesleys, George Whitefield and the rest—wrote not only with the authority of participants, but with an integrity which, if it did not always issue in what can be called "style," was even better. They were not (save, perhaps, when Charles Wesley sat down to write a hymn) men of letters, for the demands of the Revival left them no leisure for that. Nevertheless, the very exigency of their work forced a taut directness on their sentences and winged their words with urgency. The result was that, in addition to having something to say, they said it incomparably well. They speak with a particularity and a verve as refreshing as the occasional drink from a mountain spring vouchsafed a city dweller whose usual drafts come from a brass tap in the kitchen.

Scholars, of course, go directly to the original sources in their studies of this, as of any, movement. But others, even most students can hardly do that. The sheer bulk of the material precludes it. The founders of Methodism were articulate men. Their lengthy journals, countless letters, tracts, controversial pamphlets, theological treatises and sermons fill many volumes, some of which are now scarce, or available only in formidable sets. Further, as is inevitable, the importance of some of this voluminous writing diminished as the generation for which it was written receded into the past. Still, so much of what they had to say is of timeless importance and is told so well, that it deserves to be made available for every generation, and not for scholars alone, but for all who are interested in the Christian pilgrimage.

The foregoing considerations must be the justification for this book. Its purpose is to render accessible in convenient form the more crucial portions of the sources for the beginnings of the Methodist Revival. The point of view is biographical and historical rather than theological, but theology is included as an integral part of the movement. The method has been to select extracts which give, as far as possible in the leaders' own words, a faithful picture of the movement, beginning, as John Wesley advised, "before he was born," and carrying it up through the holding of the first Conference in 1744. The editor cannot claim to have read all the sources, but he has laid the most important under contribution. These are, of course, the Journals and Letters of the Wesleys and Whitefield. From them comes the bulk of the material in this volume.

The blocks from the primary sources have been cemented together where necessary with a certain amount of the editor's own material for the sake of continuity and clarity. It has been his intention to keep such material to a minimum —where he has failed to do this, it is because he has been carried away by delight at the insights which have come as a result of the more mechanical task of selection and arrangement. For the most part, chronological arrangement has been followed, using as a framework the selections from the *Journal* of John Wesley. Into this have been inserted at the appropriate points the extracts from the other sources. Several abridgements of John Wesley's Journal have been made, but this is the first time the attempt has been made to weave together with it the main strands from other sources as well. In certain sections, however, it has seemed advisable to abandon the chronological arrangement for a topical or even a geographical one.

A certain amount of interpretation is inevitable in the process of selection itself. In certain parts of even the chronological sections, where I believe I have seen a dominating tendency at work, the selections have undoubtedly been weighted to illustrate that tendency; but I have tried not to falsify the picture as a whole, even where the proportion has been purposely altered. In general, the principle of selection has been the intrinsic importance, or at least the representative character, of the piece involved. In particular I have not tried, in presenting the portraits of the leaders, to gloss over such flaws as appear. Such a procedure would have been a betrayal both of the reader and of the subjects. It is a real disservice to the reader to create for him a false and fragile image which, in breaking, would shatter likewise, perhaps, a disciple's trust; and especially is it wrong to convey the impression that God can mightily use for His purposes only such agents as are free from all flaws. Finally, there is no need in composing portraits of men whose place in posterity's esteem is already secure, to soften those few features which strike us as less admirable than the rest. And the men whose portraits are here presented are acknowledged of all men to have served God and His purposes above the rest of their generation.

R. M. C.

THE RISE OF METHODISM:
A SOURCE BOOK

CHAPTER I

THE RECTORY FAMILY

The situation of Epworth, in Lincolnshire where Samuel Wesley was Rector while his numerous family was growing up, was not without its bearing on their fortunes. Lincolnshire fronts the North Sea on the east coast of England, just north of the bulge which is Norfolk, but with no such chalk cliffs as those which protect the coast farther south. It lies too low for that. Epworth itself is in a district long known as the Isle of Axholme, not that it was not always geographically an integral part of Great Britain, but because it lay deep in the fens, surrounded by rivers. Socially and culturally also it was an island, the rude inhabitants of which cherished rather than deplored their isolation. When Charles I, the lord of the Island, began drainage operations in the seventeenth century, the resentment of the islanders at the loss of their fishing- and hiding-places in the recesses of the fens flamed into violence against the men sent to do the work. Sheds caught fire at night and horses limped when found in the morning. Eighty years later when John Wesley was a small boy, much of the fen had been drained, but the resentment remained. The fen men were still 'agin the government' and did not hesitate to use against the Tory Rector the same tactics which their fathers had tried on the King's engineers.

In addition to the actual violence to the Rectory buildings and cattle, and threats against the safety of the inmates, the family suffered by reason of its isolation from cultivated society. This, as might be expected, bore hardest on the girls. The Rector went up frequently to London, and the boys got off to their Schools and the University; but Susannah and the girls—the latter at an age when congenial com-

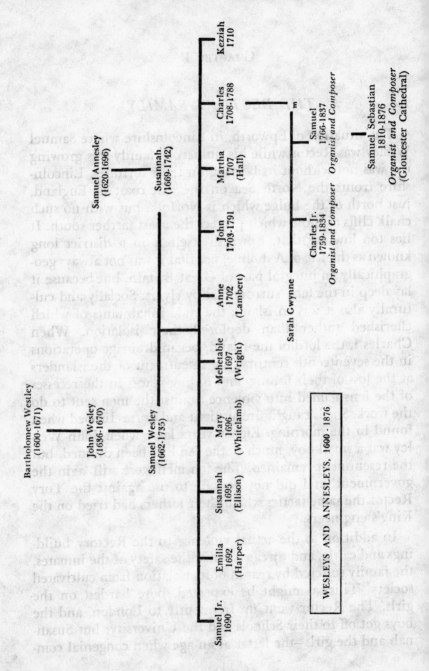

WESLEYS AND ANNESLEYS, 1600 - 1876

pany means much—never got off "the Island" for long.[1]
The Rector lacked the means, and perhaps the perceptive-
ness to alleviate the situation. To this in no small degree is
due the consistently disastrous character of their marriages.
Fortunately, since it is apart from our purpose, we need not
enter on that succession of tragic stories. For the boys, it
was different. Samuel Jr., the oldest, emerged into the larger
life of England to live out a useful career as a teacher, and
to win a modest repute as a writer. Till the death of Samuel
Sebastian Wesley in 1876 the sons and grandson of Charles
and Sarah Wesley continued, as organists and composers of
eminence, to contribute to the heritage of English church
music, so signally enriched by Charles' own poetry.

As for Charles himself, and John, they were to come forth
conquering and to conquer. As, a millennium before, Al-
fred the Christian King, having nursed his strength in the
marshes of the Isle of Athelney, emerged to roll back the
darkness of Danish heathendom, before the sword and the
Gospel, so John and Charles Wesley, armed only with their
disciplined lives and warmed hearts, issued from the Isle
of Axholme to roll back a cloud of English heathendom
before that same Gospel wonderfully renewed.

i. Dissenting Forebears

One great-grandfather and two grandfathers of the founders of Methodism were ornaments of the ministry in that
wing of the Puritan tradition which, while clinging as long
as possible to the national church, sought to rid it of "the
dregs of Popery," to raise the standard of preaching, to
mould Church and Nation into one Holy Community
which should glorify God by pure worship and saintly living after the pattern in His Word. Some of the Puritans
had left to begin afresh in New England. More stayed home
to advocate their cause in press and pulpit and Parliament,
and finally on the battlefield under Oliver Cromwell. While
Cromwell lived, their cause prospered; when his strong

leadership was removed, the nation, weary of conflict and military rule, swung back to the King, the Bishops and the Prayer Book. In 1662 a Parliament "fiercely royalist and Anglican" passed a new Act of Uniformity which became effective, as those who suffered under it significantly pointed out, on the day of St. Bartholomew, made memorable by the massacre of Huguenots in Catholic France. It required that all ministers of religion qualify by being episcopally ordained, subscribing the XXXIX Articles, and conducting public worship according to the Prayer Book only. Continued conformity under these conditions would have been apostasy to their faith for two thousand "burning and shining lights" of Puritanism, who, half in sorrow, half in triumph left their pulpits for lives of reproach and suffering. The ejected ministers were, by the vengeful "Clarendon Code," forbidden to exercise their ministry, forbidden to teach, forbidden to live near their old homes; many, detected at conducting unlawful services, faced the courts and languished in prisons.

1. *Bartholomew and John Westley.*

Bartholomew Westley (1600-1671), the great-grandfather of John and Charles, was ejected from his living at Charmouth in Dorsetshire. He was able to make a meagre living by practising as a physician, for which he may have studied at Oxford. Apparently he avoided imprisonment through the five years between his ejection and his death. His son John Westley (1636-1670) did not fare so well. Edmund Calamy has told the story in his famous *Account.*

CALAMY, CA,[2] I, 437 ff.

I must also here give an account of Mr. John Westley of Whitchurch near Blandford, M.A. . . . .

This Mr. John Westley, was the son of Mr. Bartholomew Westley of Charmouth near Lime, and the father of Mr. Samuel Westley, rector of Epworth, in the diocese of Lincoln, the author of the poem on the Life of Christ, which is dedicated to Queen Mary.

It pleased God to incline this Mr. John Westley to remember his creator in the days of his youth, and lay him under serious impressions in his tender years. He had a very humbling sense of sin, and a serious concern for his salvation, even while he was a school-boy. He began to keep a diary soon after God had begun to work upon him, and not only recorded the remarkable steps and turns of Providence that affected his outward man, but more especially, all the methods of the Spirit of Grace in his dealings with his soul; what was the frame of his heart in his attendance on the several ordinances of the Gospel, and how he found himself affected under the various methods of divine Providence, whether merciful or afflictive: and this course he continued with very little interruption, to the end of his life.

When he had finished his school-learning, he went to New-Inn-Hall in Oxon, and continued there till after he had taken the degree of M. A. During his stay there, he was taken notice of for his seriousness and diligence. He applied himself particularly to the study of the Oriental languages, in which he made no inconsiderable progress . . . He was not above two and twenty when he began to preach occasionally, and in May 1658 was sent to preach at Whitchurch. The income of this vicarage was not above thirty pounds per annum; but he was promised an augmentation of one hundred pounds a year, though the many turns and changes in public affairs which followed soon after, prevented his receiving any part of what had been promised him. A few months after he came to Whitchurch, he married a niece of Dr. Thomas Fuller. Being disappointed of the augmentation, he was necessitated to set up a school, that he might be able to maintain his growing family. Soon after the Restoration, some of his neighbours gave him a great deal of trouble and uneasiness, because he would not read the

Book of Common Prayer; and upon Dr. Gilbert Ironside's
being made Bishop of Bristol, and coming into his diocese,
he was informed by some persons of distinction, that Mr.
Westley would not gratify those who desired him to read
and use the Liturgy.

. . . In the beginning of 1662, he was seized on the Lord's
Day as he was coming out of the church, and carried to
Blandford, and committed to prison. But after he had been
some time confined, Sir Gerard Napper who was the most
furious of all his enemies, and the most forward in committing him, was so far softened by a sad disaster (having
broken his collar-bone) that he sent to some persons to
bail Mr. Westley, and told them if they would not, he
would do it himself. Thus was he set at liberty, but bound
over to appear at the Assizes, where he came off much better than he expected. The good man has recorded in his
diary the mercy of God to him in raising up several friends
to own him, inclining a solicitor to plead for him, and
restraining the wrath of man, so that even the judge though
a very choleric man spake not an angry word. The sum of
the proceedings at the Assizes as it stands in his diary is
as follows.

Clerk. Call Mr. Westley of Whitchurch.

Westley. Here.

Clerk. You were indicted for not reading the Common
Prayer. Will you traverse it? . . .

Westley. The Book was never tendered me.

Judge. Must the Book be tendered you?

Westley. So I conceive by the Act.

Judge. Are you ordained?

Westley. I am ordained to preach the Gospel.

Judge. By whom?

Westley. I have order to preach.

Judge. From whom?

Westley. I have given an account thereof already to the
bishop.

Judge. What bishop?

Westley. Of Bristol.

Judge. I say by whom were you ordained? How long was it since?

Westley. Four or five years since.

Judge. By whom then?

Westley. By those who were then empowered.

Judge. I thought so. Have you a presentation to your place?

Westley. I have.

Judge. From whom?

Westley. May it please your Lordship it is a legal presentation.

Judge. By whom was it?

Westley. By the trustees.

Judge. Have you brought it?

Westley. I have not.

Judge. Why not?

Westley. Because I did not think I should be asked any such questions here.

Judge. I would wish you to read the Common Prayer, at your peril. You will not say, "From all sedition and privy conspiracy; from all false doctrine, heresy and schism; good Lord deliver us."

Clerk. Call Mr. Meech. He was called and appeared.

Clerk. Does Mr. Westley read the Common Prayer yet?

Meech. May it please your Lordship, he never did nor he never will.

Judge. Friend how do you know that? He may bethink himself.

Meech. He never did; he never will.

Solic. We will when we see the New Book, either read it, or leave our place at Bartholomew Tide.

Judge. Are you not bound to read the Old Book till then? Let us see the Act, and reading it to himself, another cause was called.

Mr. Westley came joyfully home, though bound over to the next Assizes, and preached constantly every Lord's Day till August 17, when he delivered his farewell sermon to a weeping auditory, from Acts xx. 32. October 26, the place was by an Apparitor declared vacant, and order given to sequester the profits: but his people had given him what was his due. February 22 following, he removed with his family to Melcomb; whereupon the corporation made an order against his settlement there, imposing a fine of twenty pounds upon his landlady, and five shillings per week on him, to be levied by distress. . . . These violent proceedings forced him out of the town, and he went to Bridgwater, Ilminster, and Taunton, in all which places he met with great kindness and friendship from all the three denominations of dissenters, and was almost every day employed in preaching in the several places to which he went; and got many good acquaintances and friends, who were afterwards very kind to him and his numerous family. At length a gentleman who had a very good house at Preston, two or three miles from Melcomb, gave him free liberty to dwell in it without paying any rent. Thither he removed his family in the beginning of May, and there he continued as long as he lived. He records his coming to dwell at Preston with great wonder and thankfulness. . . .

Soon after his being fixed in his house at Preston, he was under great debates in his own mind about a removal beyond sea, either to Surinam or Maryland: but after much consideration and advice, he determined to abide in the land of his nativity, and there take his lot. About the same time also, he not a little hesitated, about hearing in the Established Church, and was much troubled in his own spirit about it: but at length by several arguments in Mr. Nye's papers he was determined: 1. Because it was the Word of God which was preached which he thought challenged attendance. 2. By separating from what was evil, and closing with what was good, he thought the testimony given would be the more convincing. 3. He looked not upon this as a part of communion with them, or an intention of closing with them, any farther than they held the Head and were unblameable in their lives. This he sets down as his judgment, August 11, 1663.

He was not a little troubled about the management of his own preaching, whether it should be carried on more openly, or more privately. Some of the neighbouring ministers, particularly Mr. Bampfield, Mr. Ince, Mr. Hallet of Shafton, and Mr. John Sacheverel, were for preaching publicly with open doors. But he thought it was his duty to beware of men, and that he was bound prudently to preserve himself at Liberty, and in a capacity of service, as long as he could, and not by the openness of one meeting hazard the liberty of all meetings. Hereby he kept himself a little longer out of the hands of his enemies than the four ministers above mentioned; for they were all indicted at the Assizes, August 7, 1663, for a riotous, routous, and unlawful assembly held at Shafton, July 23 . . . [They] were found guilty by a jury of gentlemen, and fined forty marks each, and to find security for their good behaviour. In the meantime Mr. Westley preached very frequently, not only to a few good people at Preston, but as he had opportunity at Weymouth, and other places round about. And after some time he was called by a number of serious Christians at Pool to be their pastor; and in that relation he continued to the day of his death, administering all ordinances to them as opportunity offered. But by the Oxford Act he was obliged to withdraw from Preston, for a while, and leave his family and people. But he preached wherever he was, if he could but have an auditory.

Upon his coming to the place of his retirement in March 1666, he puts this question to himself, What dost thou here at such a distance from church, wife, children, etc.? And in his answer, first sets down the Oath, and then adds, Tho' about seventeen in Devon, and seven in Dorset, and sixteen in London have taken the Oath, yet he could not do it for several reasons. Swearing to a proposition (be what it will for the matter) hath no scripture precept, precedent or allowance: and is therefore a taking the name of God in vain. 2. It is doubtful what the lawmakers intended by the words in the latter clause, and without their interpretation it cannot be understood: And for me to swear to them in my own private sense, is but juggling with God and the king, and conscience too, especially when it was declared by some magistrates, that they had no power to admit of such a private sense. 3. It was by the speaker declared at the signing of the Act, that the nation would judge the taking this Oath to be a pledge of after conformity. . . . After he had lain hid for some time, he ventured home again, and returned to his labour among his people, and among others occasionally besides those of his own peculiar charge. But notwithstanding all his prudence in managing his meeting more privately than many of his brethren, he was oft disturbed, and several times apprehended, and four times imprisoned: Once at Pool for half a year, and once at Dorchester for three months; but the other confinements were not so long. He was in many straits and difficulties, but wonderfully supported and comforted, and many times very seasonably and surprisingly relieved and delivered. The removal of many eminent Christians into another world, who were his intimate acquaintances and kind friends in this; and the great decay of serious religion among many that made a profession, and the increasing rage of the enemies of real Godliness, manifestly seized and sunk his spirits. And having filled up his part of what is behind of the afflictions of Christ in his flesh, for his body's sake which is the church, and finished the work given him to do, he was taken out of this vale of tears into the invisible world, where the wicked cease from troubling and the weary are at rest, when he had not been much longer an inhabitant here below than his blessed Master, whom he served with his whole heart, according to the best of his light. "For they that turn many to righteousness shall shine as the stars for ever and ever," though not only their persons while they are living, but also their bodies when they are dead, may here meet with contempt, as this good man's did, which the Vicar of Preston would not suffer to be buried in the church.

2. *Samuel Annesley* (1620-1696) .

Samuel Annesley put subsequent generations in his debt by being the father of Susannah Wesley. But he had a title to the admiration and gratitude of his own generation as well. In him the qualities of the earnest Nonconformist divine showed at their best. They earned for him the title, "a second St. Paul" among his colleagues. He first exercised, then retired from a chaplaincy in the Royal Navy. His first parish on land was at Cliff, in Kent, of which Adam Clarke recounts the anecdote below. During the Protectorate his abilities found fruitful outlet in London where he was Lecturer at St. Paul's and minister, upon presentation of Cromwell himself, at St. Giles' Cripplegate. His eminence and piety did not save him from ejection in 1662. Ten years later, however, on the proclamation of the royal Indulgence, he resumed his public ministry in an independent congregation which continued till his death. Ever generous of his considerable means to help the needy among the deprived ministers, and of his time in working for the welfare of struggling dissenting congregations, he was regarded by them as in some sort their dean and mentor.

CLARKE, MWF, I, 365.

. . . Not liking a seafaring life, he left the navy, and settled at Cliff, in Kent, in the place of a minister who had been sequestered for scandalous conduct, such as attending public meetings of the people for dancing, drinking and merriment on the Lord's-day. But it was *like pastor like people;* for the inhabitants of the place were so attached to their sinful leader, that when his successor came, they assailed him with spits, forks, and stones, threatening to take away his life. He told them that, "let them use him as they would, he was determined to stay with them till God should fit them by his ministry to profit by one better, who might succeed him; and solemnly declared, that when they became so prepared, he would leave the place."

In a few years his labours had surprising success, so that the people became greatly reformed. However, he kept his word, and left them; lest any seeming inconsistency of his might prove a stumbling-block to his young converts.

RECOLLECTIONS OF A GRANDFATHER. Feb. 6, 1769. WJJS,³ V, 299.

I spent an hour with a venerable woman, near ninety years of age, who retains her health, her senses, her understanding, and even her memory, to a good degree. In the last century she belonged to my grandfather Annesley's congregation, at whose house her father and she used to dine every Thursday; and whom she remembers to have frequently seen in his study, at the top of the house, with his window open, and without any fire, winter or summer. He lived seventy-seven years, and would probably have lived longer, had he not began water-drinking at seventy.

ii. The Methodical Nursery

1. *The Churchly Father.*

Had Samuel Wesley Sr. (1666-1735) followed the course marked out for him he would have been the third in the line of Wesleys to be a dissenting minister. To this end he was educated in one of the excellent academies the Dissenters had established for this purpose. But at the age of sixteen or seventeen he entered the Church of England, a step which aroused no little bitterness among his former friends, and led to some unseemly controversy in print. He left home soon afterward for Oxford (which was open to him only now that he had entered the Church) and earned his way through Exeter College where he took his degrees in due course. For the rest of his life he was a staunch Churchman. After serving in several other livings he came to Epworth in 1696. The rest of his ministry was to lie in that remote and far from opulent parish. His interests were not bounded by parish limits however. He once proposed a plan for Anglican missions, and offered to go himself to Abyssinia or the Indies. This plan, a letter from him recommending the work of the Religious Societies then numerous in the kingdom,[4] and his joy that the Holy Club came to "turn the war against the world, the flesh and the devil,"[5] show that his religious interests were broad geographically, if not ecclesiastically. As a husband and father, he had his defects: he had no money sense; he posted off to London too frequently; he spent too much time astride his usually earth-bound Pegasus; he did not always cooperate with Susannah's "methods" in the training of their children. Eager that his sons should have the best,[6] he manifested less sympathy for the fate of his daughters.[7] Of his winsomeness as a pastor there may be some doubt, but of his uprightness, courage and fidelity, none whatever. Like Moses, bowed with years and toils, he glimpsed the promised land from afar, but was not permitted to enter therein. Seven years after his death, his son John preached at Epworth from his tombstone to an attentive crowd. His comment was, "O let none think his labour of love is lost because the fruit does not immediately appear! Near forty years did my father labour here, but he saw little fruit of all his labour . . . but the seed, sown so long since, now sprung up, bringing forth repentance and remission of sins."[8] Charles Wesley wrote, three days after his father's death, "He often laid his hands upon my head, and said, 'Be steady. The Christian faith will surely revive in this kingdom; you shall see it, though I shall not'." [9]

PICTURE OF A PATRIARCH.

This selection from Samuel Wesley's long poem on the life of Christ[10] is included here because it tells us more about the writer himself than about either the Virgin Mary whom it purports to describe, or about his own wife who, Adam Clarke suggests,[11] really sat for the portrait. We simply have no data for such a detailed description of the former, and Mr. Wesley himself excludes the latter in a footnote to the passage.[12] It should be remembered however, that such a patriarchal view of the position of woman was widespread in the eighteenth century; hence its expression is typical rather than peculiar to Mr. Wesley.

She grac'd my humble roof, and blest my life
Blest me by a far greater name than wife:[13]
Yet still I bore an undisputed sway,
Nor was't her task, but pleasure to obey:
Scarce thought, much less could act what I denied;
In our low house there was no room for pride
Nor need I e'er direct what still was right,
Still studied my convenience and delight.
Nor did I for her care ungrateful prove
But only us'd my pow'r to show my love:
What e'er she asked I gave, without reproach or grudge,
For still she reason asked—and I was judge:
All my commands requests at her fair hands
And her requests to me were all commands:
To other thresholds rarely she'd incline:
Her house her pleasure was and she was mine;
Rarely abroad, or never, but with me,
Or when by pity call'd or charity.

CLARKE, MWF, I, 198 f.

"Were I," said he,[14] "to write my own life, I should begin it *before I was born*, merely for the purpose of mentioning a disagreement between my father and mother. 'Sukey,' said my father to my mother, one day after family prayer, 'why did you not say *amen* this morning to the prayer for the king?' 'Because,' said she, 'I do not believe the Prince of Orange to be king.' 'If that be the case,' said he, 'you and I must part; for if we have two kings, we must have two beds.' My mother was inflexible. My father went immediately to his study; and, after spending some time with himself, set out for London, where, being *convocation man* for the diocese of Lincoln, he remained without visiting his own house for the remainder of the year. On March 8th in the following year, 1702, King William died; and as both my father and mother were agreed as to the legitimacy of Queen Anne's title, the cause of their misunderstanding ceased. My father returned to Epworth, and conjugal harmony was restored."

SAMUEL WESLEY TO HIS ARCHBISHOP (Sharp of York) after a County election in which Mr. Wesley took the Tory (and unpopular) side. Epworth. June 7, 1705. Clarke, MWF, I, 211f.

I went to Lincoln on Tuesday night, May 29th; and the election began on Wednesday, 30th. A great part of the night our Isle people kept drumming, shouting, and firing of pistols and guns under the window where my wife lay; who had been brought to bed not three weeks. I had put the child to nurse over against my own house: the noise kept his nurse waking till one or two in the morning. Then they left off; and the nurse being heavy to sleep, overlaid the child. She waked; and finding it dead, ran over with it to my house, almost distracted; and calling my servants, threw it into their arms. They, as wise as she, ran up with it to my wife; and before she was well awake, threw it cold and dead into hers. She composed herself as well as she could, and that day got it buried.

A clergyman met me in the castle yard, and told me to withdraw, for the Isle men intended me a mischief. Another told me he had heard near twenty of them say, "If they got me in the castle yard, they would squeeze my guts out." My servant had the same advice. I went by Gainsbro', and God preserved me.

When they knew I was got home, they sent the drum and mob, with guns, etc., as usual, to compliment me till after midnight. One of them passing by on Friday evening, and seeing my children in the yard, cried out, 'O ye devils! we will come and turn ye all out of doors a begging shortly.' God convert them, and forgive them!

S. WESLEY TO THE ARCHBISHOP. Lincoln Castle, Sept. 12, 1705. Clarke, MWF, I, 218.

. . . Most of my friends advise me to leave Epworth, if e'er I should get from hence.[15] I confess I am not of that mind, because I may yet do good there; and 'tis like a coward to desert my post because the enemy fire is thick upon me. They have only wounded me yet, and, I believe, CAN'T kill me. I hope to be at home by Xmas. God help my poor family! For myself, I have but one life: but while that lasts, shall be,

Your Grace's ever obliged and most humble servant,

2. *The Mother of Methodism.*

Susannah Wesley (1669-1742) was the twenty-fifth child of Dr. Annesley. From materials she herself furnishes in a letter written much later to her son Samuel[16] we can reconstruct a picture of her as a little girl of twelve, gravely weighing the claims of the Church of England over against the Dissent of her distinguished father, and deciding in favor of the former. Some subsequent biographers[17] have judged that her decision was one of the heart more than of the head. However that may be, it abundantly appears that her new convictions were deep and lasting. She brought up her children to be, first of all, earnest Christians—but for them all, the Christian life was inseparable from the Church of England. Her incisive mind, her deep piety and her giving herself without reserve to the nurture of her children have gained for her, along with Monnica the mother of Augustine and Aletta the mother of Bernard of Clairvaux, a secure place among the great mothers of Christian history. To be sure, we would not today approve or imitate all her principles and schemes, which were characterized by even an excess of rigor untouched by any saving salt of humor. We would not start, for instance, by trying to "conquer the will of children betimes." The rare and admirable quality which animated all else involved, as she herself said,[18] "Renouncing the world in the most literal sense of the word." We may say that it involved an even greater renunciation, that of self. In respect of this selfless devotion surely, as well as the considerable intellectual gifts she brought to her task, she has merited the high esteem which later generations have accorded her.

She was the mother not only of the Methodists, but also of Methodism. From her John and Charles got their methodical discipline, by correspondence when they were at the University, she moulded John's theology and urged on him the study of "practical divinity;" when she had but lately been widowed, she bravely sped them on their mission to Georgia;[19] and finally, her guiding touch was apparent at critical moments when Methodism was but an infant movement feeling its way.[20]

SUSANNAH'S SUNDAY EVENING MEETINGS.

Much about this affair is obscure, but the situation presupposed by the following letter is evidently somewhat as follows: Mr. Wesley was making a rather extended stay in London, having left a Curate in charge of the congregation during his absence. The quality of his preaching may be judged from this, that his sermons were concerned to enforce the payment of debts as the chief if not the sole Christian duty.[21] *Under such circumstances it is not hard to see why, under the smart of finding the parishioners crowding to Susannah's informal meetings, while neglecting the Church services at which he preached, he might have denounced the former to the Rector as "conventicles" or illegal religious gatherings. Whereupon the Rector would have written to his wife to remonstrate or at least to inquire, and this letter is her spirited defense of her course. The meetings would doubtless have to be given up when the Rector returned—a sense of propriety shared by Mrs. Wesley no less than the others involved would see to that. Whether they were broken off earlier or not we have no way of knowing.*

SUSANNAH TO SAMUEL WESLEY IN LONDON. Epworth. Feb. 6, 1712. Clarke, MWF, II, 90 ff.

I heartily thank you for dealing so plainly and faithfully with me in a matter of no common concern. The main of your objections against our Sunday evening meetings are, first, that it will look particular; secondly, my sex; and lastly, your being at present in a public station and character. To all which I shall answer briefly.

As to its looking particular, I grant it does; and so does almost everything that is serious, or that may any way advance the glory of God or the salvation of souls, if it be performed out of a pulpit, or in the way of common conversation; because in our corrupt age the utmost care and diligence have been used to banish all discourse of God or spiritual concerns out of society, as if religion were never to appear out of the closet, and we were to be ashamed of nothing so much as of professing ourselves to be Christians.

To your second, I reply, that as I am a woman, so I am also mistress of a large family. And though the superior charge of the souls contained in it lies upon you, as head of the family, and as their minister; yet in your absence I cannot but look upon every soul you leave under my care as a talent committed to me, under a trust, by the great Lord of all the families of heaven and earth. And if I am unfaithful to him, or to you, in neglecting to improve these talents, how shall I answer unto him, when he shall command me to render an account of my stewardship?

As these and other such like thoughts made me at first take a more than ordinary care of the souls of my children and servants; so, knowing that our most holy religion requires a strict observation of the Lord's-day, and not thinking that we fully answered the end of the institution by only going to church, but that likewise we are obliged to fill up the intermediate spaces of that sacred time by other acts of piety and devotion; I thought it my duty to spend some part of the day in reading to and instructing my family, especially in your absence, when, having no afternoon's service, we have so much leisure for such exercises; and such time I esteemed spent in a way more acceptable to God, than if I had retired to my own private devotions.

This was the beginning of my present practice: other people coming in and joining with us was purely accidental. Our lad told his parents—they first desired to be admitted; then others who heard of it begged leave also; so our company increased to about thirty, and seldom exceeded forty last winter; and why it increased since, I leave you to judge after you have read what follows.

Soon after you went to London, Emily found in your study the account of the Danish missionaries, which hav-

ing never seen, I ordered her to read it to me. I was never,
I think, more affected with anything than with the relation of their travels; and was exceeding pleased with the
noble design they were engaged in. Their labours refreshed my soul beyond measure; and I could not forbear
spending good part of that evening in praising and adoring the divine goodness for inspiring those good men
with such an ardent zeal for his glory, that they were
willing to hazard their lives, and all that is esteemed dear
to men in this world, to advance the honour of their
master, Jesus. For several days I could think or speak of
little else. At last it came into my mind, though I am not
a man nor a minister of the gospel, and so cannot be employed in such a worthy employment as they were; yet,
if my heart were sincerely devoted to God, and if I were
inspired with a true zeal for his glory, and did really desire the salvation of souls, I might do somewhat more
than I do. I thought I might live in a more exemplary
manner in some things; I might pray more for the people,
and speak with more warmth to those with whom I have
an opportunity of conversing. However, I resolved to begin with my own children; and, accordingly, I proposed
and observed the following method. I take such a proportion of time as I can best spare every night to discourse
with each child by itself, on something that relates to its
principal concerns. On Monday I talk with Molly; on
Tuesday, with Hetty; Wednesday, with Nancy; Thursday,
with Jacky; Friday, with Patty; Saturday, with Charles;
and with Emily and Sukey together, on Sunday.

With those few neighbours who then came to me I discoursed more freely and affectionately than before. I chose
the best and most awakening sermons we had, and I spent
more time with them in such exercises. Since this our
company has increased every night, for I dare deny none
that asks admittance. Last Sunday, I believe we had above
200, and yet many went away for want of room.

But I never durst positively presume to hope that God would make use of me as an instrument in doing good; the farthest I ever durst go was, It may be: who can tell? With God all things are possible. I will resign myself to him: or, as Herbert expresses it,

> Only since God doth often make
> Of *lowly matter* for *high uses* meet,
>   I throw me at his feet;
> There will I lie until my Maker seek
> For some *mean stuff*, whereon to show his skill;
>   Then is *my* time.

And thus I rested, without passing any reflection on myself, or forming any judgment about the success or event of this undertaking.

Your third objection I leave to be answered by your own judgment. We meet not on any worldly design. We banish all temporal concerns from our society:[22] none is suffered to mingle any discourse about them with our reading or singing: we keep close to the business of the day; and as soon as it is over, they all go home. And where is the harm of this? If I and my children went a visiting on Sunday nights, or if we admitted of impertinent visits, as too many do who think themselves good Christians, perhaps it would be thought no scandalous practice, though in truth it would be so. Therefore, why any should reflect upon you, let your station be what it will, because your wife endeavours to draw people to the church, and to restrain them by reading, and other persuasions, from their profanation of God's most holy day, I cannot conceive. But if any should be so mad as to do it, I wish you would not regard it. For my part, I value no censure on this account. I have long since shook hands with the world, and I heartily wish I had never given them more reason to speak against me.

As for your proposal of letting some other person read.

Alas! you do not consider what a people these are. I do not think one man among them could read a sermon, without spelling a good part of it; and how would that edify the rest? Nor has any of our family a voice strong enough to be heard by such a number of people.

But there is one thing about which I am much dissatisfied; that is, their being present at family prayers. I do not speak of any concern I am under, barely because so many are present; for those who have the honour of speaking to the Great and Holy God, need not be ashamed to speak before the whole world; but because of my sex, I doubt if it be proper for me to present the prayers of the people to God.

Last Sunday, I fain would have dismissed them before prayers; but they begged so earnestly to stay, that I durst not deny them . . .

Besides the constant attendance on the public worship of God, our meeting has wonderfully conciliated the minds of this people towards us, so that we now live in the greatest amity imaginable; and what is still better, they are very much reformed in their behaviour on the Lord's day; and those who used to be playing in the streets now come to hear a good sermon read, which is surely more acceptable to Almighty God.

SUSANNAH TO JOHN WESLEY. July 24, 1732[23].
WJJS, III, 34ff.

DEAR SON,

According to your desire, I have collected the principal rules I observed in educating my family; which I now send you as they occurred to my mind, and you may (if you think they can be of use to any) dispose of them in what order you please.

The children were always put into a regular method of living, in such things as they were capable of, from their birth: as in dressing, undressing, changing their linen, etc. The first quarter commonly passes in sleep. After that they were, if possible, laid into their cradles awake, and rocked to sleep; and so they were kept rocking till it was time for them to awake. This was done to bring them to a regular course of sleeping; which at first was three hours in the morning, and three in the afternoon; afterwards two hours, till they needed none at all.

When turned a year old (and some before), they were taught to fear the rod, and to cry softly; by which means they escaped abundance of correction they might otherwise have had, and that most odious noise of the crying of children was rarely heard in the house, but the family usually lived in as much quietness as if there had not been a child among them.

As soon as they were grown pretty strong, they were confined to three meals a day. At dinner their little table and chairs were set by ours, where they could be overlooked; and they were suffered to eat and drink (small beer) as much as they would; but not to call for anything. If they wanted aught they used to whisper to the maid which attended them, who came and spake to me; and as soon as they could handle a knife and fork, they were set to our table. They were never suffered to choose their meat, but always made eat such things as were provided for the family.

Mornings they had always spoon-meat; sometimes on nights. But whatever they had, they were never permitted to eat at those meals of more than one thing; and of that sparingly enough. Drinking or eating between meals was never allowed, unless in case of sickness; which seldom happened. Nor were they suffered to go into the kitchen to ask any thing of the servants, when they were at meat; if it was known they did, they were certainly beat, and the servants severely reprimanded.

At six, as soon as family prayers were over, they had their

supper; at seven, the maid washed them; and, beginning at the youngest, she undressed and got them all to bed by eight; at which time she left them in their several rooms awake—for there was no such thing allowed of in our house as sitting by a child till it fell asleep.

They were so constantly used to eat and drink what was given them that, when any of them was ill, there was no difficulty in making them take the most unpleasant medicine; for they durst not refuse it, though some of them would presently throw it up. This I mention to show that a person may be taught to take any thing, though it be never so much against his stomach.

In order to form the minds of children, the first thing to be done is to conquer their will, and bring them to an obedient temper. To inform the understanding is a work of time, and must with children proceed by slow degrees as they are able to bear it; but the subjecting the will is a thing that must be done at once, and the sooner the better. For, by neglecting timely correction, they will contract a stubbornness and obstinacy which is hardly ever after conquered; and never, without using such severity as would be as painful to me as to the child. In the esteem of the world they pass for kind and indulgent whom I call cruel parents, who permit their children to get habits which they know must be afterwards broken. Nay, some are so stupidly fond as in sport to teach their children to do things which in a while after they have severely beaten them for doing. Whenever a child is corrected, it must be conquered; and this will be no hard matter to do if it be not grown headstrong by too much indulgence. And when the will of a child is totally subdued, and it is brought to revere and stand in awe of the parents, then a great many childish follies and inadvertences may be passed by. Some should be overlooked and taken no notice of, and others mildly reproved; but no wilful transgression ought ever to be forgiven children without chastisement, less or more, as the nature and circumstances of the offence require.

I insist upon conquering the will of children betimes, because this is the only strong and rational foundation of a religious education, without which both precept and example will be ineffectual. But when this is thoroughly done, then a child is capable of being governed by the reason and piety of its parents, till its own understanding comes to maturity, and the principles of religion have taken root in the mind.

I cannot yet dismiss this subject. As self-will is the root of all sin and misery, so whatever cherishes this in children insures their after-wretchedness and irreligion; whatever checks and mortifies it promotes their future happiness and piety. This is still more evident if we farther consider that religion is nothing else than the doing the will of God, and not our own; that, the one grand impediment to our temporal and eternal happiness being this self-will, no indulgences of it can be trivial, no denial unprofitable. Heaven or hell depends on this alone. So that the parent who studies to subdue it in his child works together with God in the renewing and saving a soul. The parent who indulges it does the devil's work, makes religion impracticable, salvation unattainable; and does all that in him lies to damn his child, soul and body, for ever.

The children of this family were taught, as soon as they could speak, the Lord's Prayer, which they were made to say at rising and bed-time constantly; to which, as they grew bigger, were added a short prayer for their parents and some collects; a short catechism, and some portions of Scripture, as their memories could bear. They were very early made to distinguish the Sabbath from other days, before they could well speak or go. They were as soon taught to be still at family prayers, and to ask a blessing immediately after, which they used to do by signs, before they could kneel or speak.

They were quickly made to understand they might have nothing they cried for, and instructed to speak handsomely for what they wanted. They were not suffered to ask even the lowest servant for aught without saying, 'Pray give me such a thing'; and the servant was chid if she ever let them omit that word. Taking God's name in vain, cursing and swearing, profaneness, obscenity, rude, ill-bred names, were never heard among them. Nor were they ever permitted to call each other by their proper names without the addition of Brother or Sister.

None of them were taught to read till five years old, except Kezzy, in whose case I was overruled; and she was more years learning than any of the rest had been months. The way of teaching was this: The day before a child began to learn, the house was set in order, every one's work appointed them, and a charge given that none should come into the room from nine till twelve, or from two till five; which, you know, were our school hours. One day was allowed the child wherein to learn its letters; and each of them did in that time know all its letters, great and small, except Molly and Nancy, who were a day and a half before they knew them perfectly; for which I then thought them very dull; but since I have observed how long many children are learning the horn-book, I have changed my opinion. But the reason why I thought them so then was because the rest learned so readily; and your brother Samuel, who was the first child I ever taught, learned the alphabet in a few hours. He was five years old on the 10th of February; the next day he began to learn; and, as soon as he knew the letters, began at the first chapter of Genesis. He was taught to spell the first verse, then to read it over and over, till he could read it off-hand without any hesitation; so on to the second, etc., till he took ten verses for a lesson, which he quickly did. Easter fell low that year; and by Whitsuntide he could read a chapter very well; for he read continually, and had such a prodigious memory that I cannot remember ever to have told him the same word twice.

What was yet stranger, any word he had learned in his lesson he knew wherever he saw it, either in his Bible, or any other book; by which means he learned very soon to read an English author well.

The same method was observed with them all. As soon as they knew the letters, they were put first to spell, and read one line, then a verse; never leaving till perfect in their lesson, were it shorter or longer. So one or other continued reading at school-time, without any intermission; and before we left school each child read what he had learned that morning; and, ere we parted in the afternoon, what they had learned that day.

There was no such thing as loud talking or playing allowed of, but every one was kept close to their business, for the six hours of school: and it is almost incredible what a child may be taught in a quarter of a year, by a vigorous application, if it have but a tolerable capacity and good health. Every one of these, Kezzy excepted, could read better in that time than the most of women can do as long as they live.

Rising out of their places, or going out of the room, was not permitted unless for good cause; and running into the yard, garden, or street, without leave was always esteemed a capital offence.

For some years we went on very well. Never were children in better order. Never were children better disposed to piety or in more subjection to their parents, till that fatal dispersion of them, after the fire, into several families. In these they were left at full liberty to converse with servants, which before they had always been restrained from; and to run abroad, and play with any children, good or bad. They soon learned to neglect a strict observation of the Sabbath, and got knowledge of several songs and bad things, which before they had no notion of. That civil behaviour which made them admired when at home by all which saw them was, in great measure, lost; and a clownish accent and many rude ways were learned, which were not reformed without some difficulty.

When the house was rebuilt, and the children all brought home, we entered upon a strict reform; and then was begun the custom of singing Psalms at beginning and leaving school, morning and evening. Then also that of a general retirement at five o'clock was entered upon, when the oldest took the youngest that could speak, and the second the next, to whom they read the Psalms for the day, and a chapter in the New Testament; as, in the morning, they were directed to read the Psalms and a chapter in the Old; after which they went to their private prayers, before they got their breakfast or came into the family. And, I thank God, this custom is still preserved among us.

There were several by-laws observed among us, which slipped my memory, or else they had been inserted in their proper place; but I mention them here, because I think them useful.

1. It had been observed that cowardice and fear of punishment often lead children into lying, till they get a custom of it, which they cannot leave. To prevent this a law was made, That whoever was charged with a fault, of which they were guilty, if they would ingenuously confess it, and promise to amend, should not be beaten. This rule prevented a great deal of lying, and would have done more, if one in the family would have observed it. But he could not be prevailed on, and therefore was often imposed on by false colours and equivocations; which none would have used (except one), had they been kindly dealt with. And some, in spite of all, would always speak truth plainly.

2. That no sinful action, as lying, pilfering, playing at

church, or on the Lord's day, disobedience, quarrelling, etc., should ever pass unpunished.

3. That no child should ever be chid or beat twice for the same fault; and that, if they amended, they should never be upbraided with it afterwards.

4. That every signal act of obedience, especially when it crossed upon their own inclinations, should be always commended, and frequently rewarded, according to the merits of the cause.

5. That if ever any child performed an act of obedience, or did anything with an intention to please, though the performance was not well, yet the obedience and intention should be kindly accepted; and the child with sweetness directed how to do better for the future.

6. That propriety be inviolably preserved, and none suffered to invade the property of another in the smallest matter, though it were but of the value of a farthing or a pin; which they might not take from the owner without, much less against, his consent. This rule can never be too much inculcated on the minds of children; and from the want of parents or governors doing it as they ought proceeds that shameful neglect of justice which we may observe in the world.

7. That promises be strictly observed; and a gift once bestowed, and so the right passed away from the donor, be not resumed, but left to the disposal of him to whom it was given; unless it were conditional, and the condition of the obligation not performed.

8. That no girl be taught to work till she can read very well; and then that she be kept to her work with the same application, and for the same time, that she was held to in reading. This rule also is much to be observed; for the putting children to learn sewing before they can read perfectly is the very reason why so few women can read fit to be heard, and never to be well understood.

Susannah Wesley to Mr. Annesley.[24] Epworth. Jan. 20, 1721. Clarke, MWF, I, 389 ff.

What we shall or shall not need hereafter, God only knows; but at present there hardly ever was a greater coincidence of unprosperous events in one family than is now in ours. I am rarely in health. Mr. Wesley declines apace. My dear Emily, who in my present exigencies would exceedingly comfort me, is compelled to go to service in Lincoln, where she is a teacher in a boarding-school. My second daughter, Sukey, a pretty woman, and worthy of a better fate, when, by your last unkind letters, she perceived that all her hopes in you were frustrated, rashly threw away herself upon a man (if a *man* he may be called, who is little inferior to the apostate angels in wickedness) that is not only her plague, but a constant affliction to the family. O sir! O brother! Happy, thrice happy are you, happy is my sister, that buried your children in infancy! secure from temptation, secure from guilt, secure from want or shame, or loss of friends! They are safe beyond the reach of pain or sense of misery; being gone hence, nothing can touch them further. Believe me, sir, it is better to mourn ten children dead than one living; and I have buried many. But here I must pause awhile.

The other children, though wanting neither industry nor capacity for business, we cannot put to any, by reason we have neither money nor friends to assist us in doing it . . . .

The late archbishop of York once said to me (when my master was in Lincoln castle) among other things, 'Tell me,' said he, 'Mrs. Wesley, whether you ever really wanted bread?' My lord, said I, I will freely own to your grace that, strictly speaking, I never did want bread. But then, I had so much care to get it before it was eat, and to pay for it after, as has often made it very unpleasant to me. And I think to have bread on such terms is the next degree of wretchedness to having none at all. 'You are certainly in the right,' replied my lord, and seemed for a while very thoughtful. Next morning he made me a handsome present; ...

iii. Unmethodized Irruptions

1. *The Rectory Fire.*

During the night of February 9, 1709, fire broke out in the Epworth Rectory. The material consequences were disastrous, but the whole family was saved, John (he was five at the time) only after being to all appearances inextricably trapped in his blazing room. His mother was convinced thereafter that he had been preserved by Providence for a special work, and resolved to be more than ever careful in her nurture of his powers. Thus this fearful and apparently capricious irruption into the ordered life of the family was not allowed to remain unmethodized for long. She built this irregular stone, which might easily have been a stumbling-block, into the regular courses of the rising edifice of her faith and her son's. The events of the night and his mother's teaching so burned themselves into John's mind that he regarded himself for the rest of his life as a "brand plucked from the burning." Often, when the anniversary of the fire came round, he remembered the event and its significance, sometimes making public mention of it.[25] He inscribed a similar phrase on his account of the affair with Sophy Hopkey, which nearly, but not quite, ended in his marriage with that young lady.[26] When, in 1753, ill health brought him to writing his own epitaph, he directed that the phrase be carved on his tombstone.[27] Charles Wesley's longer version of this same intended inscription included what was certainly in his brother's thought: "A brand *not once only* plucked out of the fire."[28]

Mrs. Susannah Wesley to a neighboring clergyman, and some incidents supplied by Mr. John Wesley himself. Epworth. Aug. 24, 1709. Clarke, MWF, II, 34-36.

On Wednesday night, Feb. 9, between the hours of eleven and twelve, some sparks fell from the roof of our house, upon one of the children's (Hetty's) feet. She immediately ran to our chamber, and called us. Mr. Wesley, hearing a cry of fire in the street, started up (as I was very ill, he lay in a separate room from me), and opening his door, found the fire was in his own house. He immediately came to my room, and bid me and my eldest daughters rise quickly and shift for ourselves. Then he ran and burst open the nursery door, and called to the maid to bring out the children. The two little ones lay in the bed with her; the three others, in another bed. She snatched up the youngest, and bid the rest follow; which the three elder did. When we were got into the hall, and were surrounded with flames, Mr. Wesley found he had left the keys of the doors above stairs. He ran up and recovered them, a minute before the staircase took fire. When we opened the street door, the strong North-east wind drove the flames in with such violence, that none could stand against them. But some of our children got out through the windows, the rest through a little door into the garden. I was not in a condition to climb up to the windows, neither could I get to the garden door. I endeavoured three times to force my passage through the street door, but was as often beat back by the fury of the flames. In this distress I besought our blessed Saviour for help, and then waded through the fire, naked as I was; which did me no further harm, than a little scorching my hands and my face.

When Mr. Wesley had seen the other children safe, he heard the child in the nursery cry. He attempted to go up the stairs, but they were all on fire, and would not bear his weight. Finding it impossible to give any help, he kneeled down in the hall, and recommended the soul of the child to God.

"I believe," observes Mr. John Wesley, "it was just at that time I waked; for I did not cry as they imagined, unless it was afterwards. I remember all the circumstances as distinctly as though it were but yesterday. Seeing the room was very light, I called to the maid to take me up. But none answering, I put my head out of the curtains, and saw streaks of fire on the top of the room. I got up and ran to the door, but could get no further, all the door beyond it being in a blaze. I then climbed up on a chest, which stood near the window: one in the yard saw me, and proposed running to fetch a ladder. Another answered, 'There will not be time; but I have thought of another expedient. Here I will fix myself against the wall; lift a light man, and set him upon my shoulders.' They did so; and he took me out of the window. Just then the whole roof fell in; but it fell inward, or we had all been crushed at once. When they brought me into the house where my father was, he cried out, 'Come, neighbours, let us kneel down; let us give thanks to God! He has given me all my eight children; let the house go; I am rich enough.' The next day, as he was walking in the garden, and surveying the ruins of the house, he picked up part of a leaf of his Polyglott Bible, on which just those words were legible: *Vade; vende omnia quae habes, et attolle crucem et sequere me.* "Go; sell all that thou hast; and take up thy cross, and follow me."

2. "Old Jeffrey".

When John was fourteen, and already in school at Charterhouse in London, he heard by letter of a strange visitation at the Rectory. It recurred at intervals through a couple of months in the winter 1716-17. The family ascribed the disturbances to a supernatural being whom they soon familiarly, and with a little weary contempt, called "Old Jeffrey." The phenomena described are of course not unique, and have been ascribed by students of such things to an agency called "poltergeist"—turbulent spirit—which is a descriptive rather than an explanatory name. John was naturally keenly interested at the time; nor did his interest cease with the passing of the years. It was three years before he visited his home again; at that time he made a personal investigation of the strange occurrences. His findings were published much later in the *Arminian Magazine;* they are to be found also in his *Works* (New York: 1850) VII, 474 ff. The extracts which follow come from the fuller account given by Adam Clarke.

SUSANNAH TO JOHN WESLEY. [Epworth]. Aug. 27, 1726. Clarke, MWF, I, 274.

About ten days after Nanny Marshall had heard unusual groans at the dining room door, Emily came and told me that the servants and the children had been several times frightened with strange groans and knockings about the house. I answered, that the rats John Maw had frightened from his house, by blowing a horn there, were come into ours, and ordered that one should be sent for. Molly was much displeased at it, and said, if it was any thing super-natural, it certainly would be very angry, and more trouble-some. However, the horn was blown in the garrets; and the effect was, that whereas before the noises were always in the night, from this time they were heard at all hours, day and night.

EMILY TO SAMUEL WESLEY, JR. [Epworth]. Feb. 11, 1716-17. Clarke, MWF, I, 270 ff.

Dear Brother:

I thank you for your last; and shall give you what satis-faction is in my power, concerning what has happened in our family. I am so far from being superstitious, that I was too much inclined to infidelity; so that I heartily rejoice at having such an opportunity of convincing myself, past doubt or scruple, of the existence of some beings besides those we see. A whole month was sufficient to convince any body of the reality of the thing, and to try all ways of discovering any trick, had it been possible for any such to have been used. I shall only tell you what I myself heard, and leave the rest to others.

My sister in the paper chamber had heard noises, and told me of them; but I did not much believe, till one night, about a week after the first groans were heard, which was the beginning, just after the clock had struck ten, I went down stairs to lock the doors, which I always do. Scarce had I got up the best stairs, when I heard a noise, like a person throwing down a vast coal in the middle of the fore kitchen, and all the splinters seemed to fly about from it. I was not much frighted, but went to my sister Sukey, and we together went all over the low rooms, but there was nothing out of order.

Our dog was fast asleep, and our only cat in the other end of the house. No sooner was I got upstairs, and undressing for bed, but I heard a noise among many bottles that stand under the best stairs, just like the throwing of a great stone among them, which had broke them all to pieces. This made me hasten to bed. But my sister Hetty, who sits always to wait on my father going to bed, was still sitting on the lowest step on the garret stairs, the door being shut at her back; when, soon after, there came down the stairs behind her something like a man, in a loose nightgown trailing after him, which made her fly rather than run to me in the nursery.

All this time we never told our father of it; but soon after we did. He smiled, and gave no answer; but was more careful than usual, from that time, to see us in bed, imagining it to be some of us young women that sat up late, and made a noise. His incredulity, and especially his imputing it to us, or our lovers, made me, I own, desirous of its continuance till he was convinced. As for my mother, she firmly believed it to be rats, and sent for a horn to blow them away. I laughed to think how wisely they were employed, who were striving half a day to fright away Jeffrey (for that name I gave it) with a horn.

But whatever it was, I perceived it could be made angry. For from that time it was so outrageous, there was no quiet for us after ten at night. I heard frequently, between ten and eleven, something like the quick winding up of a jack, at the corner of the room by my bed's head, just like the running of the wheels and the creaking of the iron-work. This was the common signal of its coming. Then it would knock on the floor three times, then at my sister's bed's head in the same room, almost always three together, and then stay. The sound was hollow and loud, so as none of us could ever imitate.

It would answer to my mother, if she stamped on the floor, and bid it. It would knock when I was putting the children to bed, just under me where I sat. One time, little Kezzy, pretending to scare Patty, as I was undressing them, stamped with her foot on the floor, and immediately it answered with three knocks, just in the same place. It was more loud and fierce, if any one said it was rats, or any thing natural.

I could tell you abundance more of it; but the rest will write, and therefore it would be needless. I was not much frighted at first, and very little at last; but it was never near me, except two or three times; and never followed me, as it did my sister Hetty. I have been with her when it has knocked under her; and when she has removed, it has followed, and still kept just under her feet, which was enough to terrify a stouter person.

If you would know my opinion of the reason of this, I shall briefly tell you. I believe it to be witchcraft, for these reasons. About a year since, there was a disturbance at a town near us, that was undoubtedly witches; and if so near, why may they not reach us? Then my father had for several Sundays before its coming preached warmly against consulting those that are called cunning men, which our people are given to; and it had a particular spite at my father.

Besides, something was thrice seen. The first time by my mother, under my sister's bed, like a badger, only without any head that was discernible. The same creature was sat by the dining room fire one evening; when our man went into the room, it ran by him, through the hall, under the stairs. He followed with a candle, and searched, but it was departed. The last time he saw it in the kitchen, like a white rabbit, which seems likely to be some witch; and I do so really believe it to be one, that I would venture to fire a pistol at it, if I saw it long enough. It has been heard by me and others since December. I have filled up all my room, and have only time to tell you,

I am,

Your loving sister.

From S. Wesley's Journal. Winter-1716. Clarke, MWF, I, 250.

When we were at prayers, and came to the prayers for King George and the prince, it would make a great noise over our heads constantly, whence some of the family called it a Jacobite. I have been thrice pushed by an invisible power, once against the corner of my desk in the study, a second time against the door of the matted chamber, a third time against the right side of the frame of my study door, as I was going in.

Narrative drawn up by Mr. John Wesley, and published in the *Arminian Magazine* in 1884. Clarke, MWF, I, 253.

When Robert[29] came to the top of the garret stairs, he saw a handmill, which was at a little distance, whirled about very swiftly. When he related this, he said, "Nought vexed me, but that it was empty. I thought, if it had but been full of malt, he might have ground his heart out for me."

SUSANNAH TO SAMUEL WESLEY, JR. Mar. 27, 1717.
Clarke MWF, I, 273.

I cannot imagine how you should be so curious about our unwelcome guest. For my part, I am quite tired with hearing or speaking of it: but if you come among us, you will find enough to satisfy all your scruples, and perhaps may hear or see it yourself.

CHAPTER II

THE UNIVERSITY

Introduction: The Sources.

Glimpses of the development of the future evangelists are more numerous for the extremely important University period than for their early life at home. However, since the published journals do not begin till the start of the voyage to Georgia, our picture still is a mosaic of small pieces from scattered sources. This is true even of John Wesley, and still more of Charles. John began, in 1725, to keep "a more exact account of time" in which he recorded his doings from hour to hour. This was intended to aid him in giving an account of his stewardship to God rather than for the enlightenment of his fellow men—either those of his own generation, or investigators of subsequent times. Indeed, he was at pains to hide what he wrote beneath a cipher whose mysteries were penetrated only by the labors of Nehemiah Curnock, the editor of the Standard Edition of the *Journal,* in the first decade of our own century. Even so, Curnock found the value of the Diary of this period before the *Journal* begins, to lie chiefly in its disclosure of the tenor of Wesley's inner life. Because of the fragmentary and allusive nature of this record, Curnock wisely published only samples of it.

There are letters too, for Oxford, if none for Charterhouse. Schoolboys are not noted for saving letters. The more methodical university student saved some that came from home, and a few of those he wrote to the rectory have survived. The Morgan correspondence is especially valuable. The most important of these letters stands at the beginning of the published *Journal* under the title "The Rise and Design of Oxford Methodism"; this correspondence is especially valuable for the light it throws on the ideals and activities of the "Holy Club." A letter of John Clayton, helps us further in this respect.[1] Of another sort entirely are those written by John to the members of a small circle of friends of his own age, which included the daughters of the Kirkham family in the Rectory at Stanton Harcourt, Mrs. Pendarves and several others. These are written in the "elegant" style of the age, which seems to us rather stilted; the correspondents are known by romantic pseudonyms: John Wesley was "Cyrus," Mrs. Pendarves, "Aspasia," The Kirkham girls were "Varanese" and "Sappho." Those written by "Cyrus" and others are published in the Standard Edition of the *Letters of John Wesley*.[2]

In addition to the letters, we have sundry subsequent references by John Wesley himself to his Oxford days, the most helpful of which for our purposes are the review of his spiritual development he put at the head of the conversion entry in his *Journal* (May 24, 1738) and a similar review of one aspect of his thought found in the early pages of the treatise called "A Plain Account of Christian Perfection."

In spite of the fact that it is the *inner* development of John Wesley which interests us most at this period, it may be helpful to put at the head of the extracts in this chapter an outline of the external happenings of his Oxford days.

Skeleton Chronology of John Wesley's Oxford Days.

1. From his matriculation to his taking Deacon's Orders.

1720 Matriculation at Christ's Church (age 17 years).

1721 (close) begins to keep a schedule of time, make a list of studies for 1722.

1724 (towards end) determines to enter holy orders.

1725 (April) begins to keep diary, "a more exact account of time."

April 14 first met "a religious friend."

About the same time read *Imitation of Christ* and *Holy Living and Holy Dying*. Begins in earnest the pursuit of "inward holiness."

(September) Ordained Deacon.

2. From his election as Fellow of Lincoln to his departure for Georgia.

    a. Period of non-residence.

    1726 Elected to Fellowship. Charles Wesley comes up to Christ Church.

    (April to September), his father's Curate at Epworth and Wroote.

    (November) Elected Greek Lecturer and Moderator of Classes.

    1727 (February) Master's degree.

    (August) in Lincolnshire again, Curate till 1729.

    1728 Ordination to Presbyterate.

    b. Period of residence.

    1729 (November) returns to Oxford, becomes "Curator of the Holy Club" which had been begun by Charles Wesley.

    1735 (April) death of Samuel Wesley.

    (October) Embarks with Charles for Georgia.

i. John Wesley at Charterhouse

When all that we know about John Wesley at Charterhouse is gathered together in one place, we still have very little, and some of that is of dubious value. We learn that he went up as a Foundation Scholar on the nomination of the Duke of Buckingham; that his aptitude as a scholar satisfied not only his masters, but his older brother Samuel, then head usher at Westminster School. Further, he tells us that he got little meat to eat there, because the bigger boys crowded out the smaller from getting their share; that obedient to his father's instructions, he ran "around the Charterhouse garden, which was of considerable extent, three times every morning." [3] Tyerman is concerned to defend him against charges of ambition based on a story "by an Old Member of Society." According to this story, one of the masters noted that young Wesley was always to be found with younger boys, usually haranguing them. Being questioned about this, he replied, "Better to rule in hell than to serve in heaven." [4] But the same Tyerman who is concerned to take the sting out of the imputation of ambition makes a much more sweeping charge himself: "John Wesley entered the Charterhouse a saint, and left it a sinner." [5] This he does, doubtless, to magnify the grace of God in Wesley's conversion, and perhaps is but following Wesley's own example in this matter. At any rate, we must conclude that Tyerman considerably sharpened Wesley's self-condemnation contained in the extract below.

May 24, 1738. WJJS, I, 465 f.

2. The next six or seven years were spent at school; where, outward restraints being removed, I was much more negligent than before, even of outward duties, and almost continually guilty of outward sins, which I knew to be such, though they were not scandalous in the eye of the world. However I still read the Scriptures, and said my prayers morning and evening. And what I now hoped to be saved by, was, (1) not being so bad as other people; (2) having still a kindness for religion; and (3) reading the Bible, going to church, and saying my prayers.

ii. The First Years at Oxford, 1720-1725

John Wesley did nothing during his undergraduate years to draw notice to himself in any conspicuous fashion. He did set himself, with somewhat more than average persistence and ability, to take advantage of his academic opportunities. If the strictures which, a generation later, the famous historian Gibbon levelled at his *alma mater*[6] were even partially applicable during Wesley's undergraduate days, he would have need of all his intellectual initiative and self-discipline to win through the pervasive atmosphere of indolence and frivolity to his very satisfactory academic achievement. At least he had sufficient seriousness of purpose to chide himself with a propensity to trifle away his time. As to his religious state during those years, he passed an unfavorable verdict on it, as he had on that of this Charterhouse days. We would say that he manifested an unusually tenacious loyalty to his early religious training. Nevertheless the most apt contemporary description we have is couched in primarily secular terms: "He appeared the very sensible and acute collegian — a young fellow of the finest classical taste, of the most liberal and manly sentiments."[7]

May 24, 1738. WJJS, I, 466.

3. Being removed to the University for five years, I still said my prayers both in public and in private, and read, with the Scriptures, several other books of religion, especially comments on the New Testament. Yet I had not all this while so much as a notion of inward holiness; nay, went on habitually, and for the most part very contentedly, in some or other known sin: indeed, with some intermission and short struggles, especially before and after the Holy Communion, which I was obliged to receive thrice a year. I cannot well tell what I hoped to be saved by now, when I was continually sinning against that little light I had; unless by those transient fits of what many divines taught me to call repentance.

iii. Awakening, 1725

Toward the close of 1724, John Wesley decided to seek ordination in the Church of England. We do not have the letter in which he announced this decision to his parents. Their replies we have, that from his father being given below. In this reply Mr. Wesley mentions, even before he speaks of the proposed ordination, certain steps he himself has taken "with Dr. Morley." Dr. Morley was Rector of Lincoln College where John afterward was elected Fellow. Samuel then tries to allay certain scruples in his son's heart as to the worth of the motives which had led him to this decision to enter the ministry. Taking these two hints together with the fact that ordination was prerequisite to a fellowship, we are, I believe, justified in concluding that initially, John's decision to take orders was subordinate, because instrumental, to his candidacy for a fellowship in Lincoln, the attractiveness of which to the apt, but impecunious, student we can easily understand.[8] We concur with the good Rector's judgment that to enter orders 'to eat a piece of bread' was, though not wrong, certainly insufficient. As the event was to prove, however, few men in Christian history have progressed so far beyond an originally casual view of the Christian ministry to a point where as a "calling" in the highest sense of the word, it was to absorb his whole life.

Meanwhile a change, much more important in its nature and effects than entering orders, took place in the secret recesses of John Wesley's soul. By it, his whole life found orientation about a new and dominating objective: the pursuit of holiness. The passion—for it was nothing less—which then laid hold on him, as it has on a glorious succession of saints throughout the Christian ages, was to change its form somewhat, but never thereafter to relax its grip his whole life long. So momentous was this change that some biographers profess to see in it the real conversion of John Wesley.[9] This is not the place to discuss the correctness of that view; but it is cited to underline the undoubtedly high importance of this sudden crystallization of purpose about a lofty Christian ideal.

We are unable, in the nature of the case, to describe in detail the profounder aspects of this transformation by which the "sensible and acute young collegian" became the almost terribly earnest seeker after holiness. In Curnock's happy phrase, "a book and a friend were used by the providence of God"[10] to accomplish it. Wesley himself tells us the name of the book, but not that of the friend. Curnock proposes the name of Miss Betty Kirkham to fill this gap.[11] As to the book, Wesley calls it Kempis' *Christian Pattern,* but we recognize in it the book now usually known as *The Imitation of Christ,* one of the great classics of Christian devotion. This was followed soon after by the reading of three other books: *Rules for Holy Living and Holy Dying,* by Jeremy Taylor; *A Serious Call to a Devout and Holy Life,* and *Treatise on Christian Perfection,* both by William Law. *The Imitation of Christ* comes from the fifteenth century or earlier, and is pervaded by the contemplative temper and yearning for retirement from the world which is usually associated with the pre-Reformation ideal of sanctity. The other two writers were Anglicans, Jeremy Taylor, being of the seventeenth century and William Law an older contemporary of Wesley himself. All four of the books may be said, however, to rise out of the "catholic" tradition, because they all earnestly enforce the necessity of holiness and contempt of the world. Because they teach the methodical cultivation of these ends, they supplemented the early training John had already received. While he did not read them uncritically, their cumulative effect was considerable, as Wesley's repeated mention of them shows, and their effect on his life was, according to his own estimate, both deep and lasting.

SAMUEL WESLEY, SR., TO JOHN. Wroot, Jan. 26, 1724-25. Clarke, MWF, I, 294 f.

Dear Son . . .

I did not forget you with Dr. Morley, but have moved that way as much as possible; though I must confess, hitherto, with no great prospect or hopes of success.

As for what you mention of entering into holy orders, it is indeed a great work; and I am pleased to find you think it so . . .

As for your motives you take notice of, my thoughts are: 1. It is no harm to desire getting into that office, even as Eli's sons, 'to eat a piece of bread;' for 'the labourer is worthy of his hire.' Though, 2. A desire and intention to lead a stricter life, and a belief one should do so, is a better reason; though this should by all means be begun before, or else, ten to one, it will deceive us afterwards . . . 4. The principal spring and motive, to which all the former should be only secondary, must certainly be the glory of God, and the service of his church, in the edification and salvation of our neighbour: and woe to him who with any meaner leading view, attempts so sacred a work. For which, 5, He should take all the care he possibly can, with the advice of wiser and elder men,—especially imploring with all humility, sincerity, and intention of mind, and with fasting and prayer, the direction and assistance of Almighty God and his Holy Spirit,—to qualify and prepare himself for it.

The knowledge of the languages is a very considerable help in this matter . . .

May 24, 1738. WJJS, I, 466f.

4. When I was about twenty-two,[12] my father pressed me to enter into holy orders. At the same time, the providence of God directing me to Kempis's *Christian Pattern*, I began to see, that true religion was seated in the heart,

and that God's law extended to all our thoughts as well as words and actions. I was, however, very angry at Kempis for being too strict; though I read him only in Dean Stanhope's translation. Yet I had frequently much sensible comfort in reading him, such as I was an utter stranger to before; and meeting likewise with a religious friend, which I never had till now, I began to alter the whole form of my conversation, and to set in earnest upon a new life. I set apart an hour or two a day for religious retirement. I communicated every week. I watched against all sin, whether in word or deed. I began to aim at, and pray for, inward holiness. So that now, 'doing so much, and living so good a life,' I doubted not but I was a good Christian.

Works VI,[13] 483 f.

In the year 1725, being in the twenty-third year of my age, I met with Bishop Taylor's "Rules and Exercises of Holy Living and Dying." In reading several parts of this book, I was exceedingly affected; that part in particular which relates to purity of intention. Instantly I resolved to dedicate all my life to God, all my thoughts, and words, and actions: being thoroughly convinced, there was no medium; but that every part of my life (not some only) must either be a sacrifice to God, or myself, that is, in effect, to the devil.

Can any serious person doubt of this, or find a medium between serving God and serving the devil?

In the year 1726, I met with Kempis's "Christian Pattern." The nature and extent of inward religion, the religion of the heart, now appeared to me in a stronger light than ever it had done before. I saw, that giving even all my life to God (supposing it possible to do this, and go no farther) would profit me nothing, unless I gave my heart, yea, all my heart to him.

I saw, that "simplicity of intention, and purity of affection," one design in all we speak or do, and one desire ruling all our tempers, are indeed "the wings of the soul," without which she can never ascend to the mount of God.

A year or two after, Mr. Law's "Christian Perfection" and "Serious Call" were put into my hands. These convinced me, more than ever, of the absolute impossibility of being half a Christian; and I determined, through his grace, (the absolute necessity of which I was deeply sensible of,) to be all devoted to God, to give him all my soul, my body, and my substance.

May 24, 1738. WJJS, I, 467 f.

5. Removing soon after to another College, I executed a resolution which I was before convinced was of the utmost importance,—shaking off at once all my trifling acquaintance.[14] I began to see more and more the value of time. I applied myself closer to study. I watched more carefully against actual sins; I advised others to be religious, according to that scheme of religion by which I modelled my own life. But meeting now with Mr. Law's *Christian Perfection* and *Serious Call,* although I was much offended at many parts of both, yet they convinced me more than ever of the exceeding height and breadth and depth of the law of God. The light flowed in so mightily upon my soul, that every thing appeared in a new view. I cried to God for help, and resolved not to prolong the time of obeying Him as I had never done before. And by my continued endeavour to keep His whole law, inward and outward, to the utmost of my power, I was persuaded that I should be accepted of Him, and that I was even then in a state of salvation.

6. In 1730 I began visiting the prisons; assisting the poor and sick in town; and doing what other good I could, by my presence or my little fortune, to the bodies and souls of all men. To this end I abridged myself of all superfluities, and many that are called necessaries of life.[15] I soon became a by-word for so doing, and I rejoiced that

my name was cast out as evil. The next spring I began observing the Wednesday and Friday Fasts, commonly observed in the ancient Church; tasting no food till three in the afternoon. And now I knew not how to go any further. I diligently strove against all sin. I omitted no sort of self-denial which I thought lawful; I carefully used, both in public and in private, all the means of grace at all opportunities. I omitted no occasion of doing good; I for that reason suffered evil. And all this I knew to be nothing, unless as it was directed toward inward holiness. Accordingly this, the image of God, was what I aimed at in all, my doing His will, not my own. Yet when, after continuing some years in this course, I apprehended myself to be near death, I could not find that all this gave me any comfort or any assurance of acceptance with God. At this I was then not a little surprised; not imagining I had been all this time building on the sand, nor considering that 'other foundation can no man lay than that which is laid' by God, 'even Christ Jesus.'

iv. Correspondence Course

Susannah Wesley kept her resolution "to be more *particularly* careful of the soul of this child," [16] that God had so signally rescued from death, even after he was well grown and away at the University. This care manifested itself in the correspondence she kept up with him. Sometimes she dealt in her letters with a question in the "practical divinity" the study of which she had urged on him after learning of his resolution to enter the ministry; sometimes even a more speculative topic was treated vigorously and in a way which left a lasting impression on him. For instance, through the rest of his life he believed as she had taught on the "impious assertion" of predestination; and (as will be seen below) after differing at first, he came around to her view of what constitutes saving faith.

SUSANNAH WESLEY TO JOHN. Wroote. Jan. 8, 1725.
Clarke, MWF, II, 16.

I cannot recollect the passages you mention: but believing you do the author, I positively aver that he is extremely in the wrong in that impious, not to say blasphemous, assertion, that God by an irresistible decree hath determined any man to be miserable, even in this life. His intentions, as himself, are holy, and just, and good; and all the miseries incident to men here or hereafter spring from themselves. The case stands thus:—This life is a state of probation, wherein eternal happiness or misery are proposed to our choice; the one as the reward of a virtuous, the other as a consequence of a vicious, life . . .

As the happiness of man consists in a due subordination of the inferior to the superior powers, etc., so the inversion of this order is the true source of human misery. There is in us all a natural propension towards the body and the world. The beauty, pleasures, and ease of the body strangely charm us; the wealth and honours of the world allure us; and all, under the manage of a subtle malicious adversary, give a prodigious force to present things: and if the animal life once get the ascendant of our reason, it utterly deprives us of our moral liberty, and by consequence makes us wretched. Therefore, for any man to endeavour after happiness in gratifying all his bodily appetites in opposition to his reason, is the greatest folly imaginable; because he seeks it where God has not designed he shall ever find it . . .

. . . And when, by the grace of God's Holy Spirit, we are so far conquerors, as that we never willingly offend, but still press after greater degrees of Christian perfection, sincerely endeavouring to plant each virtue in our minds, that may through Christ render us pleasing to God; we shall then experience the truth of Solomon's assertion, 'The ways of virtue are ways of pleasantness, and all her paths are peace.'

I take Kempis to have been an honest weak man, who had more zeal than knowledge, by his condemning all mirth or pleasure as sinful or useless, in opposition to so many direct and plain texts of Scripture. Would you judge of the lawfulness or unlawfulness of pleasure; of the innocence or malignity of actions? Take this rule: Whatever weakens your reason, impairs the tenderness of your conscience, obscures your sense of God, or takes off the relish of spiritual things; in short, whatever increases the strength and authority of your body over your mind; that thing is sin to you, however innocent it may be in itself. And so on the contrary.

SUSANNAH WESLEY TO JOHN. Wroote. July 18, 1725.
Clarke, MWF, II, 20 f.

I have often wondered that men should be so vain to amuse themselves by searching into the decrees of God, which no human wit can fathom; and do not rather employ their time and powers in working out their salvation, and making their own calling and election sure . . .

The doctrine of predestination, as maintained by rigid Calvinists, is very shocking, and ought utterly to be abhorred, because it charges the most holy God with being the author of sin. And I think you reason very well and justly against it; for it is certainly inconsistent with the justice and goodness of God to lay any man under either a physical or moral necessity of committing sin, and then punish him for doing it. Far be this from the Lord! Shall not the Judge of all the earth do right?

I do firmly believe that God from all eternity, hath elected some to everlasting life; but then I humbly conceive that this election is founded in his foreknowledge, according to that in the eighth of Romans, ver. 29, 30: "Whom he did foreknow, he also did predestinate to be conformed to the image of his Son: moreover, whom he did predestinate, them he also called; and whom he called,

them he also justified; and whom he justified, them he also
glorified."

SUSANNAH WESLEY TO JOHN. Epworth. Feb. 14, 1735.[17]
Clarke, MWF, II, 27.

Since God is altogether inaccessible to us but by Jesus
Christ, and since none ever was or ever will be saved but
by him is it not absolutely necessary for all people, young
and old, to be well grounded in the knowledge and faith
of Jesus Christ? By *faith,* I do not mean an assent only to
the truths of the gospel concerning him, but such an assent
as influences our practice; as makes us heartily and thankfully accept him for our God and Saviour upon his own
conditions. No faith below this can be saving. And since
this faith is necessary to salvation, can it be too frequently
or too explicitly discoursed on to young people? I think
not.

JOHN WESLEY TO HIS MOTHER. Oxford. July 29, 1725.
WJL, I, 22.

Faith is a species of belief, and belief is defined 'an assent to a proposition upon rational grounds.' Without
rational grounds there is therefore no belief, and consequently no faith.

JOHN WESLEY TO HIS MOTHER. Oxford. Nov. 22, 1725.
WJL, I, 25.

I am, therefore, at length come over entirely to your
opinion, that saving faith (including practice) is an assent
to what God has revealed because He has revealed it and
not because the truth of it may be evinced by reason.

SUSANNAH WESLEY TO JOHN. Wroote. May 14, 1727.
Clarke, MWF, II, 25.

Suffer now a word of advice. However curious you may

be in searching into the nature, or in distinguishing the properties, of the passions or virtues of human kind, for your own private satisfaction, be very cautious in giving nice distinctions in public assemblies; for it does not answer the true end of preaching, which is to mend men's lives, and not fill their heads with unprofitable speculations. And after all that can be said, every affection of the soul is better known by experience than any description that can be given of it. An honest man will more easily apprehend what is meant by being zealous for God and against sin, when he hears what are the properties and effects of true zeal, than the most accurate definition of its essence.

Dear son, the conclusion of your letter is very kind. That you were ever dutiful, I very well know. But I know myself enough to rest satisfied with a moderate degree of your affection. Indeed it would be unjust in me to desire the love of any one. Your prayers I want and wish; nor shall I cease while I live to beseech Almighty God to bless you. Adieu.

JOHN WESLEY TO HIS MOTHER. Oxford. Feb. 28, 1732. WJL, I, 120 f.

Dear mother, there is but one cause of uneasiness which I sometimes find in your behaviour towards me. You perform the noblest offices of love for me, and yet blame the Fountain from whence they flow. You have more than once said you loved me too well and would strive to love me less. Now this it is I complain of. You do not think natural affection evil in itself; far from it. But you say you have but little time to stay in the world, and therefore should not have much affection for anything in it. Most true: not any of those things which perish with the world. But am I one of those? If you think I am 'sick unto death,' love me the more, and you will the more fervently pray for me that I may be healed. If you rather incline to think that there is hope of my recovery, then what if you are to leave the world in a little time? Whom God hath joined can Death put asunder? According to your supposition that unbodied spirits still minister to those who were their kindred according to the flesh, not a moment! Certainly, not long. Yet a little while, and if you return not to me, you will certainly be overtaken by,—Your dutiful and affectionate Son.

John Wesley was not the first, nor yet the last student to write to his relatives on how busy he was. The difference in this one is that it was true—not only when he wrote, but for the rest of his life.

JOHN TO SAMUEL WESLEY, JR. Oxford. Dec. 5, 1726. WJL, I, 34.

Leisure and I have taken leave of one another: I propose to be busy as long as I live, if my health is so long indulged to me.

JOHN WESLEY TO HIS MOTHER. Oxford. Feb. 28, 1732. WJL, I, 119.

You say you 'have renounced the world.' And what have I been doing all this time? What have I done ever since I was born? Why, I have been plunging myself into it more and more. It is enough. 'Awake, thou that sleepest.' Is there not 'one Lord, one Spirit, one hope of our calling'? One way of attaining that hope? Then I am to renounce the world, as well as you. That is the very thing I want to do; to draw off my affections from this world, and fix them on a better. But How? What is the surest and the shortest way? Is it not to be humble? Surely this is a large step in the way. But the question recurs, How am I to do this? To own the necessity of it is not to be humble. In many things you have interceded for me and prevailed.

Who knows but in this too you may be successful? If you can spare me only that little part of Thursday evening which you formerly bestowed upon me in another manner, I doubt not but it would be as useful now for correcting my heart as it was then for forming my judgment.

OF MOONLIGHT AND AN ARBOUR. John Wesley to Mrs. Pendarves ("Aspasia.")

Of the some sixty letters which have been preserved from John Wesley's Oxford days, about a third are to Mrs. Pendarves. Born Mary Granville, she met the Wesley brothers at their mutual friends' the Kirkhams in Stanton. At the time of the letters (1730-1734) she was already widowed, but still young, charming and witty. Her charm and wit survived her youth, so that a biographer could say of her, " . . . at the end of her long life, when she was over eighty, people were still admiring her exquisite grace, her charming style in anecdote and retrospection."[18] In 1743 she married Dr. Delaney, Dean of Down in Ireland. She became an acceptable member of Dean Swift's circle in Dublin, and later the friend of royalty. The letter given below is a sample of the correspondence, carried on under romantic pseudonyms by the little group which included the two young Oxford clerics John and Charles Wesley (Cyrus and Araspes,) the two Kirkham girls (Varanese and Sappho,) Aspasia herself and her sister Anne Granville (Selima). The tone of John's letters, though they are ostensibly concerned with progress in spiritual matters, reveals a shy and undeclared affection. This particular bright star gradually withdrew beyond his orbit, to swing in higher circles. After lapses and resumptions their correspondence finally ceased altogether. Though not without concern for reform, Aspasia and her decanal husband would hardly have approved of the Methodist way, and there is no evidence that she and John ever met again.

Sept. 12, [1730]. WJL, I, 52.

Madam,—I am greatly ashamed that I can only think how much I am obliged to you. Your last favour leaves me utterly at a loss, and even without hope of making any suitable acknowledgement; and at the same time that it convinces me of a mistake which I should not otherwise have so easily given up, it convinces me it was possible I should enjoy an higher pleasure than even your conversation gave me. If your understanding could not appear in a stronger light than when it brightened the dear hill, the fields, the arbour, I am now forced to confess your temper could: you even then showed but half your goodness.

I spent some very agreeable moments last night in musing on this delightful subject, and thinking to how little disadvantage Aspasia or Selima would have appeared even in that faint light which the moon glimmering through the trees poured on that part of our garden where I was walking! how little would the eye of the mind that surveyed them have missed the absent sun! what darkness could have obscured gentleness, courtesy, humility, could have shaded the image of God? Sure none but that which shall never dare to approach them; none but vice, which shall ever be far away!

I could not close this reflection without adding with a sigh, When will they shine on me! when will Providence direct my wandering feet to tread again that flowery path to virtue! My dear Varanese informs me you are going yet farther from us, but cannot inform me how soon. If either this or any other ill-natured accident (to speak in the language of men) denies me the happiness of waiting upon you so soon as I sometime hoped I should, 'tis best it should be denied me: wise is He that disposes of us: I acquiesce in His disposal.

Nothing can excuse me, of all persons in the world, from entirely acquiescing in all His disposals, to whom alone I can ascribe the happiness I now enjoy, so far above my most aspiring hopes. To Him alone can I ascribe it that I have found any favour in the sight of Selima or Aspasia; that I have before me such a proof of their generous condescension as the thanks of my life will poorly repay; that I once more feel the exquisite pleasure of calling myself,— Their ever obliged and most obedient servant.

JOHN TO SAMUEL WESLEY, JR. Oxford. Nov. 17, 1731. WJL, I, 115.

Mirth, I grant, is fit for you; but does it follow that it is fit for me? Are the same tempers, any more than the same words or actions, fit for all circumstances? If you are to 'rejoice evermore' because you have put your enemies to flight, am I to do the same while they continually assault me? You are glad, because you are 'passed from death to life'; well, but let him be afraid who knows not whether he is to live or die. Whether this be my condition or no, who can tell better than myself? Him who can, whoever he be, I allow to be a proper judge whether I do well to be generally as serious as I can.

v. Practicum: The "Holy Club"

Charles Wesley came up to Christ Church in 1727 after an active schoolboy life at St. Peter's College Westminster, where he had been chosen captain of the school. He was in Oxford over two years before John returned from his three years of duty as their father's curate at Epworth and Wroote. Charles, according to his own account, lost his first year in diversions, but the next, set himself to study. John said of him during this time, "He pursued his studies diligently, and led a regular harmless life: but if I spoke to him about religion, he would warmly answer, 'What, would you have me to be a saint all at once?' and would hear no more . . . but . . . when I returned to Oxford in Novem-

ber 1729 I found him in great earnestness to save his soul."
Charles' own account continues, "Diligence led me to
serious thinking: I went to the weekly sacrament, and persuaded two or three young students to accompany me,
and to observe the method of study prescribed by the
statutes of the university. This gained me the harmless
name of Methodist."[19] In this little group may be found
the rudiments of the Holy Club. John arrived six months
later. His vigorous participation in the activities of the
little group increased their numbers and made him their
acknowledged, if not official, leader. With new participants
came new activities: William Morgan began the work in
the prisons and for the poor. John Wesley himself, according to another of the members, was responsible for the
opening, or at least the maintenance of a school for poor
children. It was from still another member, John Clayton,
that the "High Church" doctrines of the time came to per-
meate their outlook. This High Churchmanship advocated
tenets akin to the early (but not the later) positions of the
Oxford Movement of the following century, with the
exception of the latter's emphasis on the independence of
the Church from the State. The Oxford Methodists carried to a high pitch their reverence for early Christian
usages such as fasting, mortification, and the ascetic temper in general; rigid adherence to the regulations of canon
law, then widely disregarded; emphasis on the institutional mediation of grace, especially in the sacraments.
Perhaps the furthest they got in this respect was to offer
themselves to hear confessions.[20] This institutional emphasis was based on a firm belief in the Apostolic Succession in the Episcopacy, which John Wesley abandoned
only after many years, Charles never, so long as he lived.
With all this, however, went a sturdy opposition to the
claims of Rome. The eighteenth century "Oxford Movement" was completely loyal to the National Church, and
had no sort of leaning toward the Papacy.

To complete this picture of the activities of the Holy Club, we must not omit to recall that they studied much together, and that they exercised themselves in a minutely scheduled devotional life, which included private and corporate prayer and meditation, prayer for each other at fixed times, and hourly 'ejaculatory prayers' of praise, humility and petition.

That such strenuous and, from the point of view of the average student, freakish religiosity should draw down opposition on itself was inevitable. Even university officials apparently felt the reproach implied in their strictness, but the rumored disciplinary measures never actually broke over their heads. The students had their fun (not untinged with malice) at the "Methodists' " expense, but they pursued their way unswerving, encouraged by several serious men, including William Law and the now aging Rector of Epworth.

Ca. 1769. *Works*, V, 246.[21]

4. In November, 1729, four young gentlemen of Oxford,—Mr. John Wesley, fellow of Lincoln College; Mr. Charles Wesley, student of Christ Church; Mr. Morgan, commoner of Christ Church; and Mr. Kirkham, of Merton College,—began to spend some evenings in a week together, in reading, chiefly, the Greek Testament. The next year two or three of Mr. John Wesley's pupils desired the liberty of meeting with them; and afterward one of Mr. Charles Wesley's pupils. It was in 1732, that Mr. Ingham, of Queen's College, and Mr. Broughton, of Exeter, were added to their number. To these, in April, was joined Mr. Clayton, of Brazennose, with two or three of his pupils. About the same time Mr. James Hervey was permitted to meet with them, and in 1735, Mr. Whitefield.

5. The exact regularity of their lives, as well as studies, occasioned a young gentleman of Christ Church to say, "Here is a new set of Methodists sprung up;" alluding to

some ancient physicians who were so called. The name was new and quaint; so it took immediately, and the Methodists were known all over the university.

JOHN GAMBOLD[22] ON THE HOLY CLUB AND ITS HEAD. Tyerman, OM,[23] 158 f.

Mr. John Wesley was always the chief manager, for which he was very fit; for he not only had more learning and experience than the rest, but he was blest with such activity as to be always gaining ground, and such steadiness that he lost none. What proposals he made to any was sure to charm them, because he was so much in earnest; nor could they afterwards slight them, because they saw him always the same . . . To this I may add, that he had, I think, something of authority in his countenance . . . Yet he never assumed anything to himself above his companions.

It was their custom to meet most evenings, either at his chamber or one of the others, where, after some prayers, (the chief subject of which was charity,) they ate their supper together, and he read some book. But the chief business was to review what each had done that day, in pursuance of their common design, and to consult what steps were to be taken next.

They took great pains with the younger members of the University, to rescue them from bad company, and encourage them in a sober studious life.

The school was, I think, of Mr. Wesley's own setting up. At all events, he paid the mistress, and clothed some, if not all, of the children. When they went thither, they enquired how each child behaved; saw their work (for some could knit and spin) ; heard them read; heard them in their prayers and catechism; and explained part of it.

Though some practices of Mr. Wesley and his friends were much blamed,— as their fasting on Wednesday and Friday, after the custom of the Primitive Church,—their coming on those Sundays, when there was no sacrament in their own colleges, to receive it at Christ Church,—yet nothing was so much disliked as these charitable employments.

A MEMBER OF THE HOLY CLUB AT WORK. John Clayton[24] to John Wesley. Oxford. Aug. 1, 1732. WJJS, VIII, 275 ff.

Rev. and Dear Sir,

Excuse me for interrupting you from attending to the noble work you have taken in hand,[25] whilst I give you an account of the present state of our affairs in Oxford.

I cannot but think it an extraordinary piece of Providence that, when we had lost our best advocate and patron, all opposition against us should immediately cease; for, know that since you left us, nobody has thought it worth while to attack either Mr. Smith or me, or to endeavor to remove us from those principles wherein you, by the grace of God, have fixed us. I have gone every day to Lincoln, big with expectation to hear of some mighty attack made upon Mr. Smith; but, I thank God, I have always been disappointed; for not one of the Fellows has once so much as tried to shake him, or to convert him from the right way, wherein, I hope, he at present walks. Indeed, on Sunday, he met with a rub from Mr. Veesy, who refused to read Prayers for him in your chapel, for fear of contributing anything to his going to Christ Church. But Mr. Smith had the heart to desire that favour of the Rector which Mr. Veesy had denied him . . .

My little flock at Brazenose are, God be praised, true to their principles, and I hope to themselves too.

Bocardo, I fear, grows worse upon my hands. They have done nothing but quarrel ever since you left us, and they carried matters so high on Saturday that the bailiffs were sent for, who ordered Tomlyns to be fettered and put in the dungeon, where he lay some hours, and then, upon promise of his good behaviour, was released again. He has been much better ever since that time, and I hope will be the better for it all his life-time. Wisdom has never been to hear me read, notwithstanding his promise. I sent for him yesterday, but he would not come down; and when I had done reading, I went upstairs to him, and upbraided him with breaking his promise, upon which he very surlily replied, that he had thought better of it since he had seen me, and was determined never to come near Blair, lest his indignation should rise at the sight of him.

The Castle is, I thank God, in much better condition. All the felons were acquitted, except Salmon, who is referred to be tried at Warwick, to our great disappointment,—and the sheep-stealer, who is burnt in the hand, and who, I do verily believe, is a great penitent. I got Mrs. Topping a copy of her son's indictment at the assizes, which has made her mighty easy ever since; and she is now endeavouring to bring her mind into a due frame for the devout participation of the Holy Communion on Sunday next. Tempro is discharged, and I have appointed Harris to read to the prisoners in his stead. Two of the felons likewise have paid their fees, and are gone out, both of them able to read mighty well . . . .

Mrs. Trueby has been very ill this last week, so that she has made no great proficiency. I am to go down at six o'clock to hear the determination of a meeting of St. Thomas's parish, concerning [separating] Bossum and his wife. When I had promised to give a crown towards clothing the woman, and the overseer had determined to take her in upon that condition, the churchwarden would needs have him try to put the man upon me too, to get a crown towards clothing him; but, as he is able to work for his living, I don't think him a proper object of charity; nor can I at this time afford to do anything for him, because I am apprehensive that I must be forced to contribute to Salmon's relief, who will want near twenty shillings to subpoena proper witnesses to Warwick at his trial; and I cannot but think it a much greater act of charity to rescue a suffering innocent man than to relieve an idle beggar.

I have been twice at the school—namely on Tuesday and Saturday last, and intend to go again as soon as I have finished this letter. The children all go on pretty well, except Jervaise's boy, who, I find, truants till eleven o'clock in a morning. I threatened the boy what we would do to him if ever he truanted any more, and he has promised (as all children do) that he would do so no more; nay, his mother assures me that she will take care for the future that he shall not. I got a shilling for her from our Vice-Principal, and gave her sixpence myself, to preserve the gown that is in pawn from being sold; and the woman who has it has promised not to sell it, provided Jervaise will bring her sixpence a week towards redeeming it.

You cannot imagine the pleasure it is to me to know that you are engaged every morning in prayer for me. I wish for nine o'clock more eagerly than ever I did before, and I think I begin to perceive what is meant by that union of souls which is so much talked of in Père Malebranche and Madame Bourignon, which I never understood before. Good sir, continue your prayers for me, for I feel that I am benefited by them.

I thank God I have fully conquered my affection for a morning nap, and rise constantly by five o'clock at the farthest, and have the pleasure to see myself imitated by the greatest part of my pupils. I have talked with Mr. Clements, and I hope have made him a proselyte to early rising, though I cannot to constant communion.

POLEMIC FOR THE CHURCH OF ENGLAND. John Clayton to John Wesley. Oxford. Sept. 4, 1732. WJJS, VIII, 279 f.

As for Mr. Elyson, it is with great difficulty that I can get him to talk with me, he having received express orders from the Director not to converse with any one on points of faith. With much persuasion I have brought him to acknowledge that the doctrine of the Church of England is orthodox in respect to the Blessed Sacrament, and that she is catholic in her article of the Communion of Saints, but till I can bring him off from his notion of the Church's infallibility (for that is the term which he is taught to use) I find no good can be done with him, and therefore I shall enter upon that point with him tomorrow. His book is not yet come, which is a great disadvantage, for I find the man understands the faults which may be found with the Church of England better than the doctrines maintained by the Church of Rome. I generally go to him every day, but have only happened to meet his wife with him once. I find her so zealous an Anti-Papist that she almost makes the whole of Christianity to consist in opposing Popery. But I hope by God's help upon my own and my friend's prayers I shall be able so to work with them both that my labour will not be in vain either to them or myself.

Now you are gone we have in good part lost the honourable appellation of Methodists, and are talked on pretty warmly by the style and title of Super-rogation men; a good admonition to remind us that when we have done all we possibly can we are still but unprofitable servants.

THE WESLEYS AND THE MORGANS.

The facts behind the "Morgan correspondence" are these: The William Morgan who had initiated the work of the Holy Club in the prisons was the son of Richard Morgan, a substantial citizen of Dublin, connected with the Court of Exchequer. William's health had begun to fail, and rumors reaching his father ascribed his weakness to the austerities practised by the Club. The father's anxiety is mirrored in the first letter. William's health continued to worsen; he was barely able to reach home, his mind affected as well as his body, before he died. The second letter is John's explanation of the Club's procedures, written to point out that William's death was not due to any sinister effect of his connection with it. Mr. Morgan evidently was persuaded that the Wesleys at least were free from blame, for he sent his second son, Richard Jr., to be John Wesley's pupil. Young Richard, "somewhat gay," arrived in Oxford with a lavish wardrobe and leading a greyhound. He was more inclined to accept the popular theory of his brother's death than to discard suspicion and to submit himself whole-heartedly to his tutor's discipline, which tended to coincide more and more with that of the Club. It must be remembered, in explanation of John Wesley's zeal that not only did he feel himself as a Christian to be "his brother's keeper," but in virtue of the relationship he bore to Richard as tutor, he was officially responsible, according to the usage of the day, for his moral and spiritual welfare as well as his intellectual progress. This responsibility had, moreover, recently been especially emphasized in an official admonition of the Vice Chancellor to the tutors. The way Wesley strove to discharge this responsibility, is shown in the last two of the letters given here.

RICHARD MORGAN TO HIS SON WILLIAM. Dublin. Mar. 15, 1732. WJL, I, 121 f.

You shall no longer be tied to any fixed allowance; what sums are necessary for your health shall immediately be remitted. But then I must tell you, it is for those uses alone, your health and education, that I mean to supply you. You must leave me to judge for myself what portion of my substance it is fit for me to dispose of to charitable uses, of which I will be the distributor myself. You have no substance of your own; and it is but common justice that what I put into your hands should be disposed of according to my directions. I am told by a most worthy clergyman that it is sinful to do otherwise. Perhaps you may think your exhibition so much your own that you may dispose of it as you please. But that is not so; because what I put into your hands is an addition to it, to afford you physic and a comfortable subsistence with reasonable and moderate recreations, which I willingly allow you.

You may imagine I am not thus particular without some grounds. You can't conceive what a noise that ridiculous Society which you are engaged in has made here. Besides the particulars of the great follies of it at Oxford, which to my great concern I have often heard repeated, it gave me sensible trouble to hear that you were noted for your going into the villages about Holt, entering into poor people's houses, calling their children together, teaching them their prayers and catechism, and giving them a shilling at your departure.

WESLEY'S ACCOUNT OF THE ORIGIN AND PURPOSE OF THE HOLY CLUB. John Wesley to Richard Morgan. Oxford. Oct. 18, 1732. WJJS, I, 89 ff.

In November 1729, at which time I came to reside at Oxford, your son, my brother, myself, and one more agreed to spend three or four evenings in a week together. Our design was to read over the classics, which we had before read in private, on common nights, and on Sunday some book in divinity. In the summer following, Mr. M [organ] told me he had called at the jail, to see a man who was condemned for killing his wife; and that, from the talk he had with one of the debtors, he verily believed it would do much good if any one would be at the pains of now and then speaking with them. This he so frequently repeated, that on the 24th of August, 1730, my brother and I walked with him to the Castle. We were so well satisfied with our conversation there, that we agreed to go thither once or twice a week; which we had not done long, before he desired me to go with him to see a poor woman in the town who was sick. In this employment too, when we came to reflect upon it, we believed it would be worth while to spend an hour or two in a week; provided the minister of the parish in which any such person was were not against it. But that we might not depend wholly on our own judgements, I wrote an account to my father of our whole design; withal begging that he, who had lived seventy years in the world, and seen as much of it as most private men have ever done, would advise us whether we had yet gone too far, and whether we should now stand still or go forward.

Part of his answer, dated September 21, 1730, was this:

And now, as to your own designs and employments, what can I say less of them than *Valde probo;* and that I have the highest reason to bless God that He has given me two sons together at Oxford to whom He has given grace and courage to turn the war against the world and the devil, which is the best way to conquer them. They have but one more enemy to combat with, the flesh; which if they take care to subdue by fasting and prayer, there will be no more for them to do, but to proceed steadily in the same course . . . You have reason to bless God, as I do, that you have so fast a friend as Mr. Morgan, who, I see, in the most difficult service, is ready to break the ice for you . . . Go on then, in God's name, in the path to which your Saviour has directed you, and that track wherein your father has gone before you! For when I was an undergraduate at Oxford, I visited those in the Castle there, and reflect on it with great satisfaction to this day . . .

Your most affectionate and joyful father.

Soon after, a gentleman of Merton College, who was one of our little company, which now consisted of five persons, acquainted us that he had been much rallied the day before for being a member of *The Holy Club;* and that it was become a common topic of mirth at his college, where they had found out several of our customs, to which we were ourselves utter strangers.

. . . We still continued to meet together as usual; and to confirm one another, as well as we could, in our resolutions, to communicate as often as we had opportunity (which is here once a week) ; and do what service we could to our acquaintance, the prisoners, and two or three poor families in the town . . .

. . . Almost as soon as we had made our first attempts this way, some of the men of wit in Christ Church entered the lists against us; and, between mirth and anger, made a pretty many reflections upon the Sacramentarians, as they were pleased to call us . . . But . . . they had not the good fortune to gain any proselytes from the Sacrament, till a gentleman, eminent for learning, and well esteemed for piety, joining them, told his nephew that if he dared to go to the weekly communion any longer he would immediately turn him out of doors . . . This much delighted our gay opponents, who increased their number apace . . . About this time there was a meeting (as one who was present at it informed your son) of several of the officers and seniors of the college, wherein it was consulted what would be the speediest way to stop the progress of enthusiasm in it. The result we know not, only it was soon publicly reported that Dr. —— and the censors were going to blow up The Godly Club.

. . . It was a little before this time my brother and I were at London, when going into a bookseller's shop (Mr. Rivington's in St. Paul's Churchyard), after some other conversation, he asked us whether we lived in town; and upon our answering, 'No; at Oxford,'—'Then, gentlemen,' said he, 'let me earnestly recommend to your acquaintance a friend I have there, Mr. Clayton, of Brazennose.' Of this, having small leisure for contracting new acquaintance, we took no notice for the present. But in the spring following (April 20), Mr. Clayton meeting me in the street, and giving Mr. Rivington's service, I desired his company to my room, and then commenced our acquaintance. At the first opportunity I acquainted him with our whole design, which he immediately and heartily closed with; not long after, Mr. Morgan having then left Oxford, we fixed two evenings in a week to meet on, partly to talk upon that subject, and partly to read something in practical divinity.

The two points whereunto, by the blessing of God and your son's help, we had before attained, we endeavoured to hold fast: I mean, the doing what good we can; and, in order thereto, communicating as often as we have opportunity. To these, by the advice of Mr. Clayton, we have added a third,—the observing the fasts of the Church; the general neglect of which we can by no means apprehend to be a lawful excuse for neglecting them.

RICHARD MORGAN, JR. TO HIS FATHER. Oxford. Jan. 14, 1734. WJL, I, 147 f.

HONOURED SIR, — I received your kind letter of the 22nd November, which came free. I perused yours to Mr. Wesley very carefully, then sealed it and delivered it to him. When he had read it over two or three times, he desired me to breakfast with him next morning. His whole discourse turned on the contents of your letter. He said he did not know what to make of it, and was surprised that a father should show so great concern lest his son should not be wicked enough, and went on after that odd manner. He endeavoured to prove that my brother did not weaken his constitution by his great abstinence and strictness in religion; though my brasier's wife, an intimate of Mr. Wesley's, told me she has often heard Dr. Frewin say that, while he persisted in that rigid course of life, he could be of no service to him.

There is a Society of gentlemen, consisting of seven

members, whom the world calls Methodists, of whom my tutor is President. They imagine they cannot be saved if they do not spend every hour, nay minute, of their lives in the services of God. And to that end they read prayers every day in the common jail, preach every Sunday, and administer the sacrament once every month. They almost starve themselves to be able to relieve the poor and buy books for their conversion. They endeavour to reform notorious whores and allay spirits in haunted houses. They fast two days in the week, which has emaciated them to that degree that they are a frightful sight. One of them had like to have lost his life lately by a decay, which was attributed to his great abstinence. They rise every day at five of the clock, and till prayers, which began at eight, they sing psalms, and read some piece of divinity. They meet at each other's rooms at six of the clock five nights in the week, and from seven to nine read a piece of some religious book. In short, they are so particular that they are become the jest of the whole University.

When I came to college, my tutor gave me two rules in writing, which he expected I should follow. The first was to have no company but what he approved of, and the second to read no books but of his choosing. In compliance with the first, I have spent every evening of their meeting from seven to nine in their company till I received your letter. From six to seven they read over the petitions of poor people and relieve their wants, dispose of pious books, and fix the duties of the ensuing day. They told me very solemnly that, when I had acquired a pretty good stock of religion, they would take me in as an assistant. When we are all met, my tutor reads a collect to increase our attention; after that a religious book is read all the time we are together. They often cry for five minutes for their sins; then lift up their heads and eyes, and return God thanks for the great mercies He has showed them in granting them such repentance, and then laugh immoderately as if they were mad. The greatest blessing next to that is being laughed at by the world, which they esteem a sufficient proof of the goodness and justness of their actions, for which they also return thanks as aforesaid. Though some of them are remarkable for eating very heartily on gaudy-days, they stint themselves to two pence meat, and a farthing bread, and a draught of water when they dine at their own expense; and as for supper, they never eat any.

JOHN WESLEY TO RICHARD MORGAN, SR. Oxford. Jan. 15, 1734. WJL, I, 150 f.

Sir,—Going yesterday into your son's room, I providentially cast my eyes upon a paper that lay upon the table, and, contrary to my custom, read a line or two of it, which soon determined me to read the rest. It was a copy of his last letter to you; whereby, by the signal blessing of God, I came to the knowledge of his real sentiments, both with regard to myself and to several other points of the highest importance.

In the account he gives of me and those friends who are as my own soul, and who watch over it that I may not be myself a castaway, are some things true: as, that we imagine it is our bounden duty to spend our whole lives in the service of Him that gave them, or, in other words, 'whether we eat or drink, or whatever we do, to do all to the glory of God'; that we endeavor, as we are able, to relieve the poor by buying books and other necessaries for them; that some of us read prayers at the prison once a day; that I administer the sacrament once a month, and preach there as often as I am not engaged elsewhere; that we sit together five evenings in a week; and that we observe, in such manner as our health permits, the fasts of the Church. Some things are false, but taken up upon trust, so that I hope Mr. Morgan believed them true: as, that we almost starve ourselves; that one of us had like lately to have lost his life by too great abstinence; that we endeavour to reform notorious whores and to lay spirits in haunted houses; that we all rise every day at five o'clock; and that I am President of the Society. And some things are not only false, but I fear were known so to be when he related them as true (inasmuch as he had then had the repeated demonstration of both his eyes and ears to the contrary) : such as that the Society consists of seven members (I know no more than four of them) ; that from five to eight in the morning they sing psalms and read some piece of divinity; and that they are emaciated to such a degree that they are a frightful sight. As to the circumstance of the brasier's wife (no intimate of mine) I am in doubt; though she positively denies she ever said so.

To RICHARD MORGAN. Oxford. Jan. 15, 1734. WJL, I, 152.

I take religion to be, not the bare saying over so many prayers, morning and evening, in public or in private; not anything superadded now and then to a careless or worldly life; but a constant ruling habit of soul, a renewal of our minds in the image of God, a recovery of the divine likeness, a still-increasing conformity of heart and life to the pattern of our most holy Redeemer. But if this be religion, if this be that way to life which our blessed Lord hath marked out for us, how can anyone, while he keeps close to this way, be charged with running into extremes?

vi. What Parish?

The question, "In what parish shall I serve?" was posed to the Fellow of Lincoln twice during his last year at Oxford. The first came late in 1734. It took this form: "Shall I take my father's place in Epworth?" He faced it again early the next year this way: "Shall I go to Georgia as a missionary to the Indians?" That Wesley settled the first in the negative because he wanted to stay in Oxford, and a few months later settled the second in the affirmative though it would take him far away seems so inconsistent as to need explanation. The inconsistency disappears if we look deeply enough. A constant principle underlay both decisions. It was not staying in or leaving Oxford that mattered, but choosing a place for his work which would most promote his own holiness. He simply decided that Oxford was better for this purpose than Epworth, and later that Georgia was better than either.

The grounds on which Wesley made his decisions have a fundamentally selfish sound, and indeed he cannot escape blame on this count. But with justice we can say that the self-centredness of his motives was mitigated in several respects. Obviously he was not sure of himself, and desperately needed to be, before committing himself irrevocably to a parish. Further, as Fr. Piette suggests,[26] Wesley felt a responsibility to (and we may add, perhaps a need for) the little company of which he was the leader. While he obviously couldn't have taken the Holy Club with him to Epworth, he could and did take at least a part of it to Georgia. Further, we may conclude, from his ultimately applying for the living at Epworth, that the moving plea of his father did melt, at least to some extent, and for a time, the icy grip of his self-centredness. But his application came too late — the "mighty Nimrod" his father feared had got the place. And finally, as Bishop McConnell points out, "Wesley indeed said that he went to Georgia to save his own soul, but he also said that he went that he might labor wholly for the glory of the Lord."[27]

THE RECTOR'S CASE FOR ASKING JOHN TO SUCCEED HIM AT EPWORTH. Samuel Wesley to Samuel, Jr. Epworth. Dec. 4, 1734. Clarke, MWF, I, 341 ff.

. . . I urged to him among other things, the great precariousness of my own health, and sensible decay of my strength, so that he would hardly know me if he saw me

now, which will not admit of a long time for consultation.
The deplorable state in which I should leave your mother
and the family, without an almost miraculous interposi-
tion of Providence, which we are not to presume upon,
when we neglect the means, if my offer should be rejected
till it were too late. The loss of near forty years' (I hope
honest) labour in this place, where I could expect no
other, but that the field which I have been so long sowing
with (I trust) good seed, and the vineyard which I have
planted with no ignoble vine, must be soon rooted up, and
the fences of it broken down; for I think I know my successor, who, I am morally satisfied, would be no other
than Mr. P., if your brothers both slight it; and I shall
have work enough, if my life should last so long, to accomplish it; and, behold, there seems to be a price now put
into their hands, or, at least, some probability of it. If
they go on to reject it, I hope I am clear before God and
man, as to that whole affair. I hinted at one thing, which
I mentioned in my letter to your brother, whereon I depend more than upon all my own simple reasoning; and
that is, earnest prayer to Him who smiles at the strongest
resolutions of mortals, and can, in a moment, change or
demolish them; who alone can bend the inflexible sinew,
and order the irregular wills of us sinful men to his own
glory, and to our happiness; and, while the anchor holds,
I despair of nothing, but firmly believe, that he who is
best will do what is best, whether we earnestly will it, or
appear never so averse from it; and there I rest the whole
matter, and leave it with him, to whom I have committed
all my concerns, without exception and without reserve,
for soul and body, estate and family, time and eternity.

JOHN'S REFUSAL TO GO TO EPWORTH.

*The two paragraphs below are extracted from a long
letter in which John Wesley gives his father twenty-six
reasons for staying at Oxford rather than accepting his*

*father's proposal. The length of the list shows the son's
basic uneasiness over the validity of any of them.*

JOHN WESLEY TO HIS FATHER. Oxford. Dec. 10, 1734. WJL,
I, 168, 173.

5. However, when two ways of life are proposed, I should
choose to begin with that part of the question, Which of
these have I rational ground to believe will conduce most
to my own improvement? And that not only because it
is every physician's concern to heal himself first, but because it seems we may judge with more ease, and perhaps
certainty too, in which state we can most promote holiness
in ourselves than in which we can most promote it in
others.

16. From all this I conclude that, where I am most holy
myself, there I could most promote holiness in others; and
consequently that I could more promote it here than in
any place under heaven.

SAMUEL WESLEY, SR. TO JOHN. Epworth. Nov. 20, 1734.
Tyerman, SW,[28] p. 422f.

Your only argument is this: 'The question is not whether
I could do more good to others there or here, but whether
I could do more good to myself; seeing wherever I can be
most holy myself, there I can most promote holiness in
others. But I can improve myself more at Oxford than at
any other place.'

To this I answer — 1. It is not dear self, but the glory
of God, and the different degrees of promoting it, which
should be our main consideration in the choice of any
course of my life.

5. We are not to fix our eye on one single point of duty,
but to take in the complicated view of all the circumstances in every state of life that offers. Thus in the case
before us, put all circumstances together. If you are not

indifferent whether the labours of an aged father, for above forty years in God's vineyard, be lost, and the fences of it trodden down and destroyed; if you consider that Mr. M——— must in all probability succeed me if you do not, and that the prospect of that mighty Nimrod's coming hither shocks my soul, and is in a fair way of bringing down my gray hairs with sorrow to the grave; if you have any care for our family, which must be dismally shattered as soon as I am dropt; if you reflect on the dear love and longing which this poor people have for you, you may perhaps alter your mind, and bend your will to His, who has promised, if in all our ways we acknowledge Him, He will direct our paths.

Motives for going to Georgia.

Two organizations were concerned in sending the quartet of Oxford Methodists to Georgia. That both of them were philanthropic in purpose bears witness that all was not so dark in pre-Methodist England as we are sometimes led to suppose. The first of these was the Trustees of the Georgia Colony, which had been organized as a result of the interest of James Edward Oglethorpe, M. P., in a friend who had been imprisoned for debt. Out of his insistence that something should be done about the shocking conditions he discovered came a Parliamentary committee of inquiry, and a project by which some of the debtors might be given another chance in a new and fertile land. This desire to help the unfortunate was probably accompanied in the minds of those Parliamentarians where the imperial consciousness was already highly developed, by the less disinterested hope that they might serve as a bulwark against the expansion of the Spanish holdings in Florida. Oglethorpe, who was not only a philanthropist but an experienced soldier, was fitted in both respects to head the Colony. With the General the elder Wesley had, before his death, been in correspondence on several matters.

Another link with the Georgia enterprise was Dr. Burton,
of Corpus Christi College, a close friend of John Wesley,
an admirer, though not a member, of the Holy Club, and
one of the Trustees of the Colony. It is to him that the
letter given below was addressed by John. The Trustees
appointed John to his work October 10, 1735. The other
organization concerned with the mission was the Society
for the Propagation of the Gospel in Foreign Parts—usu-
ally known as the S. P. G. It had grown out of the interest
taken by Dr. Bray, the Commissary of the Bishop of Lon-
don, in getting home support for the National Church in
America. Founded in 1701, by now it already had behind
it a generation of service to Colonials and natives overseas.
It was this Society which undertook to pay Wesley's ex-
penses; he, in turn, was bound by their regulations. The
letter to Dr. Burton given below is interesting not only
because of its frank delineation of Wesley's motives in
accepting the call to Georgia, but also because it shows
that he felt celibacy to be an essential condition for his
calling. In addition we learn from it the extent to which
he shared the idea, later to be so attractively set forth by
Jean-Jacques Rousseau, but even then widely held in Eu-
rope, that the primitive peoples of the world were "chil-
dren of nature," unspoiled by civilization, and had retained
the dignity, purity and honesty of a Golden Age. Wesley's
naive view on the subject of the "noble Red Man" was to
suffer a severe change on closer acquaintance, but for the
time being he carried it a step farther than most. Preoccu-
pied as he was with discovering the true meaning of the
Gospel, he concluded that by presenting it to these un-
spoiled people, he would receive it back with its light unre-
fracted and pure as at its first proclamation. This was how
he now hoped to "save his own soul."

JOHN WESLEY TO DR. BURTON. Oct. 10, 1735. WJL, I, 188ff.

Dear Sir,—I have been hitherto unwilling to mention

the grounds of my design of my embarking for Georgia, for two reasons,—one, because they were such as I know few men would judge to be of any weight: the other, because I was afraid of making favourable judges think of me above what they ought to think; and what a snare this must be to my own soul I know by dear-bought experience.

But, on further reflection, I am convinced that I ought to speak the truth with all boldness, even though it should appear foolishness to the world, as it has done from the beginning; and that, whatever danger there is in doing the will of God, He will support me under it. In His name, therefore, and trusting in His defence, I shall plainly declare the thing as it is.

My chief motive, to which all the rest are subordinate, is the hope of saving my own soul. I hope to learn the true sense of the gospel of Christ by preaching it to the heathen. They have no comments to construe away the text; no vain philosophy to corrupt it; no luxurious, sensual, covetous, ambitious expounders to soften its unpleasing truths, to reconcile earthly-mindedness and faith, the Spirit of Christ and the spirit of the world. They have no party, no interest to serve, and are therefore fit to receive the gospel in its simplicity. They are as little children, humble, willing to learn, and eager to do the will of God; and consequently they shall know of every doctrine I preach whether it be of God. By these, therefore, I hope to learn the purity of that faith which was once delivered to the saints; the genuine sense and full extent of those laws which none can understand who mind earthly things.

A right faith will, I trust, by the mercy of God, open the way for a right practice; especially when most of those temptations are removed which here so easily beset me. Toward mortifying the desire of the flesh, the desire of sensual pleasures, it will be no small thing to be able, without fear of giving offence, to live on water and the fruits of the earth. This simplicity of food will, I trust,

be a blessed means, both of preventing my seeking that
happiness in meats and drinks which God designed should
be found only in faith and love and joy in the Holy Ghost;
and will assist me—especially where I see no woman but
those which are almost of a different species from me—to
attain such a purity of thought as suits a candidate for
that state wherein they neither marry nor are given in
marriage, but are as the angels of God in heaven.

It is not for me, who have been a grievous sinner from
my youth up, and am yet laden with foolish and hurtful
desires, to expect God should work so great things by my
hands; but I am assured, if I be once fully converted myself, He will then employ me both to strengthen my brethren and to preach His name to the Gentiles, that the very
ends of the earth may see the salvation of our God.

But you will perhaps ask: 'Cannot you save your own
soul in England as well as in Georgia?' I answer,—No;
neither can I hope to attain the same degree of holiness
here which I may there; neither, if I stay here, knowing
this, can I reasonably hope to attain any degree of holiness
at all: for whoever, when two ways of life are proposed,
prefers that which he is convinced in his own mind is less
pleasing to God and less conducive to the perfection of
his soul, has no reason from the gospel of Christ to hope
that he shall ever please God at all or receive from Him
that grace whereby alone he can attain any degree of Christian perfection.

vii. George Whitefield

Having up to this point been concerned with the life of
the Wesley brothers through their Oxford days, we turn
now to George Whitefield, the third of the triumvirate
of Methodist leaders. This section will deal with his life
through the corresponding period. He has made the task
easier in that he himself drew up and published a review
of his early life which comprehends most of what we know

about it. This review was written during his second trip to America. It bore the characteristic title: *A Short Account of God's Dealings with the Reverend Mr. George Whitefield . . . from his Infancy to the Time of his Entring* [sic] *into Holy Orders. Written by Himself on Board the Elizabeth and Sent over by him to be Published for the Benefit of the Orphan House in Georgia.*[29] The "Account" headed by this lengthy title is itself really "short"; and of course the extracts given below occupy even less space. However, they mark the crucial stages in the life of a man who was quite as influential in the early development of Methodism as the Wesleys themselves—perhaps even more so. The fact that he could, in 1740 when he had been ordained only four years, publish such a work with every confidence that it would be widely bought and read is in itself evidence of the wide interest his career as an evangelist had aroused. We shall later have occasion to notice further proofs in abundance of the influential quality of his leadership.

WHITEFIELD, SA, 8-26, *passim.*

I was born in Gloucester, in the month of December, 1714. My father and mother kept the Bell-Inn. The former died when I was two years old . . .

I can truly say I was froward from my mother's womb. I was so brutish as to hate instruction, and used purposely to shun all opportunities of receiving it. I can date some very early acts of uncleanness . . . Often have I joined with others in playing roguish tricks, but was generally, if not always, happily detected. For this I have often since, and do now bless and praise God.

But such was the free grace of God to me that tho' corruption worked so strongly in my soul, and produced such early and bitter fruits, yet I can recollect very early movings of the blessed Spirit upon my heart . . . I was always fond of being a clergyman, used frequently to imitate the ministers reading prayers, etc., part of the money I used to steal from my parents, I gave to the poor . . .

My mother was very careful of my education, and always kept me in my tender years (for which I never can sufficiently thank her) from intermeddling in the least with the public business.

When I was about twelve, I was placed in the school called St. Mary de Crypt in Gloucester. Having a good elocution and memory, I was remarked for making speeches before the corporation at their annual visitation.

During the time of my being at school, I was very fond of reading plays, and have kept myself from school for days together to prepare myself for acting them . . . However, though the first thing I had to repent of was my education in general, yet I must always acknowledge my particular thanks are due to my master for the great pains he took with me and his other scholars in teaching us to speak and write correctly.

My mother's circumstances being much on the decline, and being tractable that way, I from time to time began to assist her occasionally in the public house, till at length I put on my blue apron and my snuffers, washed mops, cleaned rooms, and, in one word, became professed and common drawer for nigh a year and an half.

Having thus lived with my mother for some considerable time, a young student, who was once my schoolfellow, and then a servitor of Pembroke College, Oxford, came to pay my mother a visit. Amongst other conversation, he told her how he had discharged all college expenses that quarter and received a penny. Upon that my mother cried out, "This will do for my son." Then, turning to me she said, "Will you go to Oxford, George?" I replied, "With all my heart."

Before I went to the University, I met with Mr. Law's *Serious Call to a Devout Life,* but had not then money to purchase it. Soon after my coming up to the University,

seeing a small edition of it in a friend's hand, I soon procured it. God worked powerfully on my soul, as he has
since upon many others, by that and his other excellent
treatise upon *Christian Perfection*.

I now began . . . to receive the Sacrament at a parish-
church near our College, and at the Castle where the
despised Methodists used to receive once a month.

The young men, so called, were then much talked of at
Oxford. I had heard of, and loved them before I came to
the University . . .

For above a twelvemonth my soul longed to be acquainted with some of them and was strongly pressed to
follow their good example, when I saw them go through
a ridiculing crowd to receive the Holy Eucharist at St.
Mary's. At length God was pleased to open a door. . . . I
thankfully embraced the opportunity. . . .

WHITEFIELD, SA, 28.

At my first reading it, [*The Life of God in the Soul of
Man*][30] I wondered what the author meant by saying,
"That some falsely placed religion in going to church,
doing hurt to no one, being constant in the duties of the
closet, and now and then reaching out their hands to give
alms to their poor neighbours".—Alas! thought I, "If this
be not religion, what is?" God soon showed me. For in
reading a few lines further, that "true religion was an
union of the soul with God, and Christ formed within
us;" a ray of divine light was instantaneously darted in
upon my soul, and from that moment, but not till then,
did I know that I must be a new creature.

WHITEFIELD, SA, 29.

From time to time Mr. Wesley permitted me to come
unto him, and instructed me as I was able to bear it.—By
degrees he introduced me to the rest of his christian breth-

ren.—They built me up daily in the knowledge and fear of God, and taught me to endure hardness like a good soldier of Jesus Christ.

I now began, like them, to live by rule, and to pick up the very fragments of my time, that not a moment of it might be lost. Whether I ate or drank, or whatsoever I did, I endeavoured to do all to the glory of God. Like them, having no weekly Sacrament (altho' the Rubrick required it) at our own college, I received every Sunday at Christ Church. I joined with them in keeping the Stations by fasting Wednesdays and Fridays, and left no means unused, which I thought would lead me nearer to Jesus Christ.

WHITEFIELD, SA, 38f.

Whilst my inward man was thus exercised, my outward man was not unemployed. I soon found what a slave I had been to my sensual appetite, and now resolved to get the mastery over it by the help of Jesus Christ.—Accordingly, by degrees I began to leave off eating fruits and such like, and gave the money I usually spent in that way to the poor.—Afterward I always chose the worst sort of food, tho' my place furnished me with variety.—I fasted twice a week. —My apparel was mean.—I thought it unbecoming a penitent to have his hair powdered.—I wore woolen gloves, a patched gown and dirty shoes;—and tho' I was then convinced that the kingdom of God did not consist in meats and drinks, yet I resolutely persisted in these voluntary acts of self-denial, because I found them great promoters of the spiritual life.

WHITEFIELD, SA, 47-49.

Soon after this the holy season of Lent came on, which our friends kept very strictly, eating no flesh during the six weeks, except on Saturdays and Sundays. I abstained frequently on Saturdays also, and ate nothing on the other days, (except on Sunday) but sage tea without sugar, and coarse bread.—I constantly walked out in the cold mornings, till part of one of my hands was quite black.—This, with my continued abstinence, and inward conflicts, at length so emaciated my body, that at Passion-week, finding I could scarce creep up stairs, I was obliged to inform my kind tutor of my condition, who immediately sent for a physician to me.

This caused no small triumph amongst the collegians, who began to cry out, "What is his fasting come to now?" But I rejoiced in this reproach, knowing that tho' I had been imprudent, and lost much of my flesh, yet I had nevertheless increased in the Spirit.

This fit of sickness continued upon me for seven weeks, and a glorious visitation it was.—The blessed Spirit was all this time purifying my soul.—All my former gross and notorious, and even my heart sins also, were now set home upon me, of which I wrote down some remembrance immediately, and confessed them before God morning and evening.—Tho' weak, I often spent two hours in my evening retirements, and prayed over my Greek Testament, and Bishop Hall's most excellent Contemplations, every hour that my health would permit. About the end of the seven weeks, and after I had been groaning under an unspeakable pressure both of body and mind for above a twelvemonth; God was pleased to set me free in the following manner.—One day, perceiving an uncommon drought, and a disagreeable clamminess in my mouth, and using things to allay my thirst, but in vain, it was suggested to me, that when Jesus Christ cried out, "I thirst", his sufferings were near at an end. Upon which, I cast myself down on the bed, crying out, I thirst! I thirst!—Soon after this, I found and felt in myself that I was delivered from the burden that had so heavily oppressed me! The spirit of mourning was taken from me, and I knew what it was truly to rejoice in God my Saviour, and, for some time, could not avoid singing psalms wherever I was; but my joy gradually became more settled, and, blessed be God, has abode and increased in my soul (saving a few casual intermissions) ever since!

Thus were the days of my mourning ended.—After a long night of desertion and temptation, the Star, which I had seen at a distance before, began to appear again, and the Day-star arose in my heart.—Now did the spirit of God take possession of my soul, and, as I humbly hope, seal me unto the day of redemption.

WHITEFIELD, SA, 52.

Not long after, God made me instrumental to awaken several young persons, who soon formed themselves into a little Society, and had quickly the honour of being despised at Gloucester, as we had been before them at Oxford: Thus, all that will live godly in Christ Jesus, must suffer persecution.

WHITEFIELD, SA, 56.

About this time God was pleased to enlighten my soul, and bring me into the knowledge of his free Grace, and the necessity of being justified in his sight by faith only; this was more extraordinary, because my friends at Oxford had rather inclined to the mystic divinity.—And one of them (a dear servant of the Lord) lately confessed he did not like me so well when at Oxford, as the rest of his brethren, because I held justification by faith *only*.—And yet he observed I had most success.—But blessed be God, most of us have now been taught this doctrine of Christ, and, I hope, shall be willing to die in the defence of it.

WHITEFIELD, SA, 58, 59.

. . . Months after came a letter from a friend at Oxford, desiring me to go to one Pebworth, who was broken out of Oxford Gaol, and was retaken at Gloucester. As soon as I read this, it appeared to me that my prayer was now answered. Immediately I went to the prison, assuredly gathering that the Lord called me thither.—I met with the person, and finding him and some others willing to hear the word of God, having gained leave of the keeper and two ordinaries, I constantly read to, and prayed with them every day I was in town.—I also begged money for them, whereby I was enabled to release some of them, and cause provision to be distributed weekly amongst them, as also to put such books into their hands as I judged most proper. —I cannot say any one of the prisoners was effectually wrought upon; however, much evil was prevented, many were convinced, and my own soul was much edified and strengthened in the love of God and man.

CHAPTER III

GEORGIA

In the period of the mission to Georgia, the published *Journals* of both John and Charles Wesley begin: John's with their embarkation, Charles' with his landing in his new "parish." For the Georgia period, use will be made of John's only—Charles' can be omitted without losing anything essential, since it assumes importance for the Revival only after he returns to England.

Charles' stay in Georgia was, to put it bluntly, brief, unfruitful and unhappy. Less than thirty-two pages of his *Journal* are devoted to it. He was ill much of the time. He had no liking, and but little capacity for the post which, in addition to his ministerial duties, he held under Oglethorpe, and which went by the rather grandiose title "Secretary for Indian Affairs." He manifested a combination of official stiffness and personal impulsiveness which kept him embroiled in a tangle of personal animosities. His *Journal* is occupied for the most part with rather obscure allusion to these difficulties, the chief of which was an estrangement, based on a deep misunderstanding, between himself and General Oglethorpe. In extenuation it can be said that this situation was not primarily his own fault. His work kept him, not in Savannah where, in all conscience, there were quarrels enough, but in an outpost of the Colony to the south called Frederica, which was even worse. The people there had a positive genius for slander, intrigue, falsehood and violence. The ringleaders seem to have been two women whose idleness gave full scope to their malicious activities. It was they who set Oglethorpe and Charles Wesley at variance by "confessing" to each in turn illicit relations with the other. Charles (who, admittedly saw more clearly the character of those with whom he had to deal than the more naive John) wrote to the latter in Savannah an indiscreet letter which was intercepted and read by their enemies. It contained two Greek words which they imagined (possibly rightly) applied to them, and which in their very incomprehensibility were grounds for greater grievance. John had to go down to straighten the tangle out, which he succeeded in doing, not without incurring real personal risk.

Though Charles' personal character was vindicated in the eyes of Oglethorpe and he was restored to that extent to his confidence, it was evident that Charles' continued presence in the Colony would serve no good purpose. So, without regret, he announced his intention to resign, and, leaving to John his work both as Secretary and minister at Frederica, he left for the return to England just under six months after his arrival.

The *Journals* of John Wesley, the first of which we now begin to use extensively, constitute one of the most remarkable documents of the eighteenth century. It was, as is well known, published in sections. The first of these is entitled, *An Extract of the Rev. Mr. John Wesley's Journal from his Embarking for Georgia to his Return to London.*[1] In the preface to this we read:

1. *It was in Pursuance of an Advice given by Bishop* Taylor *in his* Rules for Holy Living and Dying, *that about fifteen Years ago, I began to take a more exact Account than I had done before, of the manner wherein I spent my Time, writing down how I had employed every Hour. This I continued to do, wherever I was, till the Time of my leaving* England. *The Variety of Scenes which I then past thro', induced me to transcribe from time to time, the more material Parts of my Diary, adding here and there such little Reflections as occur'd to my Mind. Of this Journal thus occasionally compiled, the following is a short Extract.*

*It not being my Design to relate all those Particulars, which
I wrote for my own Use only; and which would answer no
valuable End to others, however important they were to me.*

2. *Indeed I had no Design or Desire to trouble the World
with any of my little Affairs . . . Neither shou'd I have
done it now, had not Captain* Williams's *Affidavit, publish'd* as soon as he had left England, *laid an Obligation
upon me, to do what in me lies, in Obedience to that Command of God,* Let not the Good which is in you be evil-
spoken of.[2]

From these introductory words much can be gathered
as regards both the process out of which it came, and the
reasons for its publication. It is evident that the original
daily jottings (in cipher, it will be remembered) were
gone over twice: first they were transformed into a long-
hand narrative; then those parts to be published were
"extracted" for the printer. During either or both of these
processes, he added "such little reflections" as seemed appropriate. One obvious later addition is found, for instance, in the following passage:

*I spent another hour with the amiable family this morn-
ing . . . but it will never return! For one, if not more, of
that lovely company are since removed to Abraham's
bosom!*[3]

Again, the long review of his religious development
from his early childhood on, which is set down under the
crucial date of his conversion (May 24, 1738) also has the
air of having been added after the diary entry was made.[4]

The publication of the first *Extract* was occasioned not
only by the natural interest of the public in the experiences of a returned "foreign missionary," but also by the
necessity of vindicating the missionary's character. Just as
aspersions on the Holy Club at Oxford influenced Wesley
to begin it with the letter to Mr. Morgan, so the "Williams
Affidavit" influenced the selection of material for the
Journal itself. This affidavit accusing Wesley of misde-

meanors in Georgia was sworn to by an unscrupulous land-
holder in Georgia called Williams, and was the unworthy
counter-attack of a group of men angered at Wesley's opposition to the introduction of slavery into the Colony. It
was "a tissue of palpable falsehoods . . . only of interest because their publication in England and America was the
occasion of hastening the issue of Wesley's first extract
from his Journal."[5] No date appears on the title page of
the first *Extract*, but it can be assigned to either late in
1739 or early in 1740.[6] Other dissensions influenced the
choice of material for subsequent extracts; but as the Revival spread more and more widely, what Wesley said and
did was of interest to increasing numbers of people on
their own account. So, fortunately for subsequent generations, the published *Extracts* continued to appear, till there
were twenty of them before Wesley's death, and one afterward.

Augustine Birrell, a distinguished literary critic said of
Wesley, "As a writer he has not achieved distinction."[7] We
can agree that his chief distinction lay in another realm
than the literary. Certainly his style does not conform to
the standards which dominated *belles lettres* at the end of
the nineteenth century when Mr. Birrell wrote. But if
we remember that Wesley's *Journal* was essentially an ex-
panded account book, and that practically all of his letters
were business letters—both written in the interests of the
Lord's business—we will judge them by other standards.
Certainly the egotism which made Whitefield's autobiographical publications so obnoxious to his enemies, and
even an embarrassment to his friends,[8] is completely absent from Wesley's journal. Whereas Whitefield could
never quite suppress a feeling of rather pleased surprise
that it was *himself* God was dealing with in a very extraordinary way, Wesley always seemed to feel that in so far as
he was involved in the extraordinary "work of God," he

was an instrument of only incidental importance. By any standards it would be hard to deny to Wesley's style the merits of vigor and swift cogency; even the beauty of exact and economical expression is not wanting. Francis Asbury called it "his nervous style," by which he meant, apparently, the taut, sinewy quality that always characterized it. Nor was it wanting in sweep and grandeur of conception. The man who had taken the world for his parish, and felt that he was carrying out God's own plan might be expected so to write when he was able to swing free of details and speak of first principles. For these qualities it would be hard to surpass the well known letter to one of his preachers:

Dear George:—The time is arrived for you to embark for America. You must go down to Bristol, where you will meet with Thomas Rankin, Captain Webb and his wife. I let you loose George, on the great continent of America. Publish your message in the open face of the sun, and do all the good you can. I am, dear George, Yours affectionately.[9]

As for the *Journal,* the same critic who so lightly dismissed its literary quality thinks most highly of its value as an historic document. His estimate of its worth in this respect has often been quoted, but will bear repeating here:

If you want to get into the last century, to feel its pulses throb beneath your finger, be content sometimes to leave the letters of Horace Walpole unturned ... even deny yourself your annual reading of Boswell ... and ride up and down the country with the greatest force of the eighteenth century in England. No man lived nearer the centre than John Wesley. Neither Clive nor Pitt, neither Mansfield nor Johnson ... Happily for us, his journals remain, and from them we can learn better than from anywhere else what manner of man he was, and the character of the times during which he lived.[10]

i. The Voyage Out

Oct. 14, 1735. WJJS, I, 106 ff.

. . . Mr. Benjamin Ingham, of Queen's College, Oxford; Mr. Charles Delamotte, son of a . . . merchant, in London, . . . who had offered himself some days before . . .; my brother Charles Wesley, and myself, took boat for Gravesend, in order to embark for Georgia. Our end in leaving our native country was not to avoid want, God having given us plenty of temporal blessings, nor to gain riches or honour . . .; but singly this—to save our souls, to live wholly to the glory of God. . . . In the afternoon we found the *Simmonds* off Gravesend, and immediately went on board.

Oct. 15 & 16. WJJS, I, 110f.

Wednesday and *Thursday* we spent chiefly with Mr. Morgan and Mr. Hutton, partly on board and partly on shore, in exhorting one another to 'shake off every weight, and to run with patience the race set before us.'

[Oct.] 17.—I began to learn German, in order to converse . . . with the Moravians,[11] six-and-twenty of whom we have on board. . . .

Sun. 19.—The weather being fair and calm, we had the morning service on quarter-deck. I now first preached extempore . . . we then celebrated the Holy Eucharist . . .—a little flock, which we did not doubt God would increase in due time.

Oct. 20, 1735. WJJS, I, 111 f.

Believing the denying ourselves, even in the smallest instances, might, by the blessing of God, be helpful to us, we . . . wholly left off the use of flesh and wine, and confined ourselves to vegetable food, chiefly rice and biscuit. . . . In the afternoon Mr. David Nitschmann, Bishop of the

Moravians, . . . began to learn English. O may we be not
only of one tongue, but of one mind and of one heart!

Oct. 21, 1735. WJJS, I, 112 f.

[God sending us a fair wind] we sailed from Gravesend.
When we were past about half the Goodwin Sands, the
wind suddenly failed. Had the calm continued till ebb,
the ship had probably been lost. But the gale sprang up
again in an hour, and carried us into the Downs.

We now began to be a little regular. Our common way
of living was this: From four in the morning till five each
of us used private prayer. From five to seven we read the
Bible together, carefully comparing it (that we might not
lean to our own understandings) with the writings of the
earliest ages. At seven we breakfasted. At eight were the
public prayers, at which were present usually between
thirty or forty of our eighty passengers. From nine to twelve
I commonly learned German, and Mr. Delamotte Greek.
My brother writ sermons, and Mr. Ingham read some
treatise of divinity or instructed the children. At twelve
we met to give an account to one another what we had
done since our last meeting, and what we designed to do
before our next. About one we dined. The time from dinner to four we spent with the people partly in public
reading, partly in reading to those whom each of us had
taken in charge, or in speaking to them severally, as need
required. At four were the evening prayers; when either
the Second Lesson was explained — as it always was in
the morning — or the children were catechized and instructed before the congregation. From five to six we
again used private prayer. From six to seven I read in our
cabin to two or three of the passengers, of whom there
were about eighty English on board, and each of my brethren to a few more in theirs. At seven I joined with the
Germans in their public service, while Mr. Ingham was

reading between the decks to as many as desired to hear.
At eight we met again, to exhort and instruct one another.
Between nine and ten we went to bed, where neither the
roaring of the sea nor the motion of the ship could take
away the refreshing sleep which God gave us.

Oct. 24, 1735. WJJS, I, 113f.

Having a rolling sea, most of the passengers found the
effects of it. Mr. Delamotte was exceeding sick for several
days; Mr. Ingham for about half an hour. My brother's
head ached much. Hitherto, it has pleased God, the sea has
not disordered me at all; nor have I been hindered one
quarter of an hour from reading, writing, composing, or
doing any business I could have done on shore.

During our stay in the Downs, some or other of us went,
as often as we had opportunity, on board the ship that
sailed in company with us, where also many were glad to
join in [the prayers of the Church and to hear the word
of God explained].

Oct. 31, 1735. WJJS, I, 115.

[It pleased God that the wind came fair, and] we sailed
out of the Downs. At eleven at night I was waked by a
great noise. I soon found there was no danger. But the
bare apprehension of it gave me a lively conviction what
manner of men ought those to be who are every moment
on the brink of eternity.

Jan. 25, 1736. WJJS, I, 141f.

At noon our third storm began. At four it was more
violent than any we had had before. Now, indeed, we could
say, 'The waves of the sea were mighty, and raged horribly.
They rose up to the heavens above, and clave down to hell
beneath.' The winds roared round about us, and—what I
never heard before—whistled as distinctly as if it had been

a human voice. The ship not only rocked to and fro with the utmost violence, but shook and jarred with so unequal, grating a motion, that one could not but with great difficulty keep one's hold of any thing, nor stand a moment without it. Every ten minutes came a shock against the stern or side of the ship, which one would think should dash the planks in a thousand pieces.

Jan. 25, 1736. WJJS, I, 142f.

At seven I went to the Germans. I had long before observed the great seriousness of their behaviour. Of their humility they had given a continual proof, by performing those servile offices for the other passengers which none of the English would undertake; for which they desired and would receive no pay, saying, 'It was good for their proud hearts,' and 'their loving Saviour had done more for them.' And every day had given them occasion of showing a meekness which no injury could move. If they were pushed, struck, or thrown down, they rose again and went away; but no complaint was found in their mouth. There was now an opportunity of trying whether they were delivered from the spirit of fear, as well as from that of pride, anger, and revenge. In the midst of the psalm wherewith their services began, [wherein we were mentioning the power of God,] the sea broke over, split the mainsail in pieces, covered the ship, and poured in between the decks, as if the great deep had already swallowed us up. A terrible screaming began among the English. The Germans [looked up, and without intermission] calmly sung on. I asked one of them afterward, 'Was you not afraid?' He answered, 'I thank God, no.' I asked, 'But were not your women and children afraid?' He replied mildly, 'No; our women and children are not afraid to die.'

From them I went to their crying, trembling neighbours, [and found myself enabled to speak with them in boldness and to] point out to them the difference in the hour of trial between him that feareth God and him that feareth him not. At twelve the wind fell. This was the most glorious day which I have hitherto seen.

Jan. 26, 1736. WJJS, I, 143.

We [now] enjoyed the calmer weather. I can conceive no difference comparable to that between a smooth and a rough sea, except that which is between a mind calmed by the love of God and one torn up by the storms of earthly passions.

Feb. 6, 1736. WJJS, I, 146f.

About eight in the morning, I first set my foot on American ground. It was a small uninhabited island, [but a few miles in extent] over against Tybee, [called by the English Peeper Island.] Mr. Oglethorpe led us . . . to a rising ground where we all kneeled down to give thanks [to God and beg the continuance of His Fatherly protection over us.] He then took boat for Savannah. When the rest of the people were come on shore, we . . . called our little flock together to prayers.

ii. The Missionary Pastorate

1. *Till Charles' Return to England.*

August Gottlieb Spangenberg, whose conversation with Wesley appears below had come over with the first group of Moravian settlers to Savannah in the preceding year. Later to become a Bishop and a pillar of the Moravian work both in Germany and Pennsylvania, he was at the time of the interview a young man—in fact, he was Wesley's junior by one year. But he had already a serene faith which impressed Wesley at first sight. Brought up in the Pietist tradition in Germany, he had already attained that intensely personal knowledge of redemption in Christ which was the chief characteristic of that tradition, the

*fount from which all else flowed. Implied, if not expressed,
in his questions to the novice is this judgment: unless you
do have this personal knowledge, all else is vain. Wesley
had an inkling of its importance, as his closing words show,
but it took two disillusioning years and the wise ministrations of another Moravian leader before he fully realized it.*

Feb. 7 & 8, 1736. WJJS, I, 150 f.

[Mr. Oglethorpe] returned in the evening with . . . Mr.
Spangenberg, who had conducted the first company of
Bohemian Brethren to Georgia . . . I asked Mr. Spangenberg's advice with regard to my own conduct. He told me
he could say nothing till he had asked me two or three
questions. 'Do you know yourself? Have you the witness
within yourself? Does the Spirit of God bear witness with
your spirit that you are a child of God?' I was surprised,
and knew not what to answer. He observed it, and asked,
'Do you know Jesus Christ?' I paused, and said, 'I know
He is the Saviour of the world.' 'True,' replied he; 'but do
you know He has saved you?' I answered, 'I hope He has
died to save me.' He only added, 'Do you know yourself?'
I said, 'I do.' But I fear they were vain words.

Feb. 24, 1736. WJJS, I, 168 f.

At our return the next day (Mr. Quincy being then in
the house wherein we afterward were), Mr. Delamotte
and I took up our lodging with the Germans. We had
now an opportunity, day by day, of observing their whole
behaviour. For we were in one room with them from morning to night, unless for the little time I spent in walking.
They were always employed, always cheerful themselves,
and in good humour with one another; they had put away
all anger and strife, and wrath, and bitterness, and clamour,
and evil speaking; they walked worthy of the vocation
wherewith they were called, and adorned the gospel of our
Lord in all things.

Feb. 28, 1736. WJJS, I, 170 f.

They met to consult concerning the affairs of their church: Mr. Spangenberg being shortly to go to Pennsylvania, and Bishop Nitschmann to return to Germany. After several hours spent in conference and prayer, they proceeded to the election and ordination of a bishop. The great simplicity, as well as solemnity, of the whole, almost made me forget the seventeen hundred years between, and imagine myself in one of those assemblies where form and state were not, but Paul the tent-maker or Peter the fisherman presided, yet with the demonstration of the Spirit and of power.

Mar. 7, 1736. WJJS, I, 176.

I entered upon my ministry at Savannah by preaching on the Epistle for the day, being the thirteenth of the first of Corinthians.

Mar. 30, 1736. WJJS, I, 188 f.

Mr. Ingham, coming from Frederica, brought me letters, pressing me to go thither. The next day Mr. Delamotte and I began to try whether life might not as well be sustained by one sort as by a variety of food. We chose to make the experiment with bread; and were never more vigorous and healthy than while we tasted nothing else.

Apr. 4, 1736. WJJS, I, 191 f.

About four in the afternoon I set out for Frederica in a periagua—a sort of flat-bottomed barge. The next evening we anchored near Skidoway Island, where the water, at flood, was twelve or fourteen feet deep. I wrapped myself up from head to foot in a large cloak to keep off the sand-flies and lay down on the quarter-deck. Between one and two I waked under water, being so fast asleep that I did not find where I was till my mouth was full of it. Having left my cloak, I know not how, upon deck, I swam round to the other side of the periagua, where a boat was tied, and climbed up by the rope without any hurt more than wetting my clothes. Thou art the God of whom cometh salvation: Thou art the Lord by whom we escape death.

Apr. 17, 1736. WJJS, I, 197 ff.

Not finding, as yet, any door open for the pursuing our main design,[12] we considered in what manner we might be most useful to the little flock at Savannah. And we agreed (1) to advise the more serious among them to form themselves into a sort of little society, and to meet once or twice a week, in order to reprove, instruct, and exhort one another. (2) To select out of these a smaller number for a more intimate union with each other, which might be forwarded, partly by our conversing singly with each, and partly by inviting them all together to our house; and this, accordingly, we determined to do every Sunday in the afternoon.[13]

May 5, 1736. WJJS, I, 210 f.

I was asked to baptize a child of Mr. Parker's, a second Bailiff of Savannah; but Mrs. Parker told me, 'Neither Mr. Parker nor I will consent to its being dipped.' I answered, 'If you "certify that" your "child is weak, it will suffice" (the rubric says) "to pour water upon it." ' She replied, 'Nay, the child is not weak; but I am resolved it shall not be dipped.' This argument I could not confute. So I went home, and the child was baptized by another person.

May 9, 1736. WJJS, I, 212 f.

I began dividing the public prayers, according to the original appointment of the Church (still observed in a few places in England). The morning service began at five;

the Communion Office (with the sermon), at eleven; the evening service about three; and this day I began reading prayers in the court-house—a large and convenient place.

May 10, 1736. WJJS, I, 213 f.

I began visiting my parishioners in order, from house to house; for which I set apart the time when they cannot work, because of the heat, viz. from twelve till three in the afternoon.

Frederica. June 19, 1736. WJJS, I, 233 f.

Mr. Oglethorpe returned from the south, and gave orders on Sunday, the 20th, that none should profane the day (as was usual before) by fishing or fowling upon it. In the afternoon I summed up what I had seen or heard at Frederica inconsistent with Christianity, and, consequently, with the prosperity of the place. The event was as it ought: some of the hearers were profited, and the rest deeply offended.

Frederica. June 22, 1736. WJJS, I, 234.

Observing much coldness in Mr. Horton's behaviour, I asked him the reason of it. He answered, 'I like nothing you do. All your sermons are satires upon particular persons, therefore I will never hear you more; and all the people are of my mind, for we won't hear ourselves abused.

'Beside, they say they are Protestants. But as for you, they cannot tell what religion you are of. They never heard of such religion before. They do not know what to make of it. And then your private behaviour—all the quarrels that have been here since you came have been long of you. Indeed, there is neither man nor woman in the town who minds a word you say. And so you may preach long enough; but nobody will come to hear you.'

He was too warm for hearing an answer. So I had nothing to do but to thank him for his openness, and walk away.

Savannah. June 30, 1736. WJJS, I, 238 f.

I hoped a door was opened for going up immediately to the Choctaws, the least polished, that is, the least corrupted, of all the Indian nations. But upon my informing Mr. Oglethorpe of our design, he objected, not only the danger of being intercepted, or killed by the French there; but much more, the inexpediency of leaving Savannah destitute of a minister. These objections I related to our brethren in the evening, who were all of opinion we ought not to go yet.

July 26, 1736. WJJS, I, 251 f.

My brother and I set out for Charlestown, in order to his embarking for England. . . .

2. *Missionary Trials.*

The departure of Charles Wesley for England of course increased both the area and the number of people for which the three remaining were responsible. John Wesley and Benjamin Ingham agreed to exercise by turns care over the religious concerns of Frederica. Ingham, who was already an ordained Priest of the Church of England, put heart and vigor not only into this work, but also into preparing himself for that among the Indians which had been the primary objective of their journey across the sea. He made good headway in the study of their language with a half-breed woman as his teacher. Finally he got an Indian school started in a house built for him at Irene, northwest of Savannah. A few months later, that is in February, 1737, it was decided that he should leave for England to stir up interest and get recruits for their work. He never got back to Georgia.[14]

Charles Delamotte, though only an inexperienced youth of twenty-one, and though he had obtained but a reluctant consent from his parents, attached himself to John Wesley

just a few days before their start. His insistence on making
the voyage was an early tribute to Wesley's power of evok-
ing a quick and almost adoring loyalty in those about him.
Tyerman says he came as Wesley's servant,[15] but we must
not understand by that a hired menial. When John travelled about from point to point in his scattered "parish,"[16]
Delamotte sometimes travelled with him. He was during
1737 entrusted with the care of a school.[17]

During at least one of Wesley's absences from Savannah, he shared with other lay members of the congregation the responsibility for the leadership of its religious
life. He remained in Georgia after John's departure, doubtless expecting (as did John himself) that he would return.
The next June, however, he returned to England.[18]

Aug. 28, 1736. WJJS, I, 267 f.

I set apart (out of the few we had) such books [as were
of most general use], towards a library at Frederica. [In
the afternoon I walked with Mark Hird to the Fort . . .
on the other side of the island.] About five we set out
homeward; but [the night overtaking us, and] my guide
not being perfect in the way, we were soon lost in the
woods. [We walked, however, straight forward, and crept
where we could not walk,] till between nine and ten
o'clock; when, being heartily tired and thoroughly wet
with dew, we lay down and slept sound till morning.

About daybreak, on *Sunday* the 29th, [we fixed on one
of the brightest stars, and resolved to steer straight towards
it, as long as it appeared. About six we lost sight of our
star, but] found ourselves soon after sunrise in the Great
Savannah, near Frederica. By this good providence I was
delivered from another fear, that of lying in the woods;
which I find by experience is, in fair weather, and to a
person in tolerable health, a mere 'lion in the way.'

Savannah. Sept. 20, 1736. WJJS, I, 276 ff.

We ended the *Apostolical Canons,* of which I must confess I once thought more highly than I ought to think. [Of them Bishop Beveridge observes that they are the decrees of the several Synods, which met at several places, and on several occasions, in the second and third age after Christ; and are therefore] called Apostolical, because partly grounded upon, partly agreeing with, the traditions delivered down from the Apostles.

He further observes, . . . (*Codex Canonum Ecclesiae Primitivae,* p. 159; and why did he not observe it in the first page of the book?), 'they contain the discipline used in the Church at the time when they were collected; not when the Council of Nice met, for then many parts of it were useless and obsolete.'

Oct. 12, 1736. WJJS, I, 279 f.

We considered if anything could yet be done for the poor people of Frederica; and I submitted to the judgment of my friends, which was that I should take another journey thither; Mr. Ingham undertaking to supply my place at Savannah for the time I should stay there.

Oct. 13, WJJS, I, 282 ff.

[I] . . . came thither early on Saturday morning, and found few things better than I expected.

[Oct.] 16.—The morning and evening prayers, which were read for a while after my leaving the place, had been long discontinued, and from that time every thing grew worse and worse. [Mr. Tackner had thrown off the form as well as the power of godliness; and so had most of his neighbours who ever had pretensions to it.]

I was at first a little surprised and discouraged; but I soon re-collected my spirits, and remembered my calling, and the word which cannot fail: 'Greater is He that is in you than he that is in the world.' I began with earnest crying to God to maintain His own cause, and after the evening prayers were ended invited a few to my house, as I did every night while I stayed at Frederica. I read to them out of the exhortations of Ephrem Syrus—the most awakened writer, I think, of all the ancients. We concluded our reading and conversation with a psalm; and I trust our God gave us His blessing.

Oct. 18, 1736. WJJS, I, 284 f.

Finding there were several Germans at Frederica, who, not understanding the English tongue, could not join in our public service, I desired them to meet me at my house; which they did every day at noon from thenceforward. We first sang a German hymn; then I read a chapter in the New Testament; then explained it to them as well as my little skill in the tongue would allow. After another hymn and the Lord's Prayer, I concluded with the Blessing.

Nov. 23, 1736. WJJS, I, 297 f.

Mr. Oglethorpe sailed for England, leaving Mr. Ingham, Mr. Delamotte and me at Savannah, but with less prospect of preaching to the Indians than we had the first day we set foot in America. Whenever I mentioned it, it was immediately replied, 'You cannot leave Savannah without a minister.' To this indeed my plain answer was, 'I know not that I am under any obligation to the contrary. I never promised to stay here one month. I openly declared both before, at, and ever since my coming hither that I neither would nor could take charge of the English any longer than till I could go among the Indians.' If it was said, 'But did not the Trustees of Georgia appoint you to be minister of Savannah?' I replied, 'They did; but it was not done by my solicitation: it was done without either my desire or knowledge. Therefore, I cannot conceive that appointment to lay me under any obligation of continuing there any longer than till a door is opened to the heathen; and this I expressly declared at the time I consented to accept of that appointment.' But though I had no other obligation not to leave Savannah now, yet that of love I could not break through; I could not resist the importunate request of the more serious parishioners 'to watch over their souls yet a little longer till some one came who might supply my place.' And this I the more willingly did because the time was not come to preach the gospel of peace to the heathen; all their nations being in a ferment: and Paustoobee and Mingo Mattaw having told me, in terms, in my own house, 'Now our enemies are all about us, and we can do nothing but fight; but if the beloved ones should ever give us to be at peace, then we would hear the great Word.'

Savannah. Dec. 9, 1736. WJJS, I, 301.

Hearing a poor woman was dangerously ill, I went to her immediately. She told me . . . that she had many things to say. But the time was past; for her weakness prevented her saying more, and on Friday the 10th God required her soul of her.

Savannah. Dec. 22, 1736. WJJS, I, 304.

Mr. Delamotte and I, with a guide . . . set out to walk to the Cowpen. When we had walked two or three hours . . . he did not know where we were. In an hour or two we came to a cypress-swamp, directly across our path, through which likewise we were to walk, the water being about breast high. A mile or two beyond, we were out of all path and out of all our knowledge. However, we went on till past sunset, and then sat down on the driest spot we could find, intending after a while to make a fire, and so stay there till morning. But finding our tinder was all wet, we were at a stand. I advised to walk on still; but both my companions, being faint and tired, were for lying down, which we accordingly did about six o'clock. The ground was wet as well as our clothes, which in a short time (it being a sharp frost) were as hard as the tree we lay against. However, I slept till six in the morning. There fell a heavy dew in the night, so that when we rose the side that had been uppermost was white as snow. In less than an hour we came to a plantation, [and after resting a little to Mrs. Musgrave's]. Nor did any of us receive any hurt at all, but came home in the evening [in perfect health].

Dec. 28, 1736. WJJS, I, 307 f.

[Mr. Delamotte] and I with a better guide set out for Frederica by land . . . In the evening [we] came to Fort Argyle. [It stands pleasantly on the high back of the river Ogeechy, having woods at a little distance on every side.] Here we were obliged to stay till the next afternoon. Then we went on to Cooanoochi river, over which we swam our horses by the side of the small canoe in which we crossed it ourselves. We made a fire on the bank . . . and, notwithstanding the rain, slept quietly till the morning.

Jan. 1, 1737. WJJS, I, 309.

Our provisions fell short, our journey being longer than we expected; but having a little barbecued bear's flesh (that is, dried in the sun) [which we had reserved for such an occasion], we boiled it, and found it very wholesome . . . food.

Jan. 2, 1737. WJJS, I, 309 f.

We came to the settlement of the Scotch Highlanders at Darien . . . This people utterly shames our countrymen: in sobriety, industry, frugality, patience; in sincerity and openness of behaviour; in justice and mercy of all kinds . . .

Mr. McLeod, their minister, is a serious, prudent, reso-
lute, and (I hope) a pious man.

Jan. 26, 1737. WJJS, I, 313.

. . . I took my final leave of Frederica. It was not any
apprehension of my own danger, though my life had been
threatened many times, but an utter despair of doing good
there, which made me content with the thought of seeing
it no more.

In my passage home, [i.e., to Savannah] having procured
a celebrated book (*The Works of Nicholas Machiavel*),
I set myself carefully to read and consider it. I began with
a prejudice in his favour, having been informed he had
often been misunderstood and greatly misrepresented. I
weighed the sentiments that were less common, transcribed
the passages wherein they were contained, compared one
passage with another, and endeavoured to form a cool,
impartial judgement. And my cool judgement is, that if all
the other doctrines of devils which have been committed
to writing since letters were in the world were collected
together in one volume, it would fall short of this; and
that, should a Prince form himself by this book, so calmly
recommending hypocrisy, treachery, lying, robbery, op-
pression, adultery, whoredom, and murder of all kinds,
Domitian or Nero would be an angel of light compared
to that man.

Savannah. Jan. 31, 1737. WJJ *Works*[19] III, 34.

Our general method is this:—A young gentleman[20] who
came with me, teaches between thirty and forty children
to read, write, and cast accounts. Before school in the
morning, and after school in the afternoon, he catechises
the lowest class, and endeavours to fix something of what
was said in their understandings as well as their memories.
In the evening, he instructs the larger children. On Saturday, in the afternoon, I catechise them all. The same I do

on Sunday before the Evening service. And in the church, immediately after the Second lesson, a select number of them having repeated the Catechism, and been examined in some part of it, I endeavour to explain at large, and to enforce, that part, both on them and the congregation.

Some time after the Evening service, as many of my parishioners as desire it, meet at my house, (as they do also on Wednesday evening,) and spend about an hour in prayer, singing, and mutual exhortation. A smaller number (most of those who design to communicate the next day) meet here on Saturday evening; and a few of these come to me on the other evenings, and pass half an hour in the same employment.

Savannah. Mar. 24, 1737. WJJS, I, 340.

About nine in the morning a fire broke out in the house of Mr. Robert Hows [a tithing-man], which in less than an hour consumed it. The next day a collection was made for him in the town, and the generality of the people showed a surprising willingness to give a little out of their little for the relief of a necessity greater than their own.

To JAMES HUTTON. Savannah. June 16, 1737. WJL, I, 222.

DEAR SIR, — I think our Lord is beginning to lift up His standard against the flood of iniquity which hath long covered the earth. Even in this place it hath pleased Him in some measure to stir up His might and come and help us. There is a strange *motus animorum,* as it seems, continually increasing. Those 'who fear the Lord speak often together,' and many of them are not ashamed of the gospel of Christ in the midst of an adulterous and sinful generation. The enemy hath great wrath, and rageth much. May it be a sign that his time is short!

Who, then, will rise up with me against the ungodly? You, I trust, for one, when the time is come. Till then, strive mightily with God, you and all your father's house, that I may not, when I have preached to others, be myself a castaway!

iii. Miss Sophy

More space, perhaps, is devoted in this section to Wesley's affection for Sophy Hopkey and its painful end than is demanded by its importance for his future development; but not more than it merits for its intrinsically appealing story of a heart in turmoil.

Sophia Christiana Hopkey, being niece to his wife, lived in the household of Mr. Causton, the chief magistrate of Savannah. The information we have of Mr. Causton indicates a vigorous, but in business matters, unscrupulous character. His administration was characterized by sundry petty oppressions; he was later deprived of his office in Savannah and his accounts regarded as unsatisfactory by the Trustees of the Colony.[21] Their home was not of the sort to make "Miss Sophy's" lot an easy one. Doubtless the presence of an attractive unmarried girl in such a rough community would have been an embarrassment to her uncle and aunt in any case. Oglethorpe may have felt the same way about the presence of an attractive unmarried minister. Anyhow, it is obvious that they engaged in what they thought was a perfectly benevolent conspiracy to promote a match between the two. Propinquity worked for them, and they helped it along all they could. It was Oglethorpe who planned their journey together from Frederica to Savannah, during which their friendship deepened into love. They were in the company of boatmen much of the time; but there were many chances for them to be alone together. As for the hapless pair's own feelings, Sophy's seem to have been a mixture of receptiveness and awe. Very properly, having received no direct proposal, she gave no unequivocal answer. In this she was not only wise beyond her years, but deserves our highest admiration

for refraining from pressing the advantage she had over
Wesley, bemused as he was. As for Wesley, he was head
over heels in love, yet from his timid advances he always
drew back before the decisive point. This was not the
only occasion he was to act so.[22] The recurrence of this
"behaviour pattern" has led psychologists confidently to
declare it a result of a "mother-fixation." This is a satisfactory account only if we are willing to deny validity to
the reason Wesley himself gives, which involved nothing
less than fidelity to his calling. Many expressions of this
sprinkle the record, enough to convince the student of
what the late Professor George Croft Cell aptly called his
"towering vocational consciousness." That, since he had
imbibed Clayton's High Church ideas, he considered celibacy an essential precondition of his "priesthood," is certain.[23] It is both hazardous and gratuitous to go farther
than this; to do so betrays an unawareness of the persistence in Christendom of an ideal whose ascendency is almost as old as the Faith itself. It has, it is true, disappeared
from most of Protestantism,[24] it has led and still leads to
abuses in Catholicism when forced on those who have no
vocation to it, and Wesley himself later gave it up; but all
these facts together do not prove that it is an aberration
wherever it appears.

It is useless to speculate on whether it would have been
a good match. Whatever Sophy's attractions may have been,
she certainly was not, like "Varanese," to whom he was
still writing, Wesley's intellectual equal; on the other
hand she certainly would have made him a better wife than
the woman he ultimately married. That Wesley later regarded himself as in this instance too "a brand plucked
out of the burning" indicates not that he had come to
think life with Miss Sophy as his wife was a fate he had
done well to escape, but that he had been delivered from
that betrayal of his vocation which marriage with anyone
would have constituted; or perhaps the "burning" here

referred not so much to marriage as to the "inordinate affection" which had brought him so close to that betrayal, and which he so earnestly deprecated in himself.[25]

Wesley and Sophy first met March 13th, 1736. That spring she seems to have been nothing more to him than a parishioner who would profit by instruction. Early in July she and a Miss Fossett came to the service at five in the morning and accompanied him afterward to the parsonage. Frequently thereafter, Sophy had breakfast and a French lesson as well as religious instruction with him, without Miss Fossett. She spent some time during the early autumn at Frederica. Our first extract finds Wesley attending to the pastoral duties which devolved on him there after Charles' departure. He was much distressed because during her absence Sophy had lost so much of the ground his careful tutelage had brought her over.

Frederica. Oct. 19, 1736. WJJS, I, 285.

In the evening I asked Miss Sophy if she was still determined to go to England. On her answering 'Yes,' I offered several arguments drawn from the topics of religion against it. But they did not appear to make any impression. Then I pressed her upon the head of friendship. Upon which she burst into tears, and said, 'Now my resolution begins to stagger'; as it did more and more every day.

Oct. 24, 1736. WJJS, I, 286 f.

I had a long conversation with Mr. Oglethorpe, in consequence of which I told her: 'Miss Sophy, Mr. Oglethorpe thinks it best that you should return to Savannah immediately.' She fell into a great passion of tears, and said she could not bear the thought of it. I talked with her near an hour, told her Mr. Causton's engagement to make good whatever I should promise her, so that she had only to make her own terms; and I left her a little more composed.

Oct. 25, 1736. WJJS, I, 287.

I asked Mr. Oglethorpe in what boat she should go. He said, 'She can go in none but yours, and indeed there is none so proper.' I saw the danger to myself, but yet had a good hope I should be delivered out of it, (1) because it was not my choice which brought me into it; (2) because I still felt in myself the same desire and design to live a single life; and (3) because I was persuaded should my desire and design be changed, yet her resolution to live single would continue.

Oct. 25, 1736. WJJS, I, 289.

We set out about noon. The afternoon, and so the greater part of the following days, we spent partly in using Bishop Patrick's *Prayers,* and partly in reading the first volume of Fleury's *History of the Church,* a book I chose for her sake chiefly, as setting before her such glorious examples of truth and patience, in the sufferings of those ancient worthies, 'who resisted unto blood, striving against sin.'

Oct. 26, 1736. WJJS, I, 289 f.

In the evening, the wind being contrary, we landed on the south end of St. Katherine's Island. And here we were obliged to stay till Friday; so that I had time to observe her behaviour more nearly.

Oct. 28, 1736. WJJS, I, 290.

In the afternoon, after walking some time, we sat down in a little thicket by the side of a spring. Here we entered upon a close conversation on Christian holiness. The openness with which she owned her ignorance of it, and the earnest desire she showed for fresh instruction, as it much endeared her to me, so it made me hope she would one day prove an eminent pattern of it.

Oct. 29, 1736. WJJS, I, 290.

We ventured to set out, though the wind was very high. The waves dashed over the boat every moment, and the cold was extremely piercing. She showed no concern, nor made any complaint, but appeared quite cheerful and satisfied.

It was not without some difficulty that in the afternoon we landed on St. Katherine's again. Observing in the night, the fire we lay by burning bright, that Miss Sophy was broad awake, I asked her, 'Miss Sophy, how far are you engaged to Mr. Mellichamp?' She answered, 'I have promised him either to marry him or to marry no one at all.' I said (which indeed was the expression of a sudden wish, not of any formed design), 'Miss Sophy, I should think myself happy if I was to spend my life with you.' She burst out into tears and said, 'I am every way unhappy. I won't have Tommy; for he is a bad man. And I can have none else.' She added, 'Sir, you don't know the danger you are in. I beg you would speak no word more on this head.' And after a while, 'When others have spoken to me on the subject, I felt an aversion to them. But I don't feel any to you. We may converse on other subjects as freely as ever.' Both my judgement and will acquiesced in what she said, and we ended our conversation with a psalm.

Oct. 31, 1736. WJJS, I, 291.

We came to Thunderbolt. Here we agreed that I should walk to Savannah and meet her at the landing. She went to Mr. Causton's directly. About five Mr. Causton came to my house, largely protesting his obligations to me, and repeated again and again that whatever I desired with regard to Miss Sophy he would consent to. After talking again with her upon it, I desired, (1) that she should come to my house every morning and evening; (2) that at his house she should come into no company but by her own choice; (3) That she should be no more upbraided with Mellichamp,[26] nor should he be mentioned before her.

Nov. 1, 1736. WJJS, I, 291 f.

She was eighteen years old. And from the beginning of our intimate acquaintance till this day, I verily believe she used no guile: not only because even now I know no instance to the contrary, nor only because the simplicity of her behaviour was a constant voucher for her sincerity; but because of the entire openness of all her conversation, answering whatever question I proposed, without either hesitation or reserve, immediately and directly. Another thing I was much pleased with in her was, that whenever we were conversing or reading, there was such a stillness in her whole behaviour, scarce stirring hand or foot, that 'she seemed to be, all but her attention, dead.' Yet at other times she was all life—active, diligent, indefatigable; always doing something, and doing with all her might whatever her hand found to do. For indeed, if the weakness of her body did not, her sense of honour would not hinder her doing anything.

Nov. 1, 1736. WJJS, I, 294.

The temper of her heart towards God is best known by Him 'who seeth in secret.' What appeared of it was a deep, even reverence, ripening into love, and a resignation unshaken in one of the severest trials which human nature is exposed to. The utmost anguish never wrung from her a murmuring word. She saw the hand of God, and was still. She said indeed, 'If it be possible, Father!' But added, 'Not as I will, but as Thou wilt!'

Such was the woman, according to my closest observation, of whom I now began to be much afraid. My desire and design still was to live single; but how long it would continue I knew not. I therefore consulted my friends whether it was not best to break off all intercourse with her immediately. They expressed themselves so ambiguously that I understood them to mean that I ought not to break it off. And accordingly she came to me (as had been agreed) every morning and evening.

Feb. 3, 1737. WJJS, I, 315.

I was now in a great strait. I still thought it best for me to live single. And this was still my design; but I felt the foundations of it shaken more and more every day. Insomuch that I again hinted at a desire of marriage, though I made no direct proposal. For indeed it was only a sudden thought, which had not the consent of my own mind. Yet I firmly believe, had she (Miss Sophy) closed with me at that time, my judgement would have made but a faint resistance. But she said 'she thought it was best for clergymen not to be encumbered with worldly cares, and that it was best for her, too, to live single, and she was accordingly resolved never to marry.' I used no argument to induce her to alter her resolution.

Upon reflection, I thought this a very narrow escape; and after much consideration, I went to Mr. Töltschig, the pastor of the Moravians, and desired his advice, whether I had not best, while it was yet in my power, break off so dangerous an acquaintance. He asked, 'What do you think would be the consequence if you should?' I said, 'I fear her soul would be lost, being surrounded with dangers, and having no other person to warn her of and arm her against them.' He added, 'And what do you think would be the consequence if you should not break it off?' I said, 'I fear I should marry her.' He replied short, 'I don't see why you should not.'[27]

I went home amazed to the last degree; and it was now first that I had the least doubt whether it was best for me to marry or not, which I never before thought would bear a question. I immediately related what had occurred to

Mr. Ingham and Delamotte. They utterly disapproved of Mr. Töltschig's judgement, and in the evening went, as I desired they would, and talked largely with him and Antone (the Moravian Bishop Seifart) about it. It was midnight when I went to them; but even then they did not seem to be fully assured.

Feb. 6, 1737. WJJS, I, 316.

. . . I writ two or three lines which I desired Miss Bovey to give Miss Sophy. They were, I think, in these words: 'Feb. 6. I find, Miss Sophy, I can't take fire into my bosom, and not be burnt. I am therefore retiring for a while to desire the direction of God. Join with me, my friend, in fervent prayer, that He would show me what is best to be done.'

Feb. 14, 1737. WJJS, I, 318.

About seven in the morning, I told her in my own garden, 'I am resolved, Miss Sophy, if I marry at all, not to do it till I have been among the Indians.'

Feb. 15, 1737. WJJS, I, 319.

The next morning she told me, 'People wonder what I can do so long at your house; I am resolved not to breakfast with you any more. And I won't come to you any more alone.'

Feb. 26, 1737. WJJS, I, 323.

Calling at Mrs. Causton's (Saturday 26th), she was there alone. This was indeed an hour of trial. Her words, her eyes, her air, her every motion and gesture, were full of such a softness and sweetness! I know not what might have been the consequence had I then but touched her hand. And how I avoided it I know not. Surely God is over all!

Feb. 27, 1737. WJJS, I, 323 f.

After all the company but Miss Sophy was gone, Mr. Delamotte went out and left us alone again. Finding her still the same, my resolution failed. At the end of a very serious conversation, I took her by the hand, and, perceiving she was not displeased, I was so utterly disarmed, that that hour I should have engaged myself for life, had it not been for the full persuasion I had of her entire sincerity, and in consequence of which I doubted not but she was resolved (as she had said) 'never to marry while she lived.'

A moment's reflection when she was gone convinced me that I had done foolishly. And I once more resolved by God's help to be more wary for the future. Accordingly, though I saw her every day in the following week, I touched her not.

Mar. 3, 1737. WJJS, I, 324 f.

Yet on Thursday evening (March 3), after we came from her, Mr. Delamotte was deeply concerned. I had never seen him in such uneasiness before. He said, with many tears, 'He found we must part, for he could not live in that house when I was married to Miss Sophy.' I told him, 'I had no intention to marry her.' He said, 'I did not know my own heart; but he saw clearly it would come to that very soon, unless I broke off all intercourse with her.' I told him, 'This was a point of great importance, and therefore not to be determined suddenly.' He said 'I ought to determine as soon as possible; for I was losing ground daily.' I felt what he said to be true, and therefore easily consented to set aside the next day for that purpose.

Mar. 4, 1737. WJJS, I, 325 f.

Having both of us sought God by deep consideration, fasting, and prayer, in the afternoon we conferred together,

but could not come to any decision. We both apprehended
Mr. Ingham's objection to be the strongest, the doubt
whether she was what she appeared. But this doubt was
too hard for us to solve. At length we agreed to appeal
to the Searcher of hearts. I accordingly made three lots.
In one was writ 'Marry'; in the second, 'Think not of it
this year.' After we had prayed to God to 'give a perfect
lot,' Mr. Delamotte drew the third, in which were these
words, 'Think of it no more.' Instead of the agony I had
reason to expect, I was enabled to say cheerfully, 'Thy will
be done.' We cast lots once again to know whether I ought
to converse with her any more; and the direction I received from God was, 'Only in presence of Mr. Delamotte.'

I saw and adored the goodness of God, though what He
required of me was a costly sacrifice.

It was indeed the giving up at once whatever this world
affords of agreeable—not only honour, fortune, power
(which indeed were nothing to me, who despised them
as the clay in the streets), but all the truly desirable con-
veniences of life—a pleasant house, a delightful garden,
on the brow of a hill at a small distance from the town,
another house and garden in the town; and a third a few
miles off, with a large tract of fruitful land adjoining to it.
And above all, what to me made all things else vile and
utterly beneath a thought, such a companion as I never
expected to find again, should I live one thousand years
twice told. So that I could not but cry out: *O Lord God,
Thou God of my fathers, plenteous in mercy and truth,
behold I give Thee, not thousands of rams or ten thousands of rivers of oil, but the desire of my eyes, the joy of
my heart, the one thing upon earth which I longed for!
O give me Wisdom, which sitteth by Thy throne, and reject me not from among Thy children!*

Today I writ to the Trustees an account of our year's
expenses . . .

Mar. 9, 1737. WJJS, I, 329f.

About ten I called on Mrs. Causton. She said, 'Sir, Mr. Causton and I are exceedingly obliged to you for all the pains you have taken about Sophy. And so is Sophy too; and she desires you would publish the banns of marriage between her and Mr. Williamson on Sunday.' She added, 'Sir, you don't seem to be well pleased. Have you any objection to it?' I answered, 'Madam, I don't seem to be awake. Surely I am in a dream.' She said, 'They agreed on it last night between themselves after you were gone. And afterwards Mr. Williamson asked Mr. Causton's and my consent, which we gave him; but if you have any objection to it, pray speak. Speak to her. She is at the Lot. Go to her. She will be very glad to hear anything Mr. Wesley has to say. Pray go to her and talk to her yourself.' I said, 'No, madam; if Miss Sophy is engaged, I have nothing to say. It will not signify for me to see her any more.'

Mar. 9, 1737. WJJS, I, 334 f.

I came home and went into my garden. I walked up and down, seeking rest but finding none. From the beginning of my life to this hour I had not known one such as this. God let loose my inordinate affection upon me, and the poison thereof drank up my spirit. I was as stupid as if half awake, and yet in the sharpest pain I ever felt. To see her no more: that thought was as the piercings of a sword; it was not to be borne, nor shaken off. I was weary of the world, of light, of life. Yet one way remained, to seek to God—a very present help in time of trouble. And I did seek after God, but I found Him not. I forsook Him before: now He forsook me. I could not pray. Then indeed the snares of death were about me; the pains of hell overtook me. Yet I struggled for life; and though I had neither words nor thoughts, I lifted up my eyes to the Prince that is highly exalted, and supplied the place of them as I could: and about four o'clock He so far took the cup from me that I drank so deeply of it no more.

Mar. 10, 1737. WJJS, I, 336 f.

In the afternoon Mr. Delamotte and I went to the Lot, where I read them Bishop Hall's *Meditations on Heaven;* during which Miss Sophy fixed her eyes on Mr. Williamson and me alternately for above half an hour, with as steady an observation as if she had been drawing our pictures. Mr. Williamson afterwards told me, 'He should always be glad of my advice, and hoped I would still favour them with my conversation, which he should look upon as a particular happiness both to her and him.' I answered, 'I hope we shall all be happy, in the place we have been reading of.' Of which indeed I had so strong a persuasion that I returned rejoicing and wondering at myself. The next morning she set out for Purrysburg, and on Saturday, March 12, 1737, was married there; this being the day which completed the year from my first speaking to her!

iv. Retreat

Wesley's repelling of Miss Sophy from the Communion was the action that brought the thunders of the colonists' animosity about his head, but the tension had been building up from other causes also, and since the very beginning of his stay in Georgia. The first thing he did after landing was to stave in some casks of rum which had been landed[28] contrary to the intentions of Oglethorpe, who hoped to keep strong drink and slavery out of the Colony. It is not difficult to imagine the mutterings and hard looks which would follow this bold stroke. We have already had occasion to notice in connection with the Williams affidavit how Wesley's opposition to slavery turned some of the landholders against him.[29] The stiffness of his Churchmanship both puzzled and angered his parishioners.[30] Wesley was, in his ecclesiastical procedure, trying to live up to the letter of the Canons of his Church, to the instructions of the S. P. G., and to his own high standards of clerical responsibility. But his punctiliousness ran counter to the general practise of that time even at home; and was certain to rub the tempers of the unruly colonists the wrong way. If he had deliberately tried to goad the colonists to hostile action, he could hardly have chosen a better way than repelling Sophy Williamson from the Communion. Her uncle was, as Chief Magistrate, in a position to make his wrath felt. Granted that Wesley was in what he did quite within the letter of the Canon Law, it must be said nevertheless that he acted in this matter with complete insensitiveness to the emotional factors involved. He was hardly able himself to separate his hurt affection from his pastoral duty toward her—and so should not have been surprised when others too failed to make the distinction, and struck back, clumsily, but with the crowd's instinctive knowledge of how to wound. They succeeded in making Wesley's position in the Colony untenable, and (what they most wanted) ending his usefulness among them. Wesley, in leaving before the questionable legal proceedings against him had dragged out their weary course, reversed himself by transgressing the letter of the law, but doing the only thing humanly possible under the circumstances. The whole affair was painful in the extreme, but the discredit which falls to Wesley is due, not to lack of fidelity or honor, but to an egregious error in human judgment.[31]

May 7, 1737. WJJS, I, 355 f.

I was in doubt whether I could admit Miss Sophy to the Communion till she had, in some manner or other, owned her fault and declared her repentance. I doubted the more, because I was informed she had left off fasting, and because she neglected all the morning prayers, though still acknowledging her obligation to both, which made a wide difference between her neglect and that of others. But after much consideration, I resolved to take Mr. Delamotte's advice, and to bear with her till I had spoken with her once more.

July 5, 1737. WJJS, I, 366.

. . . I sent the following note to Mrs. Williamson, which I wrote in the most mild and friendly manner I could, both in pursuance of my resolution to proceed with all mildness, and because Mrs. Williamson told me she was so much grieved already.

"If the sincerity of friendship is best to be known from the painful offices, then there could not be a stronger proof of mine than that I gave you on Sunday: except that which I am going to give you now, and which you may perhaps equally misinterpret.

"Would you know what I dislike in your past or present behaviour? You have always heard my thoughts as freely as you asked them. Nay, much more freely; you knew it well, and so you shall do, as long as I can speak or write.

"In your present behaviour I dislike (1) your neglect of half the public service, which no man can compel you to; (2) your neglect of fasting, which you once know to be a help to the mind, without any prejudice to the body; (3) your neglect of almost half the opportunity of communicating which you have lately had.

"But these things are small in comparison of what I dislike in your past behaviour. For, (1) You told me over and over you had entirely conquered your inclination for Mr. Mellichamp. Yet at that very time you had not conquered it. (2) You told me frequently, you had no design to marry Mr. Williamson. Yet at the very time you spoke you had the design. (3) In order to conceal both these things from me, you went through a course of deliberate dissimulation. Oh how fallen! How changed! Surely there was a time when in Miss Sophy's life there was no guile.

"Own these facts, and own your fault, and you will be in my thoughts as if they had never been. If you are otherwise minded, I shall still be your friend, though I cannot expect you should be mine."

Aug. 3, 1737. WJJS, I, 376.

We returned to Savannah. [Aug.] 7.—I repelled Mrs. Williamson from the Holy Communion.

Aug. 8, 1737. WJJS, I, 377.

Mr. Recorder of Savannah issued out the warrant following:

GEORGIA, SAVANNAH SS.

"To all Constables, Tithingmen, and others, whom these may concern:

"YOU, and each of you, are hereby required to take the body of John Wesley, Clerk:

"And bring him before one of the bailiffs of the said town, to answer the complaint of William Williamson and Sophia his wife, for defaming the said Sophia, and refusing to administer to her the Sacrament of the Lord's Supper, in a public congregation, without cause; by which the said William Williamson is damaged one thousand pounds sterling: And for so doing, this is your warrant, certifying what you are to do in the premises. Given under my hand and seal the 8th day of August, *Anno Dom.* 1737.

THO. CHRISTIE."

Aug. 16, 1737. WJJS, I, 382.

. . . Mrs. Williamson was induced to swear to and sign [the memorable] affidavit, insinuating much more than it asserted; but asserting that Mr. Wesley had many times proposed marriage to her, all which proposals she had rejected.

Aug. 22, 1737. WJJS, I, 383 ff.

Mrs. Williamson's affidavit was next read, of which I desired a copy. Mr. Causton answered that I might have one from any of the newspapers, [for it would be printed in them all immediately.

[The affidavit was as follows:

PROVINCE OF GEORGIA, SAVANNAH Ss.

["SOPHIA Christiana Williamson, the wife of William Williamson, of Savannah aforesaid, maketh oath, . . . that ever since her marriage with the said William Williamson, he, the said John Wesley, hath taken all opportunities, in her husband's absence, to persecute this Deponent and to force his private discourse to her, wherein he hath often terrified her with the danger her soul would be in if she did not continue to spend her time and converse with him, the said John Wesley, in the same manner she did before marriage. And this Deponent further saith that particularly about three months since the said John Wesley being at this Deponent's house among other company who were then busy with this Deponent's uncle, he, the said John Wesley, took an opportunity to follow this Deponent to the back door, and there told this Deponent that it was necessary for the benefit of her soul that he should still continue to converse with her; that she must not mind what the world said on such an occasion; and that she must contrive some opportunity or proper times for him to converse with her. To which this Deponent answered, 'She wondered he could desire any such thing, when he knew this Deponent's husband had so often forbidden him, and she had so often refused him so to do.'

"Signed by Sophia Christiana Williamson. Sworn before me this 16th day of August, 1737.

HENRY PARKER."

Transcribed from the copy taken and attested by Mr. Burnside.]

Then the Court delivered to the Grand Jury the following paper entitled:

A List of Grievances Presented by the Grand Jury for Savannah, This——Day of August, 1737

["That whereas the Colony of Georgia is composed of a mixed number of Christians, members of the Church of England and Dissenters, who all or most part would attend divine ordinances and communicate with a faithful pastor of the Established Church: the Rev. Mr. John Wesley, who for the present serves the cure of Savannah, has not as the law directs emitted any declaration in this place of his adherence to the principles of the Church of England. We have the more reason to complain of grievances, that the said Revd. person (as we humbly conceive) deviates from the principles and regulations of the Established Church, in many particulars inconsistent with the happiness and prosperity of this Colony, as —

"Prima, by inverting the order and method of the Liturgy,

"2. By changing or altering such passages as he thinks proper in the version of Psalms publicly authorized to be sung in the church.

"3. By introducing into the church and service at the Altar compositions of psalms and hymns not inspected or authorized by any proper judicature;

"4. By introducing novelties, such as dipping infants, etc., in the Sacrament of Baptism, and refusing to baptize the children of such as will not submit to his innovations;

"5. By restricting the benefit of the Lord's Supper to a small number of persons, and refusing it to all others who will not conform to a grievous set of penances, confessions, mortifications, and constant attendance of early and late hours of prayer, very inconsistent with the labour and employments of the Colony;

"6. By administering the Sacrament of the Lord's Supper to boys ignorant and unqualified, and that notwithstanding of their parents and nearest friends remonstrating against it, and accusing them of disobedience and other crimes, etc.;

"7. By refusing to administrate the Holy Sacrament to well-disposed and well-living persons, unless they should submit to confessions and penances for crimes which they utterly refuse and whereof no evidence is offered;

"8. By venting sundry uncharitable expressions of all who differ from him, and not pronouncing the Benediction in church, until all the hearers except his own communicants are withdrawn;

"9. By teaching wives and servants that they ought absolutely to follow the course of mortification, fastings, and diets of prayers prescribed by him, without any regard to the interest of their private families, or the commands of their respective husbands and masters;

"10. By refusing the Office of the Dead to such as did not communicate with him, or leaving out such parts of that Service as he thought proper;

"11. By searching into and meddling with the affairs of private families, by means of servants and spies employed by him for that purpose, whereby the peace both of public and private life is much endangered;

"12. By calling himself 'Ordinary,' and thereby claiming a jurisdiction which we believe is not due to him, and whereby we should be precluded from access to redress by any superior jurisdiction.

"We do with all respect and deference to the person and character of the Revd. Mr. John Westley, present these our grievances: not from any resentment, but allanerly that such relief may be afforded in time coming as shall be judged necessary for the interest of peace and religion in this Province."]

Oct. 29, 1737. WJJS, I, 397 f.

Some of the French of Savannah were present at the prayers at Highgate. The next day I received a message from them all, 'That as I read prayers to the French of Highgate, who were but few, they hoped I would do the same to those of Savannah, where was a large number who did not understand English.' Sunday, the 30th, I began so to do; and now I had full employment for that holy-day. The first English prayers lasted from five till half an hour past six. The Italian, which I read to a few Vaudois, began at nine. The second service for the English, including the sermon and the Holy Communion, continued from half an hour past ten till about half an hour past twelve. The French service began at one. At two I catechised the children. About three began the English service. After this was ended, I had the happiness of joining with as many as my largest room would hold, in reading, prayer, and singing praise. And about six the service of the Moravians, so called, began; at which I was glad to be present, not as a teacher, but a learner.

Nov. 22, 1737. WJJS, I, 399.

[Mr. Causton desired to have a conference with me. . . .] He likewise read me the affidavits made September 15, in one of which it was expressly asserted that I had assaulted Mr. Causton in his own house, calling him liar, villain, and so forth. It was at this conversation, Mr. Anderson told me I had been reprimanded in the last Court, for an enemy to and hinderer of the public peace.

I again consulted my friends, who agreed with me that the time we looked for was now come. And the next morning I went to Mr. Causton again and told him I designed to set out for England immediately. I posted up an advertisement in the Great Square to the same effect, and then quietly prepared myself for the journey.

Dec. 2, 1737. WJJS, I, 400.

I proposed to set out for Port Royal, Carolina about noon, the tide then serving. But about ten, the magistrates sent for me, and told me I must not go out of the province; for I had not answered the allegations laid against me. I replied, 'I have appeared at six or seven Courts successively in order to answer them. But I was not suffered so to do, when I desired it time after time.' Then they said, however, I must not go, unless I would give security to answer those allegations at their Court. I asked, 'What security?' After consulting together about two hours, the Recorder showed me a kind of bond, engaging me, under a penalty of fifty pounds, to appear at their Court when I should be required. He added, 'But Mr. Williamson, too, has desired of us, that you should give bail to answer his action.' I then told him plainly, 'Sir, you use me very ill, and so you do the Trustees. I will give neither any bond nor any bail at all. You know your business, and I know mine.'

In the afternoon the magistrates published an order, requiring all the officers and sentinels to prevent my going out of the province, and forbidding any person to assist me so to do. Being now only a prisoner at large, in a place where I knew by experience every day would give fresh opportunity to procure evidence of words I never said, and actions I never did, I saw clearly the hour was come for leaving this place; and as soon as evening prayers were over, about eight o'clock, the tide then serving, I shook off the dust of my feet, and left Georgia, after having preached the gospel there not as I ought, but as I was able, one year and nearly nine months.

v. Self-appraisal

The return voyage of the missionary of the S. P. G. is in sad contrast to the outward trip. Then he had comrades, now he is alone; then he was full of confidence, now doubt of himself overwhelms him. In the *Journal,* now, as before, there are notices of daily happenings, of work done (on a much smaller scale) for the souls of those aboard. But the dominant note is one of anxious self-examination. As he approaches England, he knows that an accounting will be due: to his loved ones, his friends of the Holy Club, and to his superiors in both the colonial administration and the S. P. G. But before and more important than these, must come an accounting to God. Here his self-abasement is extreme. He must acknowledge failure, total and abject. Even while our pity flows for him, we can see that if the way he had been treading was a dead-end, at least it was gain for him to have learned that he must try another; and we know that he had met those people who could say, "This is the way; walk in it!" The Moravian Peter Böhler would complete what the Moravian Spangenberg had begun.

Dec. 22, 1737. WJJS, I, 413.

I took my leave of America, though, if it please God, not for ever, going on board the *Samuel,* Captain Percy, with a young gentleman who had been a few months in Carolina, one of my parishioners of Savannah, and a Frenchman, late of Purrysburg, who was escaped thence with the skin of his teeth.

[Dec. 26.—I began instructing a negro lad in the principles of Christianity. The next day I resolved to break off living delicately, and return to my old simplicity of diet; and after I did so, neither my stomach nor my head much complained of the motion of the ship].

Jan. 24, 1738. WJJS, I, 418.

We spoke with two ships, outward-bound, from whom we had the welcome news of our wanting but one hundred and sixty leagues of the Land's End. My mind was now full of thought, part of which I writ down as follows:

"I went to America, to convert the Indians; but oh, who shall convert me? who, what is he that will deliver me from this evil heart of unbelief? I have a fair summer religion. I can talk well; nay, and believe myself, while no danger is near. But let death look me in the face, and my spirit is troubled. Nor can I say, 'To die is gain'!

"I think, verily, if the gospel be true, I am safe: for I not only have given, and do give, all my goods to feed the poor; I not only give my body to be burned, drowned, or whatever God shall appoint for me; but I follow after charity (though not as I ought, yet as I can), if haply I may attain it. I *now* believe the gospel is true. 'I show my faith by my works,' by staking my all upon it. I would do so again and again a thousand times, if the choice were still to make. Whoever sees me, sees I would be a Christian. Therefore 'are my ways not like other men's ways.' Therefore I have been, I am, I am content to be, 'a by-word, a proverb of reproach.' But in a storm I think, What if the gospel be not true?"

Deal. Jan. 29, 1738. WJJS, I, 421 ff.

Toward evening was a calm; but in the night a strong north wind brought us safe into the Downs. The day before, Mr. Whitefield had sailed out, neither of us then knowing any thing of the other.[32] At four in the morning we took boat, and in half an hour landed at Deal: it being *Wednesday*, February 1, the anniversary festival in Georgia for Mr. Oglethorpe's landing there.

It is now two years and almost four months since I left my native country, in order to teach the Georgian Indians the nature of Christianity. But what have I learned myself in the mean time? Why, what I the least of all suspected, that I, who went to America to convert others, was never myself converted to God.[33] 'I am not mad,' though I thus speak; but 'I speak the words of truth and soberness'; if haply some of those who still dream may awake, and see, that as I am, so are they.

Are they read in philosophy? So was I. In ancient or modern tongues? So was I also. Are they versed in the science of divinity? I too have studied it many years. Can they talk fluently upon spiritual things? The very same could I do. Are they plenteous in alms? Behold, I gave all my goods to feed the poor. Do they give of their labour as well as of their substance? I have laboured more abundantly than they all. Are they willing to suffer for their brethren? I have thrown up my friends, reputation, ease, country; I have put my life in my hand, wandering into strange lands; I have given my body to be devoured by the deep, parched up with heat, consumed by toil and weariness, or whatsoever God should please to bring upon me. But does all this —be it more or less, it matters not—make me acceptable to God? Does all I ever did or can know, say, give, do, or suffer, justify me in His sight? Yea, or the constant use of all the means of grace? (which, nevertheless, is meet, right, and our bounden duty). Or that I know nothing of myself; that I am, as touching outward, moral righteousness, blameless? Or (to come closer yet) the having a rational conviction of all the truths of Christianity? Does all this give me a claim to the holy, heavenly, divine character of a Christian? By no means. If the oracles of God are true, if we are still to abide by 'the law and the testimony,' all these things, though, when ennobled by faith in Christ,[34] they are holy and just and good, yet without it are 'dung and dross,' meet only to be purged away by 'the fire that never shall be quenched.'

This, then, have I learned in the ends of the earth,— that I 'am fallen short of the glory of God': that my whole heart is 'altogether corrupt and abominable'; and consequently my whole life (seeing it cannot be that an 'evil tree' should 'bring forth good fruit') : that, 'alienated' as

I am from the life of God, I am 'a child of wrath,'[35] an heir
of hell: that my own works, my own sufferings, my own
righteousness, are so far from reconciling me to an offended
God, so far from making any atonement for the least of
those sins, which 'are more in number than the hairs of my
head,' that the most specious of them need an atonement
themselves, or they cannot abide His righteous judgement:
that 'having the sentence of death' in my heart, and having
nothing in or of myself to plead, I have no hope, but that
of being justified freely, 'through the redemption that is
in Jesus': I have no hope, but that if I seek I shall find
Christ, and 'be found in Him, not having my own righteousness, but that which is through the faith of Christ, the
righteousness which is of God by faith.'

   If it be said that I have faith (for many such things have
I heard, from many miserable comforters), I answer, So
have the devils—a sort of faith; but still they are strangers
to the covenant of promise. So the apostles had even at Cana
in Galilee, when Jesus first 'manifested forth His glory';
even then they, in a sort, 'believed on Him'; but they had
not then 'the faith that overcometh the world.' The faith
I want is[36] 'A sure trust and confidence in God, that,
through the merits of Christ, my sins are forgiven, and I
reconciled to the favour of God.' I want that faith which
St. Paul recommends to all the world, especially in his
Epistle to the Romans: that faith which enables every one
that hath it to cry out, 'I live not; but Christ liveth in me;
and the life which I now live, I live by faith in the Son of
God, who loved me, and gave Himself for me.' I want that
faith which none can have without knowing that he hath
it (though many imagine they have it, who have it not);
for whosoever hath it, is 'freed from sin, the whole body
of sin is destroyed' in him: he is freed from fear, 'having
peace with God through Christ, and rejoicing in hope of
the glory of God.' And he is freed from doubt, 'having the
love of God shed abroad in his heart, through the Holy

Ghost which is given unto him'; which 'Spirit itself beareth witness with his spirit, that he is a child of God.'

WHITEFIELD'S DESCRIPTION OF WESLEY'S WORK IN GEORGIA. June 2, 1738. Whitefield, JV,[37] p. 84.

The good Mr. John Wesley has done in America, under God, is inexpressible. His name is very precious among the people; and he has laid such a foundation, that I hope neither men nor devils will ever be able to shake. Oh, that I may follow him, as he has Christ.

Sept. 29, 1749. WJJS, III, 433.

About this time I was refreshed with a friendly letter from an excellent man, whom I had not heard from for several years. Part of it was as follows:

EBENEZER, IN GEORGIA, *July* 25, 1749.

REV. AND DEAR SIR,

The sincere love to your worthy person and faithful performance of your holy office, which the Lord kindled in my heart during your presence at Savannah, hath not been abated, but rather increased, since the providence of God called you from us, and showed you another field for the labour of your ministry.

Diagram of the Major Movements
of the Wesleys, Whitefield and Böhler
1736-1739

Illustrating (1) the periods during which Whitefield and Charles
labored before John's return from Georgia; and
(2) the fact that not till December, 1738, were
all three working together in England.

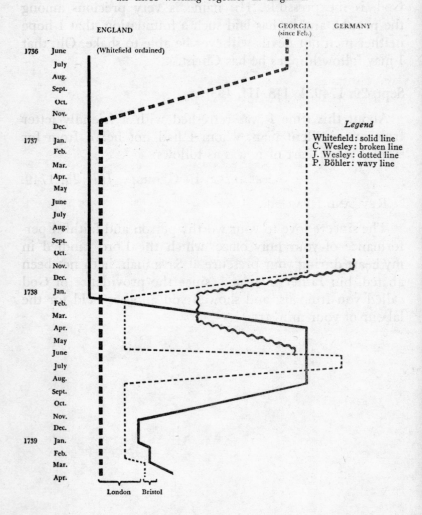

CHAPTER IV

THE NASCENT REVIVAL

The revival in which the Wesleys were to play such a conspicuous role in England was but a part of a far wider one which embraced Central Europe and North America as well. Since in a sense the Continental movement was parent to both the others, a word as to its origin and nature will not be out of place here. Even before the end of the seventeenth century the earnest Pastor Spener in Frankfort, feeling very keenly the insufficiency of the formal ministrations of the State Church, started little groups of lay people who met regularly outside of service hours for religious reading, singing, prayer and mutual edification. These groups multiplied rapidly in other German cities, and, though they did not cut themselves off from the State Church, were called "collegia pietatis," and their adherents nicknamed "Pietists." Their piety was the sort we have come to call "evangelical." They accepted the basic formulations of Protestant doctrine, especially salvation by faith, but insisted that until such a doctrine was verified in personal experience, it was worth nothing. Repentance and remission of sins must be *felt;* the new-birth must be *experienced* as the beginning of a life of devotion to the Lord Jesus. Usually this life of devotion was held to involve a commensurate detachment from earthly preoccupations such as "human learning," business, and even family affections, and a suspicion of, if not an actual hostility to "worldly pleasures." The same piety characterized the Moravians, who differed from other Pietists only in that they formed a separate religious body, without connection with a State Church.

135

A few links between the widely sundered revival spots can be traced. We have already seen the Moravians at work in Georgia. More significant still for the religious life of the Colonies was the work of Theodore Frelinghuysen, who had been reared in German Pietism, and who by his awakening sermons in the Raritan Valley of New Jersey began the American revival known as the Great Awakening. In New England, its best known leader was Jonathan Edwards. Edwards' *Narrative of Surprising Conversions* was read in England.[1] Whitefield, as is well known, linked the revival in England with that in America. In the early months of 1737 the Moravian leaders Zinzendorf and Nitschmann were in England; a year later, Peter Böhler stopped there on his way to America.

However, when we have traced all the links, personal and literary, that we can find between these distant revival spots, we are finally forced, in accounting for the contemporary revivals in Berlin and Northampton, London and Savannah, to fall back on this: "The Spirit breatheth where He will . . . thou knowest not whence He cometh and whither He goeth."

Just as the New England revival had its indigenous leadership in Jonathan Edwards, so in old England, though it owed much, no doubt, to the presence of Moravian missionaries, the nascent revival there owed more to George Whitefield than to any other Englishman. This needs to be emphasized, for it is easy to assume, that, because the Wesleys so powerfully guided and conserved the revival, they initiated it as well. But we must remember that Whitefield had labored incessantly between his ordination in the summer of 1736 and his first trip to Georgia which did not begin till just as John was landing from there in February of 1738. It would perhaps be too much to say that, when Charles landed in England, in December, 1736, he found a revival already in progress; but there was a stirring among the dry bones, and it had been caused by the eloquent preaching of "the boy parson," as Whitefield was often called. The quickening went on at an accelerated pace throughout 1737. We should not try to deny that Charles' work had something to do with it, but a study of his *Journal* for the period indicates that he was influenced by it more than he influenced it. He preached, he met with Religious Societies, he talked religion with individuals, but, as his *Journal* reveals, the 'evangelical' way of thought invaded his mind only gradually. His first work after landing shows nothing new: he exhorted "two [who were probably former Oxford Methodists] to resume all their rules for holy living." Scougal and Law (mystics both) were his mentors. There was a period when he seemed to think salvation depended on believing that only a few are saved! But in July, 1737, Whitefield's sermon *On the Nature and Necessity of the New Birth* appeared. The next month Charles is urging the same necessity on those with whom he conversed. Faith as the condition of salvation is still later in appearing—that lesson, it is safe to say, came from the Moravians (who still were disciples of Luther) and it was most effectively taught by Peter Böhler.[2]

Peter Böhler landed in England not long after John in the winter of 1737-8. He was not an uneducated man, having studied at the University of Jena. He and the Wesleys conversed in Latin. Böhler had been led to a personal experience of the forgiveness of sins in an interview with Spangenberg, then Professor at Jena. Though he had been a Lutheran pastor, he forthwith cast in his lot with the Moravians. He could not preach in England, because he knew too little English, but after the Moravian fashion, he was instant in earnest conversation on religious topics with those whom he met. He is credited with influencing about fifty individuals during his short stay in England;[3] doubtless this work, added to the preaching of Whitefield, accounts for the quickening tempo of the revival during that rushing springtime of 1738.

The impression that the Wesleys were, so to speak, at once the first fruits of the revival and its initiators, rises quite naturally out of a perusal of John's *Journal* for the four months he spent in England previous to his conversion. During this time his soul was at war with itself; so preoccupied is the *Journal* with his struggle that it seems to take place in a social vacuum. Peter Böhler, fresh from Germany, is his mentor; he produces a few "living witnesses";[4] but apart from them John Wesley seems to be struggling solitary in the presence of God alone. To be sure, he is recommending salvation by faith in both conversations and sermons; but none seem to hear except to cavil or to forbid him to preach in that pulpit again. This impression is corrected when we turn to Charles' *Journal* for the same period. His temper was less self-absorbed, more interested in other people. He gives us a vivid picture full of folk struggling toward the same end—the "inward change" as he calls it. There are Mrs. Delamotte and her family, Mr. Edmunds, "seeking Christ as in an agony," and Mr. Ainsworth, "upon the entrance to the kingdom of heaven." He does not hesitate to speak of those who had attained before him: Mrs. Turner who had "perfect peace with God;" "young Gr., who told me that on this day he first felt the beginnings of the change";[5] and above all Bray the brazier, who not only sheltered Charles' ailing body in his home, but assumed, though only an "ignorant mechanic," the role of the departed Peter Böhler as guide to his soul. All this enables us to see, not indeed, a mass revival, but a stir, a pressing of many toward salvation, an atmosphere of expectation and triumph which prevailed before the Wesleys themselves were converted. In such an atmosphere they came to their own triumph; it was an atmosphere which they breathed, but which others did more to create than they.

One factor in the revival, the importance of which was first brought to notice by Overton,[6] and later elaborated by

Simon,[7] was the existence in England, since the seventeenth century, of a number of groups called Religious Societies. Their importance for the revival lies in this, that they were the matrix out of which it grew, and that the Wesleys' Societies were, in their organization and purpose modelled closely on them. There are explicit references to "societies" in which all three of the leaders worked during this period. Further, reading between the lines, we may conclude that such "societies" were even more numerous than the actual use of the term would lead us to expect, and that the first converts came in the great majority of cases from among their membership. The first section to follow, then, deals with the characteristics of this form of religious organization which lay ready to the evangelists' hands, and the changes they introduced.

The extracts in the remaining sections of the chapter convey not only the struggle in the soul of the Wesleys, but also the increasing momentum of the revival in the circles among which they moved. In the climactic position stand the famous conversion documents. This arrangement reflects the editor's conviction that in spite of recent attempts to depreciate the value of the conversion experience (especially John's) they were of the highest importance both for their personal religious lives and for the revival as a whole. It has been contended[8] that the conversion of John Wesley was merely a passing gust of emotion, without real importance; that another point in his life (his entering Holy Orders and his "turn for the more serious," in 1725) was the really decisive one; and finally that the conversion was not an evangelical, but a mystical one. The arguments are too involved to set down here,[9] but the reader is referred to the able defense of the highest evaluation of the Aldersgate Street experience by Drs. Cell and Rattenbury.[10] The importance of John Wesley's conversion has never been better stated than in the historian Lecky's well-known words:

"It is however, scarcely an exaggeration to say that the scene which took place at that humble meeting in Aldersgate Street forms an epoch in English history. The conviction which then flashed upon one of the most powerful and most active intellects in England is the true source of English Methodism."[11]

i. The Religious Societies

The Spring of 1738 was marked in mid-course by the founding of yet another Religious Society, soon to be called, from its place of meeting, the Fetter Lane Society. This Society was started before the conversion of the Wesleys, though its special importance for the revival did not appear till some time later. In order to keep it in its proper position in the revival's development, the story of the founding has been left under the proper date in section iii.[12] However, it should be regarded as a new development in the process delineated in this section.

It was just sixty years before the beginning of the Fetter Lane Society that the first such association had been founded in London. The story of this beginning and multiplication of Societies was first told in a pamphlet of 1680 by the Rev. Josiah Woodward. It must have had a wide reading, for it was re-issued several times over a quarter of a century. In the extracts below can be seen the extreme anxiety of the Societies to remain under the guidance of the clergy of the Established Church, and defend themselves against the charge of schism. Though the movement had its warm defenders such as Woodward and Samuel Wesley Sr.,[13] the majority of the prelates seem to have regarded them askance. Archbishop Sharp's nervousness shows through the studiously non-committal tone of his letter.[14]

By 1738 the movement had declined somewhat from the highest point of its influence, which had been at the turn of the century; but it was still important enough to furnish the model for the organization of the Methodist Societies, and it was from them that most of the earliest converts came.

I have ventured to put first in this series of documents, one from the reign of Elizabeth. I do this not because the Religious Societies have a continuous history reaching back into the sixteenth century, but simply for the interesting analogies the venture of a Puritan minister shows with the movement which began only three generations later. It is one instance of a tendency which recurs in all the Christian ages when earnest folk feel the need of supplementing the ministrations of the official Church, by forming "ecclesiolae in ecclesia."

"Godly Conference" among the Puritans.

The extracts immediately following are by Richard Rogers, Puritan minister of Wethersfield in Essex. They are different accounts of the same events, the one taken from his diary,[15] the other from a volume written later for publication.[16] There is, of course, no observable continuity between the events in Rogers' congregation and the Religious Societies of the following century. But there are evident similarities; both were for mutual edification, both included lay people, both were smaller groups within the church, and both dreaded being thought separatist in tendency. An interesting persistence in terminology is found in the use of the term "godly conference" in Rogers and "religious conference" in Woodward.

KPD, p. 67 f.

The next day we met publicly with much comfort and after met privately that company which came by course that day. We conferred, after matters of judgment and knowledge ended,[17] of such things as concerned our edifying, and most of us went home to a neighbour's house where I urged them to see the necessity of this covenant making which I had lately entered into, they consenting that they had especial cause to complain that they had much decayed in fervent and earnest desire of pleasing God. And this was acknowledged amongst us with tears, which we determined to be further proceeded with . . .[18]

RST, p. 515 f.

In the year 1588, there met in a Christian man's house certain well minded persons, which dwelt in one town together with whom also the preacher of the place did meet at the same time. Their meeting was for the continuance of love, and for the edifying one another, after some bodily repast and refreshing. And yet know, that they were no Brownists;[19] for they were diligent and ordinary frequenters of public assemblies with the people of God. Neither were their meetings Conventicles, for the disturbing of the state of the Church and peace thereof; as many imagine that there can be no private fellowship among Christians, but it is to such ends: the contrary may be seen by their conference. These with one consent, fell into communication how the case stood betwixt God and themselves.

Some accusing and complaining of themselves, that they had not used their long continued peace and liberty of the Gospel to the end for which God did send both, but that they had been dim lights. The rest consenting, and by occasions offered among them all, (well nigh twenty persons) sundry reasons and proofs were set down to make their complaints more weighty, and also to show, what evil fruit they did see to proceed from a dead and unprofitable course of living: and yet the persons spoken of, did as far exceed the common sort of them that profess the Gospel, as the common professors do exceed them in religion which know not the Gospel.

When they had proceeded thus far, it was demanded whether there were no way to come out of this wearisome and unprofitable life, which (in their own judgment) did not seem to be such as embraced the Gospel . . . and betwixt them they agreed upon certain, with such good liking, after they heard and conceived them, that it might appear that their heavy hearts were much eased, when they did but see a way to be delivered from that yoke of bondage, their plentiful tears being turned into cheerful countenance. The conclusion was this, they did covenant faithfully and seriously, to set upon these remedies forthwith and speedily; thinking that such a weighty matter had need of no delay; and thereupon desired the Preacher to set down the sum of their conference and communication together, for the better putting of them in remembrance of it to practise it; as also that they might see what the sum of their conference was; which, seeing they agreed unto, they called a covenant.

Now it may be, ye look to hear what fruit came of this; surely even this meeting was a great whetting them on to enjoy the public ministry more cheerfully and faithfully afterwards; and this mean with others, both public and private did knit them in that love, the bond whereof could not be broken, either on their part which now sleep in the Lord, while they here lived, nor in them which yet remain, by any adversary power unto this day. And this I set down to this end, as well that godly conference may be had in more account among Christians; as principally, to show what hindrances there are . . . and how necessary it is that all good remedies should be used to continue the same.

The Religious Societies whose "rise and progress" is described below not only furnished the matrix for the revival, but nourished other offshoots of wide usefulness which continue to this day: The Society for the Promotion of Christian Knowledge, founded in 1698, and the Society for the Propagation of the Gospel in Foreign Parts, which came into being three years later, and which, as we have seen, was the agency under which John Wesley went to Georgia. Another closely allied movement (more ephemeral and less highly regarded) was the Societies for the Reformation of Manners—manners meaning in this case, public morals rather than etiquette. Their purpose was to encourage the repression of open blasphemy, drunkenness and prostitution, by the officers of the law. Woodward lent the support of his pen to these also, dedicating a special pamphlet to them.[20] Though they had some support in high places, they soon languished. Their methods were too exclusively external, and their use of informers (who were suspected of profiting from the fines levied on their victims) precluded popular support. The continuity of the Religious Societies with the early Methodist Societies is seen in several respects: their avowed purpose was to cultivate "holiness of heart and life"; and they earnestly promoted benevolent enterprises for which the funds came from the members. The word "steward" which they used for the administrators of these projects is still a familiar one in Methodist circles.

WOODWARD, RS,[21] p. 142 ff.

It is now about twenty years ago,[22] that several young men of the Church of England in the Cities of London and Westminster, were about the same time touched with a very affecting sense of their sins, and began to apply themselves in a very serious manner, to religious thoughts and purposes. . . I was, about that time, made privy to the spiritual sorrows of one of them . . .

In this mournful season, these disconsolate convicted persons often resorted to their ministers for spiritual advice and succour . . . And many times it fell out (as the same person informed me), that several of them met together at the house of their spiritual physician, seeking cure for their wounded spirits; and so contracted a little acquaintance by those providential interviews . . .

The benefit of Dr. Horneck's awakening sermons, and the morning lectures on the Lord's Day in Cornhill, preached by Mr. Smithies, (chiefly designed for the in-

struction of youth) . . . occasioned much of this happy
work upon the spirits of these young men . . .

Upon their frequent application to these and other Ministers, it was advised, that since their troubles arose from
the same spiritual cause, and that their inclinations and
resolutions centered in the same purpose of a holy life; they
should meet together once a week, and apply themselves
to a good discourse, and things wherein they might edify
one another. And for the better regulation of their meetings, several rules and orders were prescribed.

Upon this, they met together, and kept to their rules;
and at every meeting (as it was advised) they considered
the wants of the poor; which in time amounted to such
considerable sums, that thereby many poor families have
been relieved, some poor people set into a way of trade
suitable to their capacities, sundry prisoners set at liberty,
some poor scholars furthered in their subsistence at the
University, several orphans maintained, with many other
good works.

It seemed proper for the better management of their
common stock for charitable uses to choose two Stewards
as the managers of their charity. And the first two Stewards,
that I find (after diligent search) were in the year 1678.

Woodward, RS, p. 158 ff.

As to that which is feared by some sober and good people,
namely that it may degenerate in time to a sect, and intro-
duce a division; be it considered, that as this would indeed
be a very detestable thing, so they have most industriously
fenced themselves against it by their monthly Communion;
their use of many of the public prayers constantly in their
assemblies; their setting up public Prayers in many churches
in the city, and frequenting them in great bodies, where
they appear the most devout part of the congregation; and
their utter disclaiming of all schism and faction; and finally
their humble deference to their ministers, (without whose

approbation no rule, prayer, nor practice is allowed among them).

There is such love amongst those of them that have fallen under my observation, that scarce any natural brothers are so vigorously affectionate. I have often beheld their meeting and parting embraces with admiration; and those who are newly admitted are soon contracted into the same fellowship of Christian brotherhood.

It is required of such as desire to join themselves to them, that they give the Society a solemn account of their sense of spiritual things, with the real motives which lead them to this undertaking, and what they seriously purpose as to their future life. This is many times done in writing . . .

And thus by exhorting and encouraging one another to Christian duty, the piety of many of them has appeared very eminent and exemplary; insomuch that it is evident, even to demonstration that their zeal hath in many places given new life to the celebration of the Lord's Supper, public Prayer, Singing of Psalms, and Christian conference, duties which were in many places almost disused, or performed in a cool and languishing manner.

This is (as far as human eye can see) the real and only design of these Societies, who seem with one heart to attempt by the most pious and peaceable methods, to put a stop to our overflowing wickedness, remove our plagues, and to dispose us into a meetness for the blessings and gracious presence of God; by whose blessing they have of late years so increased amongst us, that there are twenty-five distinct bodies of them, with the compass of the Bills of Mortality. And besides, those that have been some time erected in the University of Cambridge, and in the City of Gloucester, etc. there are others newly formed in Shadwell, Greenwich, and even as far as Dublin in the kingdom of Ireland; where, from three to four persons, with which they began, they are now increased to nine or ten Societies, containing about three hundred persons.

Woodward, RS, p. 199 ff.

A specimen of the Orders of the Societies before mentioned . . .

1. That the sole design of this Society being to promote real holiness of heart and life: it is absolutely necessary that the persons who enter into it do seriously resolve to apply themselves in good earnest to all means proper to make them wise unto salvation.

2. That in order to their being of one heart and one mind, in this design, every member of this Society shall own and manifest himself to be of the Church of England, and frequent the Liturgy and other public holy exercises of the same . . .

3. That the members of this Society shall meet together one evening in the week, at a convenient place, in order to encourage each other in practical holiness, by discoursing on spiritual subjects, and reading God's holy Word; and to pray to Almighty God, and praise his Name together.

5. That it be left to every person's discretion to contribute at every weekly meeting what he thinks fit towards a public stock for pious and charitable uses: and the money thus collected shall be kept by the two Stewards . . .

7. That every one that absents himself four meetings together (without giving a satisfactory account to the Stewards) shall be looked upon as disaffected to the Society.

9. It is hereby recommended to every person concerned in this Society, to consider the many inconveniences (and many times sins) which attend Ale-house-games, and wholly decline them. And to shun all unnecessary resort to such houses and taverns; and wholly to avoid lewd play-houses.

10. That the respective members of this Society shall heartily endeavor through God's grace:

   i. To be just in all their dealings, even to an exemplary strictness.

   ii. To pray many times every day: remembering our continual dependence upon God both for spiritual and temporal things.

iii. To partake of the Lord's Supper at least once a month . . .

iv. To practise the profoundest meekness and humility.

xii. To examine themselves every night, what good or evil they have done in the day past.

xvii. To pray for the whole Society in their private Prayers.

DIRECTIONS FOR RELIGIOUS CONFERENCE
Woodward, RS, p. 225 ff.

I premise that it may be very expedient, and what would much promote the pious design of these Societies: That an orthodox and pious minister should be chosen by each Society as the director and visitor of it. Who may frequently be present at their assemblies to preserve order, excite zeal, and resolve doubts.

This director may be chosen every year (when the Stewards are) by majority of votes . . .

[After giving a long list of Scripture verses for meditation on Christian duties]: These are duties of the greatest importance, and are all suited to the rules of these Societies. And I have kept to the number forty, that I might assign one distinct subject of discourse for every weekly conference in the year, reserving the discourses on twelve of them to be spent upon the subject of the Lord's Supper . . .

Thus every person knowing for a whole week before, what will be the subject of the discourse at the conference, may better prepare for it by suitable reading, meditation and prayer.

And at the time of conference, one of the stewards (in the absence of the director) may propose the following questions, for the sake of method: . . . Wherein consists the nature of this duty? What directions do you propose in order to make the practice of it more sure and easy? What discouragement do any of you find in the practise of it?

What motives may encourage our practise of this duty, and our perseverance in it?

A LETTER CONCERNING THE RELIGIOUS SOCIETIES BY SAMUEL WESLEY. 1699. Clarke, MWF, I, 144 ff.

Sir,

Having in conversation accidentally mentioned those religious societies which have been for some time erected in and about the cities of London and Westminster, and of late in some other places, you were pleased to desire a more particular account concerning them, of their orders and manner of life, and what my thoughts were as to what we then heard objected against them.

I cannot tell whether I can give you a better character of those persons who compose these religious societies, and their design and employment in them, than what Tertullian and other ancient writers have left us of the first Christians, in the best and purest ages of the church: I am sure I cannot speak more truth of them in fewer words.

'They often meet together,' say the ancients of those first Christians, 'ad confoederandam disciplinam; and to pray and sing hymns to Christ as God.' 'We assemble ourselves,' says Tertullian, 'to the repetition of the Holy Scriptures; we support our faith by religious discourse; we excite our hope, we fix our confidence, we increase our knowledge, by the exhortations of our teachers; we gather a stock for the poor according to every man's ability, which we expend, not in riotous feasting, but in helping the indigent and orphans, and aged, and those who are persecuted for the cause of God.'

There are a great many parishes in this kingdom, which consist of several thousands, some of some myriads of souls: now, what one man, or two, or three, is sufficient for such a multitude? what strength to visit them? what memory, unless very extraordinary, to retain but their names? Those

who have but one or two thousand, will find their cares
heavy enough, especially now they have neither the cate-
chists of the ancients to assist them, nor those clerks which
are mentioned in the Rubrick, and seem to have been designed for that end, at the reformation: and may not we
say of these great numbers, as the disciples did to our
Saviour when they saw the multitude, From whence shall
we buy bread that these may eat? But would not these things
be rendered much more easy to the careful pastor, when
such considerable bodies should act [in subornation to him,
and with direction from him,] to promote those great ends,
for which he has so solemnly dedicated himself to God?

In short, it seems a necessary consequence, both from
what success the design has already had, and from the very
nature of it, that, if it went forward in such manner and
with such limitations as are proposed, it would be so far
from injuring the church, that these several societies would
be so many new bulwarks against its enemies, would give
it daily more strength, and beauty, and reputation, and it
may be, more than many wish to see it ever have.

'Tis not there[23] proper to discourse of many things which
fall under their care, nor is there any room for Christian
conversation, if it were decent to practise it. Pious discourse
must be owned as necessary as it is a delightful employment
to all good Christians; and yet what more generally and
shamefully neglected, and even by the accursed rules of
civility exploded out of the world?

It cannot be denied but that there may and will be some
persons in these societies of more heat than light, more
zeal and warmth than judgment and discretion; but where
was ever any body of men without some of such a character? They are of like passions with other men, and why
may not they expect the same allowances? But since the
very rules of their institution do strictly oblige them to the
practice of humility and charity, and to avoid censorious-
ness and spiritual pride, the common rocks of those who

make a more than ordinary profession of religion, I see not what human prudence can provide any farther in this matter.

I had like to have forgot one considerable advantage of these religious societies, if they should once come to be more common amongst us; and that is, that out of them it would be easy to form societies for reformation; for persons must be first truly and deeply concerned for religion themselves, before they are likely to be so concerned for others as to be willing to sacrifice all to make them better. That there is need of a general reformation of manners has not been denied even by those who have had the most need of it themselves; and that the governors, both in church and state, do most earnestly desire it, we can no less doubt, without the highest affront to both, when they have, by so many repeated acts, solemnly declared as much to the nation.

ARCHBISHOP SHARP TO (PERHAPS) SAMUEL WESLEY. Feb. 27, 1699. Clarke, MWF, I, 155 ff.

Rev. Sir,

I had the favour of yours, which that I did not answer sooner you might impute to the many affairs of sundry kinds (some of them small enough but unavoidable), which do still take up our time.

It is a nice case you write about, and I dare not take upon me to give any directions in it.

I myself have always been averse to such sort of confederacies or combinations, whether of clergy or others, as are now on foot everywhere, whether they be those called religious societies, or those of a later standing, which go under the name of Societies for Reformation; as doubting whether they be legal in themselves (though, with submission, I think it may bear a dispute whether they come under those conventicles that are forbid in the 12th and 73rd canons), and apprehending, likewise, that some time or other we may feel ill consequences from them. And for these reasons I refused my subscription the last year to that book which was writ for the recommending these societies, though I was earnestly, by letters from two of the bishops, pressed to join my hands with theirs.

But though these be my private sentiments, I find many of the bishops of another mind.

The truth is, the societies of London have been so industrious in spreading their books, and the success they have had (as they say) in this way has made such a noise every where, that the whole nation almost hath taken the alarm. And so eagerly in many places are the minds of the people set upon these new methods, that it may justly be doubted whether it be in the bishop's power to stifle or suppress these societies, though he should use his utmost endeavours to do it.

WHITEFIELD'S PRESCRIPTION FOR REVITALIZING THE RELIGIOUS SOCIETIES.

Whitefield, it will be noted, wrote this letter during his second voyage to America, and hence only after *the events subsequently narrated, including the founding of the Fetter Lane Society. It is included here in violation of chronological order for the sake of bringing the material on the Religious Societies together in one place. He indicates his anxiety over the listless formality into which the Societies have fallen, and proposes these remedies: Membership should be dependent on an awakened state of soul rather than communion with the Church of England; the formal "conference" described by Woodward should be replaced by a period of spontaneous and very personal soul-searching, confession and testimony. To further this end, smaller groups should be formed within the Society. Now this was just what had been done, with the advice of Peter Böhler, in the founding of the Fetter Lane Society, with which*

Whitefield was intimately associated soon after his return from Georgia.[24] *The new wine of the revival was bursting the old wineskins of the rigidly prescribed procedure of the old Societies.*

WHITEFIELD *Works,* [25] IV, 26 ff.

. . . You ought to be very cautious, my brethren, whom you admit to fellowship with you. Examine them again and again, not barely whether they receive the sacrament, and go to church; but whether they be in the faith . . . By no means receive them into your brotherhood, unless they can produce sufficient evidence of their having tasted the good words of life, and felt the powers of the world to come . . . Such a society, consisting of a few solid Christians is far preferable to one that is filled with a multitude of such as do not bring forth fruit unto holiness . . .

Further my brethren, content not yourselves with reading, singing and praying together; but set some time apart to confess your faults and communicate your experiences one to another. For want of this (which I take to be one chief design of private meetings) most of the old societies in London, I fear, are sunk into a dead formality, and have only a name to live. They meet on a sabbath evening, read a chapter, and sing a psalm, but seldom, if ever, acquaint each other with the operation of God's spirit upon their souls; notwithstanding this was the great end and intention of those who first began these societies.

. . . My brethren, let not your coming together be thus altogether in vain, but plainly and freely tell one another what God has done for your souls. To this end, you would do well, as others have done, to form yourselves into little companies of four or five each, and meet once a week to tell each other what is in your hearts: that you may then also pray for and comfort each other, as need shall require. None but those that have experienced it can tell the unspeakable advantages of such a union and communion of souls . . .

No one, I think, that truly loves his own soul and his brethren as himself, will be shy of opening his heart, in order to have their advice, reproof, admonition, and prayers, as occasions may require . . . Pharisees and unbelievers will pray, read, and sing psalms; but none, save an Israelite indeed, will endure to have his heart searched out.

ii. George Whitefield and Charles Wesley

1. *George Whitefield.*

The chronological data in Whitefield's *Further Account* are not sufficiently precise to permit them to be placed exactly where they belong in chronological order with the daily dated material from Charles Wesley's *Journal*. For this reason I have placed two sample passages from his *Further Account* at the beginning; some notices of his further activities (preaching, mainly) will come in Charles' *Journal*. It appears from the *Further Account* that only a few of the twenty months which he spent in England between his ordination to the diaconate and his first trip to Georgia were confined to the work of a settled parish. Some of his friends among the "Oxford Methodists" (especially Kinchin) helped him to get a start. He did some parish visiting; but his genius was not the sort to be long confined by parish boundaries. The holy restlessness (like that of the early Irish missionaries who felt impelled to leave home and kindred to be wanderers and pilgrims for Christ's sake) which kept him on the move for the rest of his life, showed itself early. A kind of impromptu itinerating began as he was asked here and there to preach. Ever-increasing crowds heard his sermons and his name was soon on thousands of lips. He took an interest in the Religious Societies ("a sweet knot of religious Friends") ; he took collections for prisoners (already he was the "spiritual pickpocket") but it was his preaching which was the most effective instrument for the awakening then beginning. His sermons, some of which were published during this period, give, in print, but a poor idea of the emotional warmth and dramatic impact of his spoken discourses. England had had searching preaching under the Puritans; from the better Anglican divines she had often had preaching characterized by moral earnestness or literary excellence, or both. Never before had she had sermons of such passionate and vivid emotional power as Whitefield here at the very beginning of his career delivered in the hearing of people from the most varied walks of life. From the highest to the lowest ranks of society, men, women, and children heard him gladly.

WGFA,[26] p. 27.

About this time [i.e., the summer before he embarked for the first Georgia trip] I was prevailed upon to print my sermon, *On the Nature and Necessity of our Regeneration or New-Birth in Christ Jesus,* which under God began the awakening at London, Bristol, Gloucester and Gloucestershire. The Dissenters, I found, were surprised to see a Sermon on such a subject from a clergyman of the Church of England.

WGFA, p. 32.

Many . . . serious Dissenters . . . told me, "That if the Doctrine of the New Birth and Justification by Faith was preached powerfully in the Church, there would be but few Dissenters in England."

WGFA, p. 33.

I had a sweet knot of religious friends, with whom I first attempted to pray extempore . . . I was their mouth unto God and he only knows what enlargement I felt in that divine employ. Once we spent a whole night in prayer and praises.

2. *Charles Wesley.*

Charles Wesley returned from Georgia with the intention of returning thither as a missionary, if not as Oglethorpe's secretary. But the illnesses sprung from seeds sown there continued to plague him, bringing him close to death's door, and forcing him to renounce his intention to return. Here we see him actively engaged in "personal work" with Religious Societies, with individual relatives and friends, and preaching wherever asked.

Apr. 6, 1737. WCJ, I, 70.

I had some conversation with M. G. about the fewness of those that are saved. How little is she advanced in the school of Christ, who is not convinced of this truth!

Apr. 30—I got back to Mr. Sarney's, weary and faint, and in a fever, through want of sleep.

May 2—Between one and two in the morning, I betook myself to my usual bed, the floor. Charles Gr. breakfasted with me, and owned with tears, he had never felt any true joy but in religion. I earnestly recommended Law to him.

Aug. 25, 1737. WCJ, I, 73.

After giving the sacrament to a sick woman, I breakfasted with Mr. Chadwick. We had some close talk about the new birth, with which he was greatly moved. I took the opportunity of recommending regular retirement, and religious acquaintance. I preached at Ludgate, dined with M. Musgrave, and called in the afternoon at Mrs. Delamotte's. The Cambridge youth was there; but we had no very useful conversation.

Aug. 31, 1737. WCJ, I, 74.

I talked at large upon my state with Mr. Law, at Putney. The sum of his advice was, "Renounce yourself; and be not impatient."

Sept. 12—I returned to town, and spent an hour with Hetty, in discoursing on the inward change, and reading Law. She received all his sayings with the utmost readiness.

Sept. 16, 1737. WCJ, I, 75.

Calling accidentally in the evening at my sister Kezia's room, she fell upon my neck, and in a flood of tears begged me to pray for her. Seeing her so softened, I did not know but this might be her time, and sat down. She anticipated me, by saying she had felt here what she never felt before, and believed now there was such a thing as the new creature. She was full of earnest wishes for divine love; owned there was a depth in religion she had never fathomed; that she was not, but longed to be, converted; would give up all to obtain the love of God: renewed her request with great vehemence that I would pray for her; often repeating, "I am weak, I am exceeding weak." I prayed over her, and blessed God from my heart; then used Pascal's prayer for conversion, with which she was much affected, and begged me to write it out for her. After supper, (at which I could not eat for joy,) I read Mr. Law's account of Redemption. She was greatly moved, full of tears and sighs, and eagerness for more. Poor Mrs. Gambold was quite unaffected: her time being not yet come.

Oct. 30, 1737. WCJ, I, 78.

I waked them at five, and attended them to Forster-Lane, where we heard Mr. Whitefield, and communicated together. I preached at St. Helen's "the one thing needful." In the afternoon I carried her and her brother to Mr. Chadwick's, (my usual lodgings,) and thence to Ironmonger's-Lane. After preaching the same sermon here, we drank tea at Mr. Chadwick's, and then took coach for College Street. They were much delighted with the singing there, and edified, I hope, by George Whitefield's example. It was near eleven before I left them at their own house.

The word "Methodist" below is still a descriptive term, referring to an outlook and a way of life rather than an organized body. It is reminiscent of "Oxford Methodism" now reaching beyond the university constituency, but only a little changed in teaching and practise.

Nov. 4, 1737. WCJ, I, 79 f.

I heard an excellent sermon at St. Antholine's, on holiness, or likeness to God; and passed the evening with B. D.; who then told me the reason why I was not sent for 'to Blendon, was, Mrs. Delamotte's fear of my making Hetty run mad: and when I gave them notice of my coming, she sent her up to town, that I might not see her; which Providence made the means of my having so many hours with her alone.

Nov. 5—I met and turned back with Betty, to hear Mr. Whitefield preach, not with the persuasive words of man's wisdom, but with the demonstration of the Spirit and with power. The churches will not contain the multitudes that throng to hear him.

Nov. 7—I read over *Pietas Hallensis;* and desired our Orphan-house might be begun in the power of faith.

Nov. 10—In obedience to a summons from Miss Betsy this morning, I took coach for Greenwich, and walked the rest of the way to Blendon. We had some animating discourse before Mrs. Delamotte came in. Then we fell into talk of the new birth, which she did not at all relish; but continued still cold, averse, and prejudiced against the truth.

Nov. 13, 1737. WCJ, I, 79 f.

I preached at Bexley, on the love of God. Mrs. Delamotte thanked me for my sermon with tears; owned she had loved Charles too well; and was quite altered in her behaviour towards me. We had farther conversation on the love of God. Mr. Delamotte confessed there could be no happiness in anything else.

Nov. 14—Little Molly burst into tears upon my telling her God loved her. The whole family now appear not far from the kingdom of God.

Nov. 20—At St. Helen's I preached the circumcision of heart. The next day my flux returned.

Nov. 22—Mr. Oglethorpe advised me to go to Tiverton. I went to take my leave of our friends at Blendon. Mrs. Delamotte was quite open, and not afraid that her son should be called a Methodist.

iii. John and Charles Wesley: the "Great Change"

From February to May, 1738, the Wesley brothers were reunited in England—reunited in their work, and in their seeking. During this momentous period in the revival, Whitefield was to be absent on the first of his several trips to America. We can omit reference to his activities till his return to England the following autumn. The arrival of Peter Böhler, for a short stay on his trip from Germany to America was of the utmost consequence. He played an inconspicuous but effective part in guiding the revival; first in importance is his masterly touch as the Wesleys' spiritual guide; scarcely less so, as it later turned out, was his part in founding the Fetter Lane Society, to be for a time the school and laboratory of the new-born evangelists.

Here, because the progress of the revival is really the topic of our study, the journals of the two brothers have been intercalated in chronological sequence; to distinguish between John's account and Charles' the reader has but to look at the reference at the head of each extract. WJJS standing of course for John's and WCJ for Charles' *Journal*.

London. Feb. 3, 1738. WJJS, I, 432 ff.

In the evening I came once more to London, whence I had been absent two years and near four months.

Many reasons I have to bless God, though the design I went upon did not take effect, for my having been carried into that strange land, contrary to all my preceding resolutions. Hereby I trust He hath in some measure 'humbled me and proved me, and shown me what was in my heart.'

Hereby God has given me to know many of His servants; particularly those of the church of Herrnhut. Hereby my passage is opened to the writings of holy men in the German, Spanish, and Italian tongues. I hope, too, some good may come to others hereby. All in Georgia have heard the word of God. Some have believed, and begun to run well. A few steps have been taken towards publishing the glad tidings both to the African and American heathen. Many children have learned 'how they ought to serve God,' and to be useful to their neighbour. And those whom it most concerns have an opportunity of knowing the true state of their infant colony, and laying a firmer foundation of peace and happiness to many generations.

Feb. 4—I told my friends some of the reasons which a little hastened my return to England. They all agreed it would be proper to relate them to the Trustees of Georgia.

Accordingly the next morning I waited on Mr. Oglethorpe, but had not time to speak on that head. In the afternoon I was desired to preach at St. John the Evangelist's. I did so on those strong words, 'If any man be in Christ, he is a new creature.' I was afterwards informed, many of the best in the parish were so offended, that I was not to preach there any more.

London. Feb. 7, 1738. WJJS, I, 436 ff.

(A day much to be remembered.) At the house of Mr. Weinantz, a Dutch merchant, I met Peter Böhler, Schulius, Richter, and Wensel Neisser, just then landed from Germany. Finding they had no acquaintance in England, I offered to procure them a lodging, and did so near Mr.

Hutton's, where I then was. And from this time I did not willingly lose any opportunity of conversing with them, while I stayed in London.

Feb. 8—I went to Mr. Oglethorpe again, but had no opportunity of speaking as I designed. Afterwards I waited on the Board of Trustees, and gave them a short but plain account of the state of the Colony: an account, I fear, not a little differing from those which they had frequently received before; and for which I have reason to believe some of them have not forgiven me to this day.

Feb. 12—I preached at St. Andrew's, Holborn, on 'Though I give all my goods to feed the poor, and though I give my body to be burned, and have not charity, it profiteth me nothing.' Oh, hard sayings! Who can hear them? Here too, it seems, I am to preach no more.

Oxford. Feb. 17, 1738. WJJS, I, 439.

I set out for Oxford with Peter Böhler, where we were kindly received by Mr. Sarney, the only one now remaining here of many who, at our embarking for America, were used to 'take sweet counsel together,' and rejoice in 'bearing the reproach of Christ.'

Oxford. Feb. 18, 1738. WJJS, I, 439 f.

We went to Stanton Harcourt, to Mr. Gambold, and found my old friend recovered from his *mystic* delusion, and convinced that St. Paul was a better writer than either Tauler or Jacob Behmen. The next day I preached once more at the Castle (in Oxford) to a numerous and serious congregation.

All this time I conversed much with Peter Böhler; but I understood him not, and least of all when he said, *Mi frater, mi frater, excoquenda est ista tua philosophia.* 'My brother, my brother, that philosophy of yours must be purged away.'

Oxford. Feb. 20, & 22, 1738. WCJ, I, 82.

I began teaching Peter Böhler English.

I waked much better. At five I had some close conversation with Peter Böhler, who pressed upon our scholars the necessity of combining, and instanced in many awakened, but fallen asleep again, for want of it. He talked much of the necessity of prayer and faith.

Feb. 24—At six in the evening, an hour after I had taken my electuary, the tooth-ache returned more violently than ever. I smoked tobacco; which set me a vomiting, and took away my senses and pain together. At eleven I waked in extreme pain, which I thought would quickly separate soul and body. Soon after Peter Böhler came to my bedside. I asked him to pray for me. He seemed unwilling at first, but, beginning very faintly, he raised his voice by degrees, and prayed for my recovery with strange confidence. Then he took me by the hand, and calmly said, "You will not die now." I thought within myself, "I cannot hold out in this pain till morning. If it abates before, I believe I may recover." He asked me, "Do you hope to be saved?" "Yes." "For what reason do you hope it?" "Because I have used my best endeavours to serve God." He shook his head, and said no more. I thought him very uncharitable, saying in my heart, "What, are not my endeavours a sufficient ground of hope? Would he rob me of my endeavours? I have nothing else to trust to."

The resort to "offense" as a criterion for judging the effectiveness of a sermon is an indication of the turmoil in John Wesley's soul. He is still beating the air. He never shrank from giving offense when that was essential to edification; but he later abandoned any thought that edification and offense were in direct proportion the one to the other. Such a feeling disappeared with the desperate frustration of these months.

Feb. 26, 1738. WJJS, I, 440.

I preached at six at St. Lawrence's; at ten in St. Katherine Cree's church; and in the afternoon at St. John's, Wapping. I believe it pleased God to bless the first sermon most, because it gave most offence; being indeed an open defiance of that mystery of iniquity which the world calls *prudence*, grounded on those words of St. Paul to the Galatians, 'As many as desire to make a fair show in the flesh, they constrain you to be circumcised; only lest they should suffer persecution for the cross of Christ.'

Feb. 27, 1738. WJJS, I, 440 f.

I took coach for Salisbury, and had several opportunities of conversing seriously with my fellow travellers. But endeavouring to mend the wisdom of God by the worldly wisdom of prefacing serious with light conversation, and afterward following that advice of the *Mystics*, 'Leave them to themselves,' all I had said was written on the sand. 'Lord, lay not this sin to' my 'charge!'

Feb. 28, 1738. WJJS, I, 441 f.

I saw my mother once more. The next day I prepared for my journey to my brother at Tiverton. But on *Thursday* morning, March 2, a message that my brother Charles was dying at Oxford obliged me to set out for that place immediately. Calling at an odd house in the afternoon, I found several persons there who seemed well-wishers to religion, to whom I spake plainly; as I did in the evening, both to the servants and strangers at my inn.

With regard to my own behaviour, I now renewed and wrote down my former resolutions:

1. To use absolute openness and unreserve with all I should converse with.

2. To labour after continual seriousness, not willingly

indulging myself in any the least levity of behaviour, or in laughter,—no, not for a moment.

3. To speak no word which does not tend to the glory of God; in particular, not to talk of worldly things. Others may, nay, must. But what is that to thee? And,

4. To take no pleasure which does not tend to the glory of God; thanking God every moment for all I do take, and therefore rejecting every sort and degree of it which I feel I cannot so thank Him *in* and *for*.

March 4.—I found my brother at Oxford, recovering from his pleurisy; and with him Peter Böhler, by whom (in the hand of the great God) I was, on *Sunday* the 5th, clearly convinced of unbelief, of the want of that faith whereby alone we are saved.

Immediately it struck into my mind, 'Leave off preaching. How can you preach to others who have not faith yourself?' I asked Böhler whether he thought I should leave it off or not. He answered, 'By no means.' I asked, 'But what can I preach?' He said, 'Preach faith *till* you have it; and then, *because* you have it, you *will* preach faith.'

March 6, 1738. WJJS, I, 442 ff.

Accordingly, *Monday* the 6th, I began preaching this new doctrine, though my soul started back from the work. The first person to whom I offered salvation by faith alone was a prisoner under sentence of death. His name was Clifford. Peter Böhler had many times desired me to speak to him before. But I could not prevail on myself so to do; being still (as I had been many years) a zealous asserter of the impossibility of a death-bed repentance.

[Mar.] 10—Peter Böhler returned to London.

[Mar.] 14—I set out for Manchester with Mr. Kinchin, Fellow of Corpus Christi, and Mr. Fox, late a prisoner in the city prison. Between five and six we called at Chapel-on-the-Heath, where lived a poor man, some time prisoner in the Castle of Oxford. He was not at home; but his wife came to us, to whom Mr. Kinchin spoke a few words, which so melted her heart that she burst out into tears, and we went on rejoicing and praising God.

Mar. 16, 1738. WJJS, I, 444.

The next day we dined at Birmingham, and, soon after we left it, were reproved for our negligence there (in letting those who attended us go without either exhortation or instruction) , by a severe shower of hail. At Hednesford, about five, we endeavoured to be more faithful; and all who heard seemed serious and affected.

Mar. 23, 1738. WJJS, I, 447.

I met Peter Böhler again, who now amazed me more and more by the account he gave of the fruits of living faith,— the holiness and happiness which he affirmed to attend it. The next morning I began the Greek Testament again, resolving to abide by 'the law and the testimony'; and being confident that God would hereby show me whether this doctrine was of God.

Oxford. Mar. 26, 1738. WJJS, I, 447 f.

I preached at Whitam on 'the new creature,' and went in the evening to a society in Oxford, where (as my manner then was at all societies) , after using a collect or two and the Lord's Prayer, I expounded a chapter in the New Testament, and concluded with three or four more collects and a psalm.

[Mar.] 27—Mr. Kinchin went with me to the Castle, where, after reading prayers, and preaching on 'It is appointed unto men once to die,' we prayed with the condemned man, first in several forms of prayer, and then in such words as were given us in that hour. He kneeled down in much heaviness and confusion having 'no rest in' his 'bones, by reason of' his 'sins.' After a space he rose up, and eagerly said, 'I am now ready to die. I know Christ has taken away my sins; and there is no more condemnation for me.' The same composed cheerfulness he showed when he was carried to execution; and in his last moments he was the same, enjoying a perfect peace, in confidence that he was 'accepted in the Beloved.'

The inner ferment must have been great indeed which could break through the lifelong habit of using written prayers only—a habit reinforced by prejudice strong in Anglicanism since the time when extempore prayers were the badge of the Puritan dissidents.

April 1, 1738. WJJS, I, 448 f.

Being at Mr. Fox's society, my heart was so full that I could not confine myself to the forms of prayer which we were accustomed to use there. Neither do I purpose to be confined to them any more; but to pray indifferently, with a form or without, as I may find suitable to particular occasions.

London. Apr. 22, 1738. WJJS, I, 454 ff.

I met Peter Böhler once more. I had now no objection to what he said of the nature of faith; namely, that it is (to use the words of our Church) 'a sure trust and confidence which a man hath in God, that through the merits of Christ his sins are forgiven and he reconciled to the favour of God.' Neither could I deny either the happiness or holiness which he described as fruits of this living faith. 'The Spirit itself beareth witness with our spirit that we are the children of God,' and 'He that believeth hath the witness in himself' fully convinced me of the former; as 'Whatsoever is born of God doth not commit sin,' and 'Whosoever believeth is born of God' did of the latter. But I could not comprehend what he spoke of an *instantaneous work*. I could not understand how this faith should be given in a moment: how a man could *at once* be thus turned from darkness to light, from sin and misery to righteousness and joy in the Holy Ghost. I searched the Scriptures again touching this very thing, particularly the Acts of the Apostles: but, to my utter astonishment, found scarce any instances there of other than *instantaneous* conversions; scarce any so slow as that of St. Paul, who was three days in the pangs of the new birth. I had but one retreat left; namely, '*Thus,* I grant, God wrought in the *first* ages of Christianity; but the times are changed. What reason have I to believe He works in the same manner now?'

But on *Sunday* the 23rd, I was beat out of this retreat too, by the concurring evidence of several living witnesses; who testified God had thus wrought in themselves, giving them in a moment such a faith in the blood of His Son as translated them out of darkness into light, out of sin and fear into holiness and happiness. Here ended my disputing. I could now only cry out, 'Lord, help Thou my unbelief!'

I asked Peter Böhler again whether I ought not to refrain from teaching others. He said, 'No; do not hide in the earth the talent God hath given you.' Accordingly, on *Tuesday* the 25th, I spoke clearly and fully at Blendon to Mr. Delamotte's family of the nature and fruits of faith. Mr. Broughton and my brother were there. Mr. Broughton's great objection was, he could never think that I had not faith, who had done and suffered such things. My brother was very angry, and told me I did not know what mischief I had done by talking thus. And, indeed, it did please God then to kindle a fire which I trust shall never be extinguished.

Apr. 25, 1738. WCJ, I, 84 f.

Soon after five, as we were met in our little chapel, Mrs. Delamotte came to us. We sang, and fell into a dispute whether conversion was gradual or instantaneous. My brother was very positive for the latter, and very shocking;

mentioned some late instances of gross sinners believing in a moment. I was much offended at his worse than unedifying discourse. Mrs. Delamotte left us abruptly. I stayed, and insisted, a man need not know when first he had faith. His obstinacy in favouring the contrary opinion drove me at last out of the room. Mr. Broughton was only not so much scandalized as myself.

Blendon. Apr. 26, 1738. WJJS, I, 457.

Peter Böhler walked with me a few miles, and exhorted me not to stop short of the grace of God.

London. Apr. 28, 1738. WJJS, I, 457.

In the day or two following I was much confirmed in the 'truth that is after godliness' by hearing the experiences of Mr. Hutchins, of Pembroke College, and Mrs. Fox; two living witnesses that God *can* (at least, if He *does* not always) give that faith whereof cometh salvation in a moment, as lightning falling from heaven.

Apr. 28, 1738. WCJ, I, 85.

I immediately thought it might be that I should again consider Böhler's doctrine of faith; examine myself whether I was in the faith; and if I was not, never cease seeking and longing after it, till I attained it.

May 1—After receiving the sacrament, I felt a small anticipation of peace, and said, "Now I have demonstration against the Moravian doctrine that a man cannot have peace without assurance of his pardon. I now have peace, yet cannot say of a surety that my sins are forgiven.". . .

For some days following I felt a faint longing for faith; and could pray for nothing else. My desires were quickened by a letter of Mr. Edmunds, seeking Christ as in an agony.

A "new wineskin"—the Fetter Lane Society.

This Society was the source of the innovations recommended by Whitefield to all the Religious Societies in his Letter.[27] It was only later that the Society came to be dominated by the Moravian element. At first it was composed wholly of Church of England communicants. The rules given below are as important for what they do not say as for what they do: it is not necessary to be an Anglican to belong to the Society. Important too is the division into 'bands' a device Wesley had employed (without using the name) in Georgia, and one of the many admirable things he learned from the Moravians.

London. May 1, 1738. WJJS, I, 458 f.

This evening our little society began, which afterward met in Fetter Lane. Our fundamental rules were as follows:

In obedience to the command of God by St. James, and by the advice of Peter Böhler, it is agreed by us,

1. That we will meet together once a week to 'confess our faults one to another and pray one for another, that we may be healed.'

2. That the persons so meeting be divided into several *bands,* or little companies, none of them consisting of fewer than five, or more than ten persons.

3. That every one in order speak as freely, plainly, and concisely as he can, the real state of his heart, with his several temptations and deliverances, since the last time of meeting.

4. That all the bands have a conference at eight every Wednesday evening, begun and ended with singing and prayer.

5. That any who desire to be admitted into this society be asked, 'What are your reasons for desiring this? Will you

be entirely open; using no kind of reserve? Have you any objection to any of our orders?' (which may then be read).

6. That when any new member is proposed, every one present speak clearly and freely whatever objection he has to him.

7. That those against whom no reasonable objection appears be, in order for their trial, formed into one or more distinct bands, and some person agreed on to assist them.

8. That after two months' trial, if no objection then appear, they may be admitted into the society.

9. That every fourth Saturday be observed as a day of general intercession.

10. That on the Sunday seven-night following be a general love feast, from seven till ten in the evening.

11. That no particular member be allowed to act in any thing contrary to any order of the society; and that if any persons, after being thrice admonished, do not conform thereto, they be not any longer esteemed as members.

May 3—My brother had a long and particular conversation with Peter Böhler. And it now pleased God to open his eyes; so that he also saw clearly what was the nature of that one true living faith, whereby alone, 'through grace, we are saved.'

May 4, 1738. WJJS, I, 459 f.

Peter Böhler left London, in order to embark for Carolina. O what a work hath God begun, since his coming into England! Such an one as shall never come to an end till heaven and earth pass away.

May 6, 1738. WCJ, I, 86.

By bearing witness to the truth before Miss Delamotte, Mr. Baldwin, and others, I found my desires of apprehending Christ increased.

Blendon. May 7, 1738. WJJS, I, 460.

I preached at St. Lawrence's in the morning, and afterward at St. Katherine Cree's church. I was enabled to speak strong words at both, and was therefore the less surprised at being informed I was not to preach any more in either of those churches.

May 9—I preached at Great St. Helen's, to a very numerous congregation, on 'He that spared not His own Son, but delivered Him up for us all, how shall He not with Him also freely give us all things?' My heart was now so enlarged to declare the love of God to all that were oppressed by the devil, that I did not wonder in the least when I was afterward told, 'Sir, you must preach here no more.'

May 11, 1738. WCJ, I, 86.

I was just going to remove to old Mr. Hutton's, when God sent Mr. Bray to me, a poor ignorant mechanic, who knows nothing but Christ; yet by knowing him, knows and discerns all things. Some time ago I had taken leave of Peter Böhler, confessed my unbelief and want of forgiveness, but declared my firm persuasion that I should receive the atonement before I died. His answer was, "Be it unto thee according to thy faith."

Mr. Bray is now to supply Böhler's place. We prayed together for faith. I was quite overpowered and melted into tears, and hereby induced to think it was God's will that I should go to his home, and not to Mr. Hutton's. He was of the same judgment. Accordingly I was carried thither in a chair.

His sister I found in earnest pursuit of Christ; his wife well inclined to conversion . . . I put all my hopes of ever attaining it, or eternal salvation, upon the truth of this assertion, *"I have not now the faith of the Gospel."*

May 12, 1738. WJC, I, 87.

This day (and indeed my whole time) I spent in discoursing on faith, either with those that had it, or those that sought it; in reading the Scripture, and in prayer.

JOHN WESLEY TO WILLIAM LAW.

Below is given the first of two letters to William Law, written the one ten, and the other four, days before John Wesley's conversion. Law replied to both with understandably rising irritation, for Wesley in the stress of his inner struggle, left the courtesy he almost universally observed for a high tone of reproach, as though he had completely forgotten how much he owed one who had long been a chief guide. It seems that the very greatness of the debt he owed Law was the cause of his bitterness, for he felt that he had been set on the wrong path, or at least, told how to follow the end of the right one before his feet had been set on the beginning. The ground of his complaint is most succinctly put in a comment on the Theologia Germanica[28] *(which Law had recommended to his attention) in the second letter:*[29] *"I remember something of Christ our Pattern, but nothing express of Christ our Atonement." What Wesley complained of in the* Theologia Germanica *expresses also the fundamental lack he found in Law's teaching as a whole. We may say that Wesley's phrase epitomizes as well as any single phrase could the difference between the "mystical" and the "evangelical" outlook.*

London. May 14, 1738. WJL, I, 239 f.

REVEREND SIR,—It is in obedience to what I think to be the call of God that I, who have the sentence of death in my own soul, take upon me to write to you, of whom I have often desired to learn the first elements of the gospel of Christ.

If you are born of God, you will approve of the design,

though it may be but weakly executed. If not, I shall grieve for you, not for myself. For as I seek not the praise of men, so neither regard I the contempt either of you or of any other.

For two years (more especially) I have been preaching after the model of your two practical treatises; and all that heard have allowed that the law is great, wonderful, and holy. But no sooner did they attempt to fulfil it but they found that it is too high for man, and that by doing 'the works of the law shall no flesh living be justified.'

To remedy this, I exhorted them, and stirred up myself, to pray earnestly for the grace of God, and to use all the other means of obtaining that grace which the all-wise God hath appointed. But still, both they and I were more and more convinced that this is a law by which a man cannot live; the law in our members continually warring against it, and bringing us into deeper captivity to the law of sin.

Under this heavy yoke I might have groaned till death, had not an holy man, to whom God lately directed me, upon my complaining thereof, answered at once: 'Believe, and thou shalt be saved. Believe in the Lord Jesus Christ with all thy heart, and nothing shall be impossible to thee. This faith, indeed, as well as the salvation it brings, is the free gift of God. But seek, and thou shalt find. Strip thyself naked of thy own works and thy own righteousness, and fly to Him. For whosoever cometh unto Him, He will in no wise cast out.'

Now, sir, suffer me to ask: How will you answer it to our common Lord that you never gave me this advice? Did you never read the Acts of the Apostles, or the answer of Paul to him who said, 'What must I do to be saved? Or are you wiser than he? Why did I scarce ever hear you name the name of Christ? never, so as to ground anything upon 'faith in His blood'? Who is this who is laying another foundation? If you say you advised other things as preparatory to this what is this but laying a foundation below the foundation? Is not Christ, then, the first as well as the last? If you say you advised them because you knew that I had faith already, verily you knew nothing of me; you discerned not my spirit at all. I know that I had not faith, unless the faith of a devil, the faith of Judas, that speculative, notional, airy shadow, which lives in the head, not in the heart. But what is this to the living, justifying faith in the blood of Jesus? the faith that cleanseth from sin, that gives us to have free access to the Father, to 'rejoice in hope of the glory of God,' to have 'the love of God shed abroad in our hearts by the Holy Ghost' which dwelleth in us, and 'the Spirit itself bearing witness with our spirit that we are the children of God'?

I beseech you, sir, by the mercies of God, to consider deeply and impartially, whether the true reason of your never pressing this upon me was not this—that you had it not yourself; whether that man of God was not in the right who gave this account of a late interview he had with you,— 'I began speaking to him of faith in Christ: he was silent. Then he began to speak of Mystical matters. I spake to him of faith in Christ again. He was silent. Then he began to speak of Mystical matters again. I saw his state at once.' And a very dangerous one in his judgment, whom I know to have the Spirit of God.

Once more, sir, let me beg you to consider whether your extreme roughness, and morose and sour behaviour, at least on many occasions, can possibly be the fruit of a living faith in Christ. If not, may the God of peace and love fill up what is yet wanting in you! I am, reverend sir,

Your humble servant.

May 17, 1738. WCJ, I, 88.

I experienced the power of Christ rescuing me in temptation. Today I first saw Luther on the Galatians, which Mr. Holland had accidentally lit upon. We began, and found him nobly full of faith. My friend, in hearing him, was so affected, as to breathe out sighs and groans unutterable. I marvelled that we were so soon and so entirely removed from him that called us into the grace of Christ, unto another Gospel. Who would believe our Church had been founded on this important article of justification by faith alone? I am astonished I should ever think this a new doctrine; especially while our Articles and Homilies stand unrepealed, and the key of knowledge is not yet taken away.

CHARLES WESLEY'S CONVERSION.

The story of Charles Wesley's conversion is not without its touch of the marvellous, nor is it improbable that it was enhanced by the fever from which he was suffering at the time. These details so uncongenial to the modern temper should not divert us from the central and unshakable fact that he found rest to his soul in the experience. As Dr. Rattenbury says, "God's ways with critics and poets are different."[30] We are struck most of all perhaps by that Scripture verse he read, "He hath put a new song in my mouth, even a thanksgiving unto our God. Many shall see it and fear, and shall put their trust in the Lord." How prophetic that was! Two days later he "began an hymn" on his conversion. Out of his new-found exaltation began to gush that fountain of hymnody which was to make a singing people of the Methodists. The Lord was to put many new songs in his mouth, which have continued to be the unrivalled expressions of the whole range of the Christian heart's deepest emotions. Scholars are agreed that this hymn was "almost certainly . . . the one commencing, 'Where shall my wondering soul begin.' " Simon describes it thus,

It is wistful, chastened with humility, confident in its conviction of sins forgiven, radiant with the light of a passionate love for the 'Great Deliverer', bold in its outlook on the hosts drawn up in battle array against 'the sinner's Friend,' tender in its appeal to the outcast sons of men, triumphant in its closing cry, 'Believe, and all your sin's forgiven; only believe, and yours is heaven!' Mr. Telford truly describes this hymn as the birth-song of the Evangelical Revival. So far as we know, it stands first in order of time among the hymns with which Charles Wesley enriched the psalmody of the Christian Church.[31]

THE DAY OF PENTECOST

May 21, 1738. WCJ, I, 90 ff.

I waked in hope and expectation of His coming. At nine my brother and some friends came, and sang an hymn to the Holy Ghost. My comfort and hope were hereby increased. In about half-an-hour they went: I betook myself to prayer; the substance as follows:—"O Jesus, thou hast said, 'I will come unto you;' thou hast said, 'I will send the Comforter unto you;' thou hast said, 'My Father and I will come unto you, and make our abode with you.' Thou art God who canst not lie; I wholly rely upon thy most true promise: accomplish it in thy time and manner." Having said this, I was composing myself to sleep, in quietness and peace, when I heard one come in (Mrs. Musgrave, I thought, by the voice) and say, "In the name of Jesus of Nazareth, arise, and believe, and thou shalt be healed of all thy infirmities." I wondered how it should enter into her head to speak in that manner. The words struck me to the heart. I sighed, and said within myself, "O that Christ would but speak thus to me!" I lay musing and trembling: then thought, "But what if it should be Him? I will send at least to see." I rang, and, Mrs. Turner coming, I desired her to send up Mrs. Musgrave. She went down, and, returning, said, "Mrs. Musgrave had not been here." My heart sunk within me at the word, and I hoped it might be Christ indeed. However, I sent her down again to inquire, and felt in the meantime a strange palpitation of heart. I said, yet feared to say, "I believe, I believe!" She came up again and said, "It was I, a weak, sinful creature, spoke; but the words were Christ's: he commanded me to say them, and so constrained me that I could not forbear."

I sent for Mr. Bray, and asked him whether I believed. He answered, I ought not to doubt of it: it was Christ spoke to me. He knew it; and willed us to pray together: "but first," said he, "I will read what I have casually opened upon: 'Blessed is the man whose unrighteousness is forgiven, and whose sin is covered: blessed is the man to whom the Lord imputeth no sin, and in whose spirit is no guile'." Still I felt a violent opposition and reluctance to believe; yet still the Spirit of God strove with my own and the evil spirit, till by degrees he chased away the darkness of my unbelief. I found myself convinced, I knew not how, nor when; and immediately fell to intercession.

Mr. Bray then told me, his sister had been ordered by Christ to come and say those words to me. This she afterwards confirmed, and related to me more at large the manner of her believing. At night, and nearly the moment I was taken ill, she dreamt she heard one knock at the door: she went down, and opened it; saw a person in white; caught hold of and asked him who he was; was answered, "I am Jesus Christ," and cried out, with great vehemence, "Come in, come in!"

She waked in a fright. It was immediately suggested to her, "You must not mind this: it is all a dream, an illusion." She continued wavering and uneasy all Friday till evening prayers. No sooner were they begun than she found herself full of the power of faith, so that she could scarce contain herself, and almost doubted whether she was sober. At the same time she was enlarged in love and prayer for all mankind, and commanded to go and assure me from Christ of my recovery, soul and body. She returned home repeating with all joy and triumph, "I believe, I believe:" yet her heart failed her, and she durst not say the words to me that night.

On Sunday morning she took Mr. Bray aside, burst into tears, and informed him of the matter; objecting she was a poor weak sinful creature, and should she go to a Minister? She could not do it; nor rest till she did. He asked whether she had ever found herself so before. "No, never." "Why, then," said he, "go. Remember Jonah. You declare promises, not threatenings. Go in the name of the Lord. Fear not your own weakness. Speak you the words: Christ will do the work. Out of the mouth of babes and sucklings hath he ordained strength."

They prayed together, and she then went up, but durst not come in till she had prayed again by herself. About six minutes after she had left him, he found and felt, while she was speaking the words, that Christ was with us. I never heard words uttered with like solemnity. The sound of her voice was entirely changed into that of Mrs. Musgrave. (If I can be sure of anything sensible.) I rose and looked into the Scripture. The words that first presented were, "And now, Lord, what is my hope? truly my hope is even in thee." I then cast down my eye, and met, "He hath put a new song in my mouth, even a thanksgiving unto our God. Many shall see it, and fear, and shall put their trust in the Lord." Afterwards I opened upon Isaiah xl. 1: "Comfort ye, comfort ye, my people, saith your God: speak comfortably to Jerusalem, and cry unto her, that her warfare is accomplished, that her iniquity is pardoned; for she hath received of the Lord's hand double for all her sin."

I now found myself at peace with God, and rejoiced in hope of loving Christ. My temper for the rest of the day was, mistrust of my own great, but before unknown, weakness. I saw that by faith I stood; by the continual support of faith, which kept me from falling, though of myself I am ever sinking into sin. I went to bed still sensible of my own weakness, (I humbly hope to be more and more so,) yet confident of Christ's protection.

May 22, 1738. WCJ, I, 92 f.

Under his protection I waked next morning and rejoiced in reading the 107th Psalm, so nobly describing what God had done for my soul. I fell asleep again, and waked out of a dream that I was fighting with two devils; had one under my feet; the other faced me some time, but faded, and sunk, and vanished away, upon my telling him I belonged to Christ.

To-day I saw him chiefly as my King, and found him in his power: but saw little of the love of Christ crucified, or of my sins past: though more, I humbly hope, of my own weakness and his strength. I had many evil thoughts darted into my mind, but I rejected them immediately (yet not I). At noon I rose, continually fainting, nevertheless upheld. I was greatly strengthened by Isaiah xliii, which God directed me to. "But now thus saith the Lord that created thee, O Jacob, and he that formed thee, O Israel, Fear not: for I have redeemed thee, I have called thee by thy name; thou art mine. When thou passest through the waters, I will be with thee; and through the rivers, they shall not overflow thee: when thou walkest through the fire, thou shalt not be burned; neither shall the flame kindle upon thee. For I am the Lord thy God, the Holy One of Israel, thy Saviour."

My brother coming, we joined in intercession for him. In the midst of prayer, I almost believed the Holy Ghost was coming upon him. In the evening we sang and prayed again. I found myself very weak in body, but thought I ought to pray for my friends, being the only Priest among them. I kneeled down, and was immediately strengthened, both mind and body. The enemy did not lose such an opportunity of tempting me to pride: but, God be praised, my strength did I ascribe unto Him. I was often since assisted to pray readily and earnestly, without a form. Not unto me, O Lord, not unto me, but to thy name be the glory!

London. May 19, 1738. WJJS, I, 463 f.

My brother had a second return of his pleurisy. A few of us spent Saturday night in prayer. The next day, being Whitsunday, after hearing Dr. Heylyn preach a truly Christian sermon (on 'They were all filled with the Holy Ghost') . . . , I received the surprising news that my brother had found rest to his soul. His bodily strength returned also from that hour. 'Who is so great a God as our God?'

May 23, 1738. WCJ, I, 94.

I waked under the protection of Christ, and gave myself up, soul and body, to him. At nine I began an hymn upon my conversion, but was persuaded to break off, for fear of pride. Mr. Bray coming, encouraged me to proceed in spite of Satan. I prayed Christ to stand by me, and finished the hymn. . . .

Throughout this day he has kept up in me a constant sense of my own weakness. At night I was tempted to think the reason of my believing before others was, my sincerity. I rejected the thought with horror, and remained more than conqueror, through Him that loved me.

June 3, 1738. WCJ, I, 98 f.

My deadness continued, and the next day increased. I rose exceeding heavy and averse to prayer; so that I almost resolved not to go to church; which I had not been able to do, till within these two or three days past. When I did go, the prayers and sacrament were exceeding grievous to me; and I could not help asking myself, "Where is the difference between what I am now, and what I was before believing?" I immediately answered, "That the darkness was not like the former darkness, because I was satisfied there was no guilt in it; because I was assured it would be dispersed; and because though I could not find I loved God, or feel that he loved me, yet I did and would believe he loved me notwithstanding."

JOHN WESLEY'S CONVERSION.

As Wesley's brief introduction shows, he felt this event was of special importance, and prefaced it with a resumé of his spiritual progress up to that time.[32]

London. May 24, 1738. WJJS, I, 465 ff.

What occurred on *Wednesday* 24, I think best to relate at large, after premising what may make it the better understood. Let him that cannot receive it ask of the Father of lights that He would give more light to him and me.

1. I believe till I was about ten years old I had not sinned away that 'washing of the Holy Ghost' which was given me in baptism; having been strictly educated and carefully taught that I could only be saved 'by universal obedience, by keeping all the commandments of God'; in the meaning of which I was diligently instructed. And those instructions, so far as they respected outward duties and sins, I gladly received and often thought of. But all that was said to me of inward obedience or holiness I neither understood nor remembered. So that I was indeed as ignorant of the true meaning of the law as I was of the gospel of Christ.

7. Soon after, a contemplative man convinced me still more than I was convinced before, that outward works are nothing, being alone; and in several conversations instructed me how to pursue inward holiness or a union of the soul with God. But even of his instructions (though I then received them as the words of God) I cannot but now observe (1) that he spoke so incautiously against trusting in outward works, that he discouraged me from doing them at all; (2) that he recommended (as it were, to supply

what was wanting in them) *mental prayer,* and the like exercises, as the most effectual means of purifying the soul and uniting it with God. Now these were, in truth, as much my own works as visiting the sick or clothing the naked; and the union with God thus pursued was as really my own righteousness as any I had before pursued under another name.

8. In this refined way of trusting to my own works and my own righteousness (so zealously inculcated by the Mystic writers) , I dragged on heavily, finding no comfort or help therein till the time of my leaving England. On shipboard, however, I was again active in outward works; where it pleased God of His free mercy to give me twenty-six of the Moravian brethren for companions, who endeavoured to show me 'a more excellent way.' But I understood it not at first. I was too learned and too wise. So that it seemed foolishness unto me. And I continued preaching, and following after, and trusting in, that righteousness whereby no flesh can be justified.

13. I continued thus to seek it [that is, a saving faith,] (though with strange indifference, dullness, and coldness, and unusually frequent relapses into sin) till *Wednesday,* May 24. I think it was about five this morning, that I opened my Testament on those words, τὰ μέγιστα ἡμῖν καὶ τίμια ἐπαγγέλματα δεδώρηται, ἵνα γένησθε θείας κοινωνοὶ Φύσεως. 'There are given unto us exceeding great and precious promises, even that ye should be partakers of the Divine nature' (2 Pet. i. 4) . Just as I went out, I opened it again on those words, 'Thou are not far from the kingdom of God.' In the afternoon I was asked to go to St. Paul's. The anthem was, 'Out of the deep have I called unto Thee, O Lord: Lord, hear my voice. O let Thine ears consider well the voice of my complaint. If Thou, Lord, wilt be extreme to mark what is done amiss, O Lord, who may abide it? For there is mercy with Thee; therefore shalt Thou be feared. O Israel, trust in the Lord: for with the Lord there

is mercy, and with Him is plenteous redemption. And He shall redeem Israel from all his sins.'

14. In the evening I went very unwillingly to a society in Aldersgate Street, where one was reading Luther's preface to the *Epistle to the Romans*. About a quarter before nine, while he was describing the change which God works in the heart through faith in Christ, I felt my heart strangely warmed. I felt I did trust in Christ, Christ alone for salvation; and an assurance was given me, that He had taken away *my* sins, even *mine,* and saved *me* from the law of sin and death.

15. I began to pray with all my might for those who had in a more especial manner despitefully used me and persecuted me. I then testified openly to all there what I now first felt in my heart. But it was not long before the enemy suggested, 'This cannot be faith; for where is thy joy?' Then was I taught that peace and victory over sin are essential to faith in the Captain of our salvation; but that, as to the transports of joy that usually attend the beginning of it, especially in those who have mourned deeply, God sometimes giveth, sometimes withholdeth them, according to the counsels of His own will.

16. After my return home, I was much buffeted with temptations; but cried out, and they fled away. They returned again and again. I as often lifted up my eyes, and He 'sent me help from His holy place.' And herein I found the difference between this and my former state chiefly consisted. I was striving, yea, fighting with all my might under the law, as well as under grace. But then I was sometimes, if not often, conquered; now, I was always conqueror.

May 25, 1738. WJJS, I, 477 f.

17. The moment I awaked, 'Jesus, Master,' was in my heart and in my mouth; and I found all my strength lay in keeping my eye fixed upon Him, and my soul waiting on Him continually. Being again at St. Paul's in the afternoon,

I could taste the good word of God in the anthem, which began, 'My song shall be always of the loving-kindness of the Lord: with my mouth will I ever be showing forth Thy truth from one generation to another.' Yet the enemy injected a fear, 'If thou dost believe, why is there not a more sensible change?' I answered (yet not I), 'That I know not. But this I know, I have "now peace with God." And I sin not to-day, and Jesus my Master has forbid me to take thought for the morrow.'

18. 'But is not any sort of fear,' continued the tempter, 'a proof that thou does not believe?' I desired my Master to answer for me; and opened His Book upon those words of St. Paul, 'Without were fightings, within were fears.' Then, inferred I, well may fears be within me; but I must go on, and tread them under my feet.

May 26, 1738. WJJS, I, 478 f.

My soul continued in peace, but yet in heaviness because of manifold temptations. I asked Mr. Töltschig, the Moravian, what to do. He said, 'You must not fight with them, as you did before, but flee from them the moment they appear, and take shelter in the wounds of Jesus.' The same I learned also from the afternoon anthem, which was, 'My soul truly waiteth still upon God: for of Him cometh my salvation; He verily is my strength and my salvation, He is my defense, so that I shall not greatly fall. O put your trust in Him always, ye people; pour out your hearts before Him; for God is our hope.'

May 27—Believing one reason of my want of joy was want of time for prayer, I resolved to do no business till I went to church in the morning, but to continue pouring out my heart before Him. And this day my spirit was enlarged; so that though I was now also assaulted by many temptations, I was more than conqueror, gaining more power thereby to trust and to rejoice in God my Saviour.

May 28, 1738. WJJS, I, 479 f.

I waked in peace, but not in joy. In the same even, quiet state I was till the evening, when I was roughly attacked in a large company as an enthusiast, a seducer, and a setter-forth of new doctrines. By the blessing of God, I was not moved to anger, but after a calm and short reply went away; though not with so tender a concern as was due to those who were seeking death in the error of their life.

Dummer. June 6, 1738. WJJS, I, 482 f.

I had still more comfort, and peace, and joy; on which I fear I began to presume: for in the evening I received a letter from Oxford which threw me into much perplexity. It was asserted therein, 'That no doubting could consist with the least degree of true faith; that whoever at any time felt any doubt or fear was not weak in faith, but had no faith at all; and that none hath any faith till the law of the Spirit of life has made him wholly free from the law of sin and death.'

Begging of God to direct me, I opened my Testament on I Cor. iii. I, &c., where St. Paul speaks of those whom he terms 'babes in Christ,' . . .; to whom nevertheless he says, 'Ye are God's building, ye are the temple of God.' Surely, then, these men had some degree of faith; though, it is plain, their faith was but weak.

June 7—I determined, if God should permit, to retire for a short time into Germany. I had fully proposed, before I left Georgia, so to do, if it should please God to bring me back to Europe. And I now clearly saw the time was come. My weak mind could not bear to be thus sawn asunder. And I hoped the conversing with those holy men who were themselves living witnesses of the full power of faith, and yet able to bear with those that are weak, would be a means, under God, of so establishing my soul, that I might go on from faith to faith and 'from strength to strength.'

CHAPTER V

CHARISMATA

i. Interlude

1. *Charles Wesley carries on alone.*

At the time of the conversion experiences, Whitefield was in Georgia, not to return till the end of the year. Soon after Aldersgate, John Wesley left for Germany, leaving Charles alone of the three to labor in England. Labor he did, indefatigably, to bring the love, joy and peace he had found to others. Most of what he recorded in his *Journal* for this period is "personal work." He regards himself as bound to be God's ambassador to all he meets, not only friends and kinsfolk, but also complete strangers: travelling companions, servants, those encountered by chance, perhaps once only. Cursing and swearing by such evoke a rebuke. A noteworthy feature of his ministry is an intensification of his work to prisoners. Now, because of the unshakable assurance of God's gift of forgiveness, he promises it confidently even to those who are under sentence of death. For the bravado (usually fortified by alcohol) which was the "right thing" for such wretches to exhibit to the curious crowds who attended executions, he persuaded some to substitute the triumph of the converted soul.

June 15, 1738. WCJ, I, 107 f.

I was sent for to baptize a child. It gave me occasion to speak upon faith. One of the company was full of self-righteousness. The rest were more patient of the truth, being only gross sinners.

June 16—After dinner Jack Delamotte came for me. We

took coach; and by the way he told me, that when we were last together at Blendon, in singing,

"Who for me, for me hast died,"

he found the words sink into his soul; could have sung for ever, being full of delight and joy: since then has thought himself led as it were in everything; feared nothing so much as offending God; could pray with life; and, in a word, found that he did indeed believe in the Lord Jesus.

I was in the coach with Miss Delamotte. While it stopped I got out to reprove a man for swearing. He thanked me most heartily. We took up Hetty at Blendon, and went on to Bexley.

The next day (Sat., June 17th) we saw, and prayed with, Mrs. Searl, to our mutual encouragement. Mr. Searl heard us gladly. The afternoon we passed with our friends at Blendon. Here I was stopped by the return of my pain, and forced to bed. Desires of death continually rose in me, which I laboured to check, not daring to form any wish concerning it.

June 18—The pain abated; and the next day left me.

June 21—I was concerned at having been here several days, and done nothing. I preached forgiveness to Mr. Piers's man, who seemed well disposed for receiving it, by a true simplicity. We prayed together, and went to public prayers. In the second lesson was the paralytic healed. I came home with the Miss Delamottes, Mrs. Searl and the man, who declared before us all, that God had given him faith by hearing the sick of the palsy healed. We returned hearty thanks.

The Lord gave us more matter for thanksgiving at Blendon, where I read my brother's sermon on faith.[1] When it was over, the gardener declared, faith had come to him by hearing it, and he had no doubt of his sins being forgiven. "Nay, was I to die just now," he added, "I know I should be accepted through Christ Jesus."

June 27, 1738. WCJ, I, 112.

Next day I returned to town, rejoicing that God had added to his living church seven more souls through my ministry. "Not unto me, O Lord, not unto me, but to thy name be the praise, for thy loving-mercy, and for thy truth's sake." I had hopes of seeing greater things than these, from a scripture He this day directed me to: Luke v. 9: "For he was astonished, and all that were with him, at the draught of fishes which they had taken."

London. July 10, 1738. WCJ, I, 117.

At Mr. Sparks's request, I went with him, Mr. Bray, and Mr. Burnham, to Newgate; and preached to the ten malefactors, under sentence of death; but with a heavy heart. My old prejudices against the possibility of a death-bed repentance still hung upon me; and I could hardly hope there was mercy for those whose time was so short. But in the midst of my languid discourse, a sudden spirit of faith came upon me, and I promised them all pardon, in the name of Jesus Christ, if they would then, as at the last hour, repent, and believe the Gospel. Nay, I did believe they would accept of the proffered mercy, and could not help telling them, "I had no doubt but God would give me every soul of them."

The Mr. Broughton mentioned below is Thomas Broughton, a fellow of Exeter College, Oxford. He had been a member of the Holy Club, but retained its High Church outlook, and was for this reason beginning to part company with the Wesleys. He was one of a growing number who were scandalized by the doctrine that sinners were justified by faith only, though it was clearly a part of the Anglican doctrinal formularies. The phrase "our friends" is probably an informal way of referring to the religious societies in which the greater number of converts to "the new faith" were found.

July 11, 1738. WCJ, I, 119 f.

Mr. Sparks this morning asked me whether I would preach for him at St. Helen's. I agreed to supply Mr. Broughton's place, who is now at Oxford, arming our friends against the faith.

LONDON's NEWGATE. July 18, 1738. WCJ, I, 122 f.

At night I was locked in with Bray in one of the cells. We wrestled in mighty prayer. All the criminals were present; and all delightfully cheerful. The soldier, in particular, found his comfort and joy increase every moment. . . . Yet on Wednesday, July 19th, I rose very heavy, and backward to visit them for the last time. At six I prayed and sang with them all together. The Ordinary would read prayers, and preached most miserably.

At half-hour past nine their irons were knocked off, and their hands tied. . . . By half-hour past ten we came to Tyburn, waited till eleven: then were brought the children appointed to die. I got upon the cart with Sparks and Broughton: the Ordinary endeavoured to follow, when the poor prisoners begged he might not come; and the mob kept him down.

I prayed first, then Sparks and Broughton. . . . The Black had spied me coming out of the coach, and saluted me with his looks. Read caught hold of my hand in a transport of joy. . . . None showed any natural terror of death: no fear, or crying, or tears. All expressed their desire of our following them to paradise. . . . We sang several hymns; particularly,

> "Behold the Saviour of mankind,
> Nail'd to the shameful tree;"

and the hymn entitled, "Faith in Christ," which concludes

> "A guilty, weak, and helpless worm,
> Into thy hands I fall:

Be thou my life, my righteousness,
My Jesus, and my all."

We prayed Him, in earnest faith, to receive their spirits. I could do nothing but rejoice: kissed Newington and Hudson; took leave of each in particular. Mr. Broughton bade them not be surprised when the cart should draw away. They cheerfully replied, they should not; expressed some concern how we should get back to our coach. We left them going to meet their Lord, ready for the Bridegroom. When the cart drew off, not one stirred, or struggled for life, but meekly gave up their spirits. Exactly at twelve they were turned off. I spoke a few suitable words to the crowd[2]; and returned, full of peace and confidence in our friends' happiness. That hour under the gallows was the most blessed hour of my life.

Charles Wesley was aware while reading the Journal in manuscript of the quality which was to repel so many readers after publication and to embarrass the friends of the revival. See above, p. 90; and below, p. 287f.

Aug. 3, 1738. WCJ, I, 126.

I corrected Mr. Whitefield's Journal for the press; my advice to suppress it being overruled.

Here is an early indication of the highly charged emotional atmosphere in which the meetings, especially of the Societies, took place. It was to increase as the winter months came on.

Oxford. Aug. 31, 1738. WCJ, I, 129.

At the Society I read my sermon, "The Scripture hath concluded all under sin," and urged upon each my usual question, "Do you deserve to be damned?" Mrs. Platt, with the utmost vehemence, cried out, "Yes; I do, I do!" I prayed, that if God saw there any contrite soul, he would fulfil his promise of coming and making his abode with it. "If thou hast sent thy Spirit to reprove any sinner of sin, in the name of Jesus Christ, I claim salvation for that sinner!" Again she broke out into strong cries, but of joy, not sorrow, being quite overpowered with the love of Christ. I asked her, if she believed in Jesus. She answered in full assurance of faith. We sang and rejoiced over her, (she still continued kneeling,) joined in thanksgiving; but her voice was heard above ours.

2. *John Wesley "Where the Christians Live."*

Like Paul after his experience on the Damascus Road, Wesley, after his experience in Aldersgate Street, felt the need of retirement to work out the implications of his conversion for thought and action. Unlike Paul he felt the need to confer with "flesh and blood." The Moravians who had guided him thus far might resolve certain residual perplexities and give directions for the still cloudy future. He learned much—though just how much was not apparent, even to himself, till later—from their organization of philanthropic enterprises, schools and community religious life. But the questions he most anxiously sought light on were fundamentally theological in nature, and had to do with the implications of conversion. There were several of these of course, but (if we can judge from the elements he emphasized in the reports of his interviews) two troubled him more than all the rest: can a man be justified and not have full assurance of his forgiveness; and, can a man be said to be justified if the impulse to sin remains in him?

Dr. Lee's point that Wesley was somewhat disappointed in the results of the Aldersgate Street experience is well made.[3] He expected a settled joy to ensue; and apparently he hoped he would be set beyond reach of temptation; but he was too honest, when he looked within himself, to report anything other than that the settled joy was not there, and that the stirrings of sin, alas, remained. It may well be that these defects led him to the conclusion that there was a further stage in the Christian life which he had not yet attained, a stage which he later emphasized increasingly in his preaching: Christian Perfection. But for the present he was concerned about his justification: all the fruits of the Spirit were not his—could he then really be justified in God's sight? The answers he got were not unanimous; but he was persuaded by the opinion of the greater number, especially that of Christian David[4] that a man may be justified *before* he is fully assured of it. The testimony of Arvid Gradin regarding the πληροφορία πίστεως, the full assurance of faith,[5] is interesting support of the thesis above, by reason of its close similarity to Wesley's later description of Christian Perfection.[6] So, he came back from his visit to the Moravians convinced that he was justified in God's sight, regenerate, but that there were heights of Christian experience yet unattained.

Though he saw much to admire and imitate, he did not suspend his critical faculties during his visit. This much may be gathered from the letter[7] he wrote, but did not post to his recent hosts. The one he finally did send has only commendation (a brief one) for what he had seen, followed by a factual account of the progress of the revival in England.

JOHN TO SUSANNAH WESLEY. Amsterdam. June 19, 1738. WJL, I, 247.

In the afternoon we came to Ysselstein, where we were received with open arms by the Baron Watteville and the Church which is in his house. There are about twenty (beside children) in that little community,[8] and their number increases daily, who are of one heart and one soul and have all things in common. Saturday the 17th (my birthday) was their monthly Thanksgiving Day. From about two in the afternoon till nine at night, the time was spent in prayer, praise, and such other exercises as became those who were 'all filled with the Holy Ghost.'

[Ysselstein] June 15, 1738. WJJS, II, 5 f.

Here we were at Baron Watteville's, as at home. We found with him a few German brethren and sisters, and seven or eight of our English acquaintance, who had settled here some time before. They lodged just without the town, in three or four little houses, till one should be built that would contain them all. *Saturday* the 17th was their Intercession-day. In the morning some of our English brethren desired me to administer the Lord's Supper. The rest of the day we spent, with all the brethren and sisters, in hearing the wonderful work which God is beginning to work over all the earth; and in making our requests known unto Him and giving Him thanks for the mightiness of His kingdom.

At six in the morning we took boat. The beautiful gardens lie on both sides of the river for great part of the way to Amsterdam, whither we came about five in the evening. The exact neatness of all the buildings here, the nice cleanness of the streets (which, we were informed, were all washed twice a week), and the canals which run through all the main streets, with rows of trees on either side, make this the pleasantest city which I have ever seen. Here we were entertained, with truly Christian hospitality, by Mr. Decknatel, a minister of the Mennonists,[9] who suffered us to want nothing while we stayed here, which was till the *Thursday* following.

Amsterdam. June 19, 1738. WJJS, II, 6 f.

I was at one of the societies, which lasted an hour and a half. About sixty persons were present. The singing was in Low Dutch (Mr. Decknatel having translated into Low Dutch part of the Herrnhut Hymn-book); but the words were so very near the German that any who understood the original might understand the translation. The expounding was in High Dutch. I was at another of the societies on *Tuesday,* where were present about the same number.

[Cologne] June 28, 1738. WJJS, II, 8 ff.

We went to the cathedral, which is mere heaps upon heaps: a huge, mis-shapen thing, which has no more of symmetry than of neatness belonging to it. I was a little surprised to observe that neither in this, nor in any other of the Romish churches where I have been, is there, properly speaking, any such thing as joint worship; but one prays at one shrine or altar, and another at another, without any regard to or communication with one another. As we came out of the church a procession began on the other side of the church-yard. One of our company scrupling to pull off his hat, a zealous Catholic presently cried out, 'Knock down the Lutheran dog.' But we prevented any contest by retiring into the church.

At four we took boat, [up the Rhine]. We were four nights on the water, by reason of the swiftness of the stream, up which the boat was drawn by horses. The high mountains on each side the river, rising almost perpendicular, and yet covered with vines to the very top, gave us many agreeable prospects; a religious house or old castle every now and then appearing on the brow of one of them. On *Sunday* evening, July 2, we came to Mayence;[10] and *Monday,* the 3rd, at half an hour past ten, to Frankfort.

Faint and weary as we were, we could have no admittance here, having brought no passes with us; which indeed we never imagined would have been required in a time of settled general peace. After waiting an hour at the gates we procured a messenger, whom we sent to Mr. Böhler (Peter Böhler's father); who immediately came, procured us entrance into the city, and entertained us in the most friendly manner.

July 7, 1738. WJJS, II, 12 f.

I lodged with one of the brethren at Eckershausen, an English mile from Marienborn, where I usually spent the day, chiefly in conversing with those who could speak either Latin or English; not being able, for want of more practice, to speak German readily. And here I continually met with what I sought for, viz. living proofs of the power of faith: persons saved from inward as well as outward sin but 'the love of God shed abroad in their hearts,' and from all doubt and fear by the abiding witness of 'the Holy Ghost given unto them.'

July 22, 1738. WJJS, II, 15.

In the afternoon we came to Weimar, where we had more difficulty to get through the city than is usual, even in Germany: being not only detained a considerable time at the [Erfurter] gate, but also carried before I know not what great man (I believe the Duke) in the Square; who, after many other questions, asked what we were going so far as Herrnhut for. I answered, 'To see the place where the Christians live.' He looked hard, and let us go.

July 26, 1738. WJJS, II, 16 f.

Having a desire to see Halle (two German miles off), we set out after breakfast, and came thither at two in the afternoon. But we could not be admitted into the town, when we came. The King of Prussia's tall men,[11] who kept the gates, sent us backward and forward, from one gate to another, for near two hours. I then thought of sending in a note to Professor Francke, the son of that August Hermann Francke[12] whose name is indeed as precious ointment. Oh may I follow him, as he did Christ, and 'by manifestation of the truth commend myself to every man's conscience in the sight of God'!

He was not in town. However, we were at length admitted into the Orphan House; that amazing proof that 'all things are' still 'possible to him that believeth.' There is now a large yearly revenue for its support, beside what is continually brought in by the printing-office, the books sold there, and the apothecary's shop, which is furnished with all sorts of medicines. The building reaches backward from the front in two wings for, I believe, a hundred and fifty yards. The lodging-chambers for the children, their dining-room, their chapel, and all the adjoining apartments, are so conveniently contrived, and so exactly clean, as I have never seen any before. Six hundred and fifty children, we were informed, are wholly maintained there; and three thousand, if I mistake not, taught. Surely, such a thing neither we nor our fathers have known as this great thing which God has done here!

Aug. 1, 1738. WJJS, II, 19.

At three in the afternoon I came to Herrnhut, about thirty English miles from Dresden. It lies in Upper Lusatia, on the border of Bohemia, and contains about a hundred houses, built on a rising ground, with evergreen woods on two sides, gardens and corn-fields on the others, and high hills at a small distance. It has one long street, through which the great road from Zittau to Löbau goes. Fronting the middle of this street is the Orphan House; in the lower part of which is the apothecary's shop, in the upper the chapel, capable of containing six or seven hundred people. Another row of houses runs at a small distance from either end of the Orphan House, which accordingly divides the rest of the town (beside the long street) into two squares. At the east end of it is the Count's [Zinzendorf's] house— a small, plain building like the rest; having a large garden behind it, well laid out, not for show, but for the use of the community.

We had a convenient lodging assigned us in the house appointed for strangers; and I had now abundant oppor-

tunity of observing whether what I had heard was enlarged
by the relators, or was neither more nor less than the naked
truth.

Herrnhut. Aug. 2, 1738. WJJS, II, 20.

At four in the afternoon was a lovefeast of the married
men, taking their food with gladness and singleness of heart,
and with the voice of praise and thanksgiving.

[Aug.] 3— (and so every day at eleven), I was at the
Bible Conference, wherein Mr. Müller (late master of a
great school in Zittau, till he left all to follow Christ) and
several others read together, as usual, a portion of Scripture
in the original. At five was the conference for strangers,
when several questions concerning justification were resolved. This evening Christian David[13] came thither. O
may God make him a messenger of glad tidings!

Herrnhut. Aug. 6, 1738. WJJS, II, 21 f.

After the Evening service at Herrnhut was ended, all
the unmarried men (as is their custom) walked quite
round the town, singing praise with instruments of music;
and then on a small hill, at a little distance from it, casting
themselves into a ring, joined in prayer. Thence they returned into the great Square, and, a little after eleven,
commended each other to God.

Aug. 10, 1738. WJJS, II, 28 ff.

It was on August 10 (old style) that I had an opportunity of spending some hours with CHRISTIAN DAVID. He is
a carpenter by trade, more than middle-aged, though I
believe not fifty yet. Most of his words I understood well;
if at any time I did not, one of the brethren who went
with me explained them in Latin. The substance of what
he spoke I immediately after wrote down; which was as
follows:

"Removing then to Görlitz, in Saxony, I fell into a dangerous illness. I could not stir hand or foot for twenty weeks. Pastor Schwedler came to me every day. And from him it was that the gospel of Christ came first with power to my soul.

"Here I found the peace I had long sought in vain; for I was assured *my* sins were forgiven. Not indeed all at once, but by degrees; not in one moment, nor in one hour. For I could not immediately believe that I *was* forgiven, because of the mistake I was then in concerning forgiveness. I saw not then that the first promise to the children of God is 'Sin shall no more reign over you'; but thought I was to feel it in me no more from the time it was forgiven. Therefore, although I had the mastery over it, yet I often feared it was not forgiven, because it still stirred in me, and at some times thrust sore at me that I might fall: because, though it did not reign, it did remain in me; and I was continually tempted, though not overcome . . . Neither saw I then that the being justified is widely different from the having the full assurance of faith.

"When I was recovered from my illness, I resolved to return into Moravia and preach Christ to my relations there. Thence I came back to Görlitz, where I continued five years; and there was a great awakening both in the town and country round about. In this space I made two more journeys into Moravia, where more and more came to hear me, many of whom promised to come to me, wherever I was, when a door should be opened for them.

"After my return from my third journey Count Zinzendorf sent to Görlitz, the minister of Berthelsdorf being dead, for Mr. Rothe, who was in a gentleman's family there, to be minister of that place. Mr. Rothe told him of me; and he writ to me to come to him; and when I came said, 'Let as many as will of your friends come hither; I will give them land to build on, and Christ will give them the rest.' I went immediately into Moravia, and told them God had

now found out a place for us. Ten of them followed me
then; ten more the next year; one more in my following
journey. The Papists were now alarmed, set a price upon
my head, and levelled the house I had lodged in even with
the ground. I made, however, eleven journeys thither in
all, and conducted as many as desired it to this place; the
way to which was now so well known, that many more
came of themselves.

"About this time we were in great straits, wherewith
many were much dejected. I endeavoured to comfort them
with the sense of God's love toward them. But they answered, 'Nay, it may be He hath no love towards us. It
may be we are not of the election; but God hated us from
eternity, and therefore He has suffered all these things to
come upon us.'

"The Count observing this, desired me to go to a neighbouring minister, Pastor Steinmetz, and talk with him fully
on that head, 'Whether Christ died for all?' I did so, and
by him God fully convinced me of that important truth.

". . . I went to Greenland five years ago. There I had a
correspondence by letter with a Danish minister on the
head of justification. . . . I saw that least of all ought we
so to insist on the full assurance of faith, or the destruction
of the body of sin, and the extinction of all its motions,
as to exclude those who had not attained this from the
Lord's Table, or to deny that they had any faith at all. I
plainly perceived this full assurance was a distinct gift
from justifying faith, and often not given till long after it;
and that justification does not imply that sin should not
stir in us but only that it should not *conquer*.

"And now first it was that I had that full assurance of
my reconciliation to God through Christ. For many years
I had had the forgiveness of my sins and a measure of the
peace of God; but I had not till now that witness of His
Spirit which shuts out all doubt and fear. In all my trials
I had always a confidence in Christ, who had done so great

things for me. But it was a confidence mixed with fear: I was afraid I had not done enough. There was always something dark in my soul till now."

WJJS, II, 36 f.

The same day I was with MICHAEL LINNER, the Eldest of the Church; the sum of whose conversation was this:—

"Indeed, the leading of the Spirit is different in different souls. His more usual method, I believe, is to give, in one and the same moment, the forgiveness of sins and a full assurance of that forgiveness. Yet in many He works as He did in me—giving first the remission of sins, and, after some weeks or months or years, the full assurance of it."

WJJS, II, 47 f.

ARVID GRADIN, a Swede, born in Dalecarlia, spoke to this purpose:—

"On the 22d of May last, I could think of nothing but 'He that believeth hath everlasting life.' But I was afraid of deceiving myself, and continually prayed I might not build without a foundation. Yet I had a sweet, settled peace, and for five days this scripture was always in my thoughts. On the 28th those words of our Lord were as strongly impressed upon me, 'If ye, being evil, know how to give good gifts to your children, how much more shall your heavenly Father give the Holy Ghost to them that ask Him?' At the same time I was incessantly carried out to ask that He would give me the witness of His Spirit. On the 29th I had what I asked of Him, namely, the πληροφορία πίστεως which is:

" 'Repose in the blood of Christ. A firm confidence in God, and persuasion of His favour; serene peace and steadfast tranquillity of mind, with a deliverance from every fleshly desire, and from every outward and inward sin. In a word, my heart, which before was tossed like a troubled sea, was still and quiet, and in a sweet calm.' "

Aug. 1738. WJJS, II, 49 ff.

In the present discipline of the Church of Herrnhut, all which is alterable at the discretion of the superiors, may be observed, . . .

I. The officers are: 1. The Eldest of the whole Church; beside whom there is an Eldest of every particular branch of it. There is also a distinct Eldest over the young men, and another over the boys; a female Eldest over the women in general, and another over the unmarried, and another over the girls. 2. The Teachers, who are four. 3. The Helpers (or Deacons.) 4. The Overseers (or Censors), eleven in number at Herrnhut. 5. The Monitors, who are eleven likewise. 6. The Almoners, eleven also. 7. The Attenders on the sick, seven in number. Lastly, the Servants, or Deacons of the lowest order.

II. The people of Herrnhut are divided: 1. Into five male classes, viz.: the little children, the middle children, the big children, the young men, and the married. The females are divided in the same manner. 2. Into eleven classes, according to the houses where they live. And in each class is an Helper, an Overseer, a Monitor, an Almoner, and a Servant. 3. Into about ninety bands, each of which meets twice at least, but most of them three times a week, to 'confess their faults one to another, and pray for one another, that they may be healed.'

III. The Rulers of the Church, that is, the Elders, Teachers, Helpers, have a conference every week, purely concerning the state of souls, and another concerning the institution of youth. Beside which they have one every day concerning outward things relating to the Church.

The Overseers, the Monitors, the Almoners, the Attenders on the sick, the Servants, the Schoolmasters, the young men and the children, have likewise each a conference once a week, relating to their several offices and duties.

Once a week also is a conference for strangers, at which

any person may be present, and propose any question or doubt which he desires to have resolved.

In Herrnhut is taught reading, writing, arithmetic, Latin, Greek, Hebrew, French, English, History, and Geography.

There is a Latin, French, and an English lecture every day, as well as an historical and geographical one. On Monday, Wednesday, Friday, and Saturday is the Hebrew lecture; the Greek on Tuesday and Thursday.

In the Orphan House the larger children rise at five. (The smaller, between five and six.) After a little private prayer they work till seven. Then they are at school till eight, the hour of prayer; at nine, those who are capable of it learn Latin; at ten, French; at eleven, they all walk; at twelve, they dine all together, and walk till one; at one, they work or learn writing; at three, arithmetic; at four, history; at five, they work; at six, sup and work; at seven, after a time spent in prayer, walk; at eight the smaller children go to bed, the larger to the public service. When this is ended, they work again till at ten they go to bed.

IV. Every morning, at eight, is singing and exposition of Scripture; and commonly short prayer.

At eight in the evening there is commonly only mental prayer,[14] joined with the singing and expounding.

The faithful afterwards spend a quarter of an hour in prayer, and conclude with the kiss of peace.

On Sunday morning the service begins at six; at nine the public service at Berthelsdorf; at one the Eldest gives separate exhortations to all the members of the Church, divided into fourteen little classes for that purpose, spending about a quarter of an hour with each class; at four begins the evening service at Berthelsdorf, closed by a conference in the church; at eight is the usual service; after which the young men, singing praises round the town, conclude the day.

On the first Saturday in the month the Lord's Supper is administered. From ten in the morning till two the Eldest speaks with each communicant in private concerning the state of his soul; at two they dine, then wash one another's feet; after which they sing and pray; about ten they receive in silence without any ceremony, and continue in silence till they part at twelve.

On the second Saturday is the solemn prayer-day for the children. The third is the day of general intercession and thanksgiving; and on the fourth is the great monthly conferences of all the superiors of the Church.

Herrnhut. Aug. 12, 1738. WJJS, II, 28.

Saturday the 12th was the Intercession-day, when many strangers were present, some of whom came twenty or thirty miles. I would gladly have spent my life here; but my Master calling me to labour in another part of His vineyard, on *Monday* the 14th I was constrained to take my leave of this happy place; Martin Dober and a few others of the brethren walking with us about an hour.

A VISITOR'S CRITICISMS. Written, but not sent, by John Wesley to the Moravians. London. Sept. 1738. WJL, I, 257 f.

MY DEAR BRETHREN,—I cannot but rejoice in your steadfast faith, in your love to our blessed Redeemer, your deadness to the world, your meekness, temperance, chastity, and love of one another. I greatly approve of your conferences and bands, of your method of instructing children, and in general of your great care of the souls committed to your charge.

But of some other things I stand in doubt, which I will mention in love and meekness. And I wish that, in order to remove those doubts, you would on each of those heads, (1) plainly answer whether the fact be as I suppose; and if so, (2) consider whether it be right.

Do you not wholly neglect joint fasting?

Is not the Count all in all? Are not the rest mere shadows,

calling him Rabbi, almost implicitly both believing and obeying him?

Is there not something of levity in your behaviour? Are you in general serious enough?

Are you zealous and watchful to redeem time? Do you not sometimes fall into trifling conversation?

Do you not magnify your own Church too much?

Do you believe any who are not of it to be in gospel liberty?

Are you not straitened in your love? Do you love your enemies and wicked men as yourselves?

Do you not mix human wisdom with divine, joining worldly prudence to heavenly?

Do you not use cunning, guile, or dissimulation in many cases?

Are you not of a close, dark, reserved temper and behaviour?

Is not the spirit of secrecy the spirit of your community?

Have you that childlike openness, frankness, and plainness of speech so manifest to all in the Apostles and first Christians?

JOHN WESLEY TO THE CHURCH AT HERRNHUT. Oxford. Oct. 14, 1738. WJL, I, 260.

Glory be to God, even the Father of our Lord Jesus Christ, for His unspeakable gift! for giving me to be an eye-witness of your faith and love and holy conversation in Christ Jesus! I have borne testimony thereof with all plainness of speech in many parts of Germany, and thanks have been given to God by many on your behalf.

We are endeavouring here also, by the grace which is given us, to be followers of you, as ye are of Christ. Fourteen were added to us since our return, so that we have now eight bands of men, consisting of fifty-six persons; all of whom seek for salvation only in the blood of Christ. As yet we have only two small bands of women—the one of three, the other of five persons. But here are many others who only wait till we have leisure to instruct them how they may most effectually build up one another in the faith and love of Him who gave Himself for them.

Though my brother and I are not permitted to preach in most of the churches of London, yet (thanks be to God) there are others left wherein we have liberty to speak the truth as it is in Jesus. Likewise every evening, and on set evenings in the week at two several places, we publish the word of reconciliation, sometimes to twenty or thirty, sometimes to fifty or sixty, sometimes to three or four hundred persons, met together to hear it. We begin and end all our meetings with singing and prayer; and we know that our Lord heareth our prayer, having more than once or twice (and this was not done in a corner) received our petitions in that very hour.

Nor hath He left Himself without other witnesses of His grace and truth. Ten ministers I know now in England who lay the right foundation—'The blood of Christ cleanseth us from all sin.' Over and above whom I have found one Anabaptist, and one, if not two, of the teachers among the Presbyterians here, who, I hope, love the Lord Jesus Christ in sincerity, and teach the way of God in truth.

ii. The Spirit and the Gifts are Ours

We noted at the end of section one of this chapter on Charles Wesley's work, the rising emotional intensity of the meetings of the religious societies in the late summer of 1738. Now, early in 1739 occurred a series of gatherings on which the Spirit's power was so palpably poured out as to justify Whitefield's comment, "A Pentecost season indeed."[15] Two of them are mentioned briefly but with unmistakable awareness of their tremendous significance. The first was a love feast at the Fetter Lane Society.[16] From the second, five days later, they parted "with a full conviction that God was about to do great things among us."[17] It is noteworthy that seven are mentioned as present at both occasions, probably the same seven: the Wesleys and White-field and four other clergymen of the Church of England. It was the beginning of the tumultuous work which was to spread rapidly through the rest of the year, and which was to attract much comment from both ecclesiastics and men of the world. Charges of "enthusiasm" were repeatedly hurled at the revivalists from both quarters. "Enthusiasm" was a word of many meanings, all of them derogatory. Basically it meant fanatical conduct rising out of superstition or false claims to divine inspiration. Wesley spiritedly replied to the more considerable of these charges. That there were extravagances in the movement, and for a time in Wesley's own thought and action, is undeniable; but in the struggle to refute the charges, Wesley developed criteria for distinguishing the true work of God from the dangerous and the simulated. These criteria were two: "the Law and the Testimony," that is, the Scripture record; and the ethical results so well emphasized in the letter to his brother Samuel.[18] These criteria, steadily applied, enabled Methodism to free itself from the peripheral elements as they appeared. In this chapter the claims of the "French Prophets" and of an unnamed pair of "proper enthusiasts" are seen being tested against these standards.[19] In the years to come other "lunatic fringe" movements rose and were shaken off. Through all the excitements of the revival the leaders strove to keep their followers close to the Gospel pattern. In the main they succeeded. But in 1739 leaders and people alike were hurried along as by a flood.

Sept. 16, 1738. WCJ[20] I, 130.

James Hutton came, and carried me perforce to Newgate; where we preached Christ to four condemned prisoners. At night my brother returned from Herrnhut. We took sweet counsel together, comparing our experiences.

London. Sept. 17, 18, & 19, 1738. WJJS, II, 70 ff.

I began again to declare in my own country the glad tidings of salvation, preaching three times, and afterward expounding the Holy Scripture to a large company in the Minories. On *Monday* I rejoiced to meet with our little society,[21] which now consisted of thirty-two persons. The next day I went to the condemned felons in Newgate, and offered them free salvation. In the evening I went to a society in Bear Yard, and preached repentance and remission of sins. The next evening I spoke the truth in love at a society in Aldersgate Street. Some contradicted at first, but not long; so that nothing but love appeared at our parting.

Sept. 22, 1738. WCJ, I, 130.

At Bray's I expounded Eph. i. A dispute arising about absolute predestination, I entered my protest against that doctrine.

Sept. 23, 1738. WJJS, II, 76 f.

On *Saturday* the 23rd I was enabled to speak strong words both at Newgate and at Mr. E.'s society; and the next day at St. Ann's, and twice at St. John's, Clerkenwell; so that I fear they will bear me there no longer.

[Sept.] 26.—I declared the gospel of peace to a small company at Windsor.

Sept. 27, 1738. WCJ, I, 131.

In our way to Oxford, I talked closely with my fellow-traveller, Mr. Combes . . . While we were discoursing, the fire within him, he said, diffused itself through every part; he was brim full of joy, (yet not knowing he believed,) and eager to praise God. He called upon me to join. "Was

I now in heaven, I could not think of my sins; I should only think of praising God." We sang and shouted all the way to Oxford.

Oct. 9, 1738. WJJS, II, 83 f.

I set out for Oxford. In walking I read the truly surprising narrative of the conversions lately wrought in and about the town of Northampton, in New England.[22] Surely 'this is the Lord's doing, and it is marvellous in our eyes.'

Nov. 18, 1738. WCJ, I, 136.

Sat.—I had a joyful meeting with my dear Charles Delamotte, just returned from Georgia. I found, in conversation, that he had received forgiveness five months ago,[23] and continued in peace and liberty.

WHITEFIELD IN IRELAND EN ROUTE FROM GEORGIA.

Whitefield's evident delight in these marks of official favor in Ireland was destined to be short-lived. When he got to England he found his former popularity a good deal abated, the officials cool, and most London pulpits closed against him. Several factors contributed to this. One was the unfortunate tone of his Journal recently published; another was his avowed intention to collect money for the Orphan House he had established in Georgia for needy children there. This cold reception drove him from London to Bristol, which city being near his old home, contained many of his friends. But a like fate awaited him there, and he was driven ultimately to taking the momentous step of preaching in the fields.

Nov. 20, 1738. Whitefield, JV, 114 f.

Having sent last night to inform doctor Burscough, bishop of Limerick, that I was lately arrived, at his lordship's appointment I waited on him this morning, and was received with the utmost candour and civility. At his lordship's request, I preached this morning at the cathedral, to a very numerous audience, who seemed universally affected, and full of expectation that I would preach in the afternoon; but Providence did not seem to open a door. But why should not a strange minister always offer his service? I think it is a wrong piece of modesty not to do it. For a sermon from a stranger may do more good than many from those the people are constantly used to.

After sermon the mayor sent twice to invite me, but I was preengaged to the bishop, who kindly invited both me and my friend, thanked me for my sermon, and offered me the free use of his palace, and would have insisted on my accepting of it, had I not told his lordship I was to leave Limerick in the morning. Oh, into what a wealthy place has my good God brought me! How does he every where command some or other to receive me! As I was eating at dinner, I was meditating on the divine goodness in spreading such a table for me, when last Sunday I was in danger almost of perishing with hunger. But I thought at the same time, if this were so great a blessing, what an infinitely greater one will it be, after the troubles of this life, to sit down and eat bread in the kingdom of God. O that I may be accounted worthy of that heavenly banquet!

Oxford. Nov. 28, 1738. WCJ, I, 137.

I dined in Christ-Church Hall, as one not belonging to them.

[Nov.] 29—After morning prayers, I called on Mr. Whitefield, who pressed me to accept of a College living. I read prayers, and preached at the Castle.

[Dec.] 7—I read prayers again to the poor prisoners in Bocardo.

Oxford. Dec. 5, 1738. WJJS, II, 106 f.

I began reading prayers, and preaching, in Gloucester Green Workhouse; and on *Thursday,* in that belonging

to St. Thomas's parish. On both days I preached at the
Castle. At St. Thomas's was a young woman, raving mad,
screaming and tormenting herself continually. I had a
strong desire to speak to her. The moment I began she was
still. The tears ran down her cheeks all the time I was
telling her, 'Jesus of Nazareth is able and willing to deliver
you.' O where is faith upon earth? Why are these poor
wretches left under the open bondage of Satan? Jesus,
Master!

Dec. 10, 1738. Whitefield, TF[24], 113.

Waited yesterday morning on the Archbishop of Canterbury, and the Bishop of London, and met with a favourable reception from both, but was not so civilly treated
by some of the Clergy; for five churches have been already
denied me.—However, I had an opportunity of preaching
in the morning at St. Helen's, and at Islington in the afternoon, to large congregations indeed, with great freedom
and enlargement of heart.—In the evening I went to a
society in Fetter Lane, where we had (what might not im-
properly be called) a love-feast, eating a little bread and
water, and spending about two hours in singing and prayers.

Dec. 11, 1738. WJJS, II, 114.

Hearing Mr. Whitefield was arrived from Georgia, I
hastened to London; and on *Tuesday* the 12th God gave
us once more to take sweet counsel together.

Dec. 11, 1738. WCJ, I, 138.

I came in the coach to Wycombe. I lodged at Mr. Hollis's,
who entertained me with his French Prophets,[25] equal, in
his account, if not superior, to the Old-Testament ones.
While we were undressing, he fell into violent agitations,
and gobbled like a turkey-cock. I was frightened, and began exorcising him with, "Thou deaf and dumb devil,"

&c. He soon recovered out of his fit of inspiration. I prayed, and went to bed, not half liking my bedfellow. I did not sleep very sound with Satan so near me. I got to London by one the next day. George Whitefield came to J. Bray's soon after me. I was full of vehement desire in prayer. I heard him preach to a vast throng at St. Helen's.

Jan. 1, 1739. WJJS, II, 121 ff.

Mr. Hall, Kinchin, Ingham, Whitefield, Hutchins, and my brother Charles were present at our lovefeast in Fetter Lane, with about sixty of our brethren. About three in the morning, as we were continuing instant in prayer, the power of God came mightily upon us, insomuch that many cried out for exceeding joy, and many fell to the ground. As soon as we were recovered a little from that awe and amazement at the presence of His majesty we broke out with one voice, 'We praise Thee, O God; we acknowledge Thee to be the Lord.'

Jan. 5, 1739. Whitefield, TF, 115.

Held a conference at Islington, concerning several things of importance, with seven ministers of Jesus Christ, despised Methodists, whom God in his providence brought together.—We continued in fasting and prayer till three o'clock, and then parted with a full conviction that God was about to do great things among us.

London. Jan. 7, 1739. WCJ, I, 139.

I was offended much at some orders which Bray, &c., were imposing on the society.

Islington. Jan. 17, 1739. WJJS, II, 130.

I was with two persons, who I doubt are properly enthusiasts. For, first, they think to attain the end without the means; which is enthusiasm, properly so called. Again, they think themselves inspired by God, and are not. But false, imaginary inspiration is enthusiasm. That theirs is only imaginary inspiration appears hence: it contradicts the Law and the Testimony.

Bermondsey. Jan. 21, 1739. Whitefield, TF, 118.

Preached twice with great freedom in my heart and clearness in my voice to two thronged congregations, especially in the afternoon, when, as I was informed, near a thousand people stood out in the church-yard, and hundreds more returned home that could not come in.—This put me first upon thinking of preaching without doors. I mentioned it to some friends, who looked upon it as a *mad* notion. However we kneeled down and prayed that nothing may be done rashly.

Islington. Jan. 28, 1739. WJJS, II, 136 f.

I went (having been long importuned thereto) about five in the evening, with four or five of my friends, to a house where was one of those commonly called French prophets. After a time, she came in. She seemed about four or five and twenty, of an agreeable speech and behaviour. She asked why we came. I said, 'To try the spirits, whether they be of God.' Presently after she leaned back in her chair, and seemed to have strong workings in her breast, with deep sighings intermixed. Her head and hands, and, by turns, every part of her body, seemed also to be in a kind of convulsive motion. This continued about ten minutes, till, at six, she began to speak (though the workings, sighings, and contortions of her body were so intermixed with her words, that she seldom spoke half a sentence together) with a clear, strong voice, 'Father, Thy will, Thy will be done. Thus saith the Lord, if of any of you that is a father, his child ask bread, will he give him a stone? If he ask a fish, will he give him a scorpion? Ask bread of Me, My children, and I will give you bread. I will not, will not give you a scorpion. By this judge of what ye shall now hear.'

She spoke much (all as in the person of God, and mostly in Scripture words) of the fulfilling of the prophecies, the coming of Christ now at hand, and the spreading of the gospel over all the earth. Then she exhorted us not to be in haste in judging her spirit to be or not to be of God; but to wait upon God, and He would teach us, if we conferred not with flesh and blood. She added, with many enforcements, that we must watch and pray, and take up our cross, and be still before God.

Two or three of our company were much affected, and believed she spoke by the Spirit of God. But this was in no wise clear to me. The motion might be either hysterical or artificial. And the same words any person of a good understanding and well versed in the Scriptures might have spoken. But I let the matter alone; knowing this, that 'if it be not of God, it will come to nought.'

Feb. 4, 1739. Whitefield, JV, 136 f.

This has been a sabbath indeed! How has God owned me before near twelve thousand people this day! . . . How has he filled and satisfied my soul! Now know I that I did receive the Holy Ghost at imposition of hands, for I feel it as much as Elijah[26] did when Elijah dropped his mantle. Nay, others see it also; and my opposers, would they but speak, cannot but confess that God is with me of a truth. Wherefore then do they fight against God?

WHITEFIELD'S COMMENT AFTER PREACHING IN THE DINING ROOM OF AN INN. Feb. 8, 1739. Whitefield, JV, 140.

God forbid that the word of God should be bound, because some out of a misguided zeal deny the use of their churches.

Feb. 10, 1739. WCJ, I, 142.

I expounded to many hundreds at a Society in Beech-lane.
Feb. 11—We prayed for utterance this day. . . . I prayed
again at Mr. Stonehouse's for a blessing upon my ministry.
(Lady Crisp with my brother.) I read prayers, and preached
without notes on blind Bartimeus; the Lord being greatly
my helper. Let Him have all the glory. I returned to pray
at Mr. Stonehouse's. Miss Crisp asked to be admitted. We
had close searching talk, before I expounded to the Society.

An evangelist-errant. Feb. 13, 1739. Whitefield, TF, 127.

Thought when I rose to abide at Salisbury a few days,
but finding it quite inconsistent with my other business,
I left that place (after public worship, and paying a visit
to an old disciple, Mr. Wesley's mother) and reached Sta-
pleashwin about six at night.—After having refreshed ourselves, we intended to set forward towards Bath; but finding the people, at whose house we put up, were well-in-
clined, we altered our resolution. And our hostess having
called in many of her neighbours, I prayed, conversed, and
sung Psalms with them for a considerable time, wrote some
letters, and went to bed, not doubting but the Lord would
cause me to dwell in safety.—Who knows but some good
may have been done here this night? But what have I to
do with that? I am only to follow my Lord, who wheresoever he came, talked of the one thing needful.

Bristol. Feb. 15, 1739. Whitefield, TF, 128 f.

After having breakfasted and prayed with some religious
friends, I went . . . to the Reverend Mr. G——s, Minister
of St. Mary, Ratcliff, who, as I was informed, had promised
to lend me his church to preach in for the Orphan house.
But he, in effect, gave me a refusal, telling me, that he could
not lend his church without a special order from the Chancellor.—Upon this, I immediately waited upon the Chan-

cellor, to whom I had sent the night before.—But he told
me frankly, "that he would not give any positive leave,
neither would he prohibit any one that should lend me a
church: But he would advise me to withdraw to some other
place till he had heard from the Bishop, and not preach
on that or any other occasion." I asked him his reasons. He
answered, "Why will you press so hard upon me? The thing
has given a general dislike."—I replied, "Not the design
of the Orphan house.—Even those that disagree with me in
other particulars, approve of that.—And as for the Gospel,
when was it preached without dislike?" Soon after this,
I took my leave, and waited upon the Reverend the Dean,
who received me with great civility. When I had shown
him my Georgia accounts, and answered him a question
or two about the Colony, I asked him, "Whether there
could be any just objection against my preaching in
churches for the Orphan house?"—After a pause for a considerable time, he answered, "He could not tell." But
somebody knocking at the door, he replied, "Mr. Whitefield, I will give you an answer some other time; now I
expect company." "Will you be pleased to fix any, Sir?"
said I. "I will send to you," says the Dean. O Christian simplicity, whither art thou fled! . . .

WHITEFIELD THE INITIATOR.

*George Whitefield's Churchmanship was much less stiff
than the Wesleys' and it fell more easily before the prompt-
ings of his sympathetic heart. As a consequence it was he
who first took the step of preaching in the fields in Kingswood not far from Bristol. The King's Wood had not originally been fitted into the framework of the parish system
of the Church of England. Even now that it was the scene
of busy mining operations and the seat of a numerous population, the miners were so wild and brutal a lot, living but
little above the level of the beasts, that no effort had been
made to extend the Church's care to them. Their needs*

touched Whitefield's heart strongly. The positive pull of their need and the negative push of his exclusion from so many pulpits together overbore his lingering scruples against the violation of ecclesiastical order involved in preaching out-of-doors. Whitefield was responsible for other innovations too: he was, if his own account is accurate, the first to attain the evangelical outlook; the first to leave Church forms to pray extempore, the first to administer Communion outside a Church. But to none of these bold steps does Methodism owe so much as to his willingness, on this February day in 1739, to preach in the fields to the miners of Kingswood. Without field preaching, the message of the revival would never have got to the masses who needed it most, and in whose hearts its greatest victories were won.

Bristol. Feb. 16, 1739. Whitefield, TF, 130 f.

About one this afternoon I went, and was most delightfully entertained by an old Christian; and having long since felt my bowels yearn toward the poor colliers, who are very numerous, and yet are as sheep having no shepherd, I went upon a mount and spake to as many as came to hear; I believe there were upwards of two hundred.—Blessed be God that the ice is now broke, and I have now taken to the field.—Some may censure me.—But is there not a cause? Pulpits are denied, and the poor colliers ready to perish for lack of knowledge.

Feb. 18.—After sermon, and taking a little refreshment, I hastened to a society in Baldwin street, where many hundreds were assembled to hear me, so that the stairs and court below, besides the room itself, were crowded.—Here I continued expounding for near two hours. And then expounded for as long a time at another Society in Nicholas street, equally thronged, but with much greater power.

Bath. Feb. 22, 1739. Whitefield, JV, 153.

. . . I was edified by the pious conversation of the Reverend Mr. Griffith Jones,[27] . . . and the account he gave me of the many obstructions he had met with in his ministry, convinced me that I was but a young soldier, just entering the field . . .

JOHN WESLEY TO GEORGE WHITEFIELD. London, Feb. 26, 1739. WJL, I, 280.

My dear Brother,—Our Lord's hand is not shortened amongst us. Yesterday I preached at St. Katherine's, and at Islington, where the church was almost as hot as some of the Society rooms used to be. I think I never was so much strengthened before. The fields after service were white with people praising God. About three hundred were present at Mr. Sims's; thence I went to Mr. Bell's, then to Fetter Lane, and at nine to Mr. Bray's, where also we only wanted room. To-day I expound in the Minories at four, at Mrs. West's at six, and to a large company of poor sinners in Gravel Lane (Bishopsgate) at eight. The Society at Mr. Crouch's does not meet till eight; so that I expound, before I go to him, near St. James's Square, where one young woman has been lately filled with the Holy Ghost and overflows with joy and love. On Wednesday at six we have a noble company of women, not adorned with gold or costly apparel, but a meek and quiet spirit and good works. At the Savoy on Thursday evening we have usually two or three hundred, most of them at least thoroughly awakened. Mr. Abbot's parlour is more than filled on Friday, as is Mr. Park's room twice over; where I have commonly had more power given me than at any other place. A week or two ago a note was given me there, as near as I can remember, in these words: 'Your prayers are desired for a sick child that is lunatic, and sore vexed day and night, that our Lord would heal him, as He did those in the days of His flesh; and that He would give his parents faith and patience till his time is come.'

London. Feb. 28, 1739. WCJ, I, 144.

I met the bands at J. Bray's, and cautioned them against schism. I was violently opposed by one who should have seconded me. They urged me to go to Oxford: but I understood them, and begged to be excused.

WHITEFIELD ON HIS FIRST PREACHING TOUR IN WALES. Cardiff. Mar. 7, 1739. Whitefield, TF, 143 f.

. . . I was much refreshed with the sight of Mr. Howell Harris; whom, tho' I knew not in person, I have long since loved in the bowels of Jesus Christ, and have often felt my soul drawn out in prayer in his behalf. "A burning and shining light has he been in those parts; a barrier against profaneness and immorality, and an indefatigable promoter of the true Gospel of Jesus Christ. About three or four years[28] God has inclined him to go about doing good. He is now above twenty-five years of age. Twice he has applied (being every way qualified) for holy orders; but was refused. About a month ago he offered himself again, but was put off. Upon this, he was, and is still resolved to go on in his work; and indefatigable zeal has he shown in his Master's service. For these three years (as he told me with his own mouth) he has discoursed almost twice every day for three or four hours together; he has been, I think, in seven Counties, and has made it his business to go to wakes, &c. to turn people from such lying vanities. Many alehouse people, fiddlers, harpers, &c. (Demetrius like) sadly cry out against him for spoiling their business. He has been made the subject of numbers of sermons, has been threatened with public prosecutions, and had constables sent to apprehend him. But God has blessed him with inflexible courage; and he still continues to go on from conquering to conquer. Many call, and own him as their spiritual Father: He discourses generally in a field; but at other times, in a house, from a wall, a table, or any thing else. He has established near thirty Societies in South-Wales, and still his sphere of action is enlarged daily." When I first saw him, my heart was knit closely to him. I wanted to catch some of his fire, and gave him the right hand of fellowship with my whole heart. God loves to do great things by weak instruments, that the power may be of God, and not of man.

Newport, Wales. Mar. 9, 1739. Whitefield, JV, 166.

I think Wales is excellently well prepared for the gospel of Christ. They have many burning and shining lights both among the dissenting and church ministers, amongst whom Mr. Griffith Jones shines in particular. No less than fifty charity schools have been erected by his means. . . .

London. Mar. 12, 1739. WCJ, I, 145.

I was at Newgate with Bray. I prayed, sang, exhorted with great life and vehemence. I talked in the cells to two Papists, who renounced all merit but that of Jesus Christ. I expounded at Bray's on the day of judgment. The power of the Lord was present to wound. A woman cried out as in an agony. Another sank down overpowered. All were moved and melted, as wax before the fire. At eight I expounded on Dowgate hill. Two were then taken into the fold.

Mar. 20—A double power and blessing accompanied my word at Fetter Lane.

Bristol. Mar. 17, 1739. Whitefield, JV, 169 f.

Returned to Bristol about eight in the morning, and had the pleasure of hearing that Mr. Mayor, &c. had engaged a clergyman to preach to the poor prisoners at Newgate, rather than to agree to a petition they had presented

to have me. "Some preach Christ out of contention, supposing to add affliction to my bonds, and others of good will:
however, Christ is preached, and I therein rejoice, yea, and
will rejoice."

Bristol. Mar. 25, 1739. Whitefield, JV, 175.

About eight I went to the society in Nicholas-street. I,
with great difficulty, at last got up into the room, which
was extremely hot. God enabled me to speak with much
freedom and power; and at the close of my exhortation, I
recommended a charity-school, which was opened by this
society today. I collected at the door myself, and few passed
by without throwing in their mites. Yet a little while, and
I hope Bristol will be as famous for charity-schools as London. . . .

GEORGE WHITEFIELD TO JOHN WESLEY. Tyerman, LGWA,
I, 193 f.

Bristol, March 22, 1739.

If the brethren, after prayer for direction, think proper,[29]
I wish you would be here the latter end of next week . . .
Mr. Chapman brings a horse to London, which you may
ride. I go away, God willing, next Monday sennight. If
you were here, before my departure, it might be best. Many
are ripe for bands. I leave that entirely to you.[30] I am but
a novice; you are acquainted with the great things of God.
Come, I beseech you; come quickly. I have promised not to
leave this people till you or somebody come to supply my
place . . .

Your dutiful son and servant,

Mar. 15, 1739. WJJS, II, 150 ff.

Thursday the 15th I set out early in the morning, and
in the afternoon came to London.

During my stay here I was fully employed between our
own society in Fetter Lane and many others, where I was
continually desired to expound; so that I had no thought
of leaving London, when I received, after several others,
a letter from Mr. Whitefield, and another from Mr. Seward,
intreating me in the most pressing manner to come to Bristol without delay. This I was not at all forward to do; and
perhaps a little the less inclined to it (though I trust I do
not count my life dear unto myself, so I may finish my
course with joy) because of the remarkable scriptures which
offered as often as we inquired touching the consequence
of this removal: [though, whether this was permitted only
for the trial of our faith, God knoweth, and the event will
show. Till then, let me not be accounted superstitious if I
barely recite them in the same order as they occurred.]
'Get thee up into this mountain . . . and die in the mount
whither thou goest up, and be gathered unto thy people'
(Deut. xxxii. 49, 50).

Mar. 28, 1739. WJJS, II, 157 f.

My journey was proposed to our society in Fetter Lane.
But my brother Charles would scarce bear the mention
of it; till, appealing to the oracles of God, he received those
words as spoken to himself, and answered not again: 'Son
of man, behold, I take from thee the desire of thine eyes
with a stroke: yet shalt thou not mourn or weep, neither
shall thy tears run down.' Our other brethren, however, continuing the dispute, without any probability of their coming to one conclusion, we at length all agreed to decide it
by lot. And by this it was determined I should go. Several
afterwards desiring we might open the Bible concerning the
issue of this, we did so on the several portions of Scripture,
which I shall set down without any reflection upon them:
'Now there was long war between the house of Saul and
the house of David: But David waxed stronger and stronger,

and the house of Saul waxed weaker and weaker.' (2 Sam.
iii. 1) . . .

Mar. 28, 1739. WCJ, I, 146.

We dissuaded my brother from going to Bristol, from
an unaccountable fear that it would prove fatal to him.[31]
A great power was among us. He offered himself willingly
to whatsoever the Lord should appoint. The next day he
set out, commended by us to the grace of God. He left a
blessing behind. I desired to die with him.

USE OF THE LOT DEFENDED. From "The Principles of a
Methodist Farther Explained" (1746). *Works*, V, 316.

3. I come now to what you expatiate upon at large, as
the two grand instances of my enthusiasm. The first is
plainly this: at some rare times when I have been in great
distress of soul, or in utter uncertainty how to act in an
important case which required a speedy determination,
after using all other means that occurred, I have cast lots,
or opened the Bible. And by this means I have been relieved
from that distress or directed in that uncertainty.

So this you give as a genuine instance of my proceedings; and I suppose, of your own fairness and candour! [Mr.
Church, to whom Wesley is replying, had cited the story of
the decision to go to Bristol.] "We agreed at length, to decide it by lot." True, *at length;* after a debate of some
hours; after carefully hearing and weighing coolly all the
reasons which could be alleged on either side; our brethren
still continuing the dispute, without any probability of
their coming to one conclusion, we, at length, (the night
being now far spent,) all agreed to this. "Can there be
greater rashness and extravagance?" I cannot but think there
can. "Reason is thus, in a manner, rendered useless." No;
we had used it as far as it could go; from Saturday March
17 (when I received the first letter,) to Wednesday, 28,

when the case was laid before the society. "Prudence is set aside." Not so: but the arguments were so equal that she saw not how to determine. "And affairs of moment left to be determined by chance!" *By chance!* What a blunder, then, is that, "The lot is cast into the lap; but the whole disposal thereof is of the Lord!" [Prov. 16:33.]

This, I firmly believe, is truth and reason, and will be to the end of the world.

Among the sober churchmen who deplored the fits and fallings, the groans and swoonings, the transports of despair and joy, the reliance on dreams and impressions, which with increasing frequency characterized the revival meetings, was Samuel Wesley, Jr. To his concern for order and decency in religion was added fraternal solicitude over John's tendency to regard these manifestations as the work of God. He had been a caustic, if affectionate, critic of his brothers' evangelical fervor ever since their conversion; his death only seven months after the date of this letter found him still unreconciled to their course. John's forthright defense below maintains that the so-called extravagances are the work of God; but with great good sense, he points chiefly to the spiritual and ethical transformation of the converts as the essential factor in, and the undeniable proof of, the divine nature of the work.

JOHN TO SAMUEL WESLEY, JR. Bristol. Apr. 4, 1739.
WJL, I, 290 f.

My dear brother, the whole question turns chiefly, if not wholly on matter of fact. You deny that God does now work these effects—at least, that He works them in such a manner: I affirm both, because I have heard those facts with my ears and seen them with my eyes. I have seen, as far as it can be seen, very many persons changed in a moment from the spirit of horror, fear, and despair to the spirit of hope, joy, peace, and from sinful desires (till then reigning over them) to a pure desire of doing the will of God. These are matters of fact, whereof I have been, and almost daily am, eye or ear witness. What, upon the same evidence, as to the suddenness and reality of the change, I believe, or know, touching visions and dreams: this I know,—several persons, in whom this great change from the power of Satan unto God was wrought either in sleep, or during a strong representation to the eye of their minds of Christ either on the cross or in glory. This is the fact. Let any judge of it as they please. But that such a change was then wrought appears, not from their shedding tears only, or sighing or singing psalms, as your poor correspondent did by the woman of Oxford, but from the whole tenor of their life, till then many ways wicked, from that time holy, just, and good.

Saw you him that was a lion till then, and is now a lamb; him that was a drunkard, but now exemplarily sober; the whoremonger that was, who now abhors the very lusts of the flesh? These are my living arguments for what I assert —that God now, as aforetime, gives remission of sins and the gift of the Holy Ghost, which may be called visions. If it be not so, I am found a false witness; but, however, I do and will testify the things I have both seen and heard.

CHAPTER VI

THE FIRST UNITED SOCIETIES, 1739-1741

At the beginning of the period covered by this chapter (April 1739—April 1741) it is still possible to speak of "the revival", for it was as yet a single, if somewhat amorphous, movement; at its end, we must recognize the existence of three separate movements. Each of these movements crystallized about a tradition which was present, though undifferentiated, from the beginning. Or perhaps it would be better to say, each crystallized about personalities representing these different traditions, for certainly as precipitating factors the persons were quite as important ás the theological traditions, if not more so. The Calvinistic tradition, characteristic of the revival in Wales and the West of England crystallized into a party about John Cennick, who was quite willing that it should be so, and the more reluctant George Whitefield. What we shall call the Moravian tradition, though really speaking of a peculiar distortion of it, solidified about certain extravagant spirits in the Fetter Lane Society in London: Philip Molther and others. On the banner of the third party no short device as yet appeared—later it was to read "Arminianism." For the present it stood for fidelity to the Anglican Church and the use of its means of grace, as against the Moravians. It insisted that *all* men can be saved, that belief in predestination is incompatible with that possibility, and that Christian Perfection is possible in this life—all this as against the Calvinists. The standard-bearers were, of course John and Charles Wesley; the administrative differentia of the United Societies (as they came to be called) was that the Wesleys were in complete control.

Moravianism continued its existence in England; after the extravagances of the Fetter Lane Society subsided, it played a useful role therein. Calvinistic Methodism, being more congenial to the British temperament than Moravianism, continued an existence not only useful but vigorous. Since, however, our theme is Wesleyan Methodism, we shall not continue the story of the other two bodies after the separation.

With respect to the Church of England, the Societies, as they drew closer together, and adopted methods foreign to Anglican usage (to put it no more strongly than that) became increasingly conscious of themselves as a body, the status of which within the Church was precarious. As everybody knows, the Wesleyan Societies maintained their position in the Church till after John Wesley's death; but at the time nobody could tell how soon it might suddenly be terminated.

The chief differences were in the realm of practise. Perhaps the most important of these divisive practices was the adoption of field preaching. This drove a wedge between the Methodist and the other Anglicans because it involved circumventing those canons which required that every preacher have both the license of the Bishop of the diocese and the permission of the incumbent of the parish in which he was to preach. Since practically the whole kingdom was divided into dioceses and parishes, we may say that the effect of field preaching was that it enabled the Methodists to carry on their work, but only by flouting the parish system. This was a grievous offense, because that system was basic to the Establishment.

None of the Bishops actually forbade the Methodists to preach in his diocese, but when they were not contemptuous and indifferent, they were suspicious and hostile. As for the parish ministers, the Wesleys for a long time patiently asked in each parish for permission to preach, which usually was refused. Having thus paid their respects to ecclesiastical regularity, they proceeded to preach anyhow, not, of course in the Church, but in some convenient open place within the parish. They alleged such legal justification for this as they could find; when that wore thin, they simply said, "The Lord hath anointed me to preach."

Another innovation of which both sides were acutely conscious was the gradual introduction of the use of lay preachers. Such irregularity was understandably repugnant to the hierarchy. Any organization by its very nature, and for self-preservation, must keep in its own hands the regulation and control of its chief functionaries. Ecclesiastical bodies, even those which allow preaching by laymen, insist on the right to say who shall and who shall not exercise that office. Such control is necessary, and, on the whole salutary, in keeping up standards of education, morality and spirituality. But there are times when it fails of its purpose, and the time with which we are now dealing was one such: in morality, spirituality and zeal the Methodist preachers exceeded the hierarchy. It is significant that the usual objection alleged against the preachers was their lack of education. Wesley admitted their lack in this respect, tried hard to overcome it, and meanwhile stoutly maintained that in the things a Gospel preacher needs most to know, they were better versed than their critics. The anomaly of the preachers' position was that the Church neither regularized nor extruded them but resorted to indirect persecution in a vain attempt to put a stop to their activities.

These measures peculiar to the Methodists, and others developed later, came into being without settled plan, to meet the necessities of the moment, and were justified by those necessities and by their success in meeting them.

There were differences in doctrine too. Wesley always contended, and for the most part truly, that he was faithful to the doctrinal formulae of the Church. The one exception is the doctrine of Christian Perfection. Wesley grounded this doctrine "in the oracles of God, in the Old and New Testament"[1]; but I do not recall any instance in which he appealed to the Articles or Homilies to support it. Certainly the doctrine had formed no part of the teaching tradition of his Church, and he had to excise several parts of the Thirty-nine Articles as incompatible with it when he made his revision for American Methodists in 1784. Doubtless he would have said that he was legitimately amplifying the doctrine of sanctification implicit in the doctrinal system of any Christian Church, including his own. We can, therefore, concur in the main with his claim to differ in no respect from the doctrinal standards of the Church of England. But he did differ from the doctrines then prevalently preached in Anglican pulpits, and did not hesitate to admit it. Further, though in general he refrained from negative criticism of the ministers of the Establishment, he did in this instance charge that it was they and not he who had departed from orthodoxy. It was a latitudinarian age; churchmen in their charges against the Methodists made much less of the doctrine in their preaching than of the manner, so searching, so impassioned, and of the effects, the bizarre elements of which obscured in their eyes the deep and permanent conversion of souls. "Enthusiasm" was the great offense of the Methodist preaching in the eyes of the Anglican clergy. The continuance, even intensification, of the "scenes" attendant on the preaching through this period heightened the repugnance of those for whom order was the first law of God.

Each of the three sections into which this chapter is divided runs, chronologically speaking, through most of the period between the Spring of 1739 and that of 1741. The first centers about Bristol, where the first United Society was formed. There the controversy over Calvinism burst into flame and resulted in the two parties going their separate, if parallel ways. The second covers the same period of time at London where, after the break with the Quietism of the Fetter Lane Society, the second United Society was formed—second in time, but destined soon to become first in importance. Here too, early experiments were made in poor relief, following the admirable method of helping the needy to help themselves. In the third section, chiefly in accounts of interviews with prelates of the Establishment, we see the anxiety of the Wesleys to remain within the Anglican fold; but stronger even than this, their determination that the work should go on. The prelates themselves were non-plussed by the problem posed by these anomalous sons of the Church who were devoted to it—*but!*

i. Bristol: The First United Society;
Separation from the Calvinists

THE FIRST STEP IN THE FOUNDING OF KINGSWOOD SCHOOL. Kingswood (nr. Bristol) Mar. 29, 1739. Whitefield, JV, 177 f.

Blessed be God, I hope a good work is begun today. Having had several notices that the colliers of Kingswood were willing to subscribe, I went to dinner with them near a place called Two Mile Hill, and collected above twenty pounds in money, and got above forty pounds in subscriptions toward building them a charity-school. It was surprising to see with what cheerfulness they parted with their money on this occasion. Were I to continue here, I would endeavor to settle schools all over the wood, as also in other places, as Mr. Griffith Jones has done in Wales. But I have but just time to set it on foot. I hope God will bless the ministry of my honoured friend Mr. John Wesley, and enable him to bring it to good effect . . .

Mar. 29, 1739. WJJS, II, 166 ff.

I left London, and in the evening expounded to a small company at Basingstoke.

Mar. 31. — In the evening I reached Bristol, and met Mr. Whitefield there. I could scarce reconcile myself at first to this strange way of preaching in the fields, of which he set me an example on Sunday; having been all my life (till very lately) so tenacious of every point relating to decency and order, that I should have thought the saving of souls almost a sin if it had not been done in a church.

Apr. 1. — In the evening, Mr. Whitefield being gone, I begun expounding our Lord's Sermon on the Mount (one pretty remarkable precedent of field-preaching, though I suppose there were churches at that time also) .

JOHN WESLEY TAKES TO THE FIELDS.

First he had a struggle with his very real and strong personal repugnance at the ecclesiastical irregularity involved in this step. That he overcame it was of inestimable importance for the movement.

Bristol. Apr. 2, 1739. WJJS, II, 172 f.

At four in the afternoon I submitted to be more vile, and proclaimed in the highways the glad tidings of salvation, speaking from a little eminence in a ground adjoining to the city, to about three thousand people. The scripture on which I spoke was this (is it possible any one should be ignorant that is fulfilled in every true minister of Christ?) , 'The Spirit of the Lord is upon Me, because He hath anointed Me to preach the gospel to the poor. He hath sent Me to heal the broken-hearted; to preach deliverance to the captives, and recovery of sight to the blind; to set at liberty them that are bruised, to proclaim the acceptable year of the Lord.'

At seven I began expounding the Acts of the Apostles to a society meeting in Baldwin Street; and the next day the Gospel of St. John in the chapel at Newgate, where I also daily read the Morning Service of the Church.

WORK IN THE BANDS. Apr. 4, 1739. WJJS, II, 174.

At Baptist Mills (a sort of a suburb or village about half

a mile from Bristol) I offered the grace of God to about fifteen hundred persons from these words: 'I will heal their backsliding; I will love them freely.'

In the evening three women agreed to meet together weekly, with the same intention as those at London—viz. 'To confess their faults one to another, and pray one for another, that they may be healed.' At eight four young men agreed to meet, in pursuance of the same design. How dare any man deny this to be (as to the substance of it) a means of grace, ordained by God? Unless he will affirm (with Luther in the fury of his Solifidianism) that St. James's Epistle is an epistle of straw.

EXPOUNDING THE SCRIPTURE.

The centrality of the Bible in the work is indicated by the countless hours Wesley spent explaining it to the Society members—day after day, year after year, the process went on—the task carried by others as soon as capable ones could be found.

Bristol. Apr. 5, 1739. WJJS, II, 175 ff.

At five in the evening I began at a society in Castle Street expounding the Epistle to the Romans; and the next evening, at a society in Gloucester Lane, the first Epistle of St. John. On Saturday evening, at Weaver's Hall also I begun expounding the Epistle to the Romans; and declared that gospel to all which is the 'power of God unto salvation to every one that believeth.'

Apr. 8.—At seven in the morning I preached to about a thousand persons at Bristol, and afterward to about fifteen hundred on the top of Hanham Mount in Kingswood. I called to them in the words of the Evangelical Prophet, 'Ho! every one that thirsteth, come ye to the waters; come and buy wine and milk, without money and without price.' About five thousand were in the afternoon at Rose Green (on the other side of Kingswood); among whom I stood and cried, in the name of the Lord, 'If any man thirst, let him come unto Me and drink. He that believeth on Me, as the Scripture hath said, out of his belly shall flow rivers of living water.'

Bristol. Apr. 21, 1739. WJJS, II, 181 f.

At Weaver's Hall a young man was suddenly seized with a violent trembling all over, and in a few minutes, the sorrows of his heart being enlarged, sunk down to the ground. But we ceased not calling upon God, till He raised him up full of 'peace and joy in the Holy Ghost.'

JOHN WESLEY TO JAMES HUTTON. Bristol. Apr. 24, 1739. WJL, I, 302.

I was now in some doubt how to proceed. Our dear brethren, before I left London, and our brother Whitefield here, and our brother Chapman since, had conjured me to enter into no disputes, least of all concerning Predestination, because this people was so deeply prejudiced for it. The same was my own inclination. But this evening I received a long letter (almost a month after date) charging me roundly with 'resisting and perverting the truth as it is in Jesus' by preaching against God's decree of predestination. I had not done so yet: but I questioned whether I ought not now to declare the whole counsel of God: especially since that letter had been long handed about in Bristol before it was sealed and brought to me, together with another, wherein also the writer exhorts his friends to avoid me as a false teacher. However, I thought it best to walk gently, and so said nothing this day.

This sermon was the opening gun in a polemic against predestinarian doctrine. The letter describes it as unpremeditated, but certainly the matter was much in Wesley's mind, as we learn from the preceding extract. In spite of

Wesley's disclaimer, we may suspect that his belief in the universal atonement on which alone, in his view, revival preaching was valid, had already led him into utterances offensive to the believers in predestination. At any rate, having once begun, he continued so to preach. Opposition grew, the final result was schism. It is hard to assess the measure of responsibility for each of the parties. Nearly forty years later Wesley laid it all on Whitefield,[2] but this fails to take into account the fact that Whitefield was in this matter led rather than a leader. To be sure he was the first to preach against his colleagues by name; but it is hard, in view of this sermon and others soon to follow, to avoid the conclusion that, at least so far as sermons with a polemic edge are concerned, it was Wesley himself who began the controversy.

JOHN WESLEY TO JAMES HUTTON. Bristol. Apr. 26, 1739. WJL, I, 303.

Preaching at Newgate[3] on those words, 'He that believeth hath everlasting life,' I was led, I know not how, to speak strongly and explicitly of Predestination, and then to pray 'that if I spake not the truth of God, He would stay His hand, and work no more among us. If this was His truth, he would not delay to confirm it by signs following.' Immediately the power of God fell upon us: one, and another, and another sunk to the earth; you might see them dropping on all sides as thunderstruck. . . .

This day, I being desirous to speak little, but our brother Purdy pressing me to speak and spare not, we made four lots, and desired our Lord to show what he would have me to do. The answer was, 'Preach and print.' Let Him see to the event.

Apr. 26, 1739. WJJS, II, 184.

In the evening I was again pressed in spirit to declare that 'Christ gave Himself a ransom for all.' And almost before we called upon Him to set His seal, He answered. One was so wounded by the sword of the Spirit that you would have imagined she could not live a moment. But immediately His abundant kindness was showed, and she loudly sang of His righteousness.

The sermon recorded below is the famous one "On Free Grace" (No. LIV in the American edition). Dr. Cell points out correctly that in this sermon Wesley begins by saying, "Whatsoever good is in man or is done by man, God is the author and doer of it. Thus is his grace free in all." But that this is his "main thesis", as Dr. Cell contends, is certainly not correct, unless he is using the word in a Hegelian sense. If that is so, the "antithesis" is the main point of the sermon, as Dr. Cell himself admits on the next page.[4] For Wesley uses but one half of a page on the point that God's grace is free in all; the remaining eight pages are devoted to the withering attack on "the horrible decree" of predestination. Wesley refrained, at Whitefield's plea, from obeying the voice of the lot to print, *till the latter had left for America.[5] But letters from him there did not deter Wesley from publishing the sermon in 1740. This distressed Whitefield greatly, and led him to compose his* Answer to Mr. Wesley's Sermon on Free Grace, *which he published both in America and in England soon after his return in the spring of 1741. The effect of this controversy on the relations of the two evangelists will be considered later.[6]*

Bristol. Apr. 29, 1739. WJJS, II, 185.

I declared the free grace of God to about four thousand people from those words, 'He that spared not His own Son, but delivered Him up for us all, how shall He not with Him also freely give us all things?'

FROM THE SERMON "ON FREE GRACE." *Works* I, 488 f.

26. This is the blasphemy clearly contained in *the hor-*

rible decree of predestination! And here I fix my foot. On this I join issue with every assertor of it. You represent God as worse than the devil; more false, more cruel, more unjust. But you say, you will prove it by Scripture. Hold! What will you prove by Scripture? That God is worse than the devil? It cannot be. Whatever that Scripture proves, it never can prove this; whatever its true meaning be, this cannot be its true meaning . . . It cannot mean, whatever it mean besides, that the God of truth is a liar. Let it mean what it will, it cannot mean that the Judge of all the world is unjust. No scripture can mean that God is not love, or that his mercy is not over all his works: that is, whatever it prove besides, no scripture can prove predestination.

27. This is the blasphemy for which (however I love the persons who assert it) I abhor the doctrine of predestination; a doctrine, upon the supposition of which, if one could possibly suppose it for a moment, (call it election, reprobation, or what you please, for all comes to the same thing), one might say to our adversary the devil, "Thou fool, why dost thou roar about any longer? Thy lying in wait for souls is as needless and useless as our preaching."

May 1, 1739. WJJS, II, 186 f.

Many were offended again, and, indeed, much more than before. For at Baldwin Street my voice could scarce be heard amidst the groanings of some and the cries of others, calling aloud to Him that is 'mighty to save.' I desired all that were sincere of heart to beseech with me the Prince exalted for us, that He would 'proclaim deliverance to the captives.' And He soon showed that He heard our voice. Many of those who had been long in darkness saw the dawn of a great light; and ten persons, I afterwards found, then began to say in faith, 'My Lord and my God.'

A Quaker, who stood by, was not a little displeased at the dissimulation of those creatures, and was biting his lips and knitting his brows, when he dropped down as thunderstruck. The agony he was in was even terrible to behold. We besought God not to lay folly to his charge. And he soon lifted up his head, and cried aloud, 'Now I know thou art a prophet of the Lord.'

A DECISIVE STEP—THE ACQUISITION OF PROPERTY FOR THE SOCIETIES.

The building proposed for the land the acquisition of which is described below was a society-room. It was later, however, to be transformed into a preaching house, and to become famous as 'the New Room.' The measures proposed by Whitefield and taken by Wesley are significant for several reasons. First we should notice that it was from Whitefield that the impulse came. He was aware, of course, that he who controls the property controls the preaching that goes on there—that was the point of his proposal. Evidently, in spite of the beginnings of a rift between the society members of Bristol and the Wesleys over predestination, Whitefield at this date still wanted the control to be in John's hands, rather than the Society's, and was instrumental in placing it there. Again the step had far-reaching results in securing the freedom of Methodist preaching from congregational control. Subsequent changes have left this freedom essentially undisturbed. Finally we should notice the effect of owning property on the crystallization of a group-consciousness. Doubtless Simon goes too far when he says that Wesley (quite unconsciously of course) "so far as the Church of England was concerned . . . had reached 'the parting of the ways.' "[7] Nevertheless the fact that the two main societies of Bristol now not only had a leader but a place of their own must have powerfully promoted the growth of a "we-sense" among them.

Bristol. May 9, 1739. WJJS, II, 194 ff.

We took possession of a piece of ground, near St. James's

churchyard, in the Horsefair, where it was designed to build a room, large enough to contain both the societies of Nicholas and Baldwin Streets, and such of their acquaintance as might desire to be present with them, at such times as the Scripture was expounded. And on *Saturday* the 12th the first stone was laid, with the voice of praise and thanksgiving.

I had not at first the least apprehension or design of being personally engaged, either in the expense of this work or in the direction of it: having appointed eleven feoffees, on whom I supposed these burdens would fall of course. But I quickly found my mistake; first with regard to the expense: for the whole undertaking must have stood still had not I immediately taken upon myself the payment of all the workmen; so that, before I knew where I was, I had contracted a debt of more than a hundred and fifty pounds. And this I was to discharge how I could; the subscriptions of both societies not amounting to one quarter of the sum. And as to the direction of the work, I presently received letters from my friends in London, Mr. Whitefield in particular, backed with a message by one just come from thence, that neither he nor they would have any thing to do with the building, neither contribute any thing towards it, unless I would instantly discharge all feoffees and do every thing in my own name. Many reasons they gave for this; but one was enough, viz. 'that such feoffees always would have it in their power to control me; and, if I preached not as they liked, to turn me out of the room I had built.' I accordingly yielded to their advice, and, calling all the feoffees together, cancelled (no man opposing) the instrument made before, and took the whole management into my own hands. Money, it is true, I had not, nor any human prospect or probability of procuring it; but I knew 'the earth is the Lord's and the fulness thereof,' and in His name set out, nothing doubting.

May 13, 1739. WJJS, II, 198.

. . . Every morning I read prayers and preached at Newgate. Every evening I expounded a portion of Scripture at
one or more of the societies. On Monday, in the afternoon,
I preached abroad, near Bristol; on Tuesday, at Bath and
Two-Mile-Hill alternately; on Wednesday, at Baptist Mills;
every other Thursday, near Pensford; every other Friday,
in another part of Kingswood; on Saturday, in the afternoon, and Sunday morning, in the Bowling Green (which
lies near the middle of the city) ; on Sunday, at eleven near
Hanham Mount, at two at Clifton, and at five on Rose
Green; and hitherto, as my days, so my strength hath been.

May 20, 1739. WJJS, II, 201 ff.

Seeing many of the rich at Clifton Church, my heart was
much pained for them, and I was earnestly desirous that
some even of them might 'enter into the kingdom of
heaven.' But full as I was, I knew not where to begin in
warning them to flee from the wrath to come, till my Testament opened on these words: 'I came not to call the righteous, but sinners to repentance'; in applying which my
soul was so enlarged that methought I could have cried
out (in another sense than poor vain Archimedes) , 'Give
me where to stand and I will shake the earth.'

Perhaps it might be because of the hardness of our hearts,
unready to receive any thing unless we see it with our eyes
and hear it with our ears, that God, in tender condescension
to our weakness, suffered so many outward signs of the very
time when He wrought this inward change to be continually seen and heard among us. But although they saw 'signs
and wonders' (for so I must term them) , yet many would
not believe. They could not indeed *deny* the facts; but they
could *explain* them away. Some said, 'These were purely
natural effects; the people fainted away only because of the

heat and closeness of the room,' and *others* were 'sure it was all a cheat; they might help it if they would. Else why were these things only in their private societies? Why were they not done in the face of the sun?'

To-day, *Monday* the 21st, our Lord answered for Himself. For while I was enforcing these words, 'Be still, and know that I am God,' He began to make bare his arm, not in a close room, neither in private, but in the open air, and before more than two thousand witnesses. One, and another, and another was struck to the earth, exceedingly trembling at the presence of His power. Others cried with a loud and bitter cry, 'What must we do to be saved?' And in less than an hour seven persons, wholly unknown to me till that time, were rejoicing, and singing, and with all their might giving thanks to the God of their salvation.

In the evening I was interrupted at Nicholas Street, almost as soon as I had begun to speak, by the cries of one who was 'pricked at the heart,' and strongly groaned for pardon and peace.

June 11, 1739. WJJS, II, 216.

I received a pressing letter from London (as I had several others before) to come thither as soon as possible, our brethren in Fetter Lane being in great confusion for want of my presence and advice.

June 18, 1739. WJJS, II, 223 ff.

I left London early in the morning, and the next evening reached Bristol, and preached (as I had appointed, if God should permit) to a numerous congregation. My text now also was, 'Look unto Me, and be ye saved, all ye ends of the earth.' Howell Harris called upon me an hour or two after. He said he had been much dissuaded from either hearing or seeing me by many who said all manner of evil of me. 'But,' said he, 'as soon as I heard you preach I quickly found what spirit you was of. And before you had done I was so overpowered with joy and love that I had much ado to walk home.'

It is scarce credible what advantage Satan had gained during my absence of only eight days. Disputes had crept into our little society, so that the love of many was already waxed cold. I showed them the state they were in the next day (both at Newgate and at Baptist Mills) from those words, 'Simon, Simon, behold, Satan hath desired to have you, that he may sift you as wheat.' And when we met in the evening, instead of reviving the dispute, we all betook ourselves to prayer. Our Lord was with us. Our divisions were healed; misunderstandings vanished away; and all our hearts were sweetly drawn together and united as at the first.

GEORGE WHITEFIELD TO JOHN WESLEY. London. June 25, 1739. Tyerman, LGWA, I, 252 f.

Honoured Sir,—I cannot think it right in you to give so much encouragement to those convulsions which people have been thrown into under your ministry. Were I to do so, how many would cry out every night! I think it is tempting God to require such signs.

I hear, honoured sir, that you are about to print a sermon against predestination. It shocks me to think of it. What will be the consequences but controversy? Silence on both sides will be best. It is noised abroad already that there is a division between you and me, and my heart within me is grieved.

Kingswood. June 26, 1739. WJJS, II, 228 f.

I preached near the house we had a few days before began to build for a school, in the middle of Kingswood, under a little sycamore-tree, during a violent storm of rain, on those words, 'As the rain cometh down from heaven, and returneth not thither, but watereth the earth and maketh it bring forth and bud: ... so shall My word be that goeth out of My mouth: it shall not return unto Me void; but it shall accomplish that which I please, and it shall prosper in the thing whereto I sent it.'

Baptist Mills. July 7, 1739. WJJS, II, 239 f.

I had an opportunity to talk with him [Mr. Whitefield] of those outward signs which had so often accompanied the inward work of God. I found his objections were chiefly grounded on gross misrepresentations of matter of fact. But the next day he had an opportunity of informing himself better: for no sooner had he begun (in the application of his sermon) to invite all sinners to believe in Christ, than four persons sunk down close to him, almost in the same moment. One of them lay without either sense or motion; a second trembled exceedingly; the third had strong convulsions all over his body, but made no noise, unless by groans, the fourth, equally convulsed, called upon God, with strong cries and tears. From this time, I trust, we shall all suffer God to carry on His own work in the way that pleaseth Him.[8]

This inconspicuous entry in Whitefield's Journal signalizes the formation of the first "United Society." The two "leading Societies" were those of Nicholas Street and Baldwin Street, for the combined occupancy of which the New Room was built. The term United Society is first applied to it in Wesley's Diary—not the Journal—for the following October 30.[9] Wesley himself does not record the actual uniting at all.

Bristol. July 11, 1739. Whitefield, JV, 248.

After this, my brother Wesley and I went to the women and men's societies, settled some affairs, and united the two leading societies together. A great harmony and sweetness of soul were amongst us all. My heart was full of love for them, and they wept most sorely at my farewell exhortation and prayer. How can I be thankful enough to God, for sending me hither to see that the seed has been sown in good ground, and that by the ministry of Mr. Wesley it has received great increase. May it still increase with all the increase of God.

Bath. July 21, 1739. WJJS, II, 244 f.

I began expounding, a second time, our Lord's Sermon on the Mount. In the morning, *Sunday* the 22nd, as I was explaining 'Blessed are the poor in spirit' to about three thousand people, we had a fair opportunity of showing all men what manner of spirit we were of; for in the middle of the sermon the press-gang came, and seized on one of the hearers (ye learned in the law, what becomes of Magna Carta, and of English liberty and property? Are not these mere sounds, while, on any pretence, there is such a thing as a press-gang suffered in the land?) ; all the rest standing still, and none opening his mouth or lifting up his hand to resist them.

July 23, 1739. WJJS, II, 246.

To guard young converts from fancying that they had 'already attained, or were already perfect,' I preached on those words, 'So is the kingdom of God, as when a man casteth seed into the ground, . . . and riseth day and night, and the seed buddeth forth and springeth up, he knoweth now how . . . first the blade, then the ear, then the full corn in the ear.'

On several evenings this week, and particularly on *Friday*, many were deeply convinced; but none were delivered from that painful conviction, 'The children came to the birth, but there was not strength to bring forth.' I fear we have grieved the Spirit of the jealous God by questioning

His work; and that, therefore, He is withdrawn from us for a season. But He will return and 'abundantly pardon.'

Bristol. Oct. 20, 1739. WJJS, II, 296.

I returned to Bristol.[10] I have seen no part of England so pleasant for sixty or seventy miles together as those parts of Wales I have been in. And most of the inhabitants are indeed ripe for the Gospel. I mean (if the expression appear strange) they are earnestly desirous of being instructed in it; and as utterly ignorant of it they are as any Creek or Cherokee Indians. I do not mean they are ignorant of the name of Christ. Many of them can say both the Lord's Prayer and the Belief. Nay, and some, all the Catechism; but take them out of the road of what they have learned by rote, and they know no more (nine in ten of those with whom I conversed) either of gospel salvation or of that faith whereby alone we can be saved, than Chicali or Tomo-Chachi. Now, what spirit is he of, who had rather these poor creatures should perish for lack of knowledge than that they should be saved, even by the exhortations of Howell Harris or an itinerant preacher?

Hanham. Jan. 21, 1740. WJJS, II, 332 f.

I preached at Hanham, four miles from Bristol. In the evening I made a collection in our congregation for the relief of the poor, without Lawfords' Gate; who having no work (because of the severe frost), and no assistance from the parish wherein they lived, were reduced to the last extremity. I made another collection on *Thursday,* and a third on *Sunday;* by which we were enabled to feed a hundred, sometimes a hundred and fifty a day, of those whom we found to need it most.

Bristol. Mar. 5, 1740. WJJS, II, 338.

[On Wednesday, 5, we came to Bristol.] It was easy to observe here in how different a manner God works now from what He did last spring. He then poured along like a rapid flood, overwhelming all before Him. Whereas now—

> He deigns His influence to infuse,
> Secret, refreshing as the silent dews.

Convictions sink deeper and deeper. Love and joy are more calm, even, and steady. And God, in many, is laying the axe to the root of the tree, who can have no rest in their spirits till they are fully renewed in the image of God, in righteousness and true holiness.

Bristol. Apr. 1, 1740. WJJS, II, 340.

While I was expounding the former part of the twenty-third chapter of the Acts (how wonderfully suited to the occasion! though not by my choice) the floods began to lift up their voice. Some or other of the children of Belial had laboured to disturb us several nights before; but now it seemed as if all the host of the aliens were come together with one consent. Not only the court and the alleys, but all the street, upwards and downwards, was filled with people, shouting, cursing, and swearing, and ready to swallow the ground with fierceness and rage. The Mayor [Stephen Clutterbuck] sent order that they should disperse. But they set him at nought. The chief constable came next in person, who was, till then, sufficiently prejudiced against us. But they insulted him also in so gross a manner as, I believe, fully opened his eyes. At length the Mayor sent several of his officers, who took the ringleaders into custody, and did not go till all the rest were dispersed. Surely he hath been to us 'the minister of God for good.'

Apr. 2. The rioters were brought up to the Court, the Quarter Sessions being held that day. They began to excuse themselves by saying many things of me. But the Mayor cut them all short, saying, 'What Mr. Wesley is, is nothing to you. I will keep the peace: I will have no rioting in this city.'

Bristol. Apr. 19, 1740. WJJS, II, 343.

I received a letter from Mr. Simpson, and another from Mr. William Oxlee, informing me that our poor brethren in Fetter Lane were again in great confusion; and earnestly desiring that, if it were possible, I would come to London without delay.

Charles now comes to Bristol while John goes to London to lead the Fetter Lane Society out of its confusion. During this time the predestinarian controversy grew hotter in Kingswood. Not even John's calm firmness could appease the spirit of faction, much less the more mercurial leadership of the poet of Methodism. At any rate, the brothers were learning to divide their labors as widely as possible in a way that foreshadowed the regular itinerancy of later years.

June 24, 1740. WCJ, I, 243.

I preached Christ, the way, the truth, and the life, to one thousand little children at Kingswood. At the room I proceeded in St. John. Some were present who fancy themselves elect, and therefore sink back into their old tempers. Without meddling in the dispute, I rebuked them sharply, yet in much love. I read my Journal to the bands, as an antidote to stillness.

Bristol. Aug. 5, 1740. WCJ, I, 247.

I talked sharply to Jenny Dechamps, a girl of twelve years old; who now confessed that her fits and cryings out (above thirty of them) were all feigned, that Mr. Wesley might take notice of her.

Sept. 22, 1740. WCJ, I, 249.

I was setting out for the Downs, when one asked me to ride out toward Mr. Willis's. At the end of the town I was informed the colliers were risen. Above one thousand of them I met at Lawrence-hill. They came about me, and saluted me very affectionately, not having seen me since my sickness. The occasion of their rising, they told me, was the dearness of corn. Many seemed inclined to go back with me to the school; but the devil stirred up his oldest servants, who violently rushed upon the others, beating, and tearing, and driving them away from me. I rode up to a ruffian who was striking one of our colliers, and prayed him rather to strike me. He would not, he said, for all the world; and was quite overcome. I turned upon one who struck my horse, and he also sank into a lamb. Wherever I turned, Satan lost ground; so that he was obliged to make one general assault, and, by the few violent colliers, forced on the quiet ones into the town.

Kingswood. Nov. 4, 1740. WCJ, I, 255.

While I was testifying Christ died for all,[11] Mr. Cennick[12] in the hearing of many, gave me the lie. I calmly told him afterwards, "If I speak not the truth as it is in Jesus, may I decrease, and you increase."

Kingswood. Nov. 30, 1740. WCJ, I, 263.

The poison of Calvin has drunk up their spirit of love. Anne Ayling and Anne Davis could not refrain from railing. John Cennick never offered to stop them. Alas! we have set the wolf to keep the sheep!

Kingswood. Dec. 6, 1740. WCJ, I, 263 f.

I wrote my brother a full account of the predestinarian party, their practices and designs, particularly "to have a church within themselves, and to give themselves the sacrament in bread and water."

Kingswood. Dec. 14, 1740. WJJS, II, 407 ff.

I went to Kingswood, intending, if it should please God,

to spend some time there, if haply I might be an instrument in His hand of repairing the breaches which had been made; that we might again, with one heart and one mouth, glorify the Father of our Lord Jesus Christ.

[Dec.] 16.—In the afternoon I preached on 'Let patience have her perfect work.' The next evening Mr. Cennick came back from a little journey into Wiltshire. I was greatly surprised when I went to receive him, as usual, with open arms, to observe him quite cold; so that a stranger would have judged he had scarce ever seen me before. However, for the present I said nothing, but did him honour before the people.

[Dec.] 19.—I pressed him to explain his behaviour. He told me many stories which he had heard of me; yet it seemed to me something was still behind; so I desired we might meet again in the morning.

[Dec.] 20.—A few of us had a long conference together. Mr. C[ennick] now told me plainly he could not agree with me, because I did not preach the truth, in particular with regard to Election. We then entered a little into the controversy; but without effect.

[Dec.] 26.—I returned early in the morning to Kingswood, in order to preach at the usual hour. But my congregation was gone to hear Mr. C[ennick], so that (except a few from Bristol) I had not above two or three men and as many women, the same number I had once or twice before.

Bristol. Feb. 22, 1741. WJJS, II, 427 ff.

He [Cennick,] said, 'I have never privately accused you.' I said, 'My brethren, judge'; and read as follows:

To The Rev. Mr. George Whitefield

Jan. 17, 1741

"My Dear Brother,

"That you might come quickly,[18] I have written a second time.

"With Universal Redemption Brother Charles pleases the world; Brother John follows him in every thing. I believe no atheist can more preach against Predestination than they; and all who believe Election are counted enemies to God, and called so.

"Fly, dear brother. I am as alone; I am in the midst of the plague. If God give thee leave make haste."

Mr. C[ennick] stood up and said, 'That letter is mine; I sent it to Mr. Whitefield, and I do not retract any thing in it, nor blame myself for sending it.'

Perceiving some of our brethren began to speak with warmth, I desired he would meet me at Kingswood on Saturday, where each of us could speak more freely, and that all things might sleep till then.

Kingswood. Feb. 28, 1741. WJJS, II, 430 f.

I met the Kingswood bands again, and heard all who desired it at large; after which I read the following paper:

"By many witnesses, it appears that several members of the band society in Kingswood have made it their common practice to scoff at the preaching of Mr. John and Charles Wesley; that they have censured and spoken evil of them behind their backs, at the very time they professed love and esteem to their faces; That they have studiously endeavoured to prejudice other members of that society against them; and, in order thereto, have belied and slandered them in divers instances.

"Therefore, not for their opinions, nor for any of them (whether they be right or wrong) , but for the causes abovementioned, viz. for their scoffing at the Word and ministers of God, for their tale-bearing, back-biting, and evil-speaking, for their dissembling, lying, and slandering:

"I, John Wesley, by the consent and approbation of the band-society in Kingswood, do declare the persons abovementioned to be no longer members thereof. Neither will they be so accounted, until they shall openly confess their fault, and thereby do what in them lies to remove the scandal they have given."

Mar. 6, 1741. WJJS, II, 433.

[Discussion followed]. Then, after a short time spent in prayer, Mr. C[ennick][14] went out, and about half of those who were present, with him.

Kingswood. Mar. 17, 1741. WJJS, II, 436.

From these words, 'Shall not the Judge of all the earth do right?' I preached a sermon (which I have not done before in Kingswood School since it was built) directly on Predestination.

Bristol. Feb. 24, 1741. WJJS, II, 429 f.

The bands meeting at Bristol, I read over the names of the United Society,[15] being determined that no disorderly walker should remain therein. Accordingly I took an account of every person (1) to whom any reasonable objection was made; (2) who was not known to and recommended by some on whose veracity I could depend. To those who were sufficiently recommended, tickets[16] were given on the following days. Most of the rest I had face to face with their accusers; and such as either appeared to be innocent, or confessed their faults and promised better behaviour, were then received into the society. The others were put upon trial again, unless they voluntarily expelled themselves. About forty were by this means separated from us; I trust only for a season.

"TICKETS" AND THEIR USE. *Works* V, 181 f.[17]

IV. 1. As the society increased, I found it required still greater care to separate the precious from the vile. In order to do this, I determined, at least once in three months, to talk with every member myself, and to inquire at their own mouths, as well as of their leaders and neighbours, whether they grew in grace and in the knowledge of our Lord Jesus Christ. At these seasons I likewise particularly inquire whether there be any misunderstanding or difference among them; that every hinderance of peace and brotherly love may be taken out of the way.

2. To each of those whose seriousness and good conversation I found no reason to doubt, I gave a testimony under my own hand, by writing their name on a ticket prepared for that purpose; every ticket implying as strong a recommendation of the person to whom it was given as if I had wrote at length, "I believe the bearer hereof to be one that fears God, and works righteousness."

3. Those who bore these tickets, (these σύμβολα or *tesserae* as the ancients termed them, being of just the same force with the ἐπιστολαὶ συστατικαί, *commendatory letters*, mentioned by the Apostle,) wherever they came, were acknowledged by their brethren, and received with all cheerfulness. These were likewise of use in other respects. By these it was easily distinguished, when the society were to meet apart, who were members of it, and who not. These also supplied us with a quiet and inoffensive method of removing any disorderly member. He has no new ticket at the quarterly visitation; (for so often the tickets are changed;) and hereby it is immediately known that he is no longer of the community.

ii. London: The Second United Society; Separation from the Moravians

Apr. 1, 1739. WCJ, I, 146 ff.

I preached at St. Katherine's, where I met my old friend Mrs. Paine, of East-Grinstead. I administered the sacrament. I dined at Chrissy Anderson's; went in a coach with her and Esther to Islington; comforted in the way while singing. I expounded the good Samaritan, with divine assistance. I prayed at Fetter Lane, that the Lord might be in the midst of us; received a remarkable answer. B. Nowers, in strong pangs, groaned, screamed, roared out. I was not offended by it,—nor edified. We sang and praised God with all our might. I could not get home till eleven.

Apr. 15. At Islington in the vestry, the Churchwardens demanded my license. I wrote down my name; preached with increase of power, on the woman taken in adultery. None went out. I gave the cup. At night I waited upon Count Zinzendorf with Bray and Hutton. He received us very cordially; told us of six hundred Moors converted, two hundred Greenlanders, three hundred Hottentots. *Saluta meo nomine fratres et sorores. Christi Spiritum illis apprecor.*

We found his prayers answered at the Society. Two received forgiveness; many were filled with unutterable groanings; all received some spiritual gift. We could not part; but continued our triumph till the morning.

Apr. 18. I met Shaw at James's. He insisted that there is no priesthood; but he himself could baptize and administer the other sacrament as well as any man. At Mrs. Claggett's I met Mr. Rogers and Miss Raymond; and prayed earnestly for her.

Apr. 27. I heard G. Whitefield in Islington church-yard. The numerous congregation could not have been more affected within the walls. I exhorted them at Fetter Lane to continue steadfast in the means of grace.

May 16. I attended G. Whitefield to Blackheath. He preached in the rain to many listening sinners. At Fetter Lane a dispute arose about lay-preaching. Many, particularly Bray and Fish, were very zealous for it. Mr. Whitefield and I declared against it.

CHARLES WESLEY TAKES TO THE FIELDS OUTSIDE OF LONDON. May 29, 1739. WCJ, I, 150 f.

Franklyn, a farmer, invited me to preach in his field. I

did so, to about five hundred, on, "Repent, for the kingdom
of heaven is at hand." I returned to the house rejoicing.

May 31. A Quaker sent me a pressing invitation to preach
at Thackstead. I scrupled preaching in another's parish, till
I had been refused the church. Many Quakers, and near
seven hundred others, attended while I declared in the
highways, "The Scripture hath concluded all under sin."

June 13, 1739. WCJ, I, 153.

My brother returned. We had over the Prophetess's affair
before the Society. Bray and Bowers were much humbled.
All agreed to disown the Prophetess. Brother Hall proposed
expelling Shaw and Wolf. We consented, *nem. con.*, that
their names should be erased out of the Society-book, because they disowned themselves members of the Church of
England.

Blackheath. June 14, 1739. WJJS, II, 220 f.

I went with Mr. Whitefield to Blackheath, where were,
I believe, twelve or fourteen thousand people. He a little
surprised me by desiring me to preach in his stead, which I
did (though nature recoiled[18]), on my favourite subject,
'Jesus Christ, who of God is made unto us wisdom, righteousness, sanctification, and redemption.'

I was greatly moved with compassion for the rich that
were there, to whom I made a particular application. Some
of them seemed to attend, while others drove away their
coaches from so uncouth a preacher.

June 16, 1739. WJJS, II, 222 f.

We met at Fetter Lane, to humble ourselves before God,
and own He had justly withdrawn His Spirit from us for
our manifold unfaithfulness. We acknowledged our having
grieved Him by our divisions: 'one saying, I am of Paul;
another, I am of Apollos'; by our leaning again to our

own works, and trusting in them, instead of Christ; by our resting in those little beginnings of sanctification which it had pleased Him to work in our souls; and, above all, by blaspheming His work among us, imputing it either to nature, to the force of imagination and animal spirits, or even to the delusion of the devil. In that hour we found God with us as at the first. Some fell prostrate upon the ground; others burst out, as with one consent, into loud praise and thanksgiving. And many openly testified there had been no such day as this since January the first preceding.

June 22, 1739. WCJ, I, 155.

The sower of tares is beginning to trouble us with disputes about predestination. My brother was wonderfully owned at Wapping last week, while asserting the contrary truth. To-night I asked in prayer, that if God would have all men to be saved, he would show some token for good upon us. Three were justified in immediate answer to that prayer. We prayed again; several fell down under the power of God, present to witness his universal love.

June 24, 1739. WCJ, I, 155.

St. John Baptist's day. The first scripture I cast my eye upon, was, "Then came the servant unto him, and said, Master, what shall we do?" I prayed with West, and went forth in the name of Jesus Christ. I found near ten thousand helpless sinners waiting for the word, in Moorfields.[19] I invited them in my Master's words, as well as name: "Come unto me, all ye that travail, and are heavy laden, and I will give you rest." The Lord was with me, even me, his meanest messenger, according to his promise. At St. Paul's, the Psalms, Lessons, &c., for the day, put fresh life into me. So did the sacrament. My load was gone, and all my doubts and scruples.

Aug. 26, 1739. WCJ, I, 165.

We dined at Mr. Ellis's of Elby. I met our brother Ellis, who has the blessing of believing parents; two sisters awakened; one only brother continues an abandoned prodigal. In the afternoon I preached again to a Kennington congregation. The church was full as it could crowd. Thousands stood in the church-yard. It was the most beautiful sight I ever beheld. The people filled the gradually-rising area, which was shut up on three sides by a vast perpendicular hill. On the top and bottom of this hill was a circular row of trees. In this amphitheatre they stood, deeply attentive, while I called upon them in Christ's words, 'Come unto me, all that are weary.' The tears of many testified that they were ready to enter into that rest. God enabled me to lift up my voice like a trumpet; so that all distinctly heard me. I concluded with singing an invitation to sinners.

Sept. 16, 1739. WCJ, I, 174.

Today I found power to pray for myself; confessed it good for me to be in desertion, and asked God to give me (if it was not tempting him) a sign from his word. The answer was from Isaiah liv. 7: "For a small moment have I forsaken thee; . . . but with everlasting kindness will I have mercy on thee, saith the Lord thy Redeemer."

Sept. 3, 1739. WJJS, II, 267 f.

I talked largely with my mother, who told me that, till a short time since, she had scarce heard such a thing mentioned as the having forgiveness of sins now, or God's Spirit bearing witness with our spirit; much less did she imagine that this was the common privilege of all true believers. 'Therefore,' said she, 'I never durst ask for it myself. But two or three weeks ago, while my son Hall was pronouncing those words, in delivering the cup to me, "The blood of our Lord Jesus Christ, which was given for thee," the words struck through my heart, and I knew God for Christ's sake had forgiven *me* all *my* sins.'

I asked whether her father (Dr. Annesley) had not the same faith; and whether she had not heard him preach it to others. She answered he had it himself; and declared, a little before his death, that for more than forty years he had no darkness, no fear, no doubt at all of his being 'accepted in the Beloved.' But that, nevertheless, she did not remember to have heard him preach—no, not once—explicitly upon it; whence she supposed he also looked upon it as the peculiar blessing of a few, not as promised to all the people of God.

Sept. 9, 1739. WJJS, II, 273.

I declared to about ten thousand, in Moorfields, what they must do to be saved. My mother went with us, about five, to Kennington, where were supposed to be twenty thousand people.[20] I again insisted on that foundation of all our hope, 'Believe in the Lord Jesus, and thou shalt be saved.' From Kennington I went to a society at Lambeth. The house being filled, the rest stood in the garden. The deep attention they showed gave me a good hope that they will not all be forgetful hearers.

Thence I went to our society at Fetter Lane, and exhorted them to love one another.

Sept. 16, 1739. WJJS, II, 278.

I preached at Moorfields to about ten thousand, and at Kennington Common to, I believe, near twenty thousand, on those words of the calmer Jews to St. Paul, 'We desire to hear of thee what thou thinkest; for as concerning this sect, we know that every where it is spoken against.' At both places I described [in very plain terms] the real difference between what is generally called Christianity, and the true old Christianity, which, under the new name of Methodism, is now also every where spoken against.

Sept. 23, 1739. WCJ, I, 179.

I missed hearing a railing sermon at St. James's. Notwithstanding all opposition, we ride on because of the word of truth.

The "Stillness" party at Fetter Lane.

We have already seen that the Fetter Lane Society was at first composed of Anglicans, and that as late as June, 1739, two members had been expelled for leaving the Church.[21] The preliminary rumblings of the stillness controversy had already been heard: John Wesley had found it necessary during his September visit to caution some of the Society against leaving off the use of the means of grace. But late in October James Hutton had introduced to the Society a young Moravian called Philip Molther. Molther had been tutor to the son of Count Zinzendorf, and recently ordained by the Count for mission work in Pennsylvania. His mind was filled with mystical, quietistic notions, which he advocated vigorously. He found a ready hearing among the ill-educated and high-strung members of the Society. The Moravians as a whole had kept pretty close to central Evangelical teaching, but they were not a stiffly creedal Church, and extravagances flared up among them from time to time. Zinzendorf himself was given to a rather sentimental blood-of-Christ mysticism. Both his and Molther's extravagances were different forms of over-emphasis on the Moravian doctrine of the substitutionary atonement, but Molther's had much more serious practical consequences. The weary controversy in the Fetter Lane Society dragged on for nearly a year. Wesley was marvellously patient—in meeting after meeting he discussed, exhorted and pled by turns, trying to rescue the deluded ones from the disastrous consequences of their errors. Only in the middle

of the following summer did he finally give up and with-
draw with the remnant of those who had been faithful.

Nov. 1, 1739. WJJS, II, 312.

I left Bristol, and on Saturday came to London. The
first person I met with there was one [Mrs. Turner] whom
I had left strong in faith and zealous of good works; but
she now told me Mr. Molther had fully convinced her she
never had any faith at all; and had advised her, till she
received faith, to be 'still,' ceasing from outward works;
which she had accordingly done, and did not doubt but in
a short time she should find the advantage of it.

In the evening Mr. Bray also was highly commending
the being 'still' before the Lord. He likewise spoke largely
of the great danger that attended the doing of outward
works, and of the folly of people that keep running about
to church and sacrament, 'as I,' said he, 'did till very lately.'

Nov. 7, 1739. WJJS, II, 314 f.

We sat an hour without speaking. The rest of the time
was spent in dispute, one having proposed a question concerning the Lord's Supper, which many warmly affirmed
none ought to receive till he had 'the full assurance of
faith.'

I observed every day more and more, the advantage Satan
had gained over us. Many of those who once knew in whom
they had believed were thrown into idle reasonings, and
thereby filled with doubts and fears, from which they now
found no way to escape. Many were induced to deny the
gift of God, and affirm they never had any faith at all,
especially those who had fallen again into sin, and, of consequence, into darkness; and almost all these had left off
the means of grace, saying they must now cease from their
own works; they must now trust in Christ alone; they were
poor sinners, and had nothing to do but to lie at His feet.

Till *Saturday* the 10th, I think I did not meet with one

woman of the society who had not been upon the point of casting away her confidence in God. I then indeed found one[22] who, when many (according to their custom) laboured to persuade her she had no faith, replied, with a spirit they were not able to resist, 'I know that the life which I now live, I live by faith in the Son of God, who loved me, and gave Himself for me; and He has never left me one moment, since the hour He was made known to me in the breaking of bread.'

What is to be inferred from this undeniable matter of fact—one that had not faith received it in the Lord's supper? Why: (1) that there are means of grace—that is, outward ordinances—whereby the inward grace of God is ordinarily conveyed to man, whereby the faith that brings salvation is conveyed to them who before had it not; (2) that one of these means is the Lord's Supper; And (3) that he who has not this faith ought to wait for it in the use both of this and of the other means which God hath ordained.

THE BEGINNINGS OF THE FOUNDERY.

The extract below is the well known historical introduction to the "Rules of the United Societies," drawn up in 1743.[23] It tells the story of the beginning of the Foundery Society, which soon became the most important one in Methodism. Perhaps it is for this reason that Wesley ignores in this recital the chronological priority of the United Society in Bristol (July 11, 1739). The Foundery Society was from the beginning under Wesley's personal control, but strictly speaking, it did not become a "United Society" till joined by the dissidents from the Fetter Lane Society the following summer.[24] Since Wesley's Journal for this period is not available, we do not know just when he began to use the property. The closest we can come to the date is found in a bit of the missing Journal preserved by Whitehead: "Nov. 11. I preached . . . at five in the evening to seven or eight thousand in the place which had been the King's Foundery for cannon."[25] Wesley acquired the property and put up a simple building for the Society's use. This building replaced the old one which had been wrecked by an explosion. It was in the section of London known as Moorfields.

Works, V, 190.[26]

1. In the latter end of the year 1739, eight or ten persons came to me in London, who appeared to be deeply convinced of sin, and earnestly groaning for redemption. They desired (as did two or three more the next day) that I would spend some time with them in prayer, and advise them how to flee from the wrath to come; which they saw continually hanging over their heads. That we might have more time for this great work, I appointed a day when they might all come together, which from thenceforward they did every week, namely, on Thursday, in the evening. To these, and as many more as desired to join with them, (for their number increased daily,) I gave those advices, from time to time, which I judged most needful for them; and we always concluded our meeting with prayer suited to their several necessities.

2. This was the rise of the United Society, first in London, and then in other places. Such a society is no other than "a company of men having the form and seeking the power of godliness, united in order to pray together, to receive the word of exhortation, and to watch over one another in love, that they may help each other to work out their salvation."

Dec. 24, 1739. WJJS, II, 328.

After spending part of the night at Fetter Lane, I went to a smaller company, where also we exhorted one another with hymns and spiritual songs, and poured out our hearts to God in prayer.[27]

Dec. 13, 1739. WJJS, II, 326 f.

During my short stay here [Bristol] I received several unpleasing accounts of the state of things in London, a part of which I have subjoined:

"Many of our sisters are shaken: J[enn]y C[hambers] says that she never had faith. Betty and Esther H[opson] are grievously torn by reasonings; the former, I am told, is going to Germany. On Wednesday night there are but few come to Fetter Lane till near nine o'clock. And then, after the names are called over, they presently depart. It appears plain our brethren here have neither wisdom enough to guide nor prudence enough to let it alone.

"Mr. B——n expounds much, and speaks so slightingly of the means of grace that many are much grieved to hear him; but others are greatly delighted with him. Ten or fourteen of them meet at our Brother Clarke's with Mr. Molther, and seem to consult about things as if they were the whole body. These make a mere jest of going to church or to the sacrament. They have much confounded some of our sisters, and many of our brothers are much grieved."

WJJS, II, 327 f.

In another letter, which I received a few days after this, were these words:

Dec. 14, 1739

"This day I was told, by one that does not belong to the bands, that the society would be divided. I believe Brother Hutton, Clarke, Edmonds, and Bray are determined to go on according to Mr. Molther's directions, and to *raise a church,* as they term it; and I suppose above half our brethren are on their side. But they are so very confused, they do not know how to go on; yet are unwilling to be taught, except by the Moravians.

"We long to see you; nay, even those would be glad to

see you who will not be directed by you. I believe, indeed, things would be much better if you would come to town."

[Dec.] 19. I accordingly came to London, though with a heavy heart. Here I found every day the dreadful effects of our brethren's reasoning and disputing with each other. Scarce one in ten retained his first love; and most of the rest were in the utmost confusion, biting and devouring one another. I pray God ye be not consumed one of another.

Apr. 7, 1740. WCJ, I, 213.

Yesterday Simpson declared, "No soul *can* be washed in the blood of Christ, unless it be first brought to a true believer, or one in whom Christ is fully formed. But there are only *two such Ministers* in London, which are Molther and Bell." If this is not calling man Rabbi, what is?

Apr. 21, 1740. WJJS, II, 343 f.

I set out, [from Bristol] and the next evening reached London.

[Apr.] 23. In the evening our society met; but cold, weary, heartless, dead. I found nothing of brotherly love among them now; but a harsh, dry, heavy, stupid spirit. For two hours they looked one at another, when they looked up at all, as if one half of them was afraid of the other; yea, as if a voice was sounding in their ears, 'Take ye heed every one of his neighbour; trust ye not in any brother; ...'

May 14, 1740. WCJ, I, 230.

Poor James [Hutton] was all tergiversation. O how unlike himself! The honest, plain, undesigning Jacob, is now turned a subtle, close, ambiguous Loyola. Bell was more frank, and I therefore put him upon speaking. He expressly denied the sacrament to the unjustified; that is, in effect, to all but Molther, M. Eusters, and himself; for these three are all the church Christ has in England.

May 19, 1740. WCJ, I, 233 f.

Ridley is famous for saying, "You may as well go to hell in praying as in thieving." Mr. Brown's words are, "If we read, the devil reads with us; if we pray, he prays with us; if we go to church or sacrament, he goes with us."

May 26. A woman from Islington complained to me, that she had brought Mr. Stonehouse to her mother, who lay a-dying, but waiting for redemption. Her Minister told her, "it signified nothing to pray either publicly or privately. Reading the Scriptures, or taking the sacrament, were equally useless. These outward things must all be laid aside. She had nothing to do but to be still." He refused to pray by her, and *so* left her.

June 11, 1740. WCJ, I, 239 f.

I returned to be exercised by our *still* brethren's contradiction. My brother proposed new-modelling the bands, and setting by themselves those few who were still for the ordinances. Great clamour was raised by this proposal. The noisy *still*-ones well knew that they had carried their point, by wearying out the sincere ones, scattered among them, one or two in a band of disputers, who had harassed and sawn them asunder; so that a remnant is scarcely left. They grudged us even this remnant, which would soon be all their own, unless immediately rescued out of their hands. Benjamin Ingham seconded us; and obtained that the names should be called over, and as many as were aggrieved put into new bands.

I told them plainly I SHOULD ONLY CONTINUE WITH THEM SO LONG AS THEY CONTINUED IN THE CHURCH OF ENGLAND. My every word was grievous to them. I am a thorn in their sides, and they cannot bear me.

June 12. The power of the Lord was present in his word, both to wound and heal. The adversary roared in the midst of the congregation; for to him, and not to the God of order, do I impute those horrible outcries which almost drowned my voice, and kept back the glad tidings from sinners.

July 2, 1740. WJJS, II, 363.

I went to the society; but I found their hearts were quite estranged.

[July] 4. I met a little handful of them who still stand in the old paths; but how long they may stand God knoweth, the rest being continually pressing upon them.

July 9, 1740. WJJS, II, 364 ff.

I came to an explanation once more with them all together; but with no effect at all.

[July] 15. We had yet another conference at large, but in vain; for all continued in their own opinions.

[July] 16. One desired me to look into an old book, and give her my judgement of it, particularly of what was added at the latter end. This, I found, was *The Mystic Divinity of Dionysius;* and several extracts nearly allied thereto, full of the same 'super-essential darkness.' I borrowed the book, and, going in the evening to Fetter Lane, read one of those extracts, to this effect:

"The Scriptures are good, prayer is good, communicating is good, relieving our neighbour is good; but to one who is not born of God, none of these is good, but all very evil. For him to read the Scriptures, or to pray, or to communicate, or to do any outward work, is deadly poison. First, let him be born of God. Till then let him not do any of these things. For if he does, he destroys himself."

After reading this twice or thrice over, as distinctly as I could, I asked, 'My brethren, is this right, or is it wrong?' Mr. Bell answered immediately, 'It is right; it is all right. It is the truth. To this we must all come, or we never can come to Christ.' Mr. Bray said, 'I believe our brother Bell did not hear what you read, or did not rightly understand.'

But Mr. Bell replied short, 'Yes, I heard every word; and I understand it well. I say, it is the truth; it is the very truth; it is the inward truth.'

Many then laboured to prove that my brother and I laid too much stress upon the ordinances. To put this matter beyond dispute, 'I,' said Mr. Bowes, 'used the ordinances twenty years; yet I found not Christ. But I left them off only for a few weeks, and I found Him then. And I am now as close united to Him as my arm is to my body.'

One asked whether they would suffer Mr. Wesley to preach at Fetter Lane. After a short debate it was answered, 'No; this place is taken for the Germans.'

[July] 18. A few of us joined with my mother[28] in the great sacrifice of thanksgiving; and then consulted how to proceed with regard to our poor brethren of Fetter Lane. We all saw the thing was now come to a crisis, and were therefore unanimously agreed what to do.

Fetter Lane. July 20, 1740. WJJS, II, 370.

In the evening I went with Mr. Seward to the lovefeast in Fetter Lane; at the conclusion of which, having said nothing till then, I read a paper, the substance whereof was as follows:

"About nine months ago certain of you began to speak contrary to the doctrine we had till then received. The sum of what you asserted is this:

1. That there is no such thing as *weak faith*: That there is no justifying faith where there is ever any doubt or fear, or where there is not, in the full sense, a new, a clean heart.

2. That a man ought not to use those ordinances which our Church terms 'means of grace,' before he has such a faith as excludes all doubt and fear, and implies a new, a clean heart.

"You have often affirmed that to search the Scriptures, to pray, or to communicate before we have this faith is to seek salvation by works; and that till these works are laid aside no man can receive faith.

"I believe these assertions to be flatly contrary to the Word of God. I have warned you hereof again and again, and besought you to turn back to the Law and the Testimony. I have borne with you long, hoping you would turn. But as I find you more and more confirmed in the error of your ways, nothing now remains but that I should give you up to God. You that are of the same judgement, follow me."

I then, without saying any thing more, withdrew, as did eighteen or nineteen of the society.

The entry below recounts the actual uniting of two smaller groups (the dissidents from the Fetter Lane Society and the Foundery Society) which constituted the United Society in London. The name of the site continued to designate the whole. This became the central headquarters for all of Wesleyan Methodism. The term United Society is not used in the Journal for it till April 7, 1741.[29]

July 23, 1740. WJJS, II, 371.

Our little company met at *The Foundery,* instead of Fetter Lane. About twenty-five of our brethren God hath given us already, all of whom think and speak the same thing; seven- or eight-and-forty likewise of the fifty women that were in band desired to cast in their lot with us.

THE FIRST LAY PREACHERS.

Among the innovations of the revival, the preaching of laymen equalled, and soon even surpassed in importance, the adoption of field preaching by the clergymen. The beginnings of this practice remain somewhat obscure, for it was one the leaders were not anxious to publicise. However, a reasonably clear account of the first four can be

pieced together. They were Howell Harris, Joseph Hum-
phreys, John Cennick and Thomas Maxfield.

Howell Harris began preaching in Wales independently
of the Wesleys, and at about the same time the latter were
beginning their work in Georgia. He met John Wesley at
Kingswood in 1739. Since Harris already had several years
of independent labor behind him, and had proved his
steadfastness under persecution from parson, squire, and
mob, there was no call for Wesley to do other than regard
him as a fellow soldier of the Cross, one who had served on
harder fields than himself. Either approval or disapproval
would have been simply an impertinence. They prayed to-
gether, and Harris returned to his work in Wales with
heart uplifted. As Tyerman puts it, "the first lay preacher
in the great Methodist movement was Howell Harris."[30]
But so far as I have been able to discover, there was never
any official connection between him and the Wesleys.

In 1790, over fifty years after the event, John Wesley
wrote in his Journal, "Joseph Humphreys, the first lay
preacher that assisted me in 1738."[31] At this time Hum-
phreys was a Moravian member of the Fetter Lane Society,
and was acting as a Moravian minister at Deptford. We
have no further particulars on the nature of the preaching
Wesley mentions. Of Wesley's statement Tyerman says in
one place that Humphreys was a Moravian lay preacher,[32]
in another that he suspects the correctness of the date.[33] It
would seem at any rate, that we cannot safely allow his
claim to priority on the basis of this single statement by
Wesley.

For a long time Maxfield was regarded as the first lay
preacher to assist the Wesleys. This honor was based on
the story told by Henry Moore, given below. Moore gives
no date, but tells the story along with events of 1740.

John Cennick has, I believe rightfully, been established
by Tyerman in the place long accorded to Maxfield. Tyer-
man bases his conclusion on a passage in Cennick's auto-

biography, which I have not been able thus far to consult. The story in its essentials is this: Cennick had, like Harris, begun preaching independently soon after his conversion. This was in 1737. In 1739 he was hired by Wesley to teach school in Kingswood, and, having received no restraining word from Wesley, indeed, with his tacit approval, continued to preach, sometimes in Wesley's place in Bristol.[34] It seems clear then, that he was the first layman actually to preach for Wesley, being in his employ, and this for a year before we hear of Maxfield's doing the same thing in London.[35]

Of these four men, three—Howell Harris, Joseph Humphreys and John Cennick—participated in the formal organization of Welsh Calvinistic Methodism in 1743; and the fourth, Thomas Maxfield, was one of four lay preachers to participate in the first Wesleyan Conference in 1744.[36]

This review may fittingly conclude with John Richard Green's passage on the Methodist lay preachers—a passage quite as remarkable for its lyrical quality as for its historical truth:

> *"Their voice was soon heard in the wildest and most barbarous corners of the land, among the bleak moors of Northumberland, or in the dens of London, or in the long galleries where in the pauses of his labour the Cornish miner listens to the sobbing of the sea."[37]*

Moore, LW[38] I, 414 f.

With this [*i.e.*, establishing converts in the faith] in view, Mr. Wesley had formerly appointed Mr. Cennick to reside at Kingswood. But the want of an assistant of this kind was particularly felt in London . . . therefore he appointed one whom he judged to be strong in the faith and of exemplary conversation, to meet the Society at the usual times, to pray with them, and give them such advice as might be needful. This was Mr. Maxfield, one of the first-fruits of his ministry at Bristol. This young man, being fervent in spirit, and mighty in the Scriptures, greatly profited the people . . . He began to *preach,* and the Lord so blessed the word, that many were not only deeply awakened and brought to repentance, but were also made happy in a consciousness of pardon. The Scripture marks of true conversion,—inward peace, and power to walk in all holiness,—evinced the work to be of God.

Some, however, were offended at this irregularity, as it was termed. A complaint was made in form to Mr. Wesley, and he hastened to London, in order to put a stop to it. His mother then lived in his house, adjoining to the Foundery. When he arrived, she perceived that his countenance was expressive of dissatisfaction, and inquired the cause.— "Thomas Maxfield," said he, abruptly, "has turned Preacher, I find." She looked attentively at him, and replied, "John, you know what my sentiments have been. You cannot suspect me of favoring readily anything of this kind. But take care what you do with respect to that young man, for he is as surely called of God to preach, as you are. Examine what have been the fruits of his preaching, and hear him also yourself." He did so. His prejudice bowed before the force of truth, and he could only say, "It is the Lord: Let him do what seemeth to him good."

WESLEY'S DEFENSE OF THE LAY PREACHERS. *Works,* V, 156 f.[39]

11. "But [you say] they are laymen . . ." Suffer me, however just to intimate to you some things which I would leave to your farther consideration: the scribes of old, who were the ordinary preachers among the Jews, were not priests; they were not better than laymen. Yea, many of them were incapable of the priesthood, being of the tribe of Simeon, not of Levi.

Hence, probably, it was that the Jews themselves never urged it as an objection to our Lord's preaching . . .

These are a few of the considerations that may readily occur to any thinking man on this head. But I do not rest the cause on these. I believe it may be defended a shorter way.

14. It pleased God, by two or three ministers of the Church of England, to call many sinners to repentance; who, in several parts were undeniably turned from a course of sin, to a course of holiness.

And how did they [the ministers of the places where this was done] watch over the sinners lately reformed? Even as a leopard watcheth over his prey.

15. When the ministers by whom God had helped them before came again to those places, great part of their work was to begin again; (if it could be begun again;) but the relapsers were often so hardened in sin, that no impression could be made upon them.

What could they do in a case of so extreme necessity, where many souls lay at stake?

No clergyman would assist at all. The expedient that remained was, to find some one among themselves, who was upright of heart, and of sound judgment in the things of God; and to desire him to meet the rest as often as he could, in order to confirm them, as he was able, in the ways of God, either by reading to them, or by prayer, or by exhortation.

God immediately gave a blessing hereto. In several places, by means of these plain men, not only those who had already begun to run well were hindered from drawing back to perdition; but other sinners also, from time to time, were converted from the error of their ways.

This plain account of the whole proceeding I take to be the best defense of it. I know no scripture which forbids making use of such help, in a case of such necessity. And I praise God who has given even this help to those poor sheep, when "their own shepherds pitied them not."

Works, V, 154 ff.[40]

8. "But they are . . . unlearned . . ." This is a grievous

offence, and is by many esteemed a sufficient excuse for not acknowledging the work to be of God.

The ground of this offence is partly true. Some of those who now preach are unlearned. They neither understand the ancient languages, nor any of the branches of philosophy. And yet this objection might have been spared by many of those who have frequently made it; because they are unlearned too, though accounted otherwise. They have not themselves the very thing they require in others.

It will easily be observed, that I do not depreciate learning of any kind . . . But yet I ask, where hath God declared in his word, that he cannot, or will not, make use of men that have it not? You know the Apostles themselves, all except St. Paul, were ἄνδρες ἀγράμματοι καὶ ἰδιῶται "common, unphilosophical, unlettered men."

10. And I am bold to affirm, that these unlettered men have help from God for that great work,—the saving souls from death; seeing he hath enabled, and doth enable them still, to "turn many to righteousness." Thus hath he "destroyed the wisdom of the wise, and brought to nought the understanding of the prudent."

Indeed, in the one thing which they profess to know, they are not ignorant men. I trust there is not one of them who is not able to go through such an examination, in substantial, practical, experimental divinity, as few of our candidates for holy orders, even in the university, (I speak it with sorrow and shame, and in tender love,) are able to do.

Aug. 17, 1740. WJJS, II, 377.

I enforced that necessary caution, 'Let him that standeth take heed lest he fall.' Let him that is full of joy and love take heed lest he fall into pride; he that is in calm peace, lest he fall into desire; and he that is in heaviness through manifold temptations, lest he fall into anger or impatience.

I afterwards heard a sermon setting forth the *duty* of

getting a good estate, and *keeping a good reputation.* Is it possible to deny (supposing the Bible true) that such a preacher is a 'blind leader of the blind'?

Sept. 14, 1740. WJJS, II, 384 f.

As I returned home in the evening, I had no sooner stepped out of the coach than the mob, who were gathered in great numbers about my door, quite closed me in. I rejoiced and blessed God, knowing this was the time I had long been looking for; and immediately spake to those that were next me of 'righteousness and judgement to come.' At first not many heard, the noise round about us being exceeding great. But the silence spread farther and farther till I had a quiet, attentive congregation; and when I left them they all showed much love, and dismissed me with many blessings.

[Sept.] 16. Many more, who came in among us as lions, in a short space became as lambs; the tears trickling apace down their cheeks, who at first most loudly contradicted and blasphemed. I wonder the devil has not wisdom enough to discern that he is destroying his own kingdom. I believe he has never yet, any one time, caused this open opposition to the truth of God, without losing one or more of his servants, who were found of God while they sought Him not.

Nov. 3, 1740. WJJS, II, 399.

We distributed, as every one had need, among the numerous poor of our society, the clothes of several kinds which many who could spare them had brought for that purpose.

Nov. 9, 1740. WJJS, II, 400 ff.

I had the comfort of finding all our brethren that are in band of one heart and of one mind.

[Nov.] 25. After several methods proposed for employing those who were out of business, we determined to make a trial of one which several of our brethren recommended to us. Our aim was, with as little expense as possible, to keep them at once from want and from idleness; in order to which, we took twelve of the poorest, and a teacher, into the society-room, where they were employed for four months, till spring came on, in carding and spinning of cotton. And the design answered; they were employed and maintained with very little more than the produce of their own labour.

[Nov.] 28. A gentleman [Mr. Allen] came to me full of good-will, to exhort me not to leave the Church; or (which was the same thing in his account) to use extemporary prayer; which, said he, 'I will prove to a demonstration to be no prayer at all. For you cannot do two things at once. But thinking how to pray, and praying, are two things. *Ergo*, you cannot both think and pray at once.' Now, may it not be proved by the self-same demonstration that praying by a form is no prayer at all?—e. g. 'You cannot do two things at once. But reading and praying are two things. *Ergo*, you cannot both read and pray at once.' Q. E. D.

[Dec.] 1. Finding many of our brethren and sisters offended at each other, I appointed the several accusers to come and speak face to face with the accused. Some of them came almost every day this week. And most of the offences vanished away. Where any doubt remained, I could only advise them each to look to his own heart; and to suspend their judgments of each other till God should 'bring to light the hidden things of darkness.'

Dec. 12, 1740. WJJS, II, 406 f.

Having received many unpleasing accounts concerning our little society in Kingswood, I left London, and after some difficulty and danger, by reason of much ice on the road, on *Saturday* evening came to my brother at Bristol, who confirmed to me what I did not desire to hear.

John Wesley was called to London about the middle of January by the sad news that Charles had deserted—it is not too strong a word—the work there. We do not have Charles' Journal for this period, but we can gather from other sources that finally he himself had been lured from the strait way by the attractions of quietistic faith.[41]

Jan. 22, 1741. WJJS, II, 418 ff.

I began expounding where my brother had left off, viz. at the fourth chapter of the First Epistle of St. John. He had not preached the morning before; nor intended to do it any more. 'The Philistines are upon thee, Samson.' But the Lord is not 'departed from thee.' He shall strengthen thee yet again, and thou shalt be 'avenged of them for the loss of thy eyes.'

This gesture, obviously made with conciliatory intent, might have served in actual effect to alienate still further the zealous partisans of Whitefield. Seeing a letter of their leader thus destroyed could be used against Wesley by those determined to make a party division in London like that which had already occurred in Kingswood. At this time Whitefield had not yet landed in England after his second voyage to America.

Feb. 1. A private letter, wrote to me by Mr. Whitefield, having been printed without either his leave or mine, great numbers of copies were given to our people, both at the door and in the Foundery itself. Having procured one of them, I related (after preaching) the naked fact to the congregation, and told them, 'I will do just what I believe Mr. Whitefield would were he here himself.' Upon which I tore it in pieces before them all. Every one who had received it did the same. So that in two minutes there was not a whole copy left. Ah! poor Ahithophel!

Feb. 12, 1741. WJJS, II, 424.

My brother returned from Oxford, and preached on the true way of waiting for God; thereby dispelling at once the fears of some and the vain hopes of others, who had confidently affirmed that Mr. Charles Wesley was *still* already, and would come to London no more.

A break in the triumvirate.

Below is the melancholy paragraph in which John Wesley noted in his Journal Whitefield's decision to go his own way. Fortunately it was not long before the rupture was at least partially healed, and the subsequent relations with Whitefield are an incongruous mixture of warmth and coolness, unity and division. It seems as though they could never again quite forget either that their objectives were identical, or that their gospels were different.

Tyerman points out that in the first nine sermons published by Whitefield (before the end of 1737) there was scarcely a trace of the doctrines he later championed.[42] When, then, and under what influences did he adopt them? Tyerman's first verdict, when he wrote the Life of Wesley *(in 1870) was that he adopted them only under the influence of the Puritan clergy, that is, after he reached New England late in the summer of 1740. But by the time Tyerman had made further studies in preparation for the* Life of Whitefield *(in 1876) his opinion had changed. He said, "Whitefield's Calvinism was suddenly born in England, about the month of June, 1739; but it was cradled and greatly strengthened in America, during the year 1740."[43] This is a much better formula, for though we might ascribe Whitefield's uneasiness over Wesley's polemic before he left England to sheer desire to avoid controversy, there are other facts to be accounted for which will not bear that interpretation. For example, on the long voyage over, Whitefield wrote over sixty letters, all of which he dated Nov. 10, and posted on landing. In these letters, obviously written before he ever got to New England, are numerous passages which show beyond doubt that he was no longer neutral when he left England, but had gone over to the Calvinistic side.*[44]

As the source of this "sudden" change, Tyerman suggests the Erskine brothers, powerful preachers in Scotland, especially Ralph, whose sermons Whitefield read on June 9, 1739.[45] *But such changes are rarely sudden, and I venture to think we should look farther back for its beginnings. During that spring, he had also met and admired Griffith Jones, Howell Harris and Philip Doddridge, all of whom were Calvinists. Jones was decidedly and articulately so; Harris quite definitely, though not aggressively, and Doddridge more liberal in his Calvinism. In the light of these facts it would seem as though Whitefield had gradually been approaching the Calvinist position all through the Spring of 1739; certainly he had reached it by the time he embarked for America. It was necessary for the New England ministers only to fortify it with their conversation, and furnish him with weapons for its defense through their writings. The reason for his adopting them will always remain hid from us; especially as he continued all this time to preach free grace in much the same tones as the Wesleys themselves. One hesitates to say that he adopted them to have an intellectually respectable basis for differing with those with whom he found it difficult or distasteful to coöperate on other grounds. But this very thing has happened too often in the history of the Church for us to exclude the possibility completely here.*[46] *Both were men of strong personality, who found it hard to share leadership.*

Whitefield repeatedly wrote Wesley from America, deprecating with mounting intensity the growing divergence.

On Nov. 24, 1740 he wrote, "Do not oblige me to preach against you, I had rather die."[47] But a month later he was writing his Letter to the Rev. Mr. John Wesley, in Answer to his Sermon Entitled Free-Grace, which made the break inevitable. He prefaced it with a kind of apologia which brought up the unfortunate business of Wesley's having determined to "preach and print" by lot, then said, "At my desire, you suppressed the publishing the sermon whilst I was in England; but soon sent it into the world after my departure. O that you had kept it in!"[48]

As followers of Wesley like Purdy probably must bear much of the burden of blame for his undertaking, in an over-exalted mood, the proclamation of his anti-predestinarian opinions, so the lesser men of the Calvinistic party must bear much of the blame for continuing the estrangement. Soon after Whitefield landed, John Cennick and others enthusiastically promoted a preaching house for him in Kingswood; in London, Dissenters of Calvinistic persuasion built a Tabernacle for Whitefield's preaching near the Foundery. This he deprecated.[49] This was in 1741. Before long Whitefield also was using a separate building in Bristol. He and the Wesleys were "united and yet divided."

Mar. 28, 1741. WJJS, II, 439 f.

Having heard much of Mr. Whitefield's unkind behaviour since his return from Georgia, I went to him to hear him speak for himself, that I might know how to judge. I much approved of his plainness of speech. He told me he and I preached two different gospels, and therefore he not only would not join with, or give me the right hand of fellowship, but was resolved publicly to preach against me and my brother, wheresoever he preached at all. Mr. Hall (who went with me) put him in mind of the promise he had made but a few days before, that, whatever his private opinion was, he would never publicly preach against us.

He said, that promise was only an effect of human weakness, and he was now of another mind.

THE FOUNDERY CALLED "UNITED SOCIETY" FOR THE FIRST TIME.

We have already noticed the first occurrences of the term "United Society" for the one in Bristol which met at the New Room.[50] *The extract below contains its first recorded use to designate the Foundery Society in London. It is interesting that in the first two instances where it occurs in the* Journal, *once of Bristol, and here of the Foundery, it is used in connection with a "purging" of the respective Societies. It would seem as though Wesley's exercise of discipline, a sense of the Societies' amenability to his control and the need for a name to distinguish them from those which were not so amenable were born together. In 1746 Wesley, concerned to make it clear that Methodism had broken its connection with the Moravians, wrote, "The United Society was originally so called, not after the Moravians, but because it consisted of several smaller societies united together."*[51] *The term was always used in the singular at first. But by 1743 at the latest, when the "Rules of the United Societies" were published, it was used in the plural, and applied to all the Societies under Wesley's care.*

Apr. 7, 1741. WJJS, II, 442.

In the evening, having desired all the bands to meet, I read over the names of the United Society, and marked those who were of a doubtful character, that full inquiry might be made concerning them. On *Thursday,* at the meeting of that society, I read over the names of these, and desired to speak with each of them the next day, as soon as they had opportunity. Many of them afterwards gave sufficient proof that they were seeking Christ in sincerity.

The rest I determined to keep on trial, till the doubts concerning them were removed.

iii. The Methodists and the Church

The purpose of this section is to illustrate the external relations of the Methodists for the period covered by this chapter. The main interest lies in the attitude of the non-Methodist Churchmen toward the movement. This is discovered, so far as the Church *officials* are concerned, in several interviews the Wesleys had with three of the prelates: The Bishops of London and Bristol, and the Archbishop of Canterbury. The letter to James Hervey and that to the "serious clergyman" give us Wesley's efforts to resolve doubts in the minds of two of the great body of Anglican clergymen. The title of the section is not really broad enough to include the story of the famous encounter between John Wesley and 'Beau' Nash. It is too good to be left out, however, and is included here as an illustration of another facet of the relations of Methodists with others.

INTERVIEW WITH THE BISHOP OF LONDON.

The first extract goes back, in time, to a point some two years earlier than the events last related. The situation then, it will be recalled, was like this: John had but lately returned from Germany; he and his brother were working with the Religious Societies, for there were as yet no Methodist Societies. Their work was so different from that of most clergymen that they had attracted notice to themselves. The question over "conventicles" requires a word of explanation. The Conventicle Act of the Restoration period had made it illegal for religious assemblies to meet under other than church auspices, or to use other than Prayer Book services. It was for holding meetings which did so that John Westley had suffered. The Toleration Act of 1689 had freed Dissenters from the penalties of the Conventicle Act but, paradoxically, left Anglicans still subject to them.

This was a source of real anxiety to workers in the Religious Societies. Their status was complicated by emotional factors (a deposit from the Puritan wars) as well as legal ones. The Bishop's reply shows how touchy the question was.

Oct. 21, 1738. WCJ, I, 133.

I waited with my brother on the Bishop of London,[52] to answer the complaints he had heard against us, that we preached an absolute assurance of salvation. Some of his words were, "If by 'assurance' you mean an inward persuasion, whereby a man is conscious in himself, after examining his life by the law of God, and weighing his own sincerity, that he is in a state of salvation, and acceptable to God; I don't see how any good Christian can be without such an assurance." "This," we answered, "is what we contend for: but we have been charged as Antinomians, for preaching justification by faith only." "Can any one preach otherwise, who agrees to our Church and the Scriptures?" "Indeed, by preaching it strongly, and not inculcating good works, many have been made Antinomians in theory, though not in practice; especially in King Charles's time." "But there is a heavy charge against us Bishops, by your bringing the Archbishop's authority for re-baptizing an adult." My brother answered, "That he had expressly declared the contrary: yet," added he, "if a person dissatisfied with lay-baptism should desire episcopal, I should think it my duty to administer it, after having acquainted the Bishop according to the canon." "Well; I am against it myself, where any one has had the Dissenters' baptism."

Next my brother inquired, whether his reading in a Religious Society made it a conventicle. His Lordship warily referred us to the laws: but upon our urging the question, "Are the Religious Societies conventicles?" he answered, "No; I think not: however, you can read the acts and laws as well as I: I determine nothing." We hoped his Lordship would not henceforward receive an accusation against a Presbyter, but at the mouth of two or three witnesses. He said, "No; by no means. And you may have free access to me at all times." We thanked him, and took our leave.

Dec. 21, 1738. WCJ, I, 138 f.

At St. Antholin's the Clerk asked me my name, and said, "Dr. Venn has forbidden any Methodist to preach. Do you call yourself a Methodist?" "I do not: the world may call me what they please." "Well, Sir," said he, "it is a pity the people should go away without preaching. You may preach." I did so, on good works.

Feb. 21, 1739. WCJ, I, 143 f.

With my brother I waited on the Archbishop.[53] He showed us great affection; spoke mildly of Mr. Whitefield; cautioned us to give no more umbrage than was necessary for our own defense; to forbear exceptionable phrases; to keep to the doctrines of the Church. We told him we expected persecution; would abide by the Church till her Articles and Homilies were repealed. He assured us he knew of no design in the governors of the Church to innovate; and neither should there be any innovation while he lived: avowed justification by faith only; and his joy to see us as often as we pleased.

From him we went to the Bishop of London; who denied his having condemned or even heard much of us. G. Whitefield's Journal, he said, was tainted with enthusiasm, though he was himself a pious, well-meaning youth. He warned us against Antinomianism, and dismissed us kindly.

"ALL THE WORLD . . . MY PARISH."

The James Hervey to whom the following letter was written had been a member of the Holy Club, and had fol-

lowed the subsequent career of the Wesleys with a friendly, if sometimes perturbed interest. In Holy Orders, his health did not permit him to bear the labors of a parish. When this letter was written he was being cared for in a friendly retreat in Devonshire, and able to preach only occasionally. Tyerman preserves a letter he wrote to Wesley toward the end of 1738 expressing alarm over rumors that he was preaching strange doctrines.[54] We do not have the letter to which this one is an answer, but evidently he was distressed over the fact that Wesley was working in other men's parishes. Wesley's reply contains one of his most striking phrases, the one which has been quoted perhaps oftener than any other. The letter is given in full to show the context in which it originally occurred. It was not in this setting a call to foreign missions, though that sense is not excluded. It simply shows Wesley's determination not to let canon law rob him of his spoil of souls. Just a fortnight after writing this letter, Wesley was to preach his first sermon in the field. He would have need of all the resolution expressed here, for field preaching raised the "parish question" in an acute form.

JOHN WESLEY TO JAMES HERVEY. Mar. 20, 1739. WJL, I, 285 f.

But in the meantime you think I ought to be still; because otherwise I should invade another's office if I interfered with other people's business and intermeddled with souls that did not belong to me. You accordingly ask, 'How is it that I assemble Christians, who are none of my charge, to sing psalms and pray and hear the Scriptures expounded?' and think it hard to justify doing this in other men's parishes, upon catholic principles.

Permit me to speak plainly. If by catholic principles you mean any other than scriptural, they weigh nothing with me. I allow no other rule, whether of faith or practice, than the Holy Scriptures; but on scriptural principles I do not think it hard to justify whatever I do. God in Scripture commands me, according to my power, to instruct the ignorant, reform the wicked, confirm the virtuous. Man forbids me to do this in another's parish: that is, in effect, to do it at all; seeing I have now no parish of my own, nor probably ever shall. Whom, then, shall I hear, God or man? 'If it be just to obey man rather than God, judge you. A dispensation of the gospel is committed to me; and woe is me if I preach not the gospel.' But where shall I preach it, upon the principles you mention? Why, not in Europe, Asia, Africa, or America; not in any of the Christian parts, at least, of the habitable earth: for all these are, after a sort, divided into parishes. If it be said, 'Go back, then, to the heathens from whence you came,' nay, but neither could I now (on your principles) preach to them; for all the heathens in Georgia belong to the parish either of Savannah or Frederica.

Suffer me now to tell you my principles in this matter. I look upon all the world as my parish; thus far I mean, that in whatever part of it I am I judge it meet, right, and my bounden duty to declare, unto all that are willing to hear, the glad tidings of salvation. This is the work which I know God has called me to; and sure I am that His blessing attends it. Great encouragement have I, therefore, to be faithful in fulfilling the work He hath given me to do. His servant I am; and, as such, am employed according to the plain direction of His word—'as I have opportunity, doing good unto all men.' And His providence clearly concurs with His word, which has disengaged me from all things else that I might singly attend on this very thing, 'and go about doing good.'

Encounter at Bath.

'*Beau' Nash, as a young man, had had the good fortune to attract the King's attention by a well-planned pageant in his honor. On the strength of this, and his native ingenu-*

ity, he became 'Master of Ceremonies' at Bath, the 'watering place' of fashionable circles in eighteenth century England. He ruled his kingdom with an iron hand, proscribing swords and boots and prescribing canes and shoes and stockings for the gentlemen of the place. As his position carried no income, he supported his magnificent wardrobe and sumptuous retinue as best he could from gambling. The arbiter elegantium *whom even royalty feared to offend was brought to a full stop by a little Methodist preacher and put to flight by an old woman.*

June 5, 1739. WJJS, II, 211 ff.

There was great expectation at Bath of what a noted man was to do to me there; and I was much entreated not to preach, because no one knew what might happen. By this report I also gained a much larger audience, among whom were many of the rich and the great. I told them plainly the Scripture had concluded them all under sin—high and low, rich and poor, one with another. Many of them seemed to be a little surprised, and were sinking apace into seriousness, when their champion appeared, and coming close to me, asked by what authority I did these things. I replied, 'By the authority of Jesus Christ, conveyed to me by the (now) Archbishop of Canterbury, when he laid hands upon me, and said, "Take thou authority to preach the Gospel." ' He said, 'This is contrary to Act of Parliament: this is a conventicle.' I answered, 'Sir, the conventicles mentioned in that Act (as the preamble shows) are seditious meetings; but this is not such; here is no shadow of sedition; therefore it is not contrary to that Act.' He replied, 'I say it is; and, beside, your preaching frightens people out of their wits.' 'Sir, did you ever hear me preach?' 'No.' 'How, then, can you judge of what you never heard?' 'Sir, by common report.' 'Common report is not enough. Give me leave, sir, to ask, Is not your name Nash?' 'My name is Nash.' 'Sir, I dare not judge of you by common report: I think it not enough to judge by.' Here he paused awhile, and, having recovered himself, said, 'I desire to know what this people comes here for': on which one replied, 'Sir, leave him to me; let an old woman answer him. You, Mr. Nash, take care of your body; we take care of our souls: and for the food of our souls we come here.' He replied not a word, but walked away.

Aug. 27, 1739. WJJS, II, 262.

Indeed the report now current in Bristol was that I was a Papist, if not a Jesuit. Some added that I was born and bred at Rome, which many cordially believed. Oh, ye fools, when will ye understand that the preaching of justification by faith alone, the allowing no meritorious cause of justification but the death and righteousness of Christ, and no conditional or instrumental cause but faith, is overturning Popery from the foundation? When will ye understand that the most destructive of all those errors which Rome, the mother of abominations, hath brought forth (compared to which Transubstantiation and a hundred more are 'trifles light as air'), is, 'That we are justified by works'; or (to express the same a little more decently) by faith and works? Now, do I preach this? I did for ten years: I was (fundamentally) a Papist, and knew it not. But I do now testify to all (and it is the very point for asserting which I have, to this day, been called in question), that 'no good works can be done before justification; none which have not in them the nature of sin.'

TROUBLE WITH LAY CHURCH OFFICERS. Apr. 29, 1739.
WCJ, I, 148.

At Islington vestry the Churchwardens forbade my preaching: demanded my local license. I said nothing but that "I heard them." Scions was very abusive; bidding me shake off the dust of my feet, etc.; and said, "You have all the spirit of the devil," mentioning Mr. Whitefield, Stone-house, and me by name.

June 19, 1739. WCJ, I, 154.

I was at Lambeth[55] with Mr. Piers. His Grace expressly forbade him to let any of us preach in his church: charged us with breach of the canon. I mentioned the Bishop of London's authorizing my forcible exclusion. He would not hear me; said he did not dispute. He asked me what call I had. I answered, "A dispensation of the Gospel is committed to me." "That is, to St. Paul; but I do not dispute: and will not proceed to excommunication YET." "Your Grace has taught me in your book on Church Government, that a man unjustly excommunicated is not thereby cut off from communion with Christ." "Of that I am the judge." I asked him, if Mr. Whitefield's success was not a spiritual sign, and sufficient proof of his call: recommended Gamaliel's advice. He dismissed us; Piers, with kind professions; me, with all the marks of his displeasure.

Oxford. July 3, 1739. WCJ, I, 156.

At night I had another conference with the Dean; who cited Mr. Whitefield to judgment. I said, "Mr. Dean, he shall be ready to answer your citation." He used his utmost address to bring me off from preaching abroad, from expounding in houses, from singing psalms: denied justification by faith only, and all vital religion: promised me, however, to read Law and Pascal.

INTERVIEW WITH A FORMER MENTOR. Aug. 10, 1739. WCJ, I, 159.

Today I carried J. Bray to Mr. Law, who resolved all his feelings and experiences into fits or natural affections, and advised him to take no notice of his comforts, which he had better be without than with. He blamed Mr. Whitefield's Journals, and way of proceeding; said, he had had great hopes, that the Methodists would have been dispersed by little and little into livings, and have leavened the whole lump. I told him my experience. "Then am I," said he, "far below you, (if you are right,) not worthy to bear your shoes." He agreed to our notion of faith, but would have it, that all men held it: was fully against the laymen's expounding, as the very worst thing, both for themselves and others. I told him, he was my schoolmaster to bring me to Christ; but the reason why I did not come sooner to Him, was, my seeking to be sanctified before I was justified. I disclaimed all expectation of becoming some great one.

INTERVIEW OF JOHN WESLEY WITH BISHOP BUTLER OF BRISTOL.

Field preaching had begun in Bristol just four months before. This interview points up as nothing else could the collision with ecclesiastical authority it involved. Since Bristol was Methodism's second important centre, giving up the work there at the Bishop's behest would have crippled it irremediably. It will be noted that the Bishop did not push his words farther than 'advice'; even if he had we may well doubt whether Wesley would have heeded them. The defense the latter made was, as Simon points out,[56] of a rather specious legality; it was not a sense of being within canon law, but a sense of God's call which nerved him to his defiance. Bishop Butler was perhaps the ablest of the Anglican prelates of the time. His massively reasonable attack on Deism, the famous Analogy of Religion, Natural and Revealed, to the Constitution and Course of Nature *had been published three years earlier. It is said to have demolished the arguments for Deism; but the conquest of Deism itself owed less to the Bishop than to the man he was trying to drive out of his Diocese. Wesley had two interviews with Bishop Butler. This is the part which has survived of the account of the second.[57]*

Aug. 18, 1739. WJJS, II, 256 f.

Bishop. Why, sir, our faith itself is a good work; it is a virtuous temper of mind.

Mr. Wesley. My lord, whatever faith is, our Church asserts we are justified by faith alone. But how it can be called a good work I see not: it is the gift of God, and a gift that presupposes nothing in us but sin and misery.

B. How, sir! Then you make God a tyrannical Being if He justifies some without any goodness in them preceding, and does not justify all. If these are not justified on account of some moral goodness in them, why are not those justified too?

W. Because, my lord, they '*resist His Spirit*'; because 'they will not come to Him that they might have life'; because they suffer Him not to 'work in them both to will and to do.' They cannot be saved, because they will not believe.

B. Sir, what do you mean by faith?

W. My lord, by justifying faith I mean a conviction, wrought in a man by the Holy Ghost, that Christ hath loved him and given Himself for him, and that through Christ his sins are forgiven.

B. I believe some good men have this, but not all. But how do you prove this to be the justifying faith taught by our Church?

W. My lord, from her Homily on Salvation, where she describes it thus: 'A sure trust and confidence which a man hath in God, that, through the merits of Christ, his sins are forgiven and he reconciled to the favour of God.'

B. Why, sir, this is quite another thing.

W. My lord, I conceive it to be the very same.

B. Mr. Wesley, I will deal plainly with you. I once thought you and Mr. Whitefield well-meaning men; but I cannot think so now. For I have heard more of you: matters of fact, sir. And Mr. Whitefield says in his Journal: 'There are promises still to be fulfilled in me.' Sir, the pretending to extraordinary revelations and gifts of the Holy Ghost is a horrid thing—a very horrid thing!

W. My lord, for what Mr. Whitefield says Mr. Whitefield, and not I, is accountable. I pretend to no extraordinary revelations, or gifts of the Holy Ghost: none but what every Christian may receive and ought to expect and pray for. But I do not wonder your lordship has heard facts asserted, which, if true, would prove the contrary; nor do I wonder that your lordship, believing them true, should alter the opinion you once had of me. A quarter of an hour I spent with your lordship before, and about an hour now; and perhaps you have never conversed one other hour with any one who spake in my favour. But how many with those who spake on the other side! So that your lordship could not but think as you do. But pray, my lord, what are those facts you have heard?

B. I hear you administer the sacrament in your societies.

W. My lord, I never did yet, and I believe never shall.

B. I hear, too, that many people fall into fits in your societies, and that you pray over them.

W. I do so, my lord, when any show by strong cries and tears that their soul is in deep anguish. I frequently pray to God to deliver them from it, and our prayer is often heard in that hour.

B. Very extraordinary, indeed! Well, sir, since you ask my advice, I will give it you very freely. You have no business here; you are not commissioned to preach in this diocese. Therefore I advise you to go hence.

W. My lord, my business on earth is to do what good I can. Wherever, therefore, I think I can do most good there must I stay, so long as I think so. At present I think I can do most good here; therefore, here I stay. As to my preaching here, a dispensation of the gospel is committed to me, and woe is me if I preach not the gospel wherever I am in the habitable world! Your lordship knows, being ordained a priest, by the commission I then received I am a priest of the Church Universal. And being ordained as Fellow of a College, I was not limited to any particular cure, but have an indeterminate commission to preach the word of God in any part of the Church of England. I do not therefore conceive that, in preaching here by this commission, I break any human law. When I am convinced I do, then it will be time to ask, 'Shall I obey God or man?' But if I should be convinced, in the meanwhile, that I could advance the glory of God and the salvation of souls in any other place more than in Bristol, in that hour, by God's help, I will go hence, which till then I may not do.

Sept. 13, 1739. WJJS, II, 274 ff.

A serious clergyman desired to know in what points we differed from the Church of England. I answered, "To the best of my knowledge, in none. The doctrines we preach are the doctrines of the Church of England; indeed, the fundamental doctrines of the Church, clearly laid down, both in her Prayers, Articles, and Homilies."

He asked, "In what points, then, do you differ from the other clergy of the Church of England?" I answered, "In none from that part of the clergy who adhere to the doctrines of the Church; but from that part of the clergy who dissent from the Church (though they own it not), I differ in the points following:

"First. They speak of justification, either as the same thing with sanctification, or as something consequent upon it. I believe justification to be wholly distinct from sanctification, and necessarily antecedent to it.

"Secondly. They speak of our own holiness, or good works, as the cause of our justification; or that for the sake of which, on account of which, we are justified before God. I believe neither our own holiness nor good works are any part of the cause of our justification; but that the death and righteousness of Christ are the whole and sole cause of it; or that for the sake of which, on account of which, we are justified before God.

"Thirdly. They speak of good works as a condition of justification, necessarily previous to it. I believe no good work can be previous to justification, nor, consequently, a condition of it; but that we are justified (being till that hour ungodly, and, therefore, incapable of doing any good work) by faith alone, faith without works, faith (though producing all, yet) including no good work.

"Fourthly. They speak of sanctification (or holiness) as if it were an outward thing—as if it consisted chiefly, if not wholly, in those two points: (1) the doing no harm; (2) the doing good (as it is called); that is, the using the means of grace, and helping our neighbour. I believe it to be an inward thing, namely, the life of God in the soul of man; a participation of the divine nature; the mind that was in Christ; or, the renewal of our heart after the image of Him that created us.

"Lastly. They speak of the new birth as an outward thing—as if it were no more than baptism; or, at most, a change from outward wickedness to outward goodness, from a vicious to (what is called) a virtuous life. I believe it to be an inward thing; a change from inward wickedness to inward goodness; an entire change of our inmost nature from the image of the devil (wherein we are born) to the image of God; a change from the love of the creature to the love of the Creator; from earthly and sensual to heavenly and holy affections,—in a word, a change from the tempers of the spirits of darkness to those of the angels of God in heaven.

"There is therefore a wide, essential, fundamental, irreconcilable difference between us; so that if they speak the truth as it is in Jesus, I am found a false witness before God. But if I teach the way of God in truth, they are blind leaders of the blind."[58]

Feb. 6, 1740. WJJS, II, 335 f.

I think it was the next time I was there [London] the Ordinary of Newgate came to me, and with much vehemence told me he was sorry I should turn Dissenter from the Church of England. I told him if it was so I did not know it, at which he seemed a little surprised, and offered at something by way of proof, but which needed not a reply.

Our twentieth Article defines a true Church, 'a congregation of faithful people, wherein the true word of God is preached and the sacraments duly administered.' According to this account the Church of England is that body of faithful people (or holy believers) in England among whom the pure word of God is preached and the sacraments duly administered. Who, then, are the worst Dissenters from this Church? (1) Unholy men of all kinds; swearers, Sabbath-breakers, drunkards, fighters, whoremongers, liars, revilers, evil-speakers; the passionate, the gay, the lovers of money, the lovers of dress or of praise, the lovers of pleasure more than lovers of God: all these are Dissenters of the highest sort, continually striking at the root of the Church, and themselves in truth belonging to no Church, but to the synagogue of Satan. (2) Men unsound in the faith; those who deny the Scriptures of truth, those who deny the Lord that brought them, those who deny justification by faith alone, or the present salvation which is by faith: these also are Dissenters of a very high kind; for they likewise strike at the foundation, and, were their principles universally to obtain, there could be no true Church upon earth. Lastly, those who unduly administer the sacraments; who (to instance but in one point) administer the Lord's Supper to such as have neither the power nor the form of godliness. These, too, are gross Dissenters from the Church of England, and should not cast the first stone at others.

CHAPTER VII

THE DEVELOPMENT OF DISCIPLINE

Before 1741 Wesleyan Methodism had freed itself from Quietism and Predestinarianism, two tendencies which had proved incompatible with its genius. On the other hand, it had discovered no reason of doctrinal incompatibility for separating from the Church of England. These matters being settled (basically at least—doctrinal elaboration and controversy would of course continue for a long time yet) the next significant developments to occupy our attention have to do with the development of discipline.

The great innovations of the preceding period—field preaching and the use of lay preachers—were adopted because of their effectiveness in spreading the Gospel. The administrative features which emerge in the period before us in this chapter (1741-1744), served, by contrast, the interests of discipline. "How can the new faith be expressed in a changed life?" was the question which demanded an increasingly effective answer. It must not, of course, be thought that the question of discipline had not arisen earlier, or that the spread of the Gospel ceased to be a matter of concern. The point is that better discipline was the end and aim of the most characteristic forms which emerged in this period.

These developments were the Classes, the "Rules of the United Societies," and the Conference. Wesley needed help in maintaining the Christian discipline of life in the fast-growing Societies. There division into classes, each with its leader, was the answer to that need. It was in response to the needs of discipline that the "Rules" were formulated. If leaders were to be responsible for the conduct of their class members, they must have definite standards to go by: the "Rules" furnished those standards. The preachers, too, needed supervision, and it was the Conference which filled that need most effectively. The Conference was an effective means of securing the preachers' conformity to Wesley's high standards of preaching and conduct, and a way of securing the most effective division of labor—in a word, an organ for the discipline of the preachers.

The two developments last named, the "Rules" and the Conference, were powerful factors in the formation of the "Connection," that is, the development of a high degree of cohesiveness and centralized organization among the Methodists. The "Rules" were the rules for *all* the Societies under Wesley; the Conference took in all the preachers who served under him. Henceforth the Methodists would act together or not at all. It is not too much, then, to say that the Connection itself developed out of the urgent need of the period for discipline.

This repeated stress on the drive toward discipline should not convey the impression that it was the imposition and enforcement of a soulless code, or intended to crush all Methodists into a rigid uniformity. Wesley understood those with whom he had to deal too well to wish for that. A reading of the "Rules" should very quickly dispel any such illusion. While the letter is important in the interest of definiteness, one senses immediately the animating spirit which is the essential thing. By it the "Rules" are redeemed from Levitical rigidity and those who obey them are released into a glad and loyal commitment to the common quest for holiness.

Thus far I have, for purposes of analysis, spoken of the Methodist discipline as something harsh and negative. But to think this was its only aspect would be to do poor justice to Wesley's concept. With him discipline was not thus narrowly conceived. It had its negative aspects, which might culminate in expulsion from the Society, but this was only a last resort, in cases of necessity. More important than such negative measures were the positive proclamation of the Gospel, the opportunities for building up one another in love, the evocation of repentance in the wrong-doer by forbearance and forgiveness. So, every one of these organs which I have called primarily disciplinary, exercised in the first instance the positive influences of edification at their disposal. As the "Rules" were permeated by the spirit of the Gospel as well as of the Law, so too the classes and the Conference were centres where the warm, winsome influences of the Gospel were generated and diffused to do their beneficent work. Further, some of the usages developed during this period had no disciplinary functions at all. The Watch Night services and the Love Feasts for example, promoted rather the corporate life of devotion and edification.

The most noteworthy aspect of the relations of Methodists to the rest of the world during this period is the outbreak of the first serious mob violence. In this furnace the growing company was tried, from it they emerged triumphant.

i. The Classes (Growth, 1741-1742)

Charles Wesley further breaches ecclesiastical law, justifying it by alleging a previous breach on the part of the Clergy.

Apr. 12, 1741. WCJ, I, 267.

I gave the sacrament to the bands of Kingswood, not of Bristol, in obedience, as I told them, to the Church of England, which requires a weekly sacrament at every cathedral. But as they had it not there, and on this particular Sunday were refused it at Temple-church, (I myself, with many of them, having been repelled,) I therefore administered it to them in our school; and, had we wanted an house, would justify doing it in the midst of the Wood. I strongly urged the duty of their receiving it as often as they could be admitted at the churches.

JOHN WESLEY TO CHARLES. London. Apr. 21, 1741.
WJL, I, 352 ff.

It is not possible for me to set out yet. I must go round and glean after G. Whitefield.[1] I will take care of the books you mention. My Journal is not written yet. The bands and Society are my first care. The bands are purged; the Society is purging: and we continually feel whose hand is in the work.

I am not clear that Brother Maxfield should not expound at Greyhound Lane;[2] nor can I as yet do without him. Our clergymen have miscarried full as much as the laymen; and that the Moravians are other than laymen I know not.

As yet I dare in no wise join with the Moravians: (1) Because their general scheme is Mystical, not scriptural,— refined in every point above what is written, immeasurably beyond the plain gospel. (2) Because there is darkness and closeness in all their behaviour, and guile in almost all their words. (3) Because they not only do not practise, but utterly despise and decry, self-denial and the daily cross. (4) Because they, upon principle, conform to the world in wearing gold and gay or costly apparel . . . (6) Because they are by no means zealous of good works; or, at least only to their own people . . . For these reasons chiefly I will rather, God being my helper, stand quite alone than join with them—I mean, till I have full assurance that they will spread none of these errors among the little flock committed to my charge.

Oh my brother, my soul is grieved for you; . . . Fair words have stolen away your heart . . . 'No English man or woman is like the Moravians!'[3] So the matter is come to a fair issue. Five of us did still stand together a few months since: but two are gone to the right hand (poor Hutchings and Cennick); and two more to the left (Mr. Hall and you).

Lord, if it be Thy gospel which I preach, arise and maintain Thine own cause!

May 2, 1741. WJJS, II, 451 f.

I had a conversation of several hours with P. Böhler and Mr. Spangenberg. Our subject was, a new creature. . . .

I asked him, 'Is there still an old man in you?' He said, 'Yes; and will be as long as I live.' I said, 'Is there, then, corruption in your heart?' He replied, 'In the heart of my old man there is; but not in the heart of my new man.' I asked, 'Does the experience of your brethren agree with yours?' He answered, 'I know what I have now spoken is the experience of all the brethren and sisters throughout our Church.'

A few of our brethren and sisters sitting by then spoke what they experienced. He told them, with great emotion, his hand trembling much, 'You all deceive your own souls. There is no higher state than that I have described. You are in a very dangerous error. You know not your own hearts. You fancy your corruptions are taken away, whereas they are only covered. Inward corruption never can be taken away till our bodies are in the dust.'

Was there inward corruption in our Lord? Or, cannot the servant be as his Master?

London. May 14, 1741. WJJS, II, 455 ff.

Hearing that one [Nanny Morris] was in a high fever, of whom I had for some time stood in doubt, I went to her, and asked how she did. She replied, 'I am very ill—but I am very well.'

In the evening [Friday 15th] I called upon her again . . . She answered, smiling and looking up, 'There is the Lamb; and where He is, what is temptation? I have no darkness, no cloud. The enemy may come; but he hath no part in me.' I said, 'But does not your sickness hinder you?' She replied, 'Nothing hinders me. It is the Spirit of my Father that worketh in me; and nothing hinders that Spirit. My body indeed is weak and in pain: but my soul is all joy and praise.'

[May] 16.—I mentioned this to Peter Böhler. But he told me, 'There is no such state on earth. Sin will and must always remain in the soul. The old man will remain till death. The old nature is like an old tooth: You may break off one bit, and another, and another; but you can never get it all away: the stump of it will stay as long as you live; and sometimes will ache too.'

May 7, 1741. WJJS, II, 453 f.

I reminded the United Society that many of our brethren and sisters had not needful food; many were destitute of convenient clothing; many were out of business, and that without their own fault; and many sick and ready to perish: that I had done what in me lay to feed the hungry, to clothe the naked, to employ the poor, and to visit the sick; but was not, alone, sufficient for these things, and therefore desired all whose hearts were as my heart:

1. To bring what clothes each could spare, to be distributed among those that wanted most.

2. To give weekly a penny, or what they could afford, for the relief of the poor and sick.

My design, I told them, is to employ, for the present,[4] all the women who were out of business, and desire it, in knitting.

To these we will first give the common price for that work they do; and then add, according as they need.

Twelve persons are appointed to inspect these, and to visit and provide things needful for the sick.

Each of these is to visit all the sick within their district, every other day; and to meet on Tuesday evening, to give an account of what they have done, and consult what can be done farther.

July 11, 1741. WCJ, I, 286.

I preached at Bristol, then among the colliers, a third time at Bath, a fourth at Sawford, and yet again in the Wood. Let God have the glory. Preaching five times a day, when he calls me to it, no more wearies the flesh than preaching once.

Oxford. July 25, 1741. WJJS, II, 478 ff.

It being my turn[5] (which comes about once in three years), I preached at St. Mary's, before the University. The harvest truly is plenteous. So numerous a congregation (from whatever motives they came) I have seldom seen at Oxford. My text was the confession of poor Agrippa, 'Almost thou persuadest me to be a Christian.'[6] I have 'cast my bread upon the waters.' Let me 'find it again after many days'!

In the afternoon I set out (having no time to spare), and on *Sunday* the 26th preached at the Foundery on the 'liberty' we have 'to enter into the holiest by the blood of Jesus.'

A "MOTHER IN ISRAEL". July 31, 1741. WJJS, II, 482 f.

Hearing that one of our sisters (Jane Muncy) was ill, I went to see her.

She was one of the first women [meeting in the] bands at Fetter Lane; and, when the controversy concerning the means of grace began, stood in the gap and contended earnestly for the ordinances once delivered to the saints. When, soon after, it was ordered that the unmarried men and women should have no conversation with each other, she again withstood to the face those who were 'teaching for doctrines the commandments of men.' Nor could all the sophistry of those who are, without controversy, of all men living the wisest in their generation, induce her either to deny the faith she had received, or to use less plainness of speech, or to be less zealous in recommending and careful in practising good works. Insomuch that many times, when she had been employed in the labour of love till eight or nine in the evening, she then sat down and wrought with her hands till twelve or one in the morning; not that she wanted anything herself, but that she might have to give to others for necessary uses.

From the time that she was made leader of one or two bands she was more eminently a pattern to the flock: in self-denial of every kind, in openness of behaviour, in simplicity and godly sincerity, in steadfast faith, in constant attendance on all the public and all the private ordinances of God. And as she had laboured more than they all, so God now called her forth to suffer. She was seized at first with a violent fever, in the beginning of which they removed her to another house. Here she had work to do which she knew not of. The master of the house was one who 'cared for none of these things.' But he observed her, and was convinced. So that he then began to understand and lay to heart the things that bring a man peace at the last.

In a few days the fever abated, or settled, as it seemed, into an inward imposthume; so that she could not breathe without violent pain, which increased day and night. When I came in she stretched out her hand and said, 'Art thou come, thou blessed of the Lord? Praised be the name of my Lord for this.' I asked, 'Do you faint, now you are chastened of Him?' She said, 'Oh no, no, no; I faint not; I murmur not; I rejoice evermore.' I said, 'But can you in everything give thanks?' She replied, 'Yes; I do, I do.' I said, 'God will make all your bed in your sickness.' She cried out, 'He does, He does; I have nothing to desire. He is ever with me, and I have nothing to do but to praise Him.'

In the same state of mind, though weaker and weaker in body, she continued till Tuesday following, when, several of those who had been in her band being present, she fixed her eyes upon them, and fell into a kind of agonizing prayer that God would keep them from the Evil One. But in the afternoon, when I came, she was quite calm again, and all her words were prayer and praise. The same spirit she breathed when Mr. Maxfield called the next day; and soon after he went she slept in peace. 'A mother in Israel' hast thou been, and 'thy works shall praise thee in the gates'!

THE ORIGIN OF CLASSES.

Wesley did indeed have cause to "bless God" for the classes. The burden of supervision was becoming much too great for any one man to carry. This new device enabled him to share his burden. The Societies at large had reason for thankfulness too. As numbers increased, the personal touch threatened to disappear. The classes, of not more than a dozen members each, were ideally conceived for the edification, encouragement and correction of new converts. A new meaning was given by the class-meeting to that saying of Ecclesiastes, "Woe to him that is alone, for when he falleth he hath not another to help him up." It takes but a little exercise of the sympathetic imagination to see what a world of hope would open to one left forlorn in that hard eighteenth century world simply from knowing that, say, ten other people were vitally interested in him, and that he was in turn partially responsible for them. That responsibility took on the qualities of a family tie as the class grew older in years and experience shared.

The members of a class often stayed together for years. Under such circumstances hypocrisy and evasion were not possible. Whereas the bands consisted of Christians who had made some progress in the Christian life, the class, ideally at least, consisted of all ages and stages of experience. The classes gradually superseded the bands in spite of Wesley's insistence on maintaining the latter.

The class leader had need of wisdom, knowledge of the human heart, patience, courage and, above all, tenderness.

It is never easy to know when frank rebuke is needed rather than forbearance and encouragement; it is harder still to be severe "in love" as needed, but no more. He had somehow to evoke the "togetherness" of the group, and make it last through, it might be, many years of intimate association and self-revelation.

Dr. Leslie Church, in his Early Methodist People *has gone through many of the records of the flourishing time of the class-meetings. He records the verdict of a veteran class leader in 1784: "Upon the whole, I think this to be the most useful means (excepting preaching) that we (Methodists) enjoy; it is instructive, it unites us together, it stirs us up to press forward; the enemy's schemes are brought to light and defeated and our souls in general abundantly comforted and strengthened."[7]*

The proceedings of a class-meeting were of the informal intimate sort not to be taken down in stenographic records. I gather that the usage was not uniform; but the structure of the meeting (apart from the hymns and prayers) depended on questions from the leader, in which, to be sure, lurked possible inquisitorial dangers. Dr. Church gives us the description of the class-meeting of John Dale, of Gateshead Fell. It comes to us through Dale's grandson who later became leader of the same class. As a child he was often allowed to stay in the room while the class met, "and describes his grandfather taking his seat, after singing and prayer and calling 'the members one after another, who came and stood before him while he inquired how their souls prospered, and conversed with them about their experience of the grace of God.' "[8] As the class "grew together" however, or for other reasons, it would become (in Dr. Church's words) "more and more the family circle, and less and less the law-court."[9]

The first extract below is inserted chiefly for the sake of the date. It gives the brief mention in the Journal *of the*

first stage only of the evolution of the class. The second ex-
tract is a later description of the classes fully developed in
form and function.

Bristol. Feb. 15, 1742. WJJS, II, 528.

Many met together to consult on a proper method for
discharging the public debt; and it was at length agreed,
(1) that every member of the society who was able should
contribute a penny a week; (2) that the whole society
should be divided into little companies or classes—about
twelve in each class; and (3) that one person in each class
should receive the contribution of the rest, and bring it in
to the stewards, weekly.

Works, V, 179 f.[10]

II. 3. At length, while we were thinking of quite another
thing, we struck upon a method for which we have cause
to bless God ever since. I was talking with several of the
society in Bristol concerning the means of paying the debts
there, when one stood up and said, "Let every member
of the society give a penny a week till all are paid." Another answered, "But many of them are poor, and cannot
afford to do it." "Then," said he, "put eleven of the poorest
with me; and if they can give any thing, well: I will call
on them weekly; and if they can give nothing, I will give
for them as well as for myself. And each of you call on
eleven of your neighbours weekly; receive what they give,
and make up what is wanting." It was done. In a while,
some of these informed me, they found such and such a
one did not live as he ought. It struck me immediately,
"This is the thing; the very thing we have wanted so long."
I called together all the leaders of the classes, (so we used
to term them and their companies,) and desired, that each
would make a particular inquiry into the behaviour of
those whom he saw weekly. They did so. Many disorderly

walkers were detected. Some turned from the evil of their ways. Some were put away from us. Many saw it with fear, and rejoiced unto God with reverence.

4. As soon as possible, the same method was used in London and all other places. Evil men were detected and reproved. They were borne with for a season. If they forsook their sins, we received them gladly; if they obstinately persisted therein, it was openly declared that they were not of us. The rest mourned and prayed for them, and yet rejoiced, that, as far as in us lay, the scandal was called away from the society.

5. It is the business of the leader, (1) To see each person in his class, once a week at the least, in order to inquire how their souls prosper; to advise, reprove, comfort or exhort, as occasion may require; to receive what they are willing to give, toward the relief of the poor. (2) To meet the minister and the stewards of the society, in order to inform the minister of any that are sick, or of any that are disorderly and will not be reproved; to pay to the stewards what they have received of their several classes in the week preceding.

6. At first they visited each person at his own house; but this was soon found not so expedient. And that on many accounts: (1) It took up more time than most of the leaders had to spare. (2) Many persons lived with masters, mistresses, or relations, who would not suffer them to be thus visited. (3) At the houses of those who were not so averse, they often had no opportunity of speaking to them but in company. And this did not at all answer the end proposed, of exhorting, comforting, or reproving. (4) It frequently happened that one affirmed what another denied. And this could not be cleared up without seeing them together. (5) Little misunderstandings and quarrels of various kinds frequently arose among relations or neighbours; effectually to remove which, it was needful to see them all face to face. Upon all these considerations it was agreed, that those of

each class should meet all together. And by this means a more full inquiry was made into the behaviour of every person. Those who could not be visited at home, or no otherwise than in company, had the same advantage with others. Advice or reproof was given as need required, quarrels made up, misunderstandings removed: and after an hour or two spent in this labour of love, they concluded with prayer and thanksgiving.

7. It can scarce be conceived what advantages have been reaped from this little prudential regulation. Many now happily experienced that Christian fellowship of which they had not so much as an idea before. They began to "bear one another's burdens," and naturally to "care for each other." As they had daily a more intimate acquaintance with, so they had a more endeared affection for, each other. And "speaking the truth in love, they grew up unto him in all things, who is the Head, even Christ; from the whole body, fitly joined together, and compacted by that which every joint supplied, according to the effectual working in the measure of every part, increased unto the edifying itself in love."

ii. Some Methodist Usages

The Origin of Watch Nights.

The first mention in the Journal *of a Watch Night Service which uses that term is under date of April 9, 1742; Wesley then tells us that the first one had been held in London.[11] Similar meetings had been held previously, though the name was not used. Of the last evening of 1740 Wesley says, "We concluded the year, wrestling with God in prayer."[12] Simon says that Wesley had found similar meetings among the Moravians.[13] As in use among the Methodists, however, it sprang from an occurrence in Kingswood. Wesley's approbation of it is one of many instances when he seized upon a spontaneous suggestion or occurrence originated by others, regulated it and turned it to*

good use. The story of the beginnings at Kingswood is a
poignant one. A miner called James Rogers, whose fiddling
had led the revels at the ale-house, became convinced after
his conversion that this was wrong. He determinedly re-
moved temptation to continue this by destroying his be-
loved fiddle, and began instead to lead prayer meetings at
the schoolhouse. As Wesley ordered them held in other
places as well, singing, preaching and prayer filled the time
from ten-thirty till near midnight; the first moments of the
new day were spent in singing one of several hymns written
by Charles Wesley for just such services. "Oft have we
passed the guilty night" evidently was written for the Kings-
wood miners; "Hearken to the solemn voice" was one the
singing of which brought a peculiar awe on the gathering.[14]
The practise of the ancient Christians which Wesley found
to support this practise was their holding of "vigils."[15]

Works, V, 181.[16]

III. 1. About this time, I was informed that several persons in Kingswood frequently met together at the school;
and, when they could spare the time, spent the greater part
of the night in prayer and praise, and thanksgiving. Some
advised to put an end to this; but, upon weighing the thing
thoroughly, and comparing it with the practice of the
ancient Christians, I could see no cause to forbid it. Rather,
I believed it might be made of more general use. So I sent
them word, I designed to watch with them on the Friday
nearest the full moon, that we might have light thither
and back again. I gave public notice of this the Sunday before, and withal, that I intended to preach; desiring they,
and they only, would meet me there, who could do it without prejudice to their business or families. On Friday abundance of people came. I began preaching between eight
and nine; and we continued till a little beyond the noon
of night, singing, praying, and praising God.

2. This we have continued to do once a month ever since,

in Bristol, London, and Newcastle, as well as Kingswood; and exceeding great are the blessings we have found therein: it has generally been an extremely solemn season; when the word of God sunk deep into the heart, even of those who till then knew him not.

"LETTER DAYS." *Works,* V, 182.[17]

V. The thing which I was greatly afraid of all this time, and which I resolved to use every possible method of preventing, was, a narrowness of spirit, a party zeal, a being straitened in our own bowels; that miserable bigotry which makes many so unready to believe that there is any work of God but among themselves. I thought it might be a help against this, frequently to read, to all who were willing to hear, the accounts I received from time to time of the work which God is carrying on in the earth, both in our own and other countries, not among us alone, but among those of various opinions and denominations. For this I allotted one evening in every month; and I find no cause to repent my labour. It is generally a time of strong consolation to those who love God, and all mankind for his sake; as well as of breaking down the partition walls which either the craft of the devil or the folly of men has built up; and of encouraging every child of God to say, (O when shall it once be!) "Whosoever doeth the will of my Father which is in heaven, the same is my brother and sister, and mother."

LOVE FEASTS.

Wesley first came into contact with Love Feasts among the Moravians in Georgia. He attended one near the end of his stay there.[18] From the Moravians came the feature, distinctive of the Love Feast, of distributing bread and water to those present. This, together with the fact that for long only band members were allowed to be present,[19]

*must have induced some Methodists to look on it as a kind
of Sacrament, though Wesley would have repudiated the
suggestion, and always urged his followers to receive the
Lord's Supper at the Churches. Continuing a feature of the
primitive Agapé, with which Wesley connected it, and
which was partly for the purpose of feeding the hungry,
the Love Feasts were often marked by an offering for the
poor. The element of thanksgiving to God for his goodness
seems to have been prominent in the prayers.*

Works, V, 183.[20]

VI. 5. In order to increase in them a grateful sense of all
his mercies, I desired that, one evening in a quarter, all
the men in band, on a second, all the women would meet;
and on a third, both men and women together; that we
might together "eat bread," as the ancient Christians did,
"with gladness and singleness of heart." At these love-feasts
(so we termed them, retaining the name, as well as the
thing, which was in use from the beginning) our food is
only a little plain cake and water. But we seldom return
from them without being fed, not only with the "meat
which perisheth," but with "that which endureth to everlasting life."

THE SELECT BANDS.

*The bands, it will be remembered, were groups of those
who had received justification and who had made some advance in the Christian life. Still more advanced were those
in the Select Bands. They were pressing on to perfection;
Wesley gathered them together to advise them in their
quest, and so that in return, he might have their advice on
perplexing problems, especially those having to do with
discipline. The Select Bands seem to have existed in the
larger cities only. Apparently what were in 1748 (the date*

of the extract below) called Select Bands were earlier called
Select Societies. At least this is the term used in the minutes
of the first Conference (1744) of a grouping which had the
same rules and functions.[21]

Works, V, 184 f.[22]

(VIII) 2. I saw it might be useful to give some advices
to all those who continued in the light of God's countenance, which the rest of their brethren did not want, and
probably could not receive. So I desired a small number of
such as appeared to be in this state, to spend an hour with
me every Monday morning. My design was, not only to
direct them how to press after perfection; to exercise their
every grace, and improve every talent they had received;
and to incite them to love one another more, and to watch
more carefully over each other; but also to have a select
company, to whom I might unbosom myself on all occasions, without reserve; and whom I could propose to all
their brethren as a pattern of love, of holiness, and of good
works.

3. They had no need of being incumbered with many
rules; having the best rule of all in their hearts. No peculiar
directions were therefore given to them, excepting only
these three:—

First. Let nothing spoken in this society be spoken again.
(Hereby we had the more full confidence in each other).

Secondly. Every member agrees to submit to his minister
in all indifferent things.

Thirdly. Every member will bring, once a week, all he
can spare toward a common stock.

4. Everyone here has an equal liberty of speaking, there
being none greater or less than another. I could say freely
to these, when they were met together, "Ye may all pro-
phesy one by one," (taking that word in its lowest sense,)

"that all may learn, and all may be comforted." And I often found the advantage of such a free conversation, and that "in the multitude of counsellors there is safety." Any who is inclined to do so is likewise encouraged to pour out his soul to God. And here especially we have found, that "the effectual fervent prayer of a righteous man availeth much."

iii. The Conference
(Struggles and Development, 1742-1744).

Mar. 19, 1742. WJJS, II, 534 f.

I rode once more to Pensford,[23] at the earnest request of several serious people. The place where they desired me to preach was a little green spot near the town. But I had no sooner begun than a great company of rabble, hired (as we afterwards found) for that purpose, came furiously upon us, bringing a bull, which they had been baiting, and now strove to drive in among the people. But the beast was wiser than his drivers; and continually ran either on one side of us or the other, while we quietly sang praise to God, and prayed for about an hour. The poor wretches, finding themselves disappointed, at length seized upon the bull, now weak and tired, after having been so long torn and beaten, both by dogs and men; and, by main strength, partly dragged and partly thrust him in among the people. When they had forced their way to the little table on which I stood, they strove several times to throw it down, by thrusting the helpless beast against it; who, of himself, stirred no more than a log of wood. I once or twice put aside his head with my hand, that the blood might not drop upon my clothes; intending to go on as soon as the hurry should be a little over. But, the table falling down, some of our friends caught me in their arms and carried me right away on their shoulders; while the rabble wreaked their vengeance on the table, which they tore bit from bit. We went a little way off, where I finished my discourse without any noise or interruption.

London. Mar. 25, 1742. WJJS, II, 535.

I appointed several earnest and sensible men to meet me, to whom I showed the great difficulty I had long found of knowing the people who desired to be under my care. After much discourse, they all agreed there could be no better way to come to a sure, thorough knowledge of each person than to divide them into classes, like those at Bristol, under the inspection of those in whom I could most confide. This was the origin of our classes at London, for which I can never sufficiently praise God, the unspeakable usefulness of the institution having ever since been more and more manifest.

Apr. 9, 1742. WJJS, II, 536.

We had the first watch-night in London. We commonly choose for this solemn service the Friday night nearest the full moon, either before or after, that those of the congregation who live at a distance may have light to their several homes. The service begins at half an hour past eight, and continues till a little after midnight. We have often found a peculiar blessing at these seasons. There is generally a deep awe upon the congregation, perhaps in some measure owing to the silence of the night, particularly in singing the hymn, with which we commonly conclude:

> *Hearken to the solemn voice,*
> *The awful midnight cry!*
> *Waiting souls, rejoice, rejoice,*
> *And feel the Bridegroom nigh.*

Birstall.[24] May 25, 1742. WJJS, III, 11 ff.

I set out early in the morning with John Taylor (since

settled in London), and *Wednesday* the 26th, in the evening, reached Birstall, six miles beyond Wakefield.

John Nelson had wrote to me some time before; but at that time I had little thought of seeing him. Hearing he was at home, I sent for him to our inn; whence he immediately carried me to his house, and gave me an account of the strange manner wherein he had been led on, from the time of our parting at London.

I preached at noon, on the top of Birstall Hill, to several hundreds of plain people; and spent the afternoon in talking severally with those who had tasted of the grace of God.

Newcastle. May 28, 1742. WJJS, III, 13 f.

We came to Newcastle about six, and, after a short refreshment, walked into the town. I was surprised: so much drunkenness, cursing, and swearing (even from mouths of little children) do I never remember to have seen and heard before, in so small a compass of time. Surely this place is ripe for Him who 'came not to call the righteous, but sinners to repentance.'

[May] 29. I was informed that one Mr. Hall[25] had been there about a year before, and had preached several times; but I could not learn that there was the least fruit of his labour; nor could I find any that desired to hear him again, nor any that appeared to care for such matters.

Newcastle. May 30, 1742. WJJS, III, 14 f.

At seven I walked down to Sandgate, the poorest and most contemptible part of the town, and, standing at the end of the street with John Taylor, began to sing the hundredth Psalm. Three or four people came out to see what was the matter, who soon increased to four or five hundred. I suppose there might be twelve to fifteen hundred before I had done preaching; to whom I applied those solemn words: 'He was wounded for our transgressions, He was bruised for our iniquities: the chastisement of our peace was upon Him; and by His stripes we are healed.'

Observing the people, when I had done, to stand gaping and staring upon me with the most profound astonishment, I told them, 'If you desire to know who I am, my name is John Wesley. At five in the evening, with God's help, I design to preach here again.'

At five the hill on which I designed to preach was covered from the top to the bottom. I never saw so large a number of people together, either in Moorfields or at Kennington Common. I knew it was not possible for the one half to hear, although my voice was then strong and clear; and I stood so as to have them all in view, as they were ranged on the side of the hill. The word of God which I set before them was 'I will heal their backsliding, I will love them freely.' After preaching the poor people were ready to tread me under-foot, out of pure love and kindness. It was some time before I could possibly get out of the press. I then went back another way than I came; but several were got to our inn before me, by whom I was vehemently importuned to stay with them, at least, a few days; or, however, one day more. But I could not consent, having given my word to be at Birstall, with God's leave, on Tuesday night.

June 1, 1742. WJJS, III, 15.

As we were riding through Knaresborough,[26] not intending to stop there, a young man stopped me in the street and earnestly desired me to go to his house. I did so. He told me our talking with a man, as we went through the town before, had set many in a flame; and that the sermon we gave him had travelled from one end of the town to the other. While I was with him a woman came and desired to speak with me. I went to her house, whither five or six of her friends came, one of whom had been long under deep conviction. We spent an hour in prayer, and all our spirits were refreshed.

Epworth. June 5, 1742. WJJS, III, 18.

I rode for Epworth. Before we came thither, I made an end of Madam Guyon's *Short Method of Prayer,* and *Les Torrents Spirituelles.* Ah, my brethren! I can answer your riddle, now I have ploughed with your heifer. The very words I have so often heard some of you use are not your own, no more than they are God's. They are only retailed from this poor Quietist, and that with the utmost faithfulness. Oh that ye knew how much God is wiser than man! Then would you drop Quietists and Mystics together, and at all hazards keep to the plain, practical, written Word of God.

It being many years since I had been in Epworth before, I went to an inn in the middle of the town, not knowing whether there were any left in it now who would not be ashamed of my acquaintance. But an old servant of my father's, with two or three poor women, presently found me out. I asked her, 'Do you know any in Epworth who are in earnest to be saved?' She answered, 'I am, by the grace of God; and I know I am saved through faith.' I asked, 'Have you, then, the peace of God? Do you know that He has forgiven your sins?' She replied, 'I thank God, I know it well. And many here can say the same thing.'

Epworth. June 6, 1742. WJJS, III, 18 f.

A little before the service began I went to Mr. Romley, the curate, and offered to assist him either by preaching or reading prayers; but he did not care to accept of my assistance. The church was exceeding full in the afternoon, a rumour being spread that I was to preach. But the sermon on 'Quench not the Spirit' was not suitable to the expectation of many of the hearers. Mr. Romley told them one of the most dangerous ways of quenching the Spirit was by enthusiasm; and enlarged on the character of an enthusiast in a very florid and oratorical manner. After sermon John Taylor stood in the churchyard, and gave notice, as the people were coming out, 'Mr. Wesley, not being permitted to preach in the church, designs to preach here at six o'clock.'

Accordingly at six I came, and found such a congregation as I believe Epworth never saw before. I stood near the east end of the church, upon my father's tombstone, and cried, 'The kingdom of heaven is not meat and drink; but righteousness, and peace, and joy in the Holy Ghost.'

Epworth. June 9, 1742. WJJS, III, 20.

I rode over to a neighbouring town to wait upon a Justice of Peace, a man of candour and understanding; before whom (I was informed) their angry neighbours had carried a whole wagon-load of these new heretics. But when he asked what they had done there was a deep silence; for that was a point their conductors had forgot. At length one said, 'Why, they pretended to be better than other people; and, besides, they prayed from morning to night.' Mr. S[tovin] asked, 'But have they done nothing besides?' 'Yes, sir,' said an old man: 'an't please your worship, they have *converted* my wife. Till she went among them, she had such a tongue! And now she is as quiet as a lamb.' 'Carry them back, carry them back,' replied the Justice, 'and let them convert all the scolds in the town.'

Epworth. June 12, 1742. WJJS, III, 23 f.

I preached on the righteousness of the law and the righteousness of faith. While I was speaking, several dropped down as dead, and among the rest such a cry was heard of sinners groaning for the righteousness of faith as almost drowned my voice. But many of these soon lifted up their heads with joy, and broke out into thanksgiving, being assured they now had the desire of their soul—the forgiveness of their sins.

I observed a gentleman there who was remarkable for not pretending to be of any religion at all. I was informed he had not been at public worship of any kind for upwards of thirty years. Seeing him stand as motionless as a statue, I asked him abruptly, 'Sir, are you a sinner?' He replied, with a deep and broken voice, 'Sinner enough'; and continued staring upwards till his wife and a servant or two who were all in tears, put him into his chaise and carried him home.

London. July 20, 1742. WJJS, III, 29.

I found my mother on the borders of eternity. But she had no doubt or fear; nor any desire but (as soon as God should call) 'to depart, and to be with Christ.'

London. July 23, 1742. WJJS, III, 29 ff.

About three in the afternoon I went to my mother, and found her change was near. I sat down on the bed-side. She was in her last conflict; unable to speak, but, I believe, quite sensible. Her look was calm and serene, and her eyes fixed upward, while we commended her soul to God. From three to four the silver cord was loosing and the wheel breaking at the cistern; and then, without any struggle, or sigh, or groan, the soul was set at liberty. We stood round the bed, and fulfilled her last request, uttered a little before she lost her speech: 'Children, as soon as I am released, sing a psalm of praise to God.'

Aug. 1. Almost an innumerable company of people being gathered together, about five in the afternoon I committed to the earth the body of my mother, to sleep with her fathers. The portion of Scripture from which I afterward spoke was, 'I saw a great white throne, and him that sat on it, from whose face the earth and the heaven fled away; and there was found no place for them. And I saw the dead, small and great, stand before God; and the books were opened: and the dead was judged out of those things which were written in the books, according to their works.' It was one of the most solemn assemblies I ever saw, or expect to see on this side eternity.[27]

Howell Harris' Christian brotherliness had kept him from joining in the attack of Whitefield and Cennick on the Wesleys. Calvinists have an invincible repugnance to the doctrines of Christian perfection which the Wesleys professed; but evidently the letter to which this was an answer had made as large concessions as possible in that direction. Wesley found them sufficient, and in his reply used words that have become famous—though they are quoted more frequently than accurately.

JOHN WESLEY TO HOWELL HARRIS. London. Aug. 6, 1742. WJL, II, 8.

I have just read yours dated at Trevecca, October 19, 1741. And what is it that we contend about? Allow such a perfection as you have there described, and all farther dispute I account vain jangling and mere strife of words. As to the other point, we agree (1) that no man can have any power except it be given him from above; (2) that no man can merit anything but hell, seeing all other merit is in the blood of the Lamb . . . Why then, . . . what need of this great gulf to be fixed between us? Brother, is thy heart with mine, as my heart is with thy heart? If it be, give me thy hand. . . . Let us rise up together against the evildoers. Let us not weaken, but (if it be our Lord's will) strengthen one another's hands in God.

London. Sept. 4, 1742. WJJS, III, 42 f.

I was pressed to visit a poor murderer in Newgate, who was much afflicted both in body and soul. I objected, It could not be; for all the turnkeys, as well as the keeper,

were so good Christians, they abhorred the name of a
Methodist, and had absolutely refused to admit me even
to one who earnestly begged it the morning he was to die.
However, I went, and found, by a surprising turn, that all
the doors were now open to me. I exhorted the sick male-
factor to cry unto God with all his might for grace to repent and believe the Gospel. It was not long before the rest
of the felons flocked round, to whom I spoke strong words
concerning the Friend of sinners, which they received with
as great signs of amazement as if it had been a voice from
heaven. When I came down into the Common Hall (I
think they called it), one of the prisoners there asking me
a question, gave me occasion to speak among them also;
more and more still running together, while I declared
God was 'not willing any of them should perish, but that
all should come to repentance.'

London. Nov. 3, 1742. WJJS, III, 49 f.

Two of those who are called *Prophets* desired to speak
with me. They told me they were sent from God with a
message to me; which was that very shortly I should be
born'd again. One of them added they would stay in the
house till it was done, unless I turned them out. I answered
gravely, 'I will not turn you out,' and showed them down
into the society-room. It was tolerably cold; and they had
neither meat nor drink: however, there they sat from morning to evening. They then went quietly away, and I have
heard nothing from them since.

London. Feb. 5, 1743. WCJ, I, 305.

One among the classes told my brother she had a constant
sense of forgiveness, and he let her pass. I could not help
proving her farther; and then the justified sinner appeared
full of the gall of bitterness; said again and again of a
sister present, "I do not love her; I hate her," &c. I assured

her, if an angel from heaven told me she was justified, I would not believe him; for she was a murderer. As such we prayed for her; and she was convinced of unbelief. I fear we have many such believers among us.

THE "RULES OF THE UNITED SOCIETIES."

Of the next two extracts, the first is included primarily for the date. It is the notice in the Journal *of the first presentation to the Methodists of the Rules by which their lives were to be guided, and which, under the name of the General Rules, still form a part of the Methodist Discipline. The second extract comes from a little pamphlet, published at Newcastle in 1743, called* The Nature, Design and General Rules of the United Societies in London, Bristol, Kingswood and Newcastle-upon-Tyne. *Only that part of it is given which contains the Rules themselves.*[28]

The promulgation of these Rules was another step in Wesley's attempt to weed out unrepentant 'disorderly walkers' from membership in the Societies. There was some complaint by those who were then members that such rules should be imposed after they had joined; but Wesley pointed out (and he was to stress it all his life long) that the only condition for joining was "a desire to flee from the wrath to come." Continuance in membership was, however, to be dependent on the observance of the Rules. The issuing of the Rules also constitutes a long step forward in the formation of the "Connection."

Newcastle. Mar. 6, 1743. WJJS, III, 68.

I read over in the society the rules which all our members are to observe; and desired every one seriously to consider whether he was willing to conform thereto or no. That this would shake many of them I knew well; and therefore, on *Monday* the 7th, I began visiting the classes again, lest 'that which is lame should be turned out of the way.'

Simon, JWMS, p. 101 ff.

4. There is one only condition previously required in those who desire admission into these Societies, *a desire to flee from the wrath to come, to be saved from their sins.* But wherever this is really fixed in the soul, it will be shown by its fruits. It is therefore expected of all who continue therein, that they should continue to evidence their desire of salvation,

First, by doing no harm, by avoiding evil in every kind; especially that which is most generally practised. Such is:

The taking the name of God in vain;

The profaning the day of the Lord, either by doing ordinary work thereon, or by buying or selling;

Drunkenness, *buying or selling spirituous liquors;* or *drinking them* (unless in cases of extreme necessity) ;

Fighting, quarrelling, brawling; *going to law;* returning evil for evil or railing for railing; the *using many words* in buying or selling;

The buying or selling uncustomed[29] goods;

The giving or taking things on usury;

Uncharitable or unprofitable conversation;

Doing to others as we would not they should do unto us;

Doing what we know is not for the glory of God: as

The *putting on of gold, or costly apparel;*

The *taking such diversions* as cannot be used in the name of the Lord Jesus;

The *singing* those *songs,* or *reading* those *books,* which do not tend to the knowledge or love of God;

Softness, and needless self-indulgence;

Laying up treasures upon earth.

5. It is expected of all who continue in these Societies

that they should continue to evidence their desire of salvation,

Secondly, By doing good; by being, in every kind, merciful after their power; as they have opportunity, doing good of every possible sort, and as far as possible, to all men:

To their bodies, of the ability which God giveth, by giving food to the hungry, by clothing the naked, by visiting or helping them that are sick, or in prison.

To their souls, by instructing, *reproving,* or exhorting all we have any intercourse with; trampling underfoot that enthusiastic doctrine of devils, that 'we are not to do unless *our heart is free to it.*'

By doing good, especially, to them that are of the household of faith, or groaning so to be; employing them preferably to others, buying one of another, helping each other in business; and that so much the more because the world will love its own, and them only.

By all possible *diligence and frugality,* that the Gospel be not blamed.

By running with patience the race that is set before them; *denying themselves* and taking up their cross daily; submitting to bear the reproach of Christ, to be as the filth and offscouring of the world; and that men should *say all manner of evil of them falsely, for their Lord's sake.*

6. It is expected of all who desire to continue in these Societies that they should continue to evidence their desire of salvation.

Thirdly, By attending upon all the ordinances of God; such are:

The public worship of God;

The ministry of the word, either read or expounded;

The supper of the Lord;

Private prayer;

Searching the Scriptures; and fasting, or abstinence.

7. These are the General Rules of our Societies; all

which we are taught of God to observe, even in His written word; the only rule, and the sufficient rule, both of our faith and practice; and all these we know His Spirit writes on every truly awakened heart. If there be any among us who observe them not, who habitually break any one of them, let it be made known unto him who watches over that soul, as one that must give an account. I will admonish him of the error of his ways. I will bear with him for a season. But if, then, he repent not, he hath no more place among us. We have delivered our souls.

JOHN WESLEY

February 23, 1742-3.

Mar. 12, 1743. WJJS, III, 69 ff.

I concluded my second course of visiting, in which I inquired particularly into two things: (1) The case of those who had almost every night the last week cried out aloud during the preaching; (2) The number of those who were separated from us, and the reason and occasion of it.

As to the former I found:

1. That all of them (I think, not one excepted) were persons in perfect health; and had not been subject to fits of any kind, till they were thus affected.

2. That this had come upon every one of them in a moment, without any previous notice, while they were either hearing the word of God or thinking on what they had heard.

3. That in that moment they dropped down, lost all their strength, and were seized with violent pain.

This they expressed in different manners. Some said they felt just as if a sword was running through them; others, that they thought a great weight lay upon them, as if it would squeeze them into the earth. Some said they were quite choked, so that they could not breathe; others, that their hearts swelled ready to burst; and others that it was as if their heart, as if their inside, as if their whole body, was tearing all to pieces.

These symptoms I can no more impute to any natural cause than to the Spirit of God. I can make no doubt but it was Satan tearing them, as they were coming to Christ.[30] And hence proceeded those grievous cries, whereby he might design both to discredit the work of God and to affright fearful people from hearing that word whereby their souls might be saved.

As to the latter, I observed the number of those who had left the society since December 30 was seventy-six:

Fourteen of these (chiefly Dissenters) said they left it because otherwise their ministers would not give them the sacrament.

Nine more, because their husbands or wives were not willing they should stay in it.

Twelve, because their parents were not willing.

Five, because their master and mistress would not let them come.

Seven, because their acquaintance persuaded them to leave it.

Five, because people said such bad things of the society.

Nine, because they would not be laughed at.

Three, because they would not lose the poor's allowance.

Three more, because they could not spare time to come.

Two, because it was too far off.

One, because she was afraid of falling into fits.

One, because people were so rude in the street.

Two, because Thomas Naisbit was in the society.

One, because he would not turn his back on his baptism.

One, because we were mere Church of England men. And,

One, because it was time enough to serve God yet.

The number of those who were expelled the society was sixty-four:

Two for cursing and swearing.

Two for habitual Sabbath breaking.
Seventeen for drunkenness.
Two for retailing spirituous liquors.
Three for quarrelling and brawling.
One for beating his wife.
Three for habitual, wilful lying.
Four for railing and evil-speaking.
One for idleness and laziness. And,
Nine-and-twenty for lightness and carelessness.

Mar. 13, 1743. WJJS, III, 71.

I went in the morning in order to speak severally with
the members of the society at Tanfield. From the terrible
instances I met with here (and indeed in all parts of England), I am more and more convinced that the devil himself desires nothing more than this, that the people of any
place should be half-awakened and then left to themselves
to fall asleep again. Therefore I determine, by the grace
of God, not to strike one stroke in any place where I cannot
follow the blow.

Burtley. Mar. 28, 1743. WJJS, III, 72 f.

I was astonished to find it was real fact (what I would
not believe before) that three of the Dissenting ministers
(Mr. A[rthur], Mr. A[itkin], and Mr. B[ruce]) had agreed
together to exclude all those from the Holy Communion
who would not refrain from hearing us.

PORTENTS OF TROUBLE IN STAFFORDSHIRE. Wednesbury.
Apr. 15, 1743. WJJS, III, 74 f.

I rode in two days to Wednesbury, but found things
surprisingly altered. The inexcusable folly of Mr. [Robert]
W[illiams][31] had so provoked Mr. E[gginto]n[32] that his
former love was turned into bitter hatred. But he had not
yet had time to work up the poor people into the rage and

madness which afterwards appeared;[33] so that they were extremely quiet both this and the following days, while I improved the present opportunity, and exhorted them, morning and evening, to 'believe on the Lord Jesus,' and to 'work out their salvation with fear and trembling.'

Apr. 17, 1743. WJJS, III, 75.

Yet on *Sunday* the 17th the scene began to open; I think I never heard so wicked a sermon, and delivered with such bitterness of voice and manner, as that which Mr. E[gginto]n preached in the afternoon. I knew what effect this must have in a little time, and therefore judged it expedient to prepare the poor people for what was to follow; that, when it came, they might not be offended. Accordingly, on *Tuesday* the 19th I strongly enforced those words of our Lord, 'If any man come after Me, and hate not his father and mother . . . yea, and his own life, he cannot be My disciple. And whosoever doth not bear his cross, and come after Me, cannot be My disciple.'

While I was speaking a gentleman rode up very drunk, and, after many unseemly and bitter words, laboured much to ride over some of the people. I was surprised to hear he was a neighbouring clergyman. And this, too, is a man zealous for the Church! Ah, poor Church, if it stood in need of such defenders!

London. May 29, 1743. WJJS, III, 78.

(Being *Trinity Sunday*). — I began officiating at the chapel in West Street,[34] near the Seven Dials, of which (by a strange chain of providences) we have a lease for several years. I preached on the Gospel for the day, part of the third chapter of St. John; and afterwards administered the Lord's Supper to some hundreds of communicants.

John Wesley tried to be critical in examining claims to religious experience and the extraordinary accompanying effects; but Charles was more successful in his efforts. He had a clearer eye for the outcropping of the old Adam even in converts. It would not be true to say that these effects never appeared under his preaching, or that he had never regarded them as of divine origin;[35] *but he changed his mind sooner and more completely than his brother.*

June 4, 1743. WCJ, I, 314.

I went on at five expounding the Acts. Some stumbling-blocks, with the help of God, I have removed, particularly the fits. Many, no doubt, were, at our first preaching, struck down, both soul and body, into the depth of distress. Their *outward affections* were easy to be imitated. Many counterfeits I have already detected. Today, one who came from the alehouse, drunk, was pleased to fall into a fit for my entertainment, and beat himself heartily. I thought it a pity to hinder him; so, instead of singing over him, as had been often done, we left him to recover at his leisure. Another, a girl, as she began her cry, I ordered to be carried out. Her convulsion was so violent, as to take away the use of her limbs, till they laid and left her without the door. Then immediately she found her legs, and walked off. Some very unstill sisters, who always took care to stand near me, and tried which should cry loudest, since I had them removed out of my sight, have been as quiet as lambs. The first night I preached here, half my words were lost through their outcries. Last night, before I began, I gave public notice, that whosoever cried so as to drown my voice, should, without any man's hurting or judging them, be gently carried to the farthest corner of the room. But my porters had no employment the whole night; yet the Lord was with us, mightily convincing of sin and of righteousness.

June 13, 1743. WCJ, I, 315 f.

Be not over-sure that so many are justified. By their

fruits you shall know them. You will see reason to be more and more deliberate in the judgment you pass on souls. Wait for their conversation. I do not know whether we can infallibly pronounce *at the time* that any one is justified. I once thought several in that state, who, I am now convinced, were only under the drawings of the Father. . . .

June 15. I observed at Newcastle that many more of the gentry come now the stumbling-block of the fits is taken out of their way; and I am more and more convinced it was a device of Satan to stop the course of the Gospel. Since I have preached it, if I can discern anything, it never had greater success than at this time. Yet we have no fits among us, and I have done nothing to prevent them, only declared that I do not think the better of any one for crying out or interrupting my work.

London. June 18, 1743. WJJS, III, 79.

I received a full account of the terrible riots which had been in Staffordshire. I was not surprised at all; neither should I have wondered if, after the advices they had so often received from the pulpit, as well as from the episcopal chair, the zealous High Churchmen had rose, and cut all that were Methodists in pieces.

June 20. Resolving to assist them as far as I could, I set out early in the morning, and, after preaching at Wycombe about noon, in the evening came to Oxford.

THE MOB AND THE MAGISTRATES.

At first Wesley had doubts as to whether he and his people should seek the protection and redress of the law in case of violent attacks. The Rules of the United Societies as first drawn up forbade it altogether.[36] In March, 1744, Whitefield obtained redress for damage done to persons and property in a Gloucestershire riot, but only after appealing to the King's Bench. Later that same year, at

*the first Wesleyan Conference the question came up and was
given only a hesitating answer.*[37] *Later still the General
Rule on the subject was amended to prohibit only "brother
going to law with brother."*[38] *In the instance recorded below Wesley left the prosecution in the hands of one of the
local Methodists, who complained in vain; no appeal was
made.*[39]

June 21, 1743. WJJS, III, 79 f.

We rode to Birmingham; and in the morning, *Wednesday* the 22nd, to Francis Ward's, at Wednesbury.

Although I knew all that had been done here[40] was as
contrary to law as it was to justice and mercy, yet I knew
not how to advise the poor sufferers, or to procure them
any redress. I was then little acquainted with the English
course of law, having long had scruples concerning it; but,
as many of these were now removed, I thought it best to
inquire whether there could be any help from the laws of
the land. I therefore rode over to Counsellor Littleton, at
Tamworth, who assured us we might have an easy remedy
if we resolutely prosecuted, in the manner the law directed,
those rebels against God and the King.

PEACE PROPOSALS REBUFFED.

*Wesley was not reconciled to the divisions in the revival
forces, and prepared for a conference to explore the pos-
sibilities of reunion. At the same time, John Cennick,
who was then on his way over from Calvinism to Moravianism favored the step. As part of his preparation Wesley
drew up a series of doctrinal statements in which he made
considerable concessions to Calvinism.*[41] *It was of this series
that the first conference gave an affirmative answer to the
question, "Have we not unawares leaned too much toward
Calvinism?"*[42] *John's statement and the three fatiguing*

journeys were all in vain, however. The Moravians had set
conditions which showed that they really were seeking
recognition from the Established Church, not union with
the Methodists.[43] *Of the failure to meet with the Calvinists*
nothing is said in either Journal. Tyerman, without giv-
ing his authority merely says, "Whitefield, who was then
in London, seems to have declined the invitation."[44]

Aug. 7, 1743. WCJ, I, 333 f.

At four we rode on to Mitchel; my brother having summoned me to London, to confer with the heads of the Moravians and predestinarians. We had near three hundred
miles to ride in five days. I was willing to undertake this
labour for peace, though the journey was too great for us
and our weary beasts, which we have used almost every day
for these three months.

[Aug.] 12. By nine at night I hardly reached the Foundery. Here I heard the Moravians would not be present at
the conference. Spangenberg, indeed, *said* he would, but
immediately left England. My brother was come from Newcastle, John Nelson from Yorkshire, and I from the Land's-
end, to good purpose.

Aug. 22, 1743. WJJS, III, 83.

After a few of us had joined in prayer, about four I set
out, and rode softly to Snow Hill, where, the saddle slip-
ping quite upon my mare's neck, I fell over her head, and
she ran back into Smithfield. Some boys caught her and
brought her to me again, cursing and swearing all the way.
I spoke plainly to them, and they promised to amend. I
was setting forward when a man cried, 'Sir, you have lost
your saddlecloth.' Two or three more would needs help
me to put it on; but these, too, swore at almost every word.
I turned to one and another, and spoke in love. They all
took it well, and thanked me much. I gave them two or

three little books, which they promised to read over carefully.

Before I reached Kensington I found my mare had lost a shoe. This gave me an opportunity of talking closely, for near half an hour, both to the smith and his servant. I mention these little circumstances to show how easy it is to redeem every fragment of time (if I may so speak) when we feel any love to those souls for which Christ died.

Cornwall. Sept. 16, 1743. WJJS, III, 93.

I preached to four or five hundred on St. Hilary Downs, and many seemed amazed; but I could find none as yet who had any deep or lasting conviction.

In the evening, as I was preaching at St. Ives, Satan began to fight for his kingdom. The mob of the town burst into the room and created much disturbance, roaring and striking those that stood in their way as though Legion himself possessed them. I would fain have persuaded our people to stand still; but the zeal of some, and the fear of others, had no ears: so that, finding the uproar increase, I went into the midst, and brought the head of the mob up with me to the desk. I received but one blow on the side of the head; after which we reasoned the case, till he grew milder and milder, and at length undertook to quiet his companions.

Bristol. Oct. 3, 1743. WJJS, III, 97.

I returned to Bristol, and employed several days in examining and purging the society, which still consisted (after many were put away) of more than seven hundred persons. The next week I examined the society in Kingswood, in which I found but a few things to reprove.

Oct. 15, 1743. WJJS, III, 97.

The leaders brought in what had been contributed in

their several classes toward the public debt: and we found it was sufficient to discharge it, which was therefore done without delay.

Oct. 20, 1743. WCJ, I, 337.

I preached at Nottingham-cross, and met the Society we began half a year ago, increased from eleven to fifty. They have been sifted like wheat by their two potent enemies, stillness and predestination.

MOB VIOLENCE IN STAFFORDSHIRE.

The period of the most intense mob violence against the Methodists lasted from 1743 to 1745; the severest outbreaks took place in Staffordshire and Cornwall. It is noteworthy that the Wesley brothers always got to the scene of violence as soon as they could. John's courage and coolness when the "seas began to lift up their voice" were nothing short of amazing. But perhaps Charles' conduct was even more admirable. He was, by his own admission, a timid man, yet went into danger nevertheless. In Staffordshire, in the very heart of England, trouble had been brewing since Williams' unfortunate sermon in the spring. Several visits by both the brothers had failed to allay the resentment of the brutal populace.

It is hard for us at this distance to account for such violent antipathy to a movement which was doing so much good. Often the outbursts of violence seemed quite spontaneous and without deliberate planning. Perhaps they were at such times just a vigorous expression of the love of brutal sports which characterized the age. Methodist-baiting was just a better sport than bear-baiting. But often—as here in Staffordshire—there was evidence of deliberate incitement by the community authorities. Several causes lay behind this. Even where there was not a pointed attack (like Williams') on the clergy, the very presence of these

*earnest preachers was a tacit reproach on their slackness.
They then found it easy to cloak their resentment behind
a cry of "The Church in danger," for the Church had a
place in the affections of her rough sons. They were ready
to spring to her defense when she was in danger, even
though they were not so eager to serve her in other ways.
Again, the charge of Popery clung to the Methodists in a
way which is comprehensible only when we remember that
the '45' was drawing near, and the public temper was on
edge. Papists were a danger to both State and Church.*

*The Methodists of the three towns of Wednesbury, Wal-
sall and Darlaston had already suffered in body and pos-
sessions from several outbreaks before the one described
here, in which Wesley himself was caught.*

Oct. 20, 1743. WJJS, III, 98 ff.

. . . I rode to Wednesbury. At twelve I preached in a
ground near the middle of the town to a far larger congregation than was expected, on 'Jesus Christ, the same
yesterday, and today, and for ever.' I believe every one
present felt the power of God; and no creature offered to
molest us, either going or coming; but the Lord fought for
us, and we held our peace.

I was writing at Francis Ward's in the afternoon when
the cry arose, that the mob had beset the house. We prayed
that God would disperse them, and it was so. One went this
way, and another that; so that, in half an hour, not a man
was left. I told our brethren, 'Now is the time for us to go';
but they pressed me exceedingly to stay; so, that I might
not offend them, I sat down, though I foresaw what would
follow. Before five the mob surrounded the house again
in greater numbers than ever. The cry of one and all was,
'Bring out the minister; we will have the minister.' I desired one to take their captain by the hand and bring him
into the house. After a few sentences interchanged between
us the lion was become a lamb. I desired him to go and

bring one or two more of the most angry of his companions. He brought in two, who were ready to swallow the
ground with rage; but in two minutes they were as calm
as he. I then bade them make way, that I might go out
among the people. As soon as I was in the midst of them I
called for a chair, and, standing up, asked, 'What do any
of you want with me?' Some said, 'We want you to go with
us to the Justice.' I replied, 'That I will, with all my heart.'
I then spoke a few words, which God applied; so that they
cried out with might and main, 'The gentleman is an
honest gentleman, and we will spill our blood in his defence.' I asked 'Shall we go to the justice to-night, or in
the morning?' Most of them cried, 'To-night, to-night';
on which I went before, and two or three hundred followed, the rest returning whence they came.

The night came on before we had walked a mile together with heavy rain. However, on we went to Bentley
Hall, two miles from Wednesbury. One or two ran before
to tell Mr. Lane they had brought Mr. Wesley before his
Worship. Mr. Lane replied, 'What have I to do with Mr.
Wesley? Go and carry him back again.' By this time the
main body came up, and began knocking at the door. A
servant told them Mr. Lane was in bed. His son followed,
and asked what was the matter. One replied, 'Why, an't
please you, they sing psalms all day; nay, and make folks
rise at five in the morning. And what would your Worship
advise us to do?' 'To go home,' said Mr. Lane, 'and be
quiet.'

Here they were at a full stop, till one advised to go to
Justice Persehouse at Walsall. All agreed to this; so we
hastened on, and about seven came to his house. But Mr.
P[ersehouse] likewise sent word that he was in bed. Now
they were at a stand again; but at last they all thought it
the wisest course to make the best of their way home. About
fifty of them undertook to convoy me. But we had not
gone a hundred yards when the mob of Walsall came, pour-

ing in like a flood, and bore down all before them. The Darlaston mob made what defence they could; but they were weary, as well as outnumbered: so that in a short time, many being knocked down, the rest ran away, and left me in their hands.

To attempt speaking was vain, for the noise on every side was like the roaring of the sea. So they dragged me along till we came to the town, where, seeing the door of a large house open, I attempted to go in; but a man, catching me by the hair, pulled me back into the middle of the mob. They made no more stop till they had carried me through the main street, from one end of the town to the other. I continued speaking all the time to those within hearing, feeling no pain or weariness. At the west end of the town, seeing a door half open, I made toward it, and would have gone in, but a gentleman in the shop would not suffer me, saying they would pull the house down to the ground. However, I stood at the door and asked, 'Are you willing to hear me speak?' Many cried out, 'No, no! knock his brains out; down with him; kill him at once.' Others said, 'Nay, but we will hear him first.' I began asking, 'What evil have I done? Which of you all have I wronged in word or deed?' And continued speaking for above a quarter of an hour, till my voice suddenly failed. Then the floods began to lift up their voice again, many crying out, 'Bring him away! bring him away!'

In the mean time my strength and my voice returned, and I broke out aloud into prayer. And now the man who just before headed the mob turned and said, 'Sir, I will spend my life for you: follow me, and not one soul here shall touch a hair of your head.' Two or three of his fellows confirmed his words, and got close to me immediately. At the same time, the gentleman in the shop cried out, 'For shame, for shame! Let him go.' An honest butcher, who was a little farther off said it was a shame they should do thus; and pulled back four or five, one after another, who were running on the most fiercely. The people then, as if it had been by common consent, fell back to the right and left; while those three or four men took me between them, and carried me through them all. But on the bridge the mob rallied again: we therefore went on one side over the mill-dam, and thence through the meadows, till, a little before ten, God brought me safe to Wednesbury, having lost only one flap of my waistcoat and a little skin from one of my hands.

I never saw such a chain of providences before; so many convincing proofs that the hand of God is on every person and thing, overruling all as it seemeth Him good.

The poor woman of Darlaston who had headed that mob, and sworn that none should touch me, when she saw her followers give way, ran into the thickest of the throng, and knocked down three or four men, one after another. But many assaulting her at once, she was soon overpowered, and had probably been killed in a few minutes (three men keeping her down and beating her with all their might) had not a man called to one of them, 'Hold, Tom, hold!' 'Who is there?' said Tom. 'What, honest Munchin? Nay, then, let her go.' So they held their hand, and let her get up and crawl home as well as she could.

From the beginning to the end I found the same presence of mind as if I had been sitting in my own study. But I took no thought for one moment before another; only once it came into my mind that if they should throw me into the river, it would spoil the papers that were in my pocket. For myself, I did not doubt that I should swim across, having but a thin coat and a light pair of boots.

The circumstances which follow, I thought, were particularly remarkable: (1) That many endeavoured to throw me down while we were going down-hill on a slippery path to the town; as well judging, that if I was once on the ground, I should hardly rise any more. But I made no stumble at all, nor the least slip till I was entirely out of their hands. (2) That although many strove to lay hold on my collar or clothes, to pull me down, they could not fasten at all; only one got fast hold of the flap of my waistcoat, which was soon left in his hand; the other flap, in the pocket of which was a bank note, was torn but half off. (3) That a lusty man just behind struck at me several times with a large oaken stick; with which, if he had struck me once on the back part of my head, it would have saved him all farther trouble. But every time the blow was turned aside, I knew not how; for I could not move to the right hand or left. (4) That another came rushing through the press, and, raising his arm to strike, on a sudden let it drop, and only stroked my head, saying, 'What soft hair he has!' (5) That I stopped exactly at the mayor's door, as if I had known it (which the mob doubtless thought I did), and found him standing in the shop, which gave the first check to the madness of the people. (6) That the very first men whose hearts were turned were the heroes of the town, the captains of the rabble on all occasions, one of them having been a prize-fighter at the beer-garden. (7) That, from first to last, I heard none give a reviling word, or call me by any opprobrious name whatever; but the cry of one and all was, 'The preacher! The preacher! The parson! The minister!' (8) That no creature, at least within my hearing, laid any thing to my charge, either true or false; having in the hurry quite forgot to provide themselves with an accusation of any kind. And lastly, that they were as utterly at a loss what they should do with me; none proposing any determinate thing; only, 'Away with him! Kill him at once!'

By how gentle degrees does God prepare us for His will! Two years ago a piece of brick grazed my shoulders. It was a year after that the stone struck me between the eyes. Last month I received one blow, and this evening two; one before we came into the town, and one after we were gone out; but both were as nothing: for though one man struck me on the breast with all his might, and the other on the mouth with such a force that the blood gushed out immediately, I felt no more pain from either of the blows than if they had touched me with a straw.

It ought not to be forgotten that, when the rest of the society made all haste to escape for their lives, four only would not stir—William Sitch, Edward Slater, John Griffiths, and Joan Parks; these kept with me, resolving to live or die together; and none of them received one blow but William Sitch, who held me by the arm, from one end of the town to the other. He was then dragged away, and knocked down; but he soon rose and got to me again. I afterwards asked him what he expected when the mob came upon us. He said, 'To die for Him who had died for us.' And he felt no hurry or fear; but calmly waited till God should require his soul of him.

I cannot close this head without inserting as great a curiosity in its kind as, I believe, was ever yet seen in England; which had its birth within a very few days of this remarkable occurrence at Walsall.

"Staffordshire.

"To all High Constables, Petty Constables, and other of His Majesty's Peace Officers, within the said County, and particularly to the Constable of Tipton (near Walsall) :

"Whereas we, his Majesty's Justices of the Peace for the said County of Stafford, have received information that several disorderly persons, styling themselves Methodist Preachers, go about raising routs and riots, to the great damage of His Majesty's liege people, and against the peace of our Sovereign Lord the King:

"These are, in his Majesty's name, to command you and every one of you, within your respective districts, to make diligent search after the said Methodist Preachers, and to bring him or them before some of us his said Majesty's Justices of the Peace, to be examined concerning their unlawful doings.

"Given under our hands and seals, this [12th] day of October, 1743.

"J. LANE.
"W. PERSEHOUSE."

(N. B.—The very Justices to whose houses I was carried, and who severally refused to see me!)

Wednesbury. Oct. 25, 1743. WCJ, I, 340.

I took several new members into the Society; and, among them, the young man whose arm was broke, and (upon trial) Munchin, the late captain of the mob. He has been constantly under the word since he rescued my brother. I asked him what he thought of him. "Think of him!" said he: "That he is a mon of God; and God was on his side, when so mony of us could not kill one mon."

Feb. 6, 1744. WCJ, I, 348.

Brother Webb would needs ride through the market-place, to see the flag and paper our enemies had set up,— and to show his courage. Had he returned with a broken head, I should not have greatly pitied him. By six our Lord brought us safe to Nottingham.

During most of this decade England was at war with France in the conflict known as the War of the Austrian Succession. Largely fought to preserve the "balance of power" it was further complicated by the fact that the "Young Pretender" was being sheltered, and his claim to the English throne backed, by the French King. "Bonnie Prince Charlie," as a Stuart, enjoyed the persistent loyalty of many of the Scottish clans, and as a Catholic felt he might have help also from the Irish. This explains the excited state of the public mind in England at the time. The Pretender tried during this year to land, but as the French fleet was caught in a storm, he did not succeed. Only after his actual landing in 1745 had proved that the help he hoped for from Scots, Irish and Jacobites all together was insufficient, was public apprehension allayed.

London. Feb. 15, 1744. WJJS, III, 116.

We were informed of the invasion intended by the French, who were expected to land every hour. I therefore exhorted the congregation, in the words of our Lord, Luke xxi. 36: 'Watch ye therefore, and pray always, that ye may be accounted worthy to escape all these things that shall come to pass, and to stand before the Son of Man.'

Feb. 18, 1744. WJJS, III, 117.

I received an account, from James Jones, of another kind of invasion in Staffordshire. The substance of it was as follows:

"On Monday, *January* 23, a great mob gathered together at Darlaston, a mile from Wednesbury. They fell upon a few people who were going to Wednesbury, and, amongst the rest, on Joshua Constable's wife, of Darlaston. Some of them threw her down, and five or six held her down, that another might force her. But she continued to resist till they changed their purpose, beat her much, and went away.

"Mon. 30.—The mob gathered again, broke into Joshua Constable's house, pulled part of it down, broke some of his goods in pieces, and carried the rest away: particularly all his shop-goods, to a considerable value. But not satisfied with this they sought for him and his wife, swearing they would knock their brains out. Their little children, meantime, as well as themselves, wandered up and down, no one daring to relieve or take them in, lest they should hazard their own lives.

"Tues. 31.—About a hundred of the mob met together on the Church Hill at Wednesbury. But hearing some of Wednesbury were resolved to defend themselves they dispersed for that time.

"*February*, Wed. 1.—Mr. Charles Wesley came to Birmingham, and the next day preached at Wednesbury. The whole congregation was quiet and attentive, nor had we any noise or interruption."

MORE VIOLENCE IN STAFFORDSHIRE. Feb. 18, 1744. WJJS, III, 118 f.

"The mob had been gathering all Monday night, and on Tuesday morning they began their work. They assaulted, one after another, all the houses of those who were called Methodists. They first broke all their windows, suffering neither glass, lead, nor frames to remain therein. Then they made their way in; and all the tables, chairs, chests of drawers, with whatever was not easily removable, they dashed in pieces, particularly shop-goods, and furniture of every kind. What they could not well break, as feather-beds, they cut in pieces, and strewed about the room. William Sitch's wife was lying in; but that was all one; they pulled away her bed too, and cut it in pieces. (Had the French come in that place, would they have done more?) All this time none offered to resist them. Indeed most part, both men and women, fled for their lives; only the children stayed, not knowing whither to go.

"Wearing apparel, and things which were of value, or easily saleable, they carried away, every man loading himself with as much as he could well carry, of whatever he liked best.

"Some of the gentlemen who had set the mob to work, or threatened to turn away collier or miner out of their service that did not come and do his part, now drew up a paper for those of the society to sign, importing that they would never invite or receive any Methodist preacher more. On this condition, they told them they would stop the mob at once; otherwise they must take what followed.

"This they offered to several; but they declared, one and all, 'We have already lost all our goods, and nothing more can follow but the loss of our lives, which we will lose too, rather than wrong our consciences.'

"On Wednesday the mob divided into two or three companies, one of which went to Aldridge, [six] miles from Wednesbury, and plundered many houses there, as they had done in several other villages. Here also they loaded themselves with clothes and goods of all sorts, as much as they could stand under. They came back through Walsall with their spoils; but the gentlemen of Walsall being apprized of their coming, raised a body of men, who met them, took what they had away, and laid it up in the Town Hall. Notice was then sent to Aldridge that every man who had been plundered might come and take his own goods.

"Mr. Wood, of Wednesbury, likewise told several they should have what could be found of their goods, on condition they would promise not to receive or hear those preachers any more.

"On Friday, in the afternoon, I went to Birmingham, designing to go to Tipton Green; but, finding the mob were still raging up and down, I returned to Birmingham, and soon after (having as yet no more place in these parts) set out for London."

The charge of being "Papists" as applied to the Methodists seems to us absurd, but it was widely enough believed to make Wesley see the wisdom of taking every possible measure to avoid confirming it. The prevalence of this charge can be in part accounted for by the excited state of public opinion in a time of danger; doubtless it was nourished too by the apparently ubiquitous wanderings of the itinerant preachers. Perhaps the early morning meetings and Watch Night services late at night summoned up

imaginary terrors fed by a sort of racial memory of the se-
cret journeyings and plottings of the Jesuit emissaries in
the days of Elizabeth.

London. Feb. 27, 1744. WJJS, III, 122.

Mon. 27.—Was the day I had appointed to go out of
town; but understanding a Proclamation was just published, requiring all Papists to go out of London before the
Friday following, I was determined to stay another week,
that I might cut off all occasion of reproach. I was the more
willing to stay, that I might procure more raiment for the
poor before I left London.

For this purpose I made a second collection, which
amounted to about thirty pounds; but perceiving that the
whole money received would not answer one-third of the
expense, I determined to go round the classes, and beg for
the rest, till I had gone through the whole society.

Surrey. Mar. 20, 1744. WJJS, III, 125.

Having received a summons from the Justices of Surrey
to appear at their court, at St. Margaret's Hill, I did so;
and asked, 'Has any one any thing to lay to my charge?'
None made any reply. At length, one of the Justices said,
'Sir, are you willing to take the oaths to his Majesty, and
to sign the declaration against Popery?' I said, 'I am'; which
I accordingly did, and returned home.

Cornwall. Apr. 16, 1744. WJJS, III, 132.

In the afternoon we came again to Trewint. I learned
that notice had been given of my preaching that evening
in Laneast church, which was crowded exceedingly. Mr.
Bennet, the minister of Laneast, carried me afterward to
his house; and (though above seventy years old) came
with me in the morning to Trewint, where I had promised
to preach at five.

Before we parted Digory Isbel informed me of an accusation against me current in those parts. It was really one which I did not expect; no more than that other, vehemently asserted at St. Ives, of my bringing the Pretender with me thither last autumn, under the name of John Downes. It was that I called myself John Wesley; whereas everybody knew Mr. Wesley was dead.

Where the Methodists were in disfavor with the authorities, they were regarded as fair game for the press gangs, who forcibly recruited them for service in the army or navy against the French. John Nelson's story of his refusal to bear arms after being "pressed" into the army is vigorously told in his Journal.

Durham. June 11, 1744. WJJS, III, 141.

I left Newcastle, and in the afternoon met John Nelson, at Durham, with Thomas Beard; another quiet and peaceable man, who had lately been torn from his trade, and wife and children, and sent away as a soldier; that is, banished from all that was near and dear to him, and constrained to dwell among lions, for no other crime, either committed or pretended, than that of calling sinners to repentance. But his soul was in nothing terrified by his adversaries. Yet the body, after a while, sank under its burden. He was then lodged in the hospital at Newcastle, where he still praised God continually. His fever increasing, he was let blood. His arm festered, mortified, and was cut off: two or three days after which, God signed his discharge, and called him up to his eternal home.

London. Mar. 22, 1744. WJJS, III, 125.

I gave the society an account of what had been done with regard to the poor. By the contributions and collections I had received about one hundred and seventy pounds; with

which above three hundred and thirty poor had been provided with needful clothing. Thirty or forty remaining
still in want, and there being some debts for the clothes
already distributed, the next day, being *Good Friday,* I
made one collection more, of about six-and-twenty pounds.
This treasure, at least, 'neither rust nor moth' shall 'corrupt,' 'nor thieves break through and steal.'

THE CONFERENCE.

*In the summer of 1744 was held the first Conference, the
beginning of an unbroken series which have been held an-
nually ever since. The initiation of the Conference marked
the climax of the succession of new departures in organization and method which were to give Methodism its characteristic form in time to come. Now all the basic institutions were in place; subsequent developments were to be
but variations of forms already constructed.*

*An earlier project for a similar gathering had not come
to fruition. In 1739 Wesley agreed with two other evangelical clergymen to meet regularly "to fix then the business
to be done the ensuing year: where, when and by whom."*[45]
*Probably the unremitting exigencies of the revival pre-
vented the realization of this scheme. By 1744 the urgency
had somewhat relaxed; more consideration could now be
given to conserving the gains. Perhaps the impulse for the
holding of this Conference came from the example set by
the Calvinistic Methodists who had formally organized the
year before.*

*For a long time the status of the Conference was tenta-
tive only. Its regular continuance was due not to any regulation in a written code, but to its proved usefulness, and
the integration furnished by Wesley's masterful personality. On his mind and will it depended for its composition
and continuance.*[46] *It achieved what might be called con-
stitutional status only in 1784 when Wesley, beginning to*

consider the possibility of his removal from the scene, drew up the Deed of Declaration, which defined the Conference and made it the heir in law to all his powers.

The importance of the Conference in furthering the work can hardly be overestimated. It gave the preachers a sense of cohesiveness; it raised the standards of, and made for agreement in, teaching and practise through the whole connection; it made possible the most efficient disposition of the forces available; and finally, it provided a way of expressing corporate disapproval of those who persistently deviated from the standards set.

Wesley himself seems hardly to have been aware at first of the importance of the measure he had initiated. No annual Minutes of Conference were published for twenty years, till in 1765 the "Penny Minutes" began.[47] In 1749, however, two pamphlets were published in Dublin, containing "some of the proceedings of the Conferences that had been held." One of the pamphlets contained the doctrinal, another the disciplinary matter, and became the "Doctrinal Minutes" and (with later accretions) the "Disciplinary Minutes" respectively.[48]

Fortunately for our knowledge of the proceedings of the earliest Conferences, we have access to material written by participants and preserved in manuscript till it was printed late in the nineteenth century.[49] For the first Conference we have minutes taken down by John Bennet, and a copy (beginning only with Wednesday's proceedings) which Wesley himself used, and which bears corrections in his own handwriting.

Chiefly from these documents comes our picture of the ten earnest men, six clergymen and four lay preachers who assembled at the Foundery in London during the last six days of June 1744. In them we can read the deliberations, in the familiar question-and-answer style, of that Mother of Conferences, who has not only maintained to this day a vigorous life of her own, but who now has, besides, in most

of those places in the world where English is spoken, a
numerous progeny, varying richly according to time and
place, but in all essentials recognizably like the Mother
from whom they sprang.

London. June 25, 1744. WJJS, III, 143 f.

Monday the 25th and the five following days we spent
in conference with many of our brethren (come from
several parts) who desire nothing but to save their own
souls, and those that hear them. And surely, as long as they
continue thus minded, their labour shall not be in vain
in the Lord.

The next week we endeavoured to purge the society of
all that did not walk according to the gospel. By this
means we reduced the number of members to less than
nineteen hundred. But number is an inconsiderable circumstance. May God increase them in faith and love!

June 25, 1744. WCJ, I, 367 f.

We opened our Conference with solemn prayer, and the
divine blessing. I preached with much assistance, and baptized Samuel Holloway; who felt in that moment the
great burden taken off. We continued in Conference the
rest of the week, settling our doctrines, practice, and discipline, with great love and unanimity.

BENNET'S MINUTES. PWHS 1. [50]

Monday, June 25, 1744

The following persons being met at the Foundery, John
Wesley, Charles Wesley, John Hodges, Henry Piers, Samuel Taylor, and John Meriton,[51] after some time spent in
prayer, the design of our meeting was proposed, namely,
to consider:—

1. What to teach;

2. How to teach; &c.

3. What to do, *i. e.,* how to regulate our Doctrine, Discipline and Practice.

But first it was inquired whether any of our Lay Brethren should be present at this Conference, and it was agreed to invite from time to time such of them as we should think proper. 'Twas then asked, Which of them shall we invite today? The answer was, Thomas Richards, Thomas Maxfield, John Bennet, and John Downes, who were accordingly brought in. Then was read as follows:—

It is desired that all things may be considered as in the immediate presence of God; That we may meet with a single eye, and as little children who have everything to learn; That every point may be examined from the foundation; That every person may speak freely whatever is in his heart; and That every question proposed may be fully debated, and bolted to the bran.

The first preliminary question was then proposed, namely, How far does each of us agree to submit to the unanimous judgement of the rest? It was answered, In speculative things each can only submit so far as his judgement shall be convinced: in every practical point so far as we can without wounding our consciences. To the second preliminary question, viz., How far should any of us mention to others what may be mentioned here? It was replied, Not one word which may be here spoken of persons should be mentioned elsewhere. Nothing at all, unless so far as we may be convinced the glory of God requires it. And from time to time we will consider on each head, Is it for the glory of God that what we have now spoken should be mentioned again?

About 7 o'clock we began to consider the doctrine of Justification,[52] the questions relating to which were as follows, with the substance of the answers thereto.

Q. 1. What is it to be justified?

A. To be pardoned and received into God's favour, and

into such a state that, if we continue therein, we shall be finally saved.

Q. 2. Is faith the condition of justification?

A. Yes: for everyone who believeth not is condemned, and every one who believes is justified.

Q. 3. But must not repentance and works meet for repentance go before faith?

A. Without doubt, if by repentance you mean conviction of sin, and by works meet for repentance, obeying God as far as we can, forgiving our brother, leaving off from evil, doing good and using His ordinances according to the power we have received.

Q. 4. What is faith?

A. Faith, in general, is a divine supernatural *Elenchus* of things not seen, *i. e.,* that is of past, future, or spiritual things; 't is a spiritual sight of God and the things of God. Therefore repentance is a low species of faith, *i. e.,* a supernatural sense of an offended God. Justifying faith is a supernatural inward sense, or sight, of God in Christ reconciling the world unto Himself. First, a sinner is convinced by the Holy Ghost, Christ loved me and gave Himself for me; this is that faith by which he is justified, or pardoned, the moment he receives it. Immediately the same spirit bears witness, Thou art pardoned, thou hast redemption in His blood; and this is saving faith, whereby the love of God is shed abroad in his heart.

Q. 5. Have all true Christians this faith? May not a man be justified and not know it?

A. That all true Christians have this faith, even such a faith as implies an assurance of God's love, appears from Rom. viii. 15, Eph. iv. 32, 2 Cor. xiii. 5, Heb. viii. 10, I John iv. 10, and last I John v. 19. And that no man can be justified and not know it, appears farther from the very nature of things, for faith after repentance is ease after pain, rest after toil, light after darkness; and from the immediate as well as distant fruits.

Q. 6. But may not a man go to heaven without it?

A. It doth not appear from Holy writ that a man who hears the Gospel can (Mark xvi. 16), whatever a heathen may do (Rom. ii. 14).

Q. 7. What are the immediate fruits of justifying faith?

A. Peace, joy, love, power over all outward sin, and power to keep down all inward sin.

Q. 8. Does any one believe who has not the witness in himself? Or any longer than he sees, loves and obeys God?

A. We apprehend not; seeing God being the very essence of faith, love and obedience the inseparable properties of it.

Q. 9. What sins are consistent with justifying faith?

A. No wilful sin. If a believer sins, he thereby forfeits his pardon. Neither is it possible he should have justifying faith again, without previously repenting.

Q. 10. Must every believer come into a state of doubt, or fear, or darkness? Will he do so unless by ignorance or unfaithfulness? Does God otherwise withdraw Himself?

A. It is certain a believer need never again come into condemnation. It seems he need not come into a state of doubt, or fear, or darkness; and that (ordinarily at least) he will not, unless by ignorance and unfaithfulness. Yet it is true that the first joy does seldom last long, that it is commonly followed by doubts and fears, and that God usually permits very great heaviness before any large manifestation of Himself.

Q. 11. Are works necessary to the continuance of faith?

A. Without doubt; for a man may forfeit the gift of God either by sins of omission or commission.

Q. 12. Can faith be lost but for want of works?

A. It cannot, but through disobedience.

Q. 13. How is faith made perfect by works?

A. The more we exert our faith, the more 't is increased: to him that hath, more and more is given.

Q. 14. St. Paul says, Abraham was not justified by works;

St. James, he was justified by works. Do not they then contradict each other?

A. No. 1. Because they do not speak of the same justification. St. Paul speaks of that justification . . . which was when he offered up Isaac on the altar. 2. Because they do not speak of the same works. St. Paul speaks of works that precede faith, St. James of works that spring from faith.

Q. 15. In what sense is Adam's sin imputed to all mankind?

A. In Adam all die, *i.e.*, 1. Our bodies then became mortal. 2. Our souls died, *i. e.*, were disunited from God. 3. And hence we are all born with a sinful, devilish nature; by reason whereof, 4. We all are children of wrath, liable to death eternal. Rom. v. 18; Eph. ii. 3.

Q. 16. In what sense is the righteousness of Christ imputed to believers or to all mankind?

A. We do not find it affirmed expressly in Scripture, that God imputes the righteousness of Christ to any; although we do find that faith is imputed unto us for righteousness. That text, "As by one man's disobedience all men were made sinners, so by the obedience of one all were made righteous," we conceive means, By the merits of Christ all men are cleared from the guilt of Adam's actual sin. We conceive farther that through the obedience and death of Christ, 1. The bodies of all men become immortal after the Resurrection; 2. Their souls recover a capacity of spiritual life; 3. And an actual seed or spark thereof. 4. All believers become children of grace; 5. Are re-united to God; and 6. Made partakers of the Divine Nature.

Q. 17. Have we not then unawares leaned too much towards Calvinism?

A. It seems we have.

Q. 18. Have we not also leaned towards Antinomianism?

A. We are afraid we have.

Q. 19. What is Antinomianism?

A. The doctrine which makes void the law through faith.

Q. 20. What are the main pillars thereof?

A. 1. That Christ abolished the moral law. 2. That Christians therefore are not obliged to observe it. 3. That one branch of Christian liberty is liberty from obeying the commandments of God. 4. That it is bondage to do a thing because it is commanded, or forbear it because it is forbidden. 5. That a believer is not obliged to use the ordinances of God, or to do good works. 6. That a preacher ought not to exhort to good works; not unbelievers because it is hurtful, not believers because it is needless.

Q. 21. What was the occasion of St. Paul writing his Epistle to the Galatians?

A. The coming of certain men among the Christians, who taught, Except ye be circumcised, and keep the whole law of Moses, ye cannot be saved.

Q. 22. What is his main design therein?

A. To prove, 1, That no man can be justified or saved by the works of the law, either moral or ritual; 2, That every believer is justified by faith in Christ, without the works of the law.

Q. 23. What does he mean by the works of the Law?

A. All works that do not spring from faith in Christ.

Q. 24. What is meant by being under the law?

A. Under the Mosaic dispensation.

Q. 25. What law has Christ abolished?

A. The ritual law of Moses.

Q. 26. What is meant by liberty?

A. Liberty, 1, from the law; 2, from sin.

ON TUESDAY MORNING, JUNE THE 26TH,

was considered the doctrine of Sanctification, with regard to which the questions asked and the substance of the answers given were as follows:—

Q. 1. What is it to be sanctified?

A. To be renewed in the image of God, in righteousness and true holiness.

Q. 2. Is faith the condition or the instrument of sanctification, or present salvation?

A. It is both the condition and the instrument of it. When we begin to believe, then salvation begins. And as faith increases, holiness increases, till we are created anew.

Q. 3. Is not every believer a new creature?

A. Not in the sense of St. Paul, 2 Cor. V. 17. All old things are passed away in him who is so a new creature, and all things become new.

Q. 4. But has every believer a new heart?

A. A great change is wrought in the heart of affections of every one as soon as he believes; yet he is still full of sin, so that he has not then a new heart in the full sense.

Q. 5. Is not every believer born of God, a temple of the Holy Ghost?

A. In a low sense he is; but he that is, in the proper sense, born of God, cannot commit sin.

Q. 6. What is implied in being made perfect in love?

A. The loving the Lord our God with all our mind and soul and strength: Deut. vi. 5, xxx. 6, Ezek. xxxvi.

Q. 7. Does this imply that he who is thus made perfect cannot commit sin?

A. St. John affirms it expressly; he cannot commit sin because he is born of God, ch. iii. 10.[53] And, indeed, how should he? seeing there is now none occasion of stumbling in him, ch. ii. 10.

Q. 8. Does it imply that all inward sin is taken away?

A. Without doubt. Or how should he be said to be saved from all his uncleannesses?

Q. 9. Can we know one that is thus saved? What is a reasonable proof of it?

A. We cannot, without the miraculous discernment of spirits, be infallibly certain of those who are thus saved.

But we apprehend these would be the best proofs which the nature of the thing admits, (unless they should be called to resist unto blood). If, 1, we had sufficient evidence of their unblamable behaviour, at least from the time of their justification. 2. If they give a distinct account of the time and manner wherein they were saved from sin, and of the circumstances thereof, with such sound speech as could not be reproved. And, 3. Upon strict inquiry from time to time, for two or three years following, it appeared that all their tempers, words, and actions were holy and unreprovable.

Q. 10. How should we treat those who think they have attained?

A. Exhort them to forget the things that are behind, to watch and pray always that God may search the ground of their hearts.

WEDNESDAY, JUNE THE 27TH,

we began to consider points of discipline, with regard to which the questions asked and the substance of the answers given were as follows:—

Q. 1. What is the Church of England?

A. According to the 20th Article, the visible Church of England is the congregation of English believers in which the pure word of God is preached, and the sacraments duly administered. But the word Church is sometimes taken in a looser sense for a congregation professing to believe. So it is taken in the 26th Article, and in the 1st, 2nd, and 3rd chapters of Revelations [the Revelation].[54]

Q. 2. What is a member of the Church of England?

A. A believer, hearing the pure word preached, and partaking of the sacraments, duly administered, in this Church.

Q. 3. What is it to be zealous for the Church?

A. To be earnestly desirous of its welfare, by the confirmation of its present members in faith, hearing and communicating; of its increase, by the addition of new members.

Q. 4. How are we to defend the doctrine [doctrines] of the Church?

A. Both by our [omit our] preaching and living.

Q. 5. Do the 8, 13, 15, 16, 17, 21, 23, and 27 Articles agree with Scripture?[55]

A. We will consider.

Q. 6. How shall we bear the most effectual testimony against that part of the clergy who either preach or live contrary to the doctrine of the Church of England?

A. Not by preaching, for they do not hear us: but by an earnest and tender address from the press.

Q. 7. How should [shall] we behave at a false or railing sermon?

A. If it only contain personal reflections, we may quietly suffer it. If it blaspheme the work and Spirit of God, it may be better to go out of Church. In either case, if opportunity serve, it would be well to speak or write to the Minister.

Q. 8. How far is it our duty to obey the Bishops?

A. In all things indifferent. And on this ground of obeying them, we should observe the canons, so far as we can with a safe conscience.

Q. 9. Do we separate from the Church?

A. We conceive not. We hold communion therewith for conscience sake, by constant attending both the word preached, and the sacraments administered therein.

Q. 10. What then do they mean who say, You separate from the Church?

A. We cannot certainly tell. Perhaps they have no determinate meaning; unless by the Church they mean themselves, i. e., that part of the clergy who accuse us of preaching false doctrine. And it is sure we do herein separate from them, by maintaining the doctrine which they deny.

Q. 11. But do you not weaken the Church?

A. Do not they who ask this by the Church mean themselves? We do not purposely weaken any man's hands, but accidentally we may thus far,—they who come to know the truth by us, will esteem such as deny it less than they did before. But the Church, in the proper sense, the congregation of English believers, we do not weaken at all.

Q. 12. Do not you entail a schism on the Church? *i. e.,* Is it not probable that your hearers after your death will be scattered into all sects and parties? Or that they will form themselves into a distinct sect?

A. 1. We are persuaded the body of our hearers will even after our death remain in the Church, unless they be thrust out. 2. We believe notwithstanding either that they will be thrust out, or that they will leaven the whole Church. 3. We do, and will do, all we can to prevent those consequences which are supposed likely to happen after our death. 4. But we cannot with good conscience neglect the present opportunity of saving souls while we live, for fear of consequences which may possibly or probably happen after we are dead.

THURSDAY, JUNE THE 28TH,

were considered other points of discipline. The substance of the questions and answers was as follows:—

Q. 1. How are the people divided who desire to be under your care?

A. Into the United Societies, the Bands, the Select Societies, and the Penitents.

Q. 2. How do these differ from each other?

A. The United Societies (which are the largest of all) consist of the awakened persons. Part of these, who are supposed to have remission of sins, are more closely united in the Bands. Those in the Bands, who seem to walk in the light of God, compose the Select Societies. Those of them who have made shipwreck of the faith, meet apart as penitents.

Q. 3. What are the Rules of the United Societies?

A. Those that follow[56] (Then they were read.)

Q. 4. What are the Rules of the Bands?

A. They are these, (which were read and considered).

Q. 5. What are the Rules of the Select Societies?

A. The same: and these three, 1. Let nothing spoken in this Society be spoken again; no, not even to the members of it. 2. Every member agrees absolutely to submit to his Minister in all indifferent things. 3. Every member till we can have all things common,[57] will bring once a week, *bonâ fide,* all he can spare towards a common stock.

Q. 6. Are there any particular [peculiar] Rules for the Penitents?

A. Not yet.

Q. 7. What officers belong to these Societies?

A. The Ministers, Assistants, Stewards, Leaders of Bands, Leaders of Classes, Visitors of the Sick, Schoolmasters,[58] Housekeepers.[59]

Q. 8. What is the office of a Minister?

A. To watch over the souls whom God commits to his charge, as he that must give an account.

Q. 9. What is it to be moved by the Holy Ghost to take upon yourself this office?

A. It can mean no less than to be immediately convinced by the Spirit of God that it is His will.

Q. 10. Is field-preaching unlawful?

A. We do not conceive that it is contrary to any law, either of God or man. Yet (to avoid giving any needless offence) we never preach without doors, when we can with any conveniency preach within.

Q. 11. Where should we endeavor to preach most?

A. 1. Where we can preach in the Church. 2. Where there is an open door, quiet and willing hearers. 3. Where there is the greatest increase of souls.

Q. 12. What is the best way of spreading the Gospel?

A. To go a little and a little farther from London, Bristol, St. Ives, Newcastle or any other Society. So a little leaven would spread with more effect and less noise, and help would always be at hand.

Q. 13. What is the best general method in preaching?

A. 1. To invite. 2. To convince. 3. Offer Christ. And lastly to build up. And to do this (in some measure) in every sermon.

FRIDAY, JUNE THE 29TH,

we considered,

Q. 1. Are Lay Assistants allowable?

A. Only in cases of necessity.

Q. 2. What is the office of our Assistants?

A. In the absence of the Minister to feed and guide, to teach and govern the flock. 1. To expound every morning and evening. 2. To meet the United Societies, the Bands, the Select Societies, and the Penitents every week. 3. To visit the classes (London [and Bristol] excepted) once a month. 4. To hear and decide all differences. 5. To put the disorderly back on trial, and to receive on trial for the Bands or Society. 6. To see that the Stewards and the Leaders, Schoolmasters and Housekeepers faithfully discharge their several offices. 7. To meet the Stewards, the Leaders of the Bands and Classes weekly, and overlook their accounts.

Q. 3. What are the Rules of an Assistant?[60]

A. 1. Be diligent, never be unemployed a moment, never be triflingly employed, [never while away time,] spend no more time at any place than is strictly necessary.

2. Be serious. Let your motto be, Holiness unto the Lord. Avoid all lightness as you would avoid hell-fire, and laughing as you would cursing and swearing.

3. Touch no woman; be as loving as you will, but hold your hands off 'em. Custom is nothing to us.

4. Believe evil of no one. If you see it done, well; else take heed how you credit it. Put the best construction on

every thing. You know the judge is always allowed [supposed] to be on the prisoner's side.

5. Speak evil of no one; else your word especially would eat as doth a canker. Keep your thoughts within your [own] breast, till you come to the person concerned.

6. Tell everyone what you think wrong in him, and that plainly, and as soon as may be, else it will fester in your heart. Make all haste therefore, to cast the fire out of your bosom.

7. Do nothing as a gentleman: you have no more to do with this character than with that of a dancing-master. You are the servant of all, therefore

8. Be ashamed of nothing but sin: not of fetching wood, or drawing water, if time permit; not of cleaning your own shoes or your neighbour's.

9. Take no money of any one. If they give you food when you are hungry, or clothes when you need them, it is good. But not silver, or gold. Let there be no pretence to say, we grow rich by the Gospel.[61]

10. Contract no debt without my knowledge.

11. Be punctual: do everything exactly at the time; and in general do not mend our rules, but keep them, not for wrath but for conscience sake.

12. Act in all things not according to your own will, but as a son in the Gospel. As such, it is your part to employ your time in the manner which we direct: partly in visiting the flock from house to house (the sick in particular); partly in such a course of Reading, Meditation and Prayer, as we advise from time to time. Above all, if you labour with us in our Lord's vineyard, it is needful you should do that part of the work [which] we prescribe [direct] at those times and places which we judge most for His glory.[62]

Q. 4. Should all our Assistants keep journals?

A. By all means, as well for our satisfaction as for the profit of their own souls.

Q. 5. Shall we now fix where each labourer shall be (if God permits) till we meet again?

A. Yes: (which was accordingly done).

Q. 6. What is the office of a Steward?

A. 1. To manage the temporal things of the Society. 2. To receive the weekly contributions of the Leaders of the Classes. 3. To expend what is needful from time to time. 4. To send relief to the poor. 5. To see that the public buildings be kept clean and in good repair. 6. To keep an exact account of Receipts and Expenses. 7. To inform the Helpers, if the rules of the house, of the school [schools], of the Bands, or of the Society, be not punctually observed: and 8. If need be, to inform the Minister hereof. 9. To tell the Helpers in love, if they think anything amiss in their doctrine or life. 10. If it be not removed, to send timely notice to the Minister. 11. To meet his fellow Steward weekly, in order to consult together on the preceding heads.

Q. 7. What are the Rules of a Steward?

A. 1. Be frugal, save everything that can be saved honestly. 2. Spend no more than you receive. Contract no debt. 3. Do nothing rashly; let every design be thoroughly weighed, before you begin to execute it. 4. Have no long accounts: pay everything within the week. 5. Give none that ask relief an ill word or ill look. Do not hurt them, if you cannot help them. 6. Expect no thanks from man. 7. Remember you are a servant of the Helper, not his master: therefore speak to him always as such.

Q. 8. What is the business of a Leader of a Band?

A. It is set down in the Rules of the Bands; as the business of a Class-leader, in the Rules of the Society.

Q. 9. What is the business of a Visitor of the sick?

A. 1. To see every person within his district thrice a week. 2. To inquire into the state of their souls, and advise them as occasion may require. 3. To inquire into their disorder, and procure advice for them. 4. To inquire if

they are in want, and relieve them if it may be, in kind.
5. To do anything for them which he can. 6. To bring his
account weekly to the Stewards.

Q. 10. What are the Rules of a Visitor?

A. Be plain and open with [in] dealing with souls. 2.
Be mild, patient, tender. 3. Be clean [cleanly] in all you
do for them. 4. Be not nice.[63]

Q. 11. Can we have a Seminary for labourers?

A. If God spare us until another Conference.

Q. 12. With whom should we correspond? When?

A. Once a month, with each Assistant, and with some
other person (at least) in each Society.

Q. 13. How shall we fix the Watch-Nights, Letter-Days,
and Love-feasts till we meet again?

A. At London, Bristol, and Newcastle thus:—

Watch-Nights	Letter-Days	Love-feasts
July 13	July 23	July 29
August 10	August 20	August 26
September 7	September 17	September 23
October 12	October 22	October 28

Q. 14. What books may an Assistant read?

A. Sallust, Caesar, Tully, Erasmus, Castellio, Terence,
Virgil, Horace, Vida, Buchanan, G. Test, Epictetus, Plato,
Ignatius, Ephrem Syrus, Homer, Greek Epigrams, Duport,
Bp. Usher's Sermons, Arndt, Boehm, Nalson, Pascal,
Frank, R. Gell, *our Tracts.*

Q. 15. How shall we exclude formality from prayer and
conversation?

A. 1. By preaching frequently on the heads. 2. By watch-
ing always, that we may speak only what we feel.

Q. 16. What shall I write next? What abridge?

A. Write a farther Appeal, Sermons: abridge and print
16 Sermons, Dr. Knight's Manual, 2 Discourses, Great
Audit, The Whole Duty of Man, Edwards.

Q. 17. Is it lawful to bear arms?[64]

A. We incline to think it is: 1. Because there is no command against it in the New Testament; 2. Because Cornelius, a soldier, is commended there, and not mentioned to have laid them down.

Q. 18. Is it lawful to use the law?

A. As defendant doubtless. And perhaps as plaintiff in some cases, seeing magistrates are an ordinance of God.[65]

ON SATURDAY, JUNE THE 30TH,

we considered:—

Q. 1. Can we unite any farther with the Moravians?

A. It seems not, were it only for this reason, they will not unite with us.

Q. 2. Can we unite any farther with Mr. Whitefield?

A. If he make any overtures towards it.

Q. 3. Shall we propose a conference with either?

A. With Mr. Whitefield, if he returns to London. The Moravians absolutely decline it.

Q. 4. Shall we send them the most material of the preceding questions, and desire their answers?

A. This can do no hurt, and may do good.

Q. 5. Can we mend our economy in temporal things?

A. We will consider this with the Stewards.

Q. 6. Have we changed in anything for the worse, since we began our Society?

A. It does not appear to us that we have.

Q. 7. Is there anything amongst us that stops the work of God?

A. Perhaps sins of omission, neglect of self-denial and taking up our cross.

Q. 8. When and where shall those of us who can meet again?

A. If God permits, Nov. 1st at Newcastle, Feb. 1st at Bristol, May 1st London.[66]

LIST OF BOOKS REFERRED TO BY SYMBOL

This list includes all the works from which extracts have been made; hence all the references found at the beginning of the several extracts may be identified here. In addition, it contains those referred to so frequently in the notes as to be designated by symbol. Other books, referred to in the notes without symbols, can easily be identified from the notes themselves, so are not included here.

Calamy CA	Edmund Calamy, *A Continuation of the Account of the Ministers . . . who were Ejected . . . after the Restoration in 1660 . . .* 2 vols. London: 1727.
Clarke MWF	Adam Clarke, *Memoirs of the Wesley Family, Collected Primarily from Original Documents.* 2nd ed. 2 vols. London: T. Tegg and Son, 1836.
KPD	M. M. Knappen, ed., *Two Elizabethan Puritan Diaries by Richard Rogers and Samuel Ward.* Chicago: American Society of Church History, 1933.
Moore LW	Henry Moore, *The Life of the Rev. John Wesley, A. M.* 2 vols. New York: 1824-5.
PWHS. 1	*Publications of the Wesley Historical Society,* No. 1. London: Published for the Wesley Historical Society, 1896.
RST	Richard Rogers, *Seven Treatises Containing Such Direction as is Gathered out of the Holie Scriptures, Leading and Guiding to True Happiness . . .* 3rd ed. London: for Thomas Man, 1610.
Simon JWLP	John S. Simon, *John Wesley: The Last Phase.* London: The Epworth Press, 1934.
Simon JWMS	John S. Simon, *John Wesley and the Methodist Societies.* 2nd ed. London: The Epworth Press, 1937.
Simon JWRS	John S. Simon, *John Wesley and the Religious Societies.* London: The Epworth Press, 1921.
Tyerman LGWA	Luke Tyerman, *The Life of the Rev. George Whitefield.* 2 vols. New York: Randolph and Co., 1877.
Tyerman LW	Luke Tyerman, *The Life and Times of the Rev. John Wesley, M. A.* 3 vols. New York: Harper and Brothers, 1872.
Tyerman OM	Luke Tyerman, *The Oxford Methodists.* New York: Harper and Brothers, 1873.
Tyerman SW	Luke Tyerman, *The Life and Times of The Rev. Samuel Wesley, M. A.* London: Simpkin, Marshall and Co., 1866.
WCJ	Thomas Jackson, ed., *The Journal of the Rev. Charles Wesley, M. A. . . . to which are Appended Selections from his Correspondence and Poetry.* 2 vols. London: Wesleyan Methodist Book Room, 1849.

WGFA	George Whitefield. *A Further Account of God's Dealings with the Rev. Mr. George Whitefield, from the Time of his Ordination to his Embarking for Georgia.* Boston: Rogers and ———, 174–. (Title page torn).
Whitefield TF	*The Two First Parts of His Life with His Journals. Revised, Corrected and Abridged by George Whitefield, A. B.* London: W. Strahan, 1756.
Whitefield JV	George Whitefield, *Journal of a Voyage from London to Savannah in Georgia.* London: Whitaker, Treacher and Arnot, 1830.
Whitefield SA	*A Short Account of God's Dealings with the Reverend Mr. George Whitefield . . . from his Infancy to the Time of his Entring [sic] into Holy Orders. Written by Himself . . .* London: W. Strahan, etc. 1740.
Whitefield Works	*The Works of the Rev. George Whitefield, M. A. . . . Prepared by Himself for the Press . . .* 6 vols. London: 1771.
Whitehead LW	John Whitehead, *The Life of the Rev. John Wesley, M. A. . . . with the Life of the Rev. Charles Wesley, M. A.* 2 vols. in 1. Philadelphia: William S. Stockton, 1845.
WJJS	Nehemiah Curnock, ed., *The Journal of the Rev. John Wesley, M. A.* Standard Edition. 8 vols. London: The Epworth Press, 1938.
WJJ *Works*	John Emory, ed., The "Journal" of John Wesley, being Vols. III and IV of *The Works of the Rev. John Wesley, A. M.* 7 vols., New York: Lane and Scott, 1850.
WJL	John Telford, ed., *The Letters of the Rev. John Wesley, A. M.* 8 vols. London: The Epworth Press, 1931.
Woodward RS	Josiah Woodward. *An Earnest Admonition to All, but Especially to Young Persons to turn to God . . . To Which is added an Account of the Rise and Progress of the Religious Societies . . . and Sundry Directions Relating to the Religious Conferences of these Societies.* London: 1697.
Works	John Emory, ed., *The Works of the Rev. John Wesley, A. M.* First American Complete . . . Edition from the Latest London Edition . . . 7 vols. New York: Lane and Scott, 1850.

NOTES

NOTES

CHAPTER I

1. Eloquent of the way they felt about it is the following extract from a poem written to Emily Wesley by her sister Hetty at a time when the former, between a period of school teaching at Lincoln and her marriage, was back at Epworth (Adam Clarke, *Memoirs of the Wesley Family*, [London: T. Tegg and Son, 1836; hereafter cited as Clarke, MWF,] II, 269):

> Fortune has fixed thee in a place
> Debarred of wisdom, wit, and grace.
> High births and virtue equally they scorn,
> As asses dull on dunghills born:
> Impervious as the stones, their heads are found,
> Their rage and hatred stedfast as the ground.
> With these unpolished wights thy youthful days
> Glide slow and dull, and Nature's lamp decays:
> O what a lamp is hid, 'midst such a sordid race!

2. Edmund Calamy, *A Continuation of the Account of the Ministers . . . who were Ejected after the Restoration in 1660.* (2 vols. London: 1727).

3. This symbol, which will recur oftener than any other, stands for *The Journal of John Wesley* (Standard Edition by Nehemiah Curnock 8 vols., London: The Epworth Press, 1909-1916. Reprint of 1938).

4. See below, p. 176ff.

5. See below, p. 82.

6. On hearing the news of his son's election to his Fellowship, he jubilantly exclaimed, "Whatever I am, my Jack is Fellow of Lincoln!" (Luke Tyerman, *The Life and Times of the Rev. John Wesley, M. A.* New York: Harper and Brothers, 1872. [hereafter cited as Tyerman, LW] I, 45.)

7. His unfeeling comment in a letter written in 1734 to General Oglethorpe was, "I thank God I creep up hill more than I did formerly, being eased of the weight of four daughters out of seven, as I hope I shall be of the fifth in a little longer." (Clarke, MWF, I, 325).

8. WJJS III, 24.

9. Clarke, MWF, I, 346.

10. Samuel Wesley, *The Life of Our Blessed Lord and Saviour Jesus Christ* (London: 1693) p. 40.

11. Clarke, MWF, II, 132 n.

12. The note runs, in part: "From her [i.e., the Virgin] I here draw the picture of a good wife; more defensibly, I'm sure than the contrary is often done by the Italian painters, who from their wives, and sometimes mistresses, usually draw their Madonnas." Samuel Wesley, *The Life of Our Blessed Lord and Saviour Jesus Christ* (London: 1693) p. 40, n.

13. That of a friend [S. W.].

14. John Wesley to Adam Clarke (subsequent to their first meeting, which was in 1782).

15. The Castle, in Lincoln, where he had been imprisoned more out of spite rising from some neighbours' political animosity, than for the ostensible cause, a debt of less than thirty pounds.

16. The letter is preserved by Dr. Whitehead in his *Life . . . of . . . John Wesley* (Philadelphia: William Stockton, 1845) I, 37.

17. *E. g.*, Richard Watson, (*The Life of the Rev. John Wesley, A.M.* New York: Emory and Waugh, 1831, p. 8) among the earlier; and Caleb Winchester, (*The Life of John Wesley,* New York: The Macmillan Company, 1921, p. 7) among the later biographers. Simon Simon, dissents. (John Simon, *John Wesley and the Religious Societies.* London: The Epworth Press, 1921, p. 26.) Hereafter cited as Simon, JWRS.

18. In a letter to John in 1732, perhaps a part of that quoted below (p. 18ff) but not given in the *Journal* whence that extract was made. See Maximin Piette, *La Réaction de John Wesley dans l'Evolution du Protestantisme* (second ed. Brussels: Catholic University of Louvain, 1927) p. 327; and Simon, JWRS p. 58.

19. "Had I twenty sons I should rejoice that they were all so employed, though I should never see their faces more." Henry Moore, *The Life of the Rev. John Wesley, A. M.* (New York: Bangs and Emory, 1824) I, 196.

20. See below, pp. 297, 299, 307, 311f.

21. Clarke, MWF, II, 96, n.

22. We may note the use, in connection with this gathering, of the word "society", which was then applied to many earnest religious groups meeting throughout the kingdom (see below p. 138ff) and to be so important in the history of Methodism, without being able to say that there was any formal organization.

23. This letter and the one just preceding were included in his *Journal* by John Wesley under the date of the day next after that of his mother's death.

24. Her brother, Samuel Annesley, Jr.

25. *E.g.*, WJJS, III, 453 f.

26. WJJS, I, 328.

27. WJJS, IV, 90.

28. Thomas Jackson, ed., *The Journal of the Rev. Charles Wesley, M.A. to which are appended Selections from his Correspondence and his Poetry.* (2 vols., London: Wesleyan Methodist Book Room, n.d. [the introduction is dated 1849] hereafter referred to as WCJ) II, 97.

29. The Rector's servant.

CHAPTER II

1. It is published as an appendix to WJJS. See below, p. 75.

2. John Telford, ed. *The Letters of the Rev. John Wesley, M.A.* Standard Edition, 8 vols. London: The Epworth Press, 1931. Herein referred to as WJL.

3. Thomas Coke and Henry Moore, *The Life of the Rev. John Wesley, A. M.* (London: G. Paramore, 1792) p. 41f.

4. Tyerman, LW, I, 20.

5. Tyerman, LW, I, 22.

6. "To the University of Oxford I acknowledge no obligation; and she will as cheerfully renounce me for a son as I am willing to disclaim her for a mother." (From the devastating passage on Oxford in his *Memoirs* quoted at length by Wylie Sypher, ed., in *Enlightened England, an Anthology of Eighteenth Century Literature* [New York: Morton and Co., 1947] p. 974f.)

7. A description by one Mr. Badcock, in the *Westminster Magazine*. Quoted in John Whitehead, *The Life of the Rev. John Wesley, M. A.* (Philadelphia: William S. Stockton, 1845) I, 235.

8. It looks in this direction also that the actual ordination to the Diaconate took place, after some scraping to provide the necessary funds, on the 19th of the following September, without creating much of a stir, so far as we can tell from the documents, in the Wesley family. John himself records it laconically in his Diary with the symbols he constantly used to express ejaculatory prayers of thanksgiving and for divine help. His ordination to the Presbyterate two years later left even less of a trace in the printed sources. See WJJS, I, 59; and WJL, I, 15.

9. Especially Maximin Piette (following Leger). *La Réaction de John Wesley dans l'Evolution du Protestantisme,* (second ed., Brussels: Catholic University of Louvain, 1927) p. 443.

10. WJJS, I, 13.

11. WJJS, I, 14 ff. After patient submission to the tyranny of dates and acute reasoning as to the identity of "Varanese". Betty Kirkham was one of the daughters of the Rectory in Stanton Harcourt, not far from Oxford, which Wesley visited just before writing his mother about the *Imitation of Christ*. G. Elsie Harrison (*Son to Susannah* [Nashville, Tenn.: Cokesbury Press, 1937] p. 72) finds difficulties in this identification and suggests Betty's sister Sally.

12. That is, in 1725.

13. *"Works"* followed by a volume number signifies an extract from the writings of John Wesley from the New York edition, 1850. This extract is from "A Plain Account of Christian Perfection," written about 1777.

14. Wesley's earnestness at this point precluded winsomeness. He describes his "fixed plan" in another place in these words: "I resolved to have no acquaintance by chance but by choice; and to choose such only, as I had reason to believe would help me on my way to heaven." The rest he shook off as courteously as he could, but unmistakably. (Sermon 86, *Works* II, 211.)

15. He describes this in more detail in a later passage which is almost certainly autobiographical: "One of them [the Oxford Methodists] had thirty pounds a year. He lived on twenty-eight, and gave away forty shillings. The next year receiving sixty pounds, he still lived on twenty-eight and gave away two and thirty. The third year he received ninety pounds, and gave away sixty-two. The fourth year he received a hundred and twenty pounds. Still he lived as before on twenty-eight; and gave to the poor ninety-two." (Sermon 94, *Works* II, 273.)

16. John Whitehead, *Life of the Rev. John Wesley*, (Philadelphia: William S. Stockton, 1845) I, 234.

17. This is the date under which Clarke prints this letter. It is tempting to think this a mistake for 1725 when the nature of faith was a live subject of discussion in other letters between mother and son.

18. C. E. Vulliamy, *Aspasia, The Life and Letters of Mary Granville, Mrs. Delaney*. (London: Geoffrey Bles, 1935), p. ix.

19. John Whitehead, *The Life of the Rev. John Wesley, M. A.* (Philadelphia: William S. Stockton, 1845) I, 72.

20. They seem to have begun tentatively with near relatives: see Emily Wesley's indignant rejection of their offer, Tyerman LW, I, 94.

21. From "A Short History of Methodism," paragraphs 4 and 5.

22. Gambold came up to Christ Church College from a Rectory in southern Wales; he joined the Holy Club in 1730, while still in his teens. Later he joined the Moravians and became one of their Bishops.

23. Here and hereafter this symbol stands for Luke Tyerman, *The Oxford Methodists*. New York: Harper and Brothers, 1873.

24. Clayton, the son of a Manchester bookseller, joined the Holy Club in 1732. His friendship with the Wesleys ceased as they left their High Church views behind.

25. Wesley was in London at the time. See Tyerman, LW, I, 83.

26. Maximin Piette, *La Réaction de John Wesley dans l'Evolution du Protestantisme*. (second ed., Brussels: Catholic University of Louvain, 1927) p. 419 ff.

27. Francis J. McConnell, *John Wesley* (New York: The Abingdon Press, 1939) p. 43. *Cf.* WJJS, I, 109.

28. Luke Tyerman, *The Life and Times of Samuel Wesley, M.A.* (London: Simpkin, Marshall and Co., 1866). Herein referred to as Tyerman, SW.

29. London: W. Strahan, 1740. Hereafter cited as Whitefield, SA.

30. By Henry Scougal, the 17th century Scottish mystic. This book, so influential in Whitefield's development, had been lent him by Charles Wesley; it had been a favorite of Susannah who called it "an excellent good book." John Wesley esteemed it so highly he published no less than six editions of it. See WJJS, I, 107, n.: and W. J. Townshend *et al.*, *A New History of Methodism* (2 vols., London: Hodder and Stoughton, 1909) I, 170.

CHAPTER III

1. See the facsimile of the original title page, WJJS, I, 81.

2. From the facsimile, WJJS, I, 83 f.

3. Entry of June 25, 1778. WJJS, VI, 202.

4. The value of the Standard Edition of the *Journal* is greatly enhanced by the inclusion of supplementary material from both preliminary stages. Material

"translated" from the cipher notes is included at the bottom of the pages; and long sections of the Ms. Journal which Wesley left unpublished are inserted in the text in square brackets. A noteworthy instance of this latter sort is the story of Miss Sophy which Wesley, with his fondness for recalling anniversaries, was transcribing into his Journal just a year after she was married (see WJJS, I, 337), but which, for obvious reasons, he did not publish. Some of this material is included below without distinguishing it from that which Wesley himself published.

5. WJJS, I, 86.

6. Curnock says probably 1739. WJJS, I, 87 n.

7. "John Wesley" *Scribner's Magazine*, XXVI (July-December, 1899), 761.

8. *Cf.* the remark of Charles Wesley, "I corrected Mr. Whitefield's Journal for the press; my advice to suppress it being overruled." WCJ, I, 126.

9. WJL, VI, 23.

10. Augustine Birrell, "John Wesley," *Scribner's Magazine*, XXVI (July-December, 1899), 761.

11. Wesley here mentions the beginning of a connection which was to have the highest significance for his religious development. The Moravians were a very special religious group whose official name was the *Unitas Fratrum*. They were connected by a line, tenuous, but continuous, of episcopal succession with the Hussite movement of the fifteenth century. It became Protestant at the Reformation, and maintained a precarious underground existence through the period of the religious wars. From this period of constriction they were now emerging, thanks to the help of Count Nicholas von Zinzendorf, a devout nobleman who invited them to settle on his estates in Saxony. We will have occasion later on to examine more closely the nature of their piety and religious tradition; just now we should notice only that to the Moravians belongs the honor of being the first Protestant body in the modern world to acknowledge their obligation as such (that is, apart from the duties of a State Church to subject peoples in dependencies abroad) to carry the Gospel to non-Christian parts of the world. The Moravians were missionaries wherever they were, but were especially noted because their work was done on principle among the most remote and neglected populations: in Greenland and among the slaves of the West Indies, among others. Another of their principles was that their missions should be self-supporting. The group on board the "Simmonds" was destined to reinforce such a mission colony already established in Georgia.

12. That is, preaching to the Indians.

13. Devices which were to be valuable in the Methodist movement. Some see in these groups models for the later Societies and Bands.

14. After John too had got back to England, Ingham worked with him for some time as a fellow evangelist; he shares with Wesley the credit for starting his fellow Yorkshireman John Nelson on his fruitful career. But as the cleavage between the Wesleys and the Moravians widened, Ingham threw in his lot with the latter. Later on he managed a number of Societies independently; however, he kept up contacts, friendly, but not closely co-operative, with both Wesleyan and Calvinistic Methodists to the end of his active career. (See the account of him in Tyerman, OM, pp. 57-154).

15. Tyerman, LW, I, 118.

16. Prof. F. J. Turner in his *Frontier in American History* (New York: 1921) advanced the suggestive thesis that the new conditions of our successive frontiers have wrought notable changes in the structure of our political institutions even in the settled East. G. P. Mode (*The Frontier Spirit in American Christianity*, New York: The Macmillan Co., 1923) has applied this suggestion to our ecclesiastical life. We might here cite an instance of the same principle's action even further back—in the mother country across the sea. The needs of this frontier mission imposed on Wesley a device much at variance with the settled "parish system" of the Anglican Church, yet destined to modify it later on: I mean the kind of "circuit" which Wesley had to care for in Georgia, and which he readily adopted when back in England. Viewed against a wider background, however, this may be regarded simply as one instance of the wholesome influence the "mission field" has had on the tendency toward rigidity too often observable in the home churches.

17. It is in connection with this responsibility that we have (in the *Wesleyan Methodist Magazine*, Vol. XXXI [1808] p. 490) the delightful story of Wesley's taking Delamotte's place as schoolmaster for a few days *barefoot*, to compose the rancor which had sprung up between those of the latter's pupils who could and those who could not afford to wear shoes to school. This is the first of a number of incidents in Wesley's life which strike an authentically Franciscan note. If, being somewhat late, it comes to us rather like one of the "Little Flowers" than a part of primitive tradition, it is not on that account without value.

18. Like Ingham, Delamotte was attracted by Moravian doctrine, especially its quietism. He remained friendly with the Wesleys, however. John records with pleasure a visit to his "old fellow-traveler" in 1782. He outlived Wesley by five years.

19. WJJ *Works* stands for the Journal of John Wesley as published in the American edition of his *Works* by John Emory, six vols. (New York: Lane and Scott, 1850). The passage here cited is not in the Standard Edition, but is included here because it illustrates important phases of the missionaries' activity.

20. Charles Delamotte.

21. WJJS, I, 182 n.

22. His vacillation in the later Grace Murray episode was very similar.

23. See above p. 79, in the letter to Dr. Burton.

24. It has not disappeared altogether. Instances come easily to mind: Conrad Beissel's community at Ephrata, Pennsylvania, in Wesley's own century; the Shakers of the nineteenth century; and in our own time several Anglican Orders and (in the Reformed tradition) a community at Taizé les Cluny, near the site in Burgundy of the great mother Abbey of the Cluniac Congregation.

25. See below, p. 119.

26. A rascally suitor who, on being refused her hand, threatened to murder any rival who should be successful.

27. Two days later (February 5) according to the diary (WJJS, I, 316), there was still more prayerful consideration of this question. When Wesley, Ingham and Delamotte were the consultants, the decision was unfavorable;

but when "the Germans" were again consulted, they were much more sympathetic. They cast lots and declared themselves "for it."

Coke and Moore in their *Life of John Wesley* (London: 1792, p. 117 f.) carry the story often repeated by subsequent writers, of his consulting the "Elders of the Moravian Church" as to whether or not he should marry Sophy Hopkey. His anxiety arose, according to this story, from Delamotte's "prejudice against the lady." He first consulted Bishop Nitschmann who, after insisting that marriage was not in itself wrong, said the expediency of this particular one needed careful consideration. When Wesley appeared before the Elders, Delamotte was sitting among them. They asked Wesley to assure them that he would abide by their decision. He gave the assurance, and they advised against the marriage. "The will of the Lord be done," he replied, and began thenceforth to break off seeing Sophy as politely as he could. Henry Moore, when, alone, he rewrote the Life he and Coke had published together, added (Henry Moore, *The Life of the Rev. John Wesley, A. M.*, [2 vols., New York: 1824-25] I, 258): "I had the whole account from himself [*i.e.*, from Wesley]; and I do not know that he ever told it to any other person."

This story as it stands is suspect for several reasons. It is true the vividness of the picture of Wesley's coming before the grave assembly, and the circumstantiality of Delamotte's sitting among them, have the ring of verisimilitude. But there are considerations still weightier than these to arouse our caution. First, there are divergences from the record written at the time and transcribed over a year later at Oxford (WJJS, I, 317 n.), called "Account of Miss Sophy." The divergences are all in the direction of a more decisive and (so at least the authors seemed to think) a more dignified Wesley. It is he (not Sophy, as the "Account" shows), who began to break off their intimacy (see below, p. 116). Nothing is said about casting lots which is mentioned twice in the record, and which determined Wesley's final course. And finally, it speaks of an unfavorable decision, by the Moravians, whereas the only one I can find recorded in the "Account" is "for it." This would, *a priori* be more consonant with the more humane attitude of the Lutheran-Pietist tradition in regard to marriage. One more consideration weighs heavily against the story as by Coke and Moore: the Bishop Nitschmann who plays the main part in it left Georgia for Germany, as we learn from other sources, less than a fortnight after Wesley had met Sophy for the first time (WJJS, I, 181; Adelaide L. Fries, *The Moravians in Georgia, 1735-1740*, [Winston Salem, North Carolina: printed for the author, 1905] p. 141). It is unthinkable that Wesley should have conceived such an affection for, and Delamotte such a prejudice against her so soon. The conclusion seems to me inescapable that the Coke-Moore story is a later, distorted conflation of the events accurately described in the diary and the "Account" for the 3rd and 5th of February 1737, narrated above.

28. WJJS, I, 149 f., diary.

29. See above, p. 90.

30. See above, pp. 99, 100.

31. The Beards characterize Wesley's stay in Georgia in one sentence, the insinuating phrases of which, without being untrue, seem to be almost studiously put together to give a completely false impression, one which falls lamentably short of the truth, and of the standards historians should set for themselves for *every* sentence. Charles and Mary Beard, *The Rise of American Civilization* (2 vols., New York: The Macmillan Co., 1927) I, 78.

32. They had knowledge of each other before Whitefield finally got out of

reach of communication with land. Whitefield was hurt as the result of their exchange. See below, n. 46, chap. VI.

33. I am not sure of this [J. W.] This comment and those in the three following notes have become famous because of their bearing on the appraisal of Wesley's subsequent view of his conversion experience. Wesley inserted them in the corrected copy for the printer of the first edition, as Umphrey Lee points out (*John Wesley and Modern Religion*, Nashville, Tennessee: Cokesbury Press p. 99). He shows correctly that Dr. Cell was not justified in the conclusion that Wesley never intended them for printing; but I believe his statement that Curnock "failed to notice" they were meant for the first edition is not warranted (see WJJS, I, 422 n., where Curnock speaks of "*errata*" in connection with these very notes).

34. I had even then the faith of a servant, though not that of a son. [J. W.]

35. I believe not. [J. W.]

36. The faith of a son. [J. W.]

37. Here and hereafter: George Whitefield, *Journal of a Voyage from London to Savannah in Georgia*. London: Whitaker, Treacher and Arnot, 1830.

CHAPTER IV

1. Wesley himself read it. See below, p. 208.

2. Just when "salvation by faith" appeared in Whitefield's preaching is a knotty point. He says that he himself made the transition from "the mystic divinity" while still a student at Oxford (see above, p. 85). But Tyerman quotes John Hutton's biographer to the effect that Whitefield called attention to the necessity of the new birth without saying how it was to be obtained. Tyerman continues, "In his first nine published sermons, [*i.e.*, till well along in 1737] there is scarce a single trace of the doctrine of salvation by faith only. Whitefield learned the doctrine afterwards." (Luke Tyerman, *The Life of the Rev. George Whitefield* [2 vols., New York: Randolph & Co., 1877] I, 101 f. Hereafter referred to as Tyerman, LGWA).

3. See WJJS, I, 436 n., and I, 460 n.

4. WJJS, I, 455. The only other exceptions I can find, are mentioned *Ibid.*, pp. 448, 457 (March 27, a condemned prisoner; and April 27 or 28: Mr. Hutchins and Mrs. Fox).

5. WCJ, I, 72 (July 7, 1737).

6. J. H. Overton, *John Wesley* (Boston and New York: Houghton Mifflin Co., 1891) p. 120 ff., and J. H. Overton and Frederic Relton, *The English Church from the Accession of George I to the End of the Eighteenth Century*, (London: the Macmillan Co., 1906) p. 74 f.

7. Simon JWRS, p. 9 ff., *et passim*.

8. Maximin Piette, *op. cit.*, p. 442 ff. Umphrey Lee, *John Wesley and Modern Religion* (Nashville, Tennessee: Cokesbury Press, 1936) p. 83 ff.

9. I cannot refrain, however, from remarking that not even the attempt to turn the Aldersgate Street experience into a mystical one can be justified

from the facts. It can be done only by operating with a very special definition of mystical experience: "the conversion of a religious man to a higher state of religious devotion" (Lee, *op. cit.*, p. 103); and by positing a misconception in Wesley's mind as to what Böhler was driving at. This in turn is supposed to be supported by "certain strange omissions and changes" in Wesley's translation of a letter in Latin from Peter Böhler (Lee, *op. cit.* p. 86). Now an examination of the letter and translation (WJJS, I, 461 f.) will show that the omissions and changes are entirely without theological significance, being such only as would be made by a man writing in haste, and endeavouring always to use as few words as possible to convey the essentials. The treatment of this translation in the *Proceedings of the Wesley Historical Society* (V, 25) is devoted to linguistic considerations only. Now, as we have seen, the whole temper of the Moravian piety was evangelical, not mystical. If (as Lee agrees is proper) we take the primacy of faith as characteristic of evangelicalism, and if Wesley understood Böhler's admonitions ("believe" plays quite as strong a part in the much-discussed letter as "love") the obvious conclusion is that Wesley's piety followed along the lines laid down by his mentor; and certainly salvation by faith was Wesley's basic doctrine through all his after life. He was an evangelical of the evangelicals, and any attempt to make him appear otherwise flies in the face of the most convincing considerations.

10. George Croft Cell, *The Rediscovery of John Wesley*, (New York: Henry Holt & Co., 1934) p. 161 ff. J. Ernest Rattenbury, *The Conversion of the Wesleys*, London: The Epworth Press, 1938.

11. W. E. H. Lecky, *A History of England in the Eighteenth Century*, (2nd ed. revised, 8 vols. London: Longmans Green and Co., 1879) II, 558.

12. May 1, 1738; see below, p. 169 f.

13. See below, pp. 144 ff and 149 ff.

14. See below, p. 151 f.

15. M. M. Knappen, ed., *Two Elizabethan Puritan Diaries by Richard Rogers and Samuel Ward* (Chicago: American Society of Church History, 1933), designated by KPD. This and the following extracts were included following a suggestion of Prof. Knappen's (*Tudor Puritanism* [Chicago: University of Chicago Press, 1939] p. 288) that these meetings were "the forerunner of the modern prayer-meeting," and using the references he gives.

16. Richard Rogers, *Seven Treatises Containing Such Directions as is Gathered out of the Holy Scriptures, Leading and Guiding to True Happiness, Both in this Life, and the Life to Come.* (3rd ed. London: for Thomas Man, 1610.) Marginal symbol, RST.

17. That is, classis business (Knappen's note).

18. The other entries in the Diary for these meetings are all for the last two months of 1587; in the *Seven Treatises* the date given is 1588. We may conclude that the accounts represent a surge of intense religious concern and activity which was not conserved by any continuing organization.

19. *I. e.*, Separatists, from Robert Browne, who first formulated their principles in the famous *Treatise of Reformation* (1582).

20. Samuel Wesley also mentions them in passing in the extract given here. See p. 151.

21. This symbol stands for a publication with a title longer than usual even in the seventeenth century. Really there are three pamphlets published together, in the last two of which we are interested. The title page reads, in part: *An Earnest Admonition to All, but Especially to Young Persons to Turn to God . . . To which is Added an Account of the Rise and Progress of the Religious Societies; and of the Societies for Reformation, Lately Erected in the Cities of London and Westminster, with a Copy of their Orders . . . and Sundry Directions Relating to the Religious Conferences of these Societies . . .* By Josiah Woodward, minister of Popler . . . Told by Ra Simpson at the Harp in St. Paul's Churchyard, 1697.

22. Woodward's work was first published in 1680, some two years after the beginning of the movement he describes. The phrase "about twenty years ago" has been inserted for purposes of this reprint, and dates the rise of the movement correctly, as about 1678. See Simon, JWRS, p. 1f.

23. In public assemblies in the church.

24. For Whitefield's intimate association with the Fetter Lane Society, see WJJS, I, 458, n. 1. The founding of the Fetter Lane Society and its rules are given below, p. 169 f.

25. *The Works of the Rev. George Whitefield, M. A.,* (6 vols., London: 1771). This extract is from the "Letter to the Religious Societies of England Written during the Voyage to Philadelphia, 1739, and Particularly recommended to those who had then lately formed themselves into Religious Societies in Scotland."

26. Here and hereafter: George Whitefield, *A Further Account of God's Dealings with the Rev. Mr. George Whitefield, from the time of his Ordination to his Embarking for Georgia.* Boston: Rogers and ————, 174–.

27. See above, p. 153 f.

28. An anonymous German work current among "the Friends of God" in the fourteenth century, and a favorite in mystical circles ever since. Luther was overjoyed when he first came across it, and regarded it as "consonant with the Gospel" (James Mackinnon, *Luther and the Reformation* [London: Longmans Green & Co., 1925] I, 212). Wesley in his final verdict however spoke of "this unscriptural writer." (Nov. 18, 1741, WJJS, II, 515.)

29. Not included in this work. See WJL, I, 241 f.

30. W. J. Townshend and others, *New History of Methodism* (London: Hodder and Stoughton, 1909) I, 239; J. Ernest Rattenbury, *The Conversion of the Wesleys* (London: The Epworth Press, 1938) p. 90.

31. Simon, JWRS, p. 191 f.

32. The whole account has not been included here—paragraphs 9-12 inclusive are omitted altogether. Those who wish to read paragraphs 2-6 in order will find them included above as follows: 2, p. 42; 3, p. 43; 4, p. 46f.; 5 and 6, p. 48f.

CHAPTER V

1. The sermon which John Wesley had been preaching at least since Böhler had persuaded him to "preach faith till he had it." Dr. Sugden thinks it goes back even farther (Edward H. Sugden, ed., *Wesley's Standard Sermons*

[2nd ed., 2 vols., London: The Epworth Press, 1935] I, 36). Written before Wesley's conversion, it required some alterations to include that experience. Thus altered it was preached at St. Mary's, Oxford, June 11, 1738, just eighteen days after his conversion. The sermon, entitled "Salvation by Faith," is regarded as a "revival manifesto," and is placed first in all the editions of the Sermons I am acquainted with.

2. Can we call this Charles' approach to field preaching? Whitefield was to make his approach in the dining room of an inn, Feb. 8, 1739. See below, pp. 212 and 213.

3. Umphrey Lee, *John Wesley and Modern Religion*. (Nashville, Tenn.: Cokesbury Press, 1936) p. 93f.

4. See below, p. 197ff.

5. See below, p. 200.

6. Curnock's note (No. 3, WJJS, II, 49) mentions this, but fails to indicate its bearing on Wesley's anxiety concerning his justification. Gradin's relation is, I think, the link between Wesley's concern about justification and his later doctrine of Christian Perfection.

7. See below, p. 203f.

8. Baron Watteville was a friend of Count Zinzendorf. He was a leader in this small Moravian community. Later he was influential in the larger affairs of that church and apparently at the same time an official in the Reformed Church (Curnock's note WJJS, II, 5).

9. A group of Baptists named for Menno Simons (d. 1561) who patiently gathered together the remnants of the shattered Anabaptist movement. Though scattered through several countries of the Continent, they were a close-knit community, bearing persecution, practising separation from the world, and a deep, non-resistant piety based on the Sermon on the Mount. In the seventeenth and eighteenth centuries they were weakened by schisms and the inroads of Socinianism, but remained fervent in charity. They influenced the beginnings of the Baptist movement in England in the seventeenth century.

10. *I.e.*, Mainz.

11. Halle was in the Brandenburg territories whose Hohenzollern Elector, Frederick William I, was the third of his line to be also King of Prussia. Realizing as had his two predecessors that the army was the foundation of Prussian power, he made it the most precise military machine in Europe. The one luxury he indulged himself in was his craze for tall soldiers: the famous "Potsdam Guard of Giants," all of whom had to be at least six feet in stature.

12. The elder Francke was, after Spener, the most important leader of Pietism —indeed he excelled the latter in administrative abilities and was responsible for the skillful operation of its large benevolent institutions. His professorate at the University there made Halle a centre of Pietism till his death in 1727.

13. Christian David, born a Roman Catholic in a Moravia predominantly Catholic, became a Lutheran, and as such, led the first emigrants out of their "Egypt" to the shelter of Zinzendorf's estates. As a carpenter he felled the first tree and built the first house at Herrnhut in 1722. As the influence of the Unitas Fratrum gradually prevailed in the settlement, he joined it. Though he had never seen a Bible till he was twenty years old, his evan-

gelical experience was clear and definite, and he became one of the most intrepid of the many missionaries who went out from Herrnhut.

14. This is unscriptural [Wesley].

15. Robert Southey, *The Life of Wesley*, (3rd ed., 2 vols., London: Longman, Brown, Green and Longmans, 1846) I, 195.

16. See below, p. 211.

17. See below, *loc. cit.*

18. See below, p. 223.

19. See below, pp. 210, 211f., 212f.; see also p. 252.

20. N.B. In the following pages where extracts from the Journals of the two Wesleys and Whitefield are cut in together, the source of any piece can easily be determined from the references. As heretofore, symbols beginning WJ indicate writing by John Wesley; those starting with WC, by Charles Wesley; while symbols for the several Journals by Whitefield begin with his name, or the symbol WG.

21. The Fetter Lane Society. Wesley, as one of the founders and its first President, felt especially close to it as the "our" shows.

22. By the Rev. Jonathan Edwards, minister of the town, first published in 1736. It is a sober, selfless account of the manner and results of God's working in the redemption of his people there.

23. This experience would have been in June, 1738, when Whitefield was in the Colony. Can we assume a connection here?

24. Here and hereafter: *George Whitefield, The Two First Parts of his Life with his Journals.* Revised, Corrected and Abridged by George Whitefield, A. B. London: W. Strahan, 1756.

25. There were many French Huguenots in England, as yet unassimilated, though the tide of refugees from Louis XIV's revocation of the Edict of Nantes had ceased to flow a generation before. For the most part these emigrants were a sober, industrious people whose loss to France was England's gain. But there is froth on every tide, and these "French Prophets" were part of a group who exploited their capacity for ecstasy and convulsions. Their puerilities were a debased imitation of the extraordinary outburst of apocalyptic utterance and reputed thaumaturgic powers among the Camisards when their revolt against intolerably cruel persecution had flamed out in the Cévennes in the first years of the century. Three of these prophet-leaders of desert warfare had appeared in London about 1707 and created quite a stir. Southey, after a vivid description of the origin of "French Prophecy," says the later and lesser heirs of the movement tried to attract followers from both the Moravians and the Methodists. (Robert Southey, *Life of Wesley* [3rd ed., 2 vols., London: Longman, Brown, Green and Longmans, 1846] I, 236).

26. *Sic.* Obviously a slip for Elisha.

27. Griffith Jones, though the holder of a church living in Wales, also did itinerant preaching, and in a sense, field preaching, for he resorted to a tombstone when the church was too small to hold his hearers. He was chiefly famous for the number of charity schools he had founded—thirty-seven of them in 1737 alone—and it may have been this example which suggested to Whitefield the idea of a similar school for the miners' children in Kings-

wood. He was a prolific writer, chiefly on theological subjects and manifested strong leanings to Calvinism.

28. From this notice on the date of the beginning of Harris' work in Wales we may conclude that the awakening there, of which he and Griffith Jones were the chief figures, antedated, or at least was quite independent of that in England itself. A similar one was in progress in Scotland under the leadership of James Robe of Kilsyth (See W. J. Townshend and others, *A New History of Methodism* [2 vols., London: Hodder and Stoughton, 1909] I, 201).

29. Before taking such an important step as going to carry on the work in Bristol, Wesley would be bound by the orders of the Fetter Lane Society to get their favorable judgment.

30. Whitefield recognized that conserving the results of the Revival by the persistent and detailed work of forming bands and working with them could be done much better by Wesley than by himself.

31. John Wesley was in poor health at the time. Fear lest his condition would be aggravated by living in a strange city and working at the tremendous task there, were at the bottom of this "unaccountable" fear; but one gets the impression that the over-excited impressibility of the Society had something to do with this "premonition" and the difficulty in coming to a decision.

CHAPTER VI

1. *Works* VI, 530.

2. In a letter to Thomas Maxfield, Feb. 14, 1778; see WJL, VI, 304.

3. Bristol had its prison called Newgate as well as London. The keeper, Abel Dagge, had been converted by Whitefield. One of Wesley's most vivid letters (WJL, IV, 127) contrasts the two Newgates after Dagge had transformed Bristol's into what was, for the time, a model prison, while London's remained one of the worst "seats of woe this side of hell."

4. G. C. Cell, *The Rediscovery of John Wesley*, (New York: Henry Holt and Co., 1935) pp. 269, 270.

5. See Tyerman, LGWA I, 470.

6. See below, p. 274ff.

7. Simon, JWRS, p. 289.

8. Nevertheless such effects were exceptional under Whitefield's preaching. He discouraged them, as did Charles (see below p. 324ff), whereas John was, at this point at least, inclined to see in them signs of direct divine intervention.

9. WJJS, II, 302.

10. From his first trip, of five days' duration, into Wales.

11. Charles' sermon themes frequently have an anti-Calvinistic slant during this period. The important words in the text are "for all."

12. Though this is the first time Cennick's name has occurred in these extracts, and he appears as an open antagonist of the Wesleys and their preaching,

he had for over a year been serving as a master in the school for miners' children at Kingswood, and had been preaching with Wesley's approbation; often indeed, in his stead (see Tyerman, LW, I, 274 f., and below p. 267). Reared in a Quaker family, he had known depths of religious despair, but had found peace and begun to preach. He subsequently threw in his lot for a time with the Calvinistic Methodists, but for most of his mature years was a Moravian.

13. Actually, Whitefield was then on the Atlantic returning to England.

14. Cennick and his friends had already formed an opposition Society (See John Simon, *John Wesley and the Methodist Societies* [2nd ed., London: The Epworth Press, 1937, hereafter cited as Simon JWMS] p. 40.) That they had gone farther toward fulfilling their intention announced by Charles Wesley (see above p. 246) I have not been able to discover. Whitefield was to land within three weeks' time from his second trip to America, ready to assume leadership of the Calvinistic Methodists. For the account of his growing Calvinist tendencies and the breach with the Wesleys, see below, p. 274ff.

15. This is the first time the term 'United Society' is used in the Journal proper. This entry is here slightly out of chronological order so as not to interrupt the story of the Calvinistic controversy.

16. This is the earliest mention of "tickets," which became a characteristic feature of early Methodism. Only holders of tickets were considered members of the Societies, and only those whose conduct passed the rigorous requirements could have tickets—which had to be renewed quarterly. No practise illustrates more clearly than this the determination of the Wesleys to keep the ethical living of the Society members on a high level. The tickets may be said to symbolize most vividly early Methodism's kinship with what Ernst Troeltsch called the 'sect-type' of religious organization rather than the 'church-type'. Membership in the latter is, according to Troeltsch's suggestive delineation, co-terminous with the population. The church-type must rely, for the raising of the ethical level, on other methods than the exclusion of offending members, for its purpose is inclusive rather than exclusive. Membership in the sect-type, on the other hand, is voluntary. To become a member of such a body, and to continue in it, one must conform to its high ethical demands. He understands that failure to do so results in his exclusion. This was the procedure of early Methodism, and the quarterly 'ticket' was concrete evidence of continued conformity.

17. From "A Plain Account of the People Called Methodists" (1748).

18. Wesley still had qualms about field preaching. Apparently doing it in *London* revived them.

19. This is Charles Wesley's first outdoor preaching in London.

20. We can only guess at the feelings stirred in Susannah Wesley's heart by the extraordinary course her younger sons had taken during the past year and a half. She may have shared in some measure the misgivings of Samuel Jr., who wrote her vigorously on the subject. Here she seems willing at least to observe the fruits of field preaching. Doubtless what she saw reconciled her, for in the crisis just ahead she seems to have exercised a quiet but effective influence over the course of events in London.

21. See above, pp. 169 and 252.

22. This almost certainly refers to his mother. See above, p. 254.

23. For the Rules themselves, see below, p. 318ff.

24. See below, p. 265.

25. Whitehead, LW, II, 78 f.

26. From "The Nature, Design and General Rules of the United Societies."

27. Simon (JWRS 328f.) believes this meeting with "a smaller company" on this date was the first Society meeting at the Foundery. Admitting that this is conjectural he offers the following as a dependable formula: "it is indisputable that in the opening months of 1740, a Society under the control of John Wesley, and distinct from the Fetter Lane Society did habitually meet in a room at the Foundery."

28. We may conclude from this that Susannah had a voice in the decision—evidently from what followed a decision to secede from the Fetter Lane Society—which was made that evening.

29. See below, p. 277.

30. Tyerman, LW, I, 220 f.

31. WJJS, VIII, 93.

32. Tyerman, LW, I, 346.

33. Tyerman, LGWA, I, 223 n.

34. Tyerman, LW, I, 274 f.

35. Simon, however, insists that Maxfield was Wesley's first 'regular' lay preacher (Simon, JWMS, pp. 23-25). Just what he means by regularity in this case is not clear.

36. Tyerman, LW, I, 402, 441.

37. John Richard Green, *A Short History of the English People* (London: Macmillan and Co., 1902) p. 737.

38. Here and hereafter: Henry Moore, *The Life of the Rev. John Wesley, A. M.* (2 vols. New York: 1824-5).

39. This extract comes from "A Farther Appeal to Men of Reason and Religion," Part III.

40. From the same treatise as the preceding.

41. See Simon, JWMS, p. 37 f.

42. Tyerman, LGWA, I, 102.

43. *Ibid.*, I, 274.

44. Whitefield, *Works*, Vol. I. He opposes the doctrine of 'sinless perfection' (p. 58); writes, "The doctrine of election is daily pressed on my heart" (p. 79); to Howell Harris he writes that their opinions on election co-incide "as face answers to face in the water" (p. 87); he repudiates free will, (p. 95); professes belief in final perseverance (p. 101). Other passages could be cited.

45. Tyerman, *loc. cit.*

46. For instance, in the prefatory matter to the *Answer to Mr. Wesley's Sermon* Whitefield brings up a matter which was probably more revealing than he intended it to be—the reprehensibly stiff and high-handed way Wesley treated his request for counsel on the whole matter of his purposes and

methods in Georgia. "The morning I sailed" (Whitefield writes) "from Deal for Gibraltar, you arrived from Georgia. Instead of giving me an opportunity to converse with you, though the ship was not far off the shore; you drew a lot, and immediately set forwards to London. You left a letter behind you, in which were words to this effect. 'When I saw God, by the wind which was carrying you out brought me in, I asked counsel of God. His answer you have enclosed.' This was a piece of paper, in which were written these words, 'Let him return to London.' When I received this, I was somewhat surprised" (Whitefield, *Works*, IV, 56). Whitefield was putting it mildly. He intended to reproach Wesley for using the lot; but in so doing, of course, he revealed how difficult he was to deal with at times, and also how this brusque repulse of two years and more back had rankled in his own heart.

47. Whitefield, *Works* I, 225.

48. *Ibid.*, IV, 56.

49. Tyerman, LGWA, I, 484.

50. See above, pp. 241 and 249.

51. "The Principles of a Methodist Farther Explained," *Works* V, 311.

52. Bishop Gibson.

53. Dr. John Potter, who, while still Bishop of Oxford, had ordained both the brothers.

54. Tyerman, OM, p. 217 f.

55. The London palace of the Archbishops of Canterbury.

56. Simon, JWRS, p. 315.

57. WJJS (Diary) II, 258.

58. Samuel Wesley, Jr. may have seen a record of this conversation. At any rate it was only some five weeks after it took place that he wrote his mother and John's; "As I told Jack, I am not afraid that the church should excommunicate him (discipline is at too low an ebb), but, that he should excommunicate the church." (Tyerman LW I, 287).

CHAPTER VII

1. Probably a guarded reference to Whitefield's active prosecution of the Calvinistic controversy.

2. This sounds as though Charles Wesley had protested against Maxfield's preaching and John was defending him.

3. This is evidently a quotation from what Charles had written to him. This paragraph conveys John's sorrowful reproach for his brothers' having succumbed to the allurements of Quietism. See Journal entry for Jan. 22, above p. 317. Happily he soon recovered.

4. This promising project was made the occasion for gross slanders by the enemies of Methodism (See WJJS II, 454, n.; and Tyerman, LW I, 357). Perhaps for this reason it was not continued for long.

5. As Fellow of Lincoln.

6. This sermon is No. 2 in the published Sermons, called "The Almost Christian." Nos. 1 and 4 were also preached before the University in 1738 and 1744 respectively. Sugden calls the first, on "Salvation by Faith" a "manifesto." (Edward Sugden, ed., *Wesley's Standard Sermons* [2nd ed., 2 vols. London: The Epworth Press, 1935] I, 36). Cell applies the term "Revival manifestoes" to all three. (George C. Cell, *The Rediscovery of John Wesley* [New York: Henry Holt and Co., 1935] p. 38). No. 3 of the published sermons was preached by Charles Wesley in the same place in 1742.

Tyerman first advanced the theory, which has been confirmed by Curnock and accepted by Sugden, that Wesley wrote another sermon, on the text "How is the faithful city become a harlot" (Is. 1:21), which he originally intended to preach on this occasion in 1741, but was dissuaded by Lady Huntingdon, who thought it too denunciatory. For the supporting evidence (which is sufficiently complex, but convincing) see Tyerman, LW I, 362 f; WJJS, II, 478 n; Sugden, *op. cit.,* I, 53f. Simon, however, is of the opinion that the one he actually preached is superior in utility (JWMS p. 56). At any rate, Wesley, not to be denied, returned to the charge three years later with the boldly critical sermon "Scriptural Christianity." This was the last time he was allowed to preach before the University.

7. Leslie F. Church, *The Early Methodist People* (London: The Epworth Press, 1948) p. 164.

8. *Ibid.,* p. 159.

9. *Ibid.,* p. 158.

10. From "A Plain Account of the People Called Methodists" written in 1748.

11. See below, p. 310.

12. WJJS, II, 412.

13. Simon, JWMS p. 66. The nearest analogy I have found is a communion service of which Wesley says "about ten [in the evening] they receive in silence without any ceremony and continue in silence till they part at twelve." See above, p. 203.

14. Simon, *op. cit.,* p. 66 f.

15. WJL, III, 287.

16. From "A Plain Account," etc.

17. From "A Plain Account", etc.

18. August 8, 1737, WJJS, I, 377 (Journal thitherto unpublished and Diary).

19. Tyerman LW, II, 341.

20. From "A Plain Account," etc.

21. Compare the extract given here with the passage found below, p. 355. One interesting phrase which occurs in the 1744 version of the rules is omitted in the later account given here: that rule which requires all members to bring what they can to a common stock says they were to do so "till we can have all things in common." In 1744 this Christian communalism formed a part of Wesley's ideal of the primitive Church, to which he was endeavoring to conform his Methodists. By 1748, when the "Plain Account" was written, this part of his plan had been abandoned.

22. From "A Plain Account," etc.

23. Near Bristol.

24. Birstall in Yorkshire may here stand for a number of places Wesley visited in brief tours of preliminary exploration in the Midlands and the North of England in the years 1741 and 1742. The trips were made on the advice and with the encouragement of Lady Huntingdon. Birstall was a small town, notable chiefly as the home of John Nelson, the sturdy stonemason who became one of Wesley's most dependable lay preachers. His zeal, his vigorous good sense and his salty wit made him a doughty champion of the Methodist cause. His *Journal* tells in highly characteristic style the story of his sufferings during the heroic days of the movement, and has become one of its classic documents. Wesley's scouting trip discovered that Moravian stillness had already spread widely in those regions. He reached Newcastle soon after this stop in Birstall, but his serious work there began only the next autumn.

25. This was, though John was probably not aware of it at the time, his brother-in-law Westley Hall, husband of Martha Wesley. A letter from John written later that same summer (Clarke, MWF, II, 337 f.) shows he had already adopted quietist views. Still later he adopted, practised and openly defended an extreme form of the antinomian consequences which often follow on such beliefs. His life degenerated into a profligacy which was at once a sore affliction to his patient wife and a scandal to the faith he professed.

26. Between Birstall and Newcastle.

27. At the committal, John altered slightly the words of the Anglican service: "Forasmuch as it hath pleased Almighty God, of his great mercy, to take unto Himself the soul of our dear *mother*." She was, in a very real sense the mother of the whole solemn concourse of Methodists who had come to the service, and of many thousands more in other parts of England.

28. The historical and explanatory points of this pamphlet have already been cited above, p. 259. The text of the Rules given here is that of the first edition given by Simon, since the text in the *Works* (V, 191 ff.) contains subsequent changes.

29. That is, smuggled.

30. In 1739 Wesley had been certain that the outcries and bodily disturbances among the hearers of the preaching were the work of the Spirit of God, who was grieved if it was questioned. Here he ascribes them to Satan— whether from some observably different quality in the phenomena or not is difficult to tell at this distance. At other times he had recourse to "natural causes" as an explanation.

31. This was the Robert Williams who was appointed at the Conference of 1769, along with Boardman, Pilmoor and Jonathan King, for service in America. Not long before that Conference, Williams had offended again in the same way, this time by preaching against the clergy in the North of Ireland (WJJS, V, 315f.) The two events may be connected. Williams was the first of the four appointed at the Conference to arrive in America, having sold his horse to pay his debts, and travelling on passage money furnished by a friend. At the first Conference in America (1773) he became, so to speak, the first Book Concern here, being allowed to distribute the Wesleys' books and pamphlets, but to print them only after obtaining their authorization. (J. M. Buckley, *A History of Methodists in the United States* [4th ed. New York: Charles Scribner's Sons, 1900] p. 141). The traits

which limited his usefulness in Europe did not do so in this country. Francis Asbury, preaching his funeral sermon in 1775, said of him, "Perhaps no one in America has been an instrument of awakening so many souls as God has awakened by him." (*Ibid.* p. 174).

32. Mr. Egginton, the Vicar, had earlier welcomed Wesley to his pulpit. Williams' sermon which caused the trouble was preached against drunkenness; Mr. Egginton was persuaded it was directed against him (Simon JWMS, p. 114 f.).

33. See below, p. 330ff.

34. Built and consecrated by French Protestants. That it had been consecrated, even by Presbyterians, was sufficient in Wesley's eyes, even at this early date, to justify holding the sacrament there.

35. See above, pp. 251, 253.

36. See above, p. 319.

37. Simon JWMS, p. 219 f., and see below, p. 360.

38. It so appears in the *Works*, V, 191.

39. Tyerman, LW I, 409 f.

40. *Loc. cit.*

41. They may be found in WJJS, III, 84 ff.

42. See below, p. 349.

43. WJJS III, 85 n.

44. Tyerman, LW, I, 420.

45. Wesley's words quoted from Whitehead in Simon, JWRS, p. 328.

46. In 1785, in defense of his having proceeded single-handed to choose the Legal Hundred, Wesley insisted that from the beginning he had retained in his own hand the choice of those who should be invited to each Conference. So long as he was possessed of such discretionary power, even though he did not always exercise it, his leadership would differ little, if at all, from complete control. By following a course admittedly extreme, but not at all incompatible with the premises, he might conceivably have brought an end to Conference simply by not summoning it. Of course what was at first a practise attained the not inconsiderable force of custom long before it reached the stage of legal prescription.

47. John Simon, *John Wesley the Master Builder*, (London: The Epworth Press, 1927) p. 179. Simon comments that until 1765 the Conference was considered a private assembly.

48. John Simon, *John Wesley and the Advance of Methodism* (London: The Epworth Press, 1925) p. 139 f. Because of the considerable extent of the additions from later Conferences, the Disciplinary Minutes came to be known familiarly as "the Large Minutes"; they are published under the title "Minutes of Several Conversations," etc. in *Works* V, 211 ff. The Doctrinal Minutes appear *Ibid.*, p. 194 ff., under the title, "Minutes of Some Late Conversations," etc.

49. In *Publications of the Wesley Historical Society*, No. 1. (London: Published for the Wesley Historical Society, 1896). Symbol: PWHS.1. Contains John

Bennet's Minutes for the Conferences of 1744, 1745, 1747 and 1748, with John Wesley's copy for that of 1746.

50. The following transcription from the valuable publication by the Wesley Historical Society (see the preceding note, No. 49) is complete for the first Conference. It proceeds without interruption for page-numbers. These are unnecessary, for the careful division of the text into days and numbered questions will make reference to the corresponding part of the original an easy matter.

51. These were all Anglican clergymen. When Wesley published this in a revised form as the first part of "Minutes of Some Late Conversations," etc. (*Works* V, 194 ff.) he gave the cures of three of them: Hodges, Wenvo; Piers, Bexley; Taylor, Quinton — all obscure parishes. Meriton came from the Isle of Man. Little is known of him save that he shared the labors and perils of the Methodists till his death.

52. The doctrine of justification and that of sanctification which was considered the next day, were the two over which the Methodists were chiefly called in question by others.

53. The reference intended is probably 1 John iii. 9 [English ed.].

54. Whereas up till Wednesday the editors of PWHS.1 have used John Bennet's own copy, beginning with that day they used Wesley's copy preserved at Headingley College. The words in square brackets are corrections by either Bennet or Wesley, the present editor having made no distinction.

55. Simon remarks that the very assembling of this Conference with the purposes they had in view constituted a breach of the Anglican Canon (No. 12) which renders them *ipso facto* excommunicate who "join together and make rules . . . in causes ecclesiastical, without the King's authority." (JWMS, p. 212). The Methodists had made rules for governing themselves as a religious body, and the Conference would add to them from time to time. Further, Question 5 presupposes an arrogation of competence to review the authority of the doctrinal standards of the Church, quite apart from legal authorization. Here are men who profess loyalty to the Church on the one hand, but on the other, take it on themselves to supplement her discipline and to call in question her doctrinal formularies. To competence in discipline and doctrine, only one thing needs to be added to make a Church: Orders. To quote Simon once more, "It is significant that the decisions of the Conference on the points in question [the agreement of the Articles with Scripture] are not recorded." (*Ibid.*, p. 211).

56. See above, p. 318ff.

57. See above, p. 308.

58. At the Kingswood School.

59. At Kingswood, the Foundery and the Orphan House. This last had been founded at Newcastle in December, 1742 on the model furnished by France's famous institution of the same name in Halle (see above, p. 195f.).

60. Some of these Rules survive today in questions asked of those seeking membership in full connection in an American Methodist Conference.

61. A truly Franciscan provision, this. We remember, moreover, that some of the preachers had families to maintain, which enhances the heroism of their renunciation of wealth for the Gospel's sake. When John Nelson's neighbours tried to dissuade him from preaching saying, "You should consider that you have a wife and children, and that your wife is big with

child," he replied, "Let God look to that." *(Extract from The Journal of John Nelson.* [16th ed., New York: Coulton and Porter, 1856] p. 104).

62. An indication, quite clear in spite of the first person plural pronoun, of the obedience Wesley expected from the preachers.

63. That is, too fastidious to be of service in sordid surroundings.

64. Perhaps this question was raised as a result of John Nelson's refusal to fight when he had been "pressed for a soldier" the preceding spring.

65. See above, p. 326f.

66. This schedule was not carried out; but at least the principle of holding regular conferences is implicit in it. The next one was held the following summer in Bristol.

INDEX

INDEX

Abbot, Mr., 217
Act of Uniformity of 1662, 4, 11
Ainsworth, Mr., 138
Aitkin, Mr., 323
Aldersgate Street Society, 183, 207
Aldridge, 340
Allen, Mr., 272
America, Methodism in, 382 (n. 31)
Amsterdam, 193-4
Analogy of Religion, Natural and Re-vealed, etc. (by Butler), 286
Anderson, Chrissy, 250
Anderson, Esther, 250
Anderson, Mr., 127
Anglican Church —
see, Church of England
Annesley, Dr. Samuel, 2, 11-12, 16, 255
Annesley, Samuel, Jr., 30
Answer to Mr. Wesley's Sermon on Free Grace (by Whitefield), 234, 379 (n. 46)
Apostolic Succession, Wesleyan views of, 58
Apostolical Canons, 103
Araspes (literary pseudonym of Charles W.), 55
Argyle, Fort (Georgia), 106
Arminian Magazine, 34, 37
Arminianism, 225
Arndt, 359
Arthur, Mr., 323
Asbury, Francis, 91, 383 (n. 31)
Aspasia (literary pseudonym of Mrs. Pendarves), 40, 55
Assistant—defined, 355-7
Axholme, Isle of, 1, 3
Ayling, Anne, 246

Baldwin, Mr., 170
Baldwin Street Society (Bristol), 216, 230, 235, 237, 241
Bampfield, Mr., 9
Baptism, 99, 125
Baptist Mills, 230-1, 238, 240-1
Baptists, 193 (see n. 9, p. 375), 205
Bands, 99 (see n. 13, p. 369), 169, 204, 218, 220, 230-1, 248, 262, 300, 306-8, 354-5, 377 (n. 30)
Basingstoke, 229
Bath, 238, 242, 282-4, 298

Bear Yard Society (London), 207
Beard, Charles and Mary, 371 (n. 31)
Bear, Thomas, 342
Beech Lane Society (London), 214
Behmen, Jacob, 161
Beissel, Conrad, 370 (n. 24)
Bell, Mr., 217, 261, 263-4
Bennet, Mr., 341
Bennett, John, 344-6, 383 (n. 49), 384 (n. 54)
Bentley Hall, 332
Berlin (Germany), 136
Bermondsey, 212
Berthelsdorf (Germany), 202
Beveridge, Bishop, 103
Bexley, 158, 187, 384 (n. 51)
Bible—used as an oracle, 182, 221-2
Birmingham, 165, 327, 339-40
Birrell, Augustine, 90-1
Birstall, 310-1
Blackheath, 251-2
Blandford, 4, 6
Blendon, 158-9, 167, 187
Boardman, 382 (n. 31)
Böhler, Peter, 129, 134, 136-8, 152, 159-62, 164-71, 296-7, 373 (n. 9), 374 (n. I)
Böhler, Mr. (Peter's father), 194
Boehm, 359
Books recommended at the first Wesleyan Conference, 359
Boswell [James], 91
Bourignon, Madame, 63
Bovey, Miss, 116
Bowers, 252
Bowes, Mr., 264
Bray, J., 138, 171, 177-8, 180, 188-9, 211, 217-9, 251-2, 257, 260, 263, 285
Bray, Dr., 77
Bridgwater, 8
Broughton, Thomas, 59, 167-8, 188-90
Brown, Mr., 262
Browne, Robert, 373 (n. 19)
Bruce, Mr., 323
Buchanan, 359
Buckingham, Duke of, 41
Burnham, Mr., 188
Burnside, Mr., 125
Burscough, Dr., 208-9

389

Date Due